lonely planet

Malawi

David Else

LONELY PLANET PUBLICATIONS
Melbourne • Oakland • London • Paris

MALAWI

Livingstonia
Time-warped missionary centre, with fascinating history, cool air, fine views and hiking opportunities.

The Ilala Lake Steamer
Venerable old passenger boat, offering the best views of Lake Malawi and snapshots of daily life along its shores.

Nkhata Bay
Busy lakeside town with 'Caribbean' feel. Go diving and canoeing, or head across the lake to Mozambique.

Likoma & Chizumulu Islands
Remote and absolutely beautiful. Likoma is crowned by a large and incongruous cathedral. Chizumulu is the perfect hideaway.

Nyika National Park
High rolling plateau, with good wildlife, first-rate hiking, exhilarating horse riding and endless views.

Vwaza Marsh Wildlife Reserve
Up-and-coming wildlife area, with easy access, walking safaris and excellent animal viewing.

TANZANIA

MOZAMBIQUE

MALAWI

ZAMBIA

NIASSA

LAKE MALAWI

LAGO

Njombe

Lumecha

Monte Quissifodo (1162m)

Monte Mecula (1738m)

Unango

Bagatha

Dias

Monte Jeci (1848m)

Monte Txinonga (1848m)

Nova Coimbra

Mariiamba

Messumba

Metengula

Nkhotakota

Mphonde

Dwangwa

Nkhotakota Wildlife Reserve

Chipata (1374m)

Malombo

Mbobo

MALAWI

Kasungu

Kasungu National Park

Kavinga

Lundazi

Jenda

Katete

Edingeni

Mzimba

Chikangawa

Mt Mpompha (1954m)

Kafukule

Kazuni

Chama

Tembwe

Chikwa

Chifunda

Mwanjawira

Chitungulu

Mbuzi

ZAMBIA

Lukusuzi National Park

Mfuwe

South Luangwa National Park

North Luangwa National Park

Mpika

Chilonga

Nsalamu

Mushupashi

Chambeshi

Duta

Mpepo

Mbali

Mulema

Chimba

Makasa

Kayambi

Nakonde

Tunduma

Chisenga

Chitipa

Nyala

Muyombe

Kalinda

Chinsali

Kampumbu

Nakonde

Ikombe

Lumbila

Matema

Ibanda

Kyela

Songwe

Kaporo

Jungi

Kambwe

Karonga

Lupingo

Manda

Chilumba

Ngara

Mt Mpanda (2071m)

Nyika National Park

Nganda Peak (2607m)

Mt Ntukuli (2580m)

Mt Vitumbi (2357m)

Nthalire

Rumphi

Bolero

Ratumbi

Vwaza Marsh Wildlife Reserve

Mwazisi

Nchenachena

Muhuju

Njakwa

Chitimba

Livingstonia

Hamiya

Ng'onga

Bwengu

Enuckiweni

Ekwendeni

Chikwina

Mzuzu

Usisya

Ruarwe

Chiweta

Tukuyu Bay

Chintheche

Bandawe

Nkhata Bay

Likoma Is

Cobué

Chizumulu Is

Mbamba Bay

Mango

Liuli

Lituhi

ELEVATION
1500m+
1200m
900m
600m
300m
0

MALAWI

Cape Maclear
Longtime backpacker favourite. Go diving, snorkelling and boating; party the night away or just lounge on the beach.

Liwonde National Park
Malawi's premier wildlife area. Excellent bird-watching and animal viewing.

Mount Mulanje
Highland wilderness, with sheer peaks, waterfalls, endless views and superb hiking.

The Lower Shire Valley
Malawi's far south. Little visited, rich in history and wilderness. Excellent bird-watching.

Lake Malawi
One of the largest lakes in Africa. A beautiful and surprisingly varied stretch of water that features fishing villages, wooded escarpments, rocky islands and idyllic beaches.

50km
30mi
0   25
0   15

MOZAMBIQUE

ZIMBABWE

Rio Lugenda

Lichinga
Meponda
Nova Guarda
Homem
Litunde
Majune

Rvia
Cuamba

Lago Amaramba
Lake Chiuta
Lake Chilwa

Mkhulumbe
Mulanje
Muloza

Lugela
Liciro
Monte Chiperone (2054m)
Marracua

Vila Nova da Fronteira

Marromeu

Lago de Cahora Bassa

Tete
Changara
Caldas Xavier
Mutando

Mount Darwin
Bindura
Shamva

Malawi
2nd edition – January 2001
First published – August 1997

Published by
Lonely Planet Publications Pty Ltd ABN 36 005 607 983
90 Maribyrnong St, Footscray, Victoria 3011, Australia

Lonely Planet Offices
Australia Locked Bag 1, Footscray, Victoria 3011
USA 150 Linden St, Oakland, CA 94607
UK 10a Spring Place, London NW5 3BH
France 1 rue du Dahomey, 75011 Paris

Photographs
Many of the images in this guide are available for licensing from
Lonely Planet Images.
email: lpi@lonelyplanet.com.au

Front cover photograph
An African fish eagle *(Haliaeetus vocifer)* catches its meal in Malawi
(David Wall)

ISBN 1 86450 095 6

Printed by Colorcraft Ltd, Hong Kong

Contents – Text

Contents – Maps

The Author

David Else

After hitchhiking through Europe for a couple of years, David Else kept heading south and first reached Africa in 1983. Since then he has travelled, trekked, worked and written all over Africa, from Cairo to Cape Town and from Sudan to Senegal, via most of the bits in between.

David has written and co-written many guidebooks for travellers to Africa, including Lonely Planet's *Trekking in East Africa, West Africa, Gambia & Senegal, Southern Africa* and *Africa on a shoestring*. He has also contributed to *East Africa* and *Tanzania, Zanzibar & Pemba*, and written a book on Zanzibar. As author of this *Malawi* book, and coordinating author of *Southern Africa*, he spent several busy months travelling through the region.

When not in Africa, David lives in the north of England, where he writes most days and then escapes as often as possible to the Derbyshire Dales or the mountains of Scotland.

FROM THE AUTHOR

Firstly – a big thank you to my wife Corinne. Although my name goes down as author of this book, and I string most of the words together, our six-month research trip through Malawi and the other countries of Southern Africa was very much a joint project. Corinne wrote several of the historical, political and background items, and in her role as Dr Corinne Else MB BCh DA she also helped compile the health section.

In the UK, thanks to Roger Gook and Janet McDougal of Footloose Adventure Travel for international flight and tour information, and to John Douglas of Malawi Tourism for regular updates.

In Malawi, my thanks go to: Mrs Harriet Chiwaula at the National Parks information desk in Lilongwe; Gillian Mann and Sarah Markes for a lively introduction to Blantyre nightlife; Carl and Jill Brussow, Jens Haugaard and Sean Conchar for advice on birds, wildlife and environmental matters; Patrick Simkin, Jon de St Pear, Joe Claven, Gertjan van Stam, Louse Kerbiriou and Stephen O'Conner for detailed notes and good stories; Chris and Pam Badger, Ted Sneed, Rob McConaghy, Lindsay Clark, Katie French, Andrea Bizzaro, Nick Dunba, Mark Sprong, Marga van der Water, Pim Kremer, Paul and Claire Norrish for much appreciated help and advice; Bill Pelle, for news from the bush; Lindsay at Ulendo Safaris and Joey at Makomo Safaris for endless help with the new phone numbers, plus all the VSOs, 'gappies' and Peace Corps volunteers who were always happy to provide information from close to the ground. Lastly, special thanks and greetings to all the citizens of Malawi that we met during our trip. *Zikomo kwambile.* It was a pleasure travelling in your land.

This Book

David Else researched and wrote the first, multi-country, edition *Malawi, Mozambique & Zambia*. He returned to Malawi to research and update this single-country edition of *Malawi*.

From the Publisher
This edition of Malawi was edited and proofed in Lonely Planet's Melbourne office by John Hinman, with expert assistance from Hilary Rogers, Justin Flynn and Adam Ford. Rod Zandbergs laid the foundations for the mapping, then passed the baton to Jody Whiteoak, who completed the mapping as well as coordinating the layout and design and drawing the chapter ends. Hunor Csutoros searched exhaustively for a reliable climate chart. Thanks to seniors Virginia Maxwell on the editing side, and designers Vince Patton and Adriana Mammarella for their guidance and careful checking, and to Adriana for her invaluable Photoshop skills. Thanks also to: Annie Horner for her persistence in tracking down images; Matt King for coordinating the illustrations; the ever-patient and wise Sarah Sloane for fielding the many technical questions; Shahara Ahmed for the map legend; and Tim Uden and Lisa Borg for the Quark support. Finally, a drum roll for Quentin Frayne who compiled the Language section.

Acknowledgments

THANKS

Many thanks to the following travellers who used the previous edition, *Malawi, Mozambique & Zambia*, and wrote to us with helpful hints, useful advice and interesting anecdotes about travelling in Malawi.

Anthony Abi-Saab, Pernilla Andren-Stridsberg, Katherine Angus, Helena Anston, Clare Baines, Saskia Beljering, John Boudette, Bo Brenstrup, Thomas Brillisauer, Jillian Brown, Jan Burgemeister, Kerrry Burke, George Casley, Dr O Cavojsky, Robert Chettle, Philippa Crocker, Katie Cuddon, James Dalton, Ronald de Hommel, Tanja de Kort, John Deacon, Luke Dealtry, Peter Ditoto, Angelika Eger, Rob Fairbairn, Laura Fargher, Bruno Fehrenbach, Imogen Franks, Aaron Frick, Rickard Fsridgh, Amy Gordon, Nick Graham, Atle van Beelen Granlund, Claudia Hammett, Amy Hardy, Andrea Harold, Peter Harrop, Dr Pradeep Henry, David Hickie, Caryl Hirons, Jonathon Mark Holder, Dennis Johnson, Hugh Johnson, Ola Jornmark, Dr Ludger Kahl, Rafael Kampel, Karen Kersten, Elizabeth Keyes, Janice Klinger, Cobus Kotze, Johan Kwant, Claire Langdon, Bent K Larsen, Magnus Larsson, Ben Lawton, Cameron Lindsay, Suzanne Martin, Margaux McDonald, Ruth McGuire, Claire McLaughlin, Patricia Milton, James Money-Kyrle, Oliver Moore, Rainer Muller, Jonas B Nielsen, John Osman, Rene Raaijmakers, Margareet & Paul Ravensbergen, Joanna Rees, Susan Reynolds, Phil Richardson, Matthias Ripp, Kevin Salvage, Michaella Schpiid, Viv Scott, Natasha Skoric, Nigel Snow, Shane Soutter, Rob Stacey, David Steinke, Reinhard Storiko, Andrew Thorburn, Martin Thormann, Oliver Thornton, Cindy Tsang, Belinda Tucker, Jaap van Maurik, Andrew van Smeerdijk, Fatima Vieira, Goetz Voland, Frank Vreys, Justine Waddington, Nigel Walder, Helen Walker, Caroline York, Daniella Zipkin

Foreword

ABOUT LONELY PLANET GUIDEBOOKS

The story begins with a classic travel adventure: Tony and Maureen Wheeler's 1972 journey across Europe and Asia to Australia. Useful information about the overland trail did not exist at that time, so Tony and Maureen published the first Lonely Planet guidebook to meet a growing need.

From a kitchen table, then from a tiny office in Melbourne (Australia), Lonely Planet has become the largest independent travel publisher in the world, an international company with offices in Melbourne, Oakland (USA), London (UK) and Paris (France).

Today Lonely Planet guidebooks cover the globe. There is an ever-growing list of books and there's information in a variety of forms and media. Some things haven't changed. The main aim is still to help make it possible for adventurous travellers to get out there – to explore and better understand the world.

At Lonely Planet we believe travellers can make a positive contribution to the countries they visit – if they respect their host communities and spend their money wisely. Since 1986 a percentage of the income from each book has been donated to aid projects and human rights campaigns.

Updates Lonely Planet thoroughly updates each guidebook as often as possible. This usually means there are around two years between editions, although for more unusual or more stable destinations the gap can be longer. Check the imprint page (following the colour map at the beginning of the book) for publication dates.

Between editions up-to-date information is available in two free newsletters – the paper *Planet Talk* and email *Comet* (to subscribe, contact any Lonely Planet office) – and on our Web site at www.lonelyplanet.com. The *Upgrades* section of the Web site covers a number of important and volatile destinations and is regularly updated by Lonely Planet authors. *Scoop* covers news and current affairs relevant to travellers. And, lastly, the *Thorn Tree* bulletin board and *Postcards* section of the site carry unverified, but fascinating, reports from travellers.

Correspondence The process of creating new editions begins with the letters, postcards and emails received from travellers. This correspondence often includes suggestions, criticisms and comments about the current editions. Interesting excerpts are immediately passed on via newsletters and the Web site, and everything goes to our authors to be verified when they're researching on the road. We're keen to get more feedback from organisations or individuals who represent communities visited by travellers.

> Lonely Planet gathers information for everyone who's curious about the planet – and especially for those who explore it first-hand. Through guidebooks, phrasebooks, activity guides, maps, literature, newsletters, image library, TV series and Web site we act as an information exchange for a worldwide community of travellers.

Research Authors aim to gather sufficient practical information to enable travellers to make informed choices and to make the mechanics of a journey run smoothly. They also research historical and cultural background to help enrich the travel experience and allow travellers to understand and respond appropriately to cultural and environmental issues.

Authors don't stay in every hotel because that would mean spending a couple of months in each medium-sized city and, no, they don't eat at every restaurant because that would mean stretching belts beyond capacity. They do visit hotels and restaurants to check standards and prices, but feedback based on readers' direct experiences can be very helpful.

Many of our authors work undercover, others aren't so secretive. None of them accept freebies in exchange for positive write-ups. And none of our guidebooks contain any advertising.

Production Authors submit their raw manuscripts and maps to offices in Australia, USA, UK or France. Editors and cartographers – all experienced travellers themselves – then begin the process of assembling the pieces. When the book finally hits the shops, some things are already out of date, we start getting feedback from readers and the process begins again ...

WARNING & REQUEST

Things change – prices go up, schedules change, good places go bad and bad places go bankrupt – nothing stays the same. So, if you find things better or worse, recently opened or long since closed, please tell us and help make the next edition even more accurate and useful. We genuinely value all the feedback we receive. Julie Young coordinates a well travelled team that reads and acknowledges every letter, postcard and email and ensures that every morsel of information finds its way to the appropriate authors, editors and cartographers for verification.

Everyone who writes to us will find their name in the next edition of the appropriate guidebook. They will also receive the latest issue of *Planet Talk*, our quarterly printed newsletter, or *Comet*, our monthly email newsletter. Subscriptions to both newsletters are free. The very best contributions will be rewarded with a free guidebook.

Excerpts from your correspondence may appear in new editions of Lonely Planet guidebooks, the Lonely Planet Web site, *Planet Talk* or *Comet*, so please let us know if you *don't* want your letter published or your name acknowledged.

Send all correspondence to the Lonely Planet office closest to you:

Australia: Locked Bag 1, Footscray, Victoria 3011
USA: 150 Linden St, Oakland, CA 94607
UK: 10A Spring Place, London NW5 3BH
France: 1 rue du Dahomey, 75011 Paris

Or email us at: talk2us@lonelyplanet.com.au

For news, views and updates see our Web site: www.lonelyplanet.com

HOW TO USE A LONELY PLANET GUIDEBOOK

The best way to use a Lonely Planet guidebook is any way you choose. At Lonely Planet we believe the most memorable travel experiences are often those that are unexpected, and the finest discoveries are those you make yourself. Guidebooks are not intended to be used as if they provide a detailed set of infallible instructions!

Contents All Lonely Planet guidebooks follow roughly the same format. The Facts about the Destination chapters or sections give background information ranging from history to weather. Facts for the Visitor gives practical information on issues like visas and health. Getting There & Away gives a brief starting point for researching travel to and from the destination. Getting Around gives an overview of the transport options when you arrive.

The peculiar demands of each destination determine how subsequent chapters are broken up, but some things remain constant. We always start with background, then proceed to sights, places to stay, places to eat, entertainment, getting there and away, and getting around information – in that order.

Heading Hierarchy Lonely Planet headings are used in a strict hierarchical structure that can be visualised as a set of Russian dolls. Each heading (and its following text) is encompassed by any preceding heading that is higher on the hierarchical ladder.

Entry Points We do not assume guidebooks will be read from beginning to end, but that people will dip into them. The traditional entry points are the list of contents and the index. In addition, however, some books have a complete list of maps and an index map illustrating map coverage.

There may also be a colour map that shows highlights. These highlights are dealt with in greater detail in the Facts for the Visitor chapter, along with planning questions and suggested itineraries. Each chapter covering a geographical region usually begins with a locator map and another list of highlights. Once you find something of interest in a list of highlights, turn to the index.

Maps Maps play a crucial role in Lonely Planet guidebooks and include a huge amount of information. A legend is printed on the back page. We seek to have complete consistency between maps and text, and to have every important place in the text captured on a map. Map key numbers usually start in the top left corner.

Although inclusion in a guidebook usually implies a recommendation we cannot list every good place. Exclusion does not necessarily imply criticism. In fact there are a number of reasons why we might exclude a place – sometimes it is simply inappropriate to encourage an influx of travellers.

Introduction

The tourist brochures bill Malawi as 'the warm heart of Africa' and, for once, the hype is true. Malawi's scenery is stunning and (although we hate to generalise) Malawians really do seem to be among the friendliest people you could meet anywhere. On top of this, Malawi offers a wonderful variety of attractions, with enough to satisfy the wants of most visitors. You can choose from a palm-lined lake shore to an airy escarpment viewpoint, from remote wilderness to a busy marketplace and from a basic camp site to a luxury hotel. Glossy shopping mall to traditional fishing village, hideaway island to popular beach, hiking trail to safari jeep, bus or train to private plane, mountain bike to dugout canoe, zebras to jackals, elephants to leopards, little bee-eaters to African fish eagles... The options are endless.

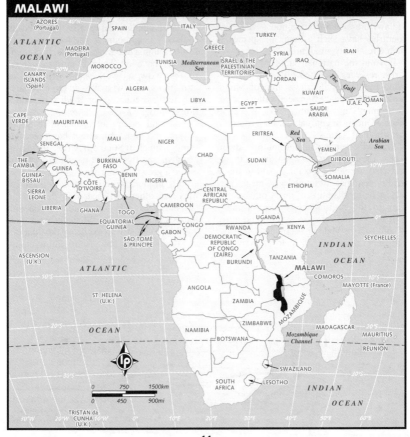

MALAWI

For most visitors, the country's main attraction is Lake Malawi, one of the Great Rift Valley lakes, stretching some 500km down the eastern border. Two of Malawi's high-profile wildlife parks, Liwonde and Lake Malawi, are on or near the lake, and there's an ever-increasing number of hotels, lodges and campgrounds being built along the southern and western shores. The diving and snorkelling here are very highly rated.

Away from the lake are several more national parks and wildlife reserves, including Kasungu, Nkhotakota, Lengwe, Vwaza Marsh and the Nyika Plateau – all different and all with something special to offer. As well as mammals and fish, the birds of Malawi are a major attraction – very few countries have such a range of species in such a relatively small area.

Beyond the national parks, Malawi has forest reserves, isolated hills and the fantastic highland wilderness area of Mount Mulanje, where you find deep valleys, sheer escarpments and dramatic peaks, as well as some of the most enjoyable hiking routes in the whole of Africa.

Malawi's compact size is another advantage – the distances between places to see and visit are never too long. Add to this a road system that, although by no means perfect, is better than that of many other countries in the region, as well as a fairly efficient public transport service and a trip of any sort in Malawi becomes a real joy. The general lack of hassle so often associated with travel in the developing world has given the country another appropriate subtitle: 'Africa for beginners'.

Since the mid-1990s, Malawi has changed considerably, following the downfall of the nonagenarian President-for-Life Dr Hastings Kamuzu Banda. Also gone is Banda's infamous and restrictive dress code, which dictated that all women had to wear a skirt and men had to have short hair. These whimsical dictates were symptomatic of a much deeper malaise – Banda's iron grip on a terrorised population. But elections in 1994 ushered in a multiparty system and a level of freedom (albeit not without significant problems) never before enjoyed in the country.

Major changes have also occurred in Malawi's neighbours to the west, east and south: Zambia and Mozambique, two countries that have long been off most travellers' routes. Now, as well as its own host of attractions, Malawi makes an obvious gateway to these countries or an ideal introduction to wider travels in the region.

Since the ending of apartheid in South Africa, the knock-on effect has been felt through much of Southern Africa, including Malawi, and this whole region has experienced a growth in tourist numbers, bringing with it an increase in hotels, hostels, activities and other facilities. But, despite the popularity, Malawi is far from over-run with tourists and travellers. Whatever your budget, Malawi is still an exclusive destination, and one that very few visitors fail to enjoy.

Facts about Malawi

HISTORY
Prehistory

Africa has long been regarded as the 'cradle of humanity', and hominid ('humanlike') species are known to have inhabited the area now called Malawi, along with many other parts of East and Southern Africa, between three and two million years ago. The oldest hominid remnant found in Malawi is a single jawbone of the species *Homo rudolfensis*, which palaeontologists calculate to be 2.5 million years old.

Most scientists agree that by about two million years ago, changing climatic and environmental conditions had resulted in the evolution of several hominid species, including *Homo habilis* and *Homo erectus*. By about 1.5 to one million years ago, the latter seems to have become dominant and developed basic tool-making skills, evolving into *Homo sapiens* (essentially the same as modern humans). This species led a nomadic existence, eventually spreading outwards from Africa to inhabit all parts of the world as it then was, slowly evolving further into various races according to local environment and other factors.

The Stone Age

Over the next million years it seems that *Homo sapiens* slowly improved the use of stone tools. At first these were large and clumsy, but by about 150,000 years ago people were using lighter stone points, spear heads, knives, saws and other finer tools useful for various hunting and gathering activities. Archaeologists classify this period of tool making as the Stone Age, divided into Early, Middle and Late stages. (The term applies to an individual group's level of technological development, rather than to a specific period of time within the whole of Africa or the world.)

In Malawi, archaeologists have found evidence to suggest that Early Stone Age settlements existed along the shore of Lake Malawi around 100,000 years ago, while Middle Stone Age sites dating from 10,000 years ago have also been discovered in this area. The evidence further suggests that the early inhabitants of this area were the same Boskopoid people who inhabited much of this part of Africa – the ancestors of the pygmies in Central Africa and the San ('Bushmen') of Southern Africa, who now survive only in isolated pockets.

The Iron Age

About 2000 years ago, these Stone Age Malawians came under pressure from the Bantu-speaking peoples (referred to as the Bantu), who were gradually migrating into the area. This movement was part of what has become known as the 'great migrations' – an important feature of East and Southern Africa's history. In the last 3000 years waves of peoples have crossed and recrossed the region, some groups searching for new territory as their populations grew, others forced to move by climatic change. The movements inevitably had a knock-on effect too, as groups being invaded from one side expanded in the other direction. Most migrations took place over hundreds of years, and were made up of many short moves (from valley to valley, or from one cultivation area to the next), with dominant peoples slowly absorbing and assimilating other groups in the process.

The Bantu migration was the most significant because this group of people had knowledge of iron working. Armed with iron tools to clear forest and cultivate more effectively, the Bantus migrated from the area that is now Cameroon, through the Congo (Zaïre) basin and onto the East and Southern African plateaus, arriving in the region around 100 BC. Over the next 1000 years they spread across present-day Uganda, Kenya and Tanzania, and southwards into Malawi, Zambia, Mozambique and eventually South Africa.

In Malawi, as in other areas, it seems that the original Stone Age inhabitants and the

Bantu newcomers co-existed for a long period (stories of 'little red men' remain part of Bantu tradition in remote areas), although the powerful new arrivals eventually became completely dominant. In Malawi, rock and cave paintings remain as permanent reminders of the Stone Age people at a number of sites, including Dedza, Fingira Cave on the Nyika Plateau, and on Hora Mountain near Mzimba. Some paintings are believed to be the work of the early Bantu inhabitants who were inspired by the designs of earlier peoples – their paintings tended to consist of abstract shapes and patterns rather than figures.

Several Iron Age sites established by the Bantu have been discovered in Malawi, particularly around the south-western shores of Lake Malawi. The Bantu also had the technology to work clay, and remains from the places they inhabited consist principally of a number of distinctive types of pottery or 'ware'. The styles vary according to geographical area and age. For example, 'Nkope ware', the earliest style of Iron Age pottery, was found in the area around Mangochi, and can be broadly dated to between the 3rd and 10th centuries AD. The latest style – 'Mwudzu ware' – dates from as recently as the late 1550s.

Early Migrations

Between the 14th and 16th centuries AD, waves of Bantu-speaking people called Tumbuka and Phoka migrated into the north of Malawi, probably from the Congo region via Tanzania, although their traditions do not agree on this. By the 17th century they had settled around the highlands of Nyika and Viphya. Meanwhile, in the south, the Maravi people (also known as Chewa or Nyanja – for more details on names, see 'The Naming of Malawi' boxed text) came in from present-day Congo

The Naming of Malawi

During colonial times the country we now call Malawi was known as Nyasaland. The derivation of both its old and new names is not entirely clear and is the subject of some dispute.

When explorer David Livingstone first reached Lake Malawi he called it Lake Nyassa. Most authorities agree that 'Nyassa' is derived from the word *nyanja*, which means 'lake' in the language of the indigenous Chewa people. There is also a Nyanja people, but in Malawi this seems to be another name for the Chewa, although other authorities refer to the Chewa and the Nyanja as separate peoples. In colonial times and the early years of independence the language of the Chewa was called Chi-Nyanja (or Chinyanja) but was renamed Chichewa in 1968 when it became the national language.

Early Portuguese explorers who reached the area in the 16th century recorded a powerful kingdom called Maravi, which seems to have covered much of southern Malawi, as well as parts of Mozambique and Zambia. They also referred to the lake and the local people as Maravi, but it is not clear if the name of the people was derived from the lake, or vice versa. It seems the Chewa/Nyanja are descended from the Maravi. In his journals, Livingstone also mentioned people called Maravi inhabiting the area, although this may have been based on the Portuguese reports.

At independence a commission was established to find a new name for the new country. 'Malaŵi' was chosen, officially inspired by the word *malavi*, which means reflected light, haze, flames or rays in Chichewa. (The word is also spelt *maravi* – 'l' and 'r' seem interchangeable in Chichewa.) This new name was seen as a reference to the sun rising over the lake, bringing a fresh light to the country. It may also be connected to the Maravi people, although no people of this name inhabit Malawi today.

The ŵ in Malaŵi is a 'soft v', and English speakers should pronounce a sound somewhere between 'w', 'v' and 'f'. Correctly, the ŵ should be used, but these days the name of the country is generally pronounced with the w (as in 'wee'), and the circumflex is often dropped.

(Zaïre) and established a large and powerful kingdom that spread all over southern Malawi and parts of present-day Mozambique and Zambia.

In the 18th century more Bantu newcomers arrived in Malawi. These included the Lambya people, who moved from southern Tanzania, and the Ngonde people, who came from the Congo (Zaïre) region. They both settled in the north of Malawi.

Later Migrations

The early 19th century brought two more significant migrations. The Yao from western Mozambique invaded the highlands of southern Malawi, killing the more peaceful local inhabitants as they went, or capturing them for sale into slavery. An important factor in their successful conquest of this area was that they were supplied firearms by Arab traders from the east coast of Africa (see 'The Horrors of Slavery' boxed text).

At about the same time, groups of Zulu people were migrating northwards as part of a great movement of populations called the *difaqane* (which translates as 'the scattering of tribes'; the Zulu word for it, *mfecane*, means 'the crushing'), initiated around 1820 by a powerful Zulu king called Shaka, who was based in present-day South Africa. A large number of displaced Zulus settled in Zimbabwe to become the Matabele. Others continued north, some as far as Tanzania. Around 1840, several groups settled in central and northern Malawi and became known as the Angoni or Ngoni. In their conquest of the local tribes, particularly the Chewa, the tendency of the Ngoni was to integrate captives into their own community, rather than selling them into slavery, as was the habit of the Yao.

The Rise of Slavery

As the Bantu had been spreading across the interior of Africa, people from Arabia were slowly moving from the Gulf, trading goods down the east coast of Africa. By AD 700 the first waves of Bantu people had reached the coast and come into contact with the Arabs. The latter traded with the local Bantu inhabitants, buying ivory, gold and slaves to take back to Arabia. Between AD 1000 and 1500 the Arab-influenced Bantu people founded several major settlements along the coast, the most notable being Kilwa, Lamu and the island of Zanzibar.

As trade flourished, Arab influence grew. A small number of Arabs settled on the coast, and there was some intermarriage – particularly in the areas now called Kenya and Tanzania. Eventually an entire culture, essentially African but with a strong Arab influence, was created. It became known as Swahili (from the Arab word for 'coast') and had its own distinct language, customs and traditions, which remain intact today.

By the 18th century the trading settlements had become powerful independent city-states, each ruled by a sultan. These city-states included Mombasa and Zanzibar, which became major import and export centres for the transport of goods between the interior of Africa and various points around the Indian Ocean.

Further south, the Swahili-Arabs established coastal trading stations at places such as Quelimane and Ilha de Moçambique, both in present-day Mozambique. In fact, Mozambique may be derived from the name of a local sultan called Mussa Mbiki.

The 'goods' carried between the interior and the coast included slaves. While slavery, and a trade in slaves, had existed in Africa for many centuries, it was not until the early 19th century that demand from outside Africa (in this case from Arabia, Persia and other regions surrounding the Indian Ocean) considerably increased the need to supply slaves from the eastern and southern parts of the continent. (A separate supply network existed in West Africa, catering for the demand for slaves from the Caribbean and the Americas.) The demand in East and Southern Africa encouraged Swahili-Arab slave traders to push deeper into the interior, in an attempt to increase the supply.

Present-day Malawi, along with parts of Zambia, became a major 'hunting ground' for the slave traders. They often used the services of powerful local tribes such as the Yao to raid and capture their unfortunate

The Horrors of Slavery

At the height of slave trading in the mid-19th century, the Swahili-Arabs together with dominant tribes are reckoned to have either killed or sold into slavery 80,000 to 100,000 Africans per year. Those taken from the areas now called Malawi and Zambia would be brought to one of the Arab trading centres, such as Nkhotakota, Karonga or Salima, where they would be sold to 'wholesalers'. They were crammed into dhows and taken across Lake Malawi. On the other side they were marched across Mozambique to the east coast, usually chained or tied to poles of wood to prevent escape. Many also carried elephant tusks, as ivory was another major commodity. Any slaves too ill to make the journey were simply abandoned, and died of dehydration or were killed by wild animals.

At the coast, the slaves were once more loaded back into dhows for the hazardous journey north to Zanzibar. They would be packed tightly, lying down in several layers in the hold of the boat and jammed in place by the deck holding the layer above. For the duration of the voyage they would have no food or water, and would lie in their own excrement. Those who died – and there were many, particularly if journeys took longer than anticipated because of poor winds – could not be removed until the journey ended.

Those who managed to survive all this were sold once more in the large slave market in Zanzibar and then shipped to places such as Arabia or India.

neighbours. Several trading centres were established in Malawi including Karonga and Nkhotakota – towns on the shore of Lake Malawi that still bear a strong Swahili-Arab influence today. (For example, large sailing boats on the lake are still built in the Arab *dhow* [design] and many of the people in the northern lake shore regions are Muslim.)

The First Europeans

The first Europeans to arrive in Malawi were Portuguese explorers who reached the African interior from the east coast (present-day Mozambique). They were active in the region east of Lake Malawi from the 16th to early 19th centuries, long before the better-known British explorers came through, but this period is only sketchily covered by most histories.

The Portuguese established trading posts in the Zambezi Valley, most notably at Tete and Vila de Sena (just to the south of present-day Malawi's southern border). By 1540 both Tete and Vila de Sena were sizeable settlements. However, although the Portuguese established trade links with the local tribes in this area, only a few ventured inland or beyond the coast and the lower Zambezi Valley. One of these was Gaspar Bocarro. In 1616 he journeyed from Tete through the valley of the Shire River (then spelt Shiray, and still pronounced '**shir**-ee' today) to Lake Chilwa – to the south of Lake Malawi, through the south of what is now Tanzania and back into Mozambique.

The most famous explorer to reach this area was David Livingstone, a Scottish missionary, even though his claim to be the first European to see Lake Malawi in 1859 is refuted by the records of another Portuguese explorer, Candido da Costa Cardoso, who sighted the lake in his travels during 1846. However, Livingstone's exploration heralded the arrival of Europeans in a way that was to change the nature of Malawi and the surrounding region forever.

Livingstone & the Missionaries

Between 1842 and 1856, Livingstone had been busy in the areas of Africa south of Malawi – exploring the Kalahari Desert and the upper reaches of the Zambezi River, and also crossing the continent from the east to the west coast.

On his return to Britain after these expeditions, he spoke at several public meetings about the 'undiscovered' interior of Africa, and particularly about the horrors of the slave trade. A speech at Cambridge University in 1857 led to the founding of the Universities Mission in Central Africa

(UMCA), the aim of which was to combat the slave trade by encouraging alternative commerce, to introduce the ideals of 'civilisation', and to establish missions for promoting the spread of Christianity.

Livingstone returned to Africa in 1858 to explore the Zambezi region in more detail. This was his second major expedition, which was to last until 1864. Livingstone and his party travelled up the River Zambezi on a small steamboat named the *Ma-Robert*, but about 500km from the mouth of the river their route was blocked by the vast gorge and series of rapids now called Cahora Bassa. Today the gorge and many of the rapids are under a lake formed by the Cahora Bassa dam in Mozambique.

The distance they had travelled was only a relatively short way up this great river, and still far from the deep African interior that Livingstone hoped to reach. The presence of the rapids meant navigation would be impossible, and thus trade and settlement unlikely, along the Zambezi. Undaunted, Livingstone interpreted the obstacle as a sign from God, radically changed his plans and, with a few team-members, followed the Shire River, a major tributary of the Zambezi, upstream into the area now known as southern Malawi.

The Shire River was navigable at first, but after about 200km the explorers reached another series of rapids and waterfalls that blocked their way. Livingstone named these the Murchison Cataracts (after a notable geographer of the day, who is also remembered by a large waterfall in Uganda); today the series of rapids are often known as the Shire Cataracts or Kapichira Rapids, after Kapichira Falls – the largest waterfall in the series. The explorers established a base camp here while Livingstone and his companion John Kirk headed further north, reaching south of Lake Malawi to Lake Chilwa. They loosely followed the footsteps of the Portuguese explorer Gaspar Bocarro, who had come this way over two centuries earlier, but Livingstone was either unaware of this predecessor or unwilling to admit that he might not have been the first European in the region.

At Lake Chilwa, the local people told Livingstone of the even larger lake to the north, so he returned to the Zambezi for more staff and supplies, then once again travelled north through the Liwonde area and past Lake Malombe. In September 1859 Livingstone and his small party finally reached Lake Malawi. Livingstone named it Lake Nyassa, and over the following weeks explored much of its western shore.

Throughout this journey, Livingstone learnt from local people that the Swahili-Arab traders and other powerful African tribes regularly raided the area around Lake Malawi for slaves. His journals record frequent sightings of dead bodies and abandoned villages. He even met a slaving party, complete with captives, and realised that a major slave route between the interior and the trading settlements on the coast of Africa passed the narrow gap of land between Lakes Malawi and Malombe (where today's town of Mangochi now stands).

Livingstone returned to the Shire River in 1861 accompanied by seven UMCA missionaries (six priests and one Charles Frederick Mackenzie, who in Cape Town had been consecrated as the Missionary Bishop of Central Africa) and a team of porters from Sesheke, a town on the Zambezi River in present-day Zambia. They retraced the earlier route, then Livingstone and a few members of the party pushed on up the Shire River and reached Lake Malawi, then spent two months exploring the western shore of the lake. In his journals Livingstone noted and named several places including Cape Maclear (after an astronomer in the then Cape Colony) and 'Maclear Harbour', which is the site of today's Cape Maclear beach – a popular tourist destination today.

Meanwhile, Charles Mackenzie attempted to establish the initial UMCA mission at a place called Magomero in the area of high ground to the north and east of the Shire River – called the Shire Highlands. Although the first mission was built, less than a year after taking up his post Mackenzie died from fever while travelling on the Lower Shire (the part of the river below the

'Dr Livingstone, I Presume'

After leaving Lake Malawi on his third expedition, Livingstone aimed for Lake Tanganyika, which he thought might be a key to the source of the Nile, and then went westwards into today's eastern Zambia, to reach Lakes Mweru and Bangweulu, which again he thought might be Nile headwaters.

Livingstone had last been seen by other Europeans in 1866, and last heard of alive in 1868, but since then there had been no news of his whereabouts, or even if he was alive or dead.

Henry Stanley, a Welsh-American journalist working for the *New York Herald*, mounted The Second Livingstone Search Expedition. He eventually tracked down Livingstone near the town of Ujiji on the banks of Lake Tanganyika in late 1871. They were both reported to be lost for words, as stiff formal behaviour was expected of gentlemen even in such remote places. Stanley greeted him with 'Dr Livingstone, I presume', which has gone down as one of history's most remembered phrases, although for the rest of his life he regretted uttering what he though was such a pompous and hollow greeting.

The two men explored Lake Tanganyika for a few months, and then Stanley tried to persuade Livingstone to return to England with him. But he was unsuccessful, and Livingstone doggedly continued alone on his quest for the source of the Nile. He returned to the area around Lake Bangweulu, where he became seriously sick and hopelessly lost. He finally died at the village of Chitambo, in the territory of the Ilala people, south-east of Lake Bangweulu in present-day Zambia, on 1 May 1873.

Two of his faithful followers called Juma and Suze (also spelt Chuma and Guze) buried his heart under a tree in Chitambo, then embalmed the rest of his body and carried it over 1000km eastwards across present-day Zambia, Malawi and Tanzania to Zanzibar. From here it was shipped back to England, to be buried in Westminster Abbey in April 1874.

In Malawi today, Livingstone is still remembered. The missionary centre of Livingstonia is named in his honour and the commercial capital, Blantyre, is named after his birthplace. Juma and Suze are also remembered, along with Livingstone, in the stained glass window of the church at Livingstonia. The *Ilala* steam-ship which still plies Lake Malawi is named after a boat used by early missionaries who came to the area after Livingstone, which in turn recalls the place where he died.

Kapichira Rapids) and was buried near the village of Chiromo. His remains were later moved to Blantyre, after some international boundary alterations meant the site of his original grave was in Portuguese territory.

Undeterred by Mackenzie's death and many other perils, more missionaries came to Malawi through the rest of the early 1860s. They built a new mission in the Lower Shire area, but suffered terribly from malaria and other illnesses, and were also in conflict with the local people. In 1864, the surviving missionaries withdrew to Zanzibar (the region's main trading centre) off the east coast of Africa, and there was a pause in missionary activity in Malawi.

Livingstone's Last Journey

Despite the problems encountered by the missionaries he'd inspired, Livingstone returned to the region around Lake Malawi once again in 1866 – his third (and last) major expedition in Africa. This time, as well as to bring to European attention the plight of African people captured for the slave trade, the main object of the expedition was to find the source of the River Nile – a geographical quest that had fascinated and baffled geographers for many centuries.

Livingstone set out from Zanzibar and crossed what is now southern Tanzania and northern Mozambique to reach Lake Malawi. He then travelled north to reach the southern end of Lake Tanganyika. During this time he fired, or was abandoned by, several of the Indian and African retainers he had recruited in Zanzibar. They made their way back to Zanzibar and reported that Livingstone had been killed by slave traders.

This story was not fully believed, so in 1867 the Livingstone Search Expedition, led by one Lieutenant Young, who had been with Livingstone on the Shire River in 1862, was sent to find the missing explorer. (This later became known as the First Livingstone Search Expedition.)

Young and his party retraced the now established route by boat up the Zambezi and Lower Shire to the Murchison Cataracts, then overland to the Upper Shire, and then by boat again onto Lake Malawi. They met several local chiefs on the west side of the lake, at towns like Nkhotakota and Karonga, where Livingstone was well-known, and discovered that Livingstone had in fact continued north in safety, and the story was a fabrication. Young decided not to follow Livingstone any further, and headed back southwards down Lake Malawi. On this return voyage down the lake, the party sheltered from a violent storm at the bay that Livingstone had earlier named Cape Maclear. Young noted that it made an excellent harbour and an ideal place for a settlement.

Despite the reports that he was alive, nothing more was heard from Livingstone for over two years. He was located by another explorer called Henry Stanley in 1871, but then disappeared again and eventually died in 1873 (see the boxed text 'Dr Livingstone, I Presume').

The Livingstonia Missionaries

If Livingstone's exploration heralded the arrival of the Europeans in Malawi, his death confirmed their presence by rekindling missionary zeal in Britain and support for missions in this part of Africa. Probably more than any other country in Africa, the history and the very existence of Malawi has been shaped and influenced by missionaries.

On the basis of his earlier experience, first with Livingstone himself, and later on the First Livingstone Search Expedition, Lieutenant Young was asked to lead the missionaries' return to Central Africa. In 1875, he returned to Lake Malawi with a group of missionaries from the Free Church of Scotland. They built a new mission at Cape Maclear, which was named Livingstonia, after the great man himself. Second-in-command of this pioneering party was Dr Robert Laws. There were six other Europeans and four freed slaves who were recruited in Cape Town. They also had a new steam-powered boat, called the *Ilala*, specially designed to be taken apart and reassembled to allow easy transfer through the Murchison Cataracts.

The Free Church mission was reinforced by new arrivals in 1876, who included James Stewart, who had also been with Livingstone on the Shire River expeditions of the early 1860s. His arrival allowed Young to return to England, and Stewart became a leading figure in this new missionary endeavour. In the same party was a William Black.

At the same time a group of missionaries from the Established Church of Scotland arrived in the Shire River area. This group also wanted to found a mission in Central Africa, and despite religious differences there was considerable cooperation between the two church groups.

Using the skills of a pioneer called Henry Henderson, who had helped Young and his party at Cape Maclear, the Established Church missionaries built a mission in the Shire Highlands, which they called Blantyre after Livingstone's birthplace. By 1891 Blantyre was a thriving community and the Church of St Michael and All Angels was completed. This important historical landmark can still be seen – for more information see the Blantyre & Limbe chapter.

Meanwhile, back at Cape Maclear, the Free Church mission on the lake shore proved to be malarial. William Black died of fever in 1877, and in the following few years three other missionaries and a local follower also died. The five were buried in a small cemetery at the foot of the hills, which is still visible today (see Cape Maclear in the Central Malawi chapter). Despite the setbacks, a high point of the mission's history was the baptism of Albert Namalambe, the first African convert, in March 1881.

Later in 1881 the mission at Cape Maclear was abandoned in favour of another site, farther north along the lake shore at a place called Bandawe. This also proved unsuitable, so in 1894 the Livingstonia Mission was moved to an area of high ground in

Hard Work

The first missionaries suffered horribly at their early sites along Lake Malawi but, inspired by their faith, they continued trying to convert the local African people to Christianity; their efforts were met with a certain degree of understandable apathy and resistance. When they realised the second site at Bandawe was unsuccessful, the missionaries' leaders in Edinburgh tabulated the progress so far in laconic and typically Scottish terms:

Liabilities: five European graves, five years expenditure (£20,000), five years hardship and toil.

Assets: one convert, one abandoned mission.

between the eastern escarpment of the Nyika Plateau and Lake Malawi. This site was successful; the mission flourished and is still there today (see Livingstonia in the Northern Malawi chapter).

The Colonial Period

The early missionaries blazed the way for various adventurers and pioneer traders, who saw Central Africa as a land of almost endless opportunity. Still following Livingstone's footsteps, these early arrivals usually disembarked from ocean-going ships at the Portuguese port of Quelimane, from where they made their way by a small river and a section of overland travel to the Zambezi River. It was not possible to go directly to the Zambezi at that time as the mouth of the river was a vast delta of channels, swamps and sandbanks some 100km wide.

Once on the Zambezi it was possible to travel by boat upstream and into the Shire River. The farthest point that could be reached was once again the Murchison Cataracts (now called Kapichira Rapids), where a small staging post was established on the site of Livingstone's original camp. From here early travellers would continue overland to Blantyre, or to a place called Matope, above the rapids from where the Upper Shire could be followed to Lake Malawi.

In 1878, in Scotland, the Livingstonia Central African Mission Company was formed by private enterprise. Its object was to develop the Zambezi and Shire river route into Central Africa, and introduce trade to the area, working alongside the Livingstonia missionaries. Blantyre became the company base and trading centre, and by 1883 it had its own bank. On the Lower Shire the company operated up and down the river using small steamboats with heroic Scottish names like *Bruce* and *Scott*, ferrying goods and passengers between the interior and the coast. (See the boxed text 'Mandala & the African Lakes Corporation' in the Blantyre & Limbe chapter.)

In 1890 a navigable channel through the Zambezi Delta was discovered and the Livingstonia Central African Mission Company established a base here, called Chinde. It was recognised as a British Concession by the Portuguese, who controlled the surrounding territory. (See the boxed text 'Chinde – Gateway to Central Africa' later in this chapter.) By 1893 the company was renamed the African Lakes Company (later the African Lakes Corporation). Trade between the coast and the new territory continued to grow, and larger Mississippi-style paddle steamers, with names like *Cobra, Scorpion* and *Mosquito*, were launched. Chiromo (then spelt Tshiromo) developed as an inland port; it was the highest point on the river that the larger boats could reliably reach (although even then in the dry season they often grounded) and it was also the first settlement along the river that could be built entirely within British territory.

The African Lakes Corporation went on to establish a successful commercial network along the upper and lower sections of the Shire River and the shores of Lake Nyasa (as Lake Malawi was still called). As intended this had a serious effect on the Arab-controlled slave trade in the area, and after several clashes (the most notable being at Karonga – see the Northern Malawi chapter) many slave traders were forced to leave the area.

The Protectorate

By the 1880s the competition among the European powers in the area (known as the 'Scramble for Africa') was fierce. Britain was the dominant power in the Lake Malawi area, but Germany and Portugal both had claims. There had also been an increase in the slave trade again following the withdrawal of British naval ships from patrol on the East African coast. These factors together convinced the British Foreign Office that there was a need for greater protection of British interests in Malawi. They were therefore happy to accept the offer made in 1889 by the financier, industrialist and empire-builder Cecil Rhodes, on behalf of his British South Africa Company (BSAC), to invest in and administer the Shire Highlands area. Thus, in 1889, the Shire district was proclaimed a British protectorate. In 1891 the British Central Africa Protectorate, administered by Rhodes' BSAC, was extended to include much of the land along the west side of the lake. Sir Harry Johnston, formerly British Consul in Mozambique, was appointed first commissioner.

The colonial authorities made several attempts to stop the slave trade, but powerful local chiefs (mostly Yao and Ngoni) continued to prey on less-warlike tribes, capture slaves and send them to the east coast of Africa for shipment elsewhere. Forts were built to house garrisons of British and Indian soldiers who patrolled the area and frequently intercepted slave traders and their captives. These included Fort Anderson (which became Mulanje town), Fort Lister (near Phalombe, on the north side of Mt Mulanje) and Fort Johnston, which became Mangochi.

In 1907 the British Central Africa Protectorate became the colony of Nyasaland, with all responsibility transferred to the British Colonial Office. These moves led to an increase in the number of settlers from Europe. The route they used was still the same as Livingstone's almost 50 years earlier: the early travellers would go from Quelimane or Chinde to Chiromo or Kapichira Falls by boat, from where they would continue by land, onto the higher ground or to Lake Malawi. The coastal territory was now formally Portuguese East Africa (later to be named Mozambique), but at the village of Chiromo these travellers entered the territory of the new British colony. Nyasaland's first post office was built at Chiromo and became a vital link in the communications network that developed across the region (for more details see the boxed text 'The Mail Runners' in the Southern Malawi chapter).

Early Protest

Initially colonial rule brought some positive effects to the African people in the region.

Chinde – Gateway to Central Africa

Chinde was a port on the east coast of Africa, south of the present-day town of Quelimane in Mozambique. It was a British possession, surrounded by Portuguese territory and used as a gateway for travellers heading up the Zambezi and Shire Rivers to the British Central Africa Protectorate (BCAP), which was to become Malawi. As the BCAP grew in importance, so Chinde also grew. In 1896 there were 20 permanent British residents (early records don't say how many locals), and by the first decade of the 20th century more than 20 ships a year were unloading here; almost 4000 passengers annually passed through Chinde on their way to the interior.

In the following years, communications were improved by the construction of a railway between Beira, a Portuguese port south of Quelimane, and Port Herald (now called Nsanje) on the Shire River about 50 km downstream from Chiromo. Blantyre became an important staging post on the route between the Zambezi and Lake Malawi, and grew in importance. Chinde declined and in 1922 (due to the effects of river erosion and a severe storm) most of the town literally slid into the sea. By 1923 Chinde was completely abandoned, and was relinquished as a British possession.

For a start, the colonisers got rid of the slave traders. The inter-tribal conflicts, which had plagued the area for so long, also ceased. Other spin-offs included improvements in health care. However, as more European settlers arrived, the demand for land grew, and vast areas were bought from local chiefs. The hapless local inhabitants on the land found themselves labelled 'squatters' or tenants of a new landlord. A 'hut tax' was introduced and traditional methods of agriculture were discouraged. As a result, increasing numbers of Africans were forced to seek work on the white-settler plantations or become migrant workers in Northern and Southern Rhodesia (present-day Zambia and Zimbabwe) and South Africa. By the end of the 19th century some 6000 Africans were leaving the country every year. (The trend continued through the colonial period: by the 1950s this number had grown to 150,000 every year.)

The first serious effort to oppose the colonial government in Nyasaland occurred in the early 20th century. This was led by the Reverend John Chilembwe, a Malawian who was educated first by a radical English missionary and later at a Baptist school in the USA, where he had become involved in a movement supporting the rights of black people.

He returned to Nyasaland in 1900 as a priest. Encouraged by his experiences abroad and unhappy about the effects of colonialism, in his preachings he started to protest about European domination of the region. His outrage was further inflamed by the forced conscription of African men into the British colonial army at the outbreak of WWI in 1914, but his verbal and written protests were largely ignored.

Finally, in January 1915, he and his followers attacked the manager of a large estate neighbouring his mission near Magomero in the Shire Highlands. The manager, William Livingstone, was brutally decapitated, although his family was spared. Chilembwe followed up the attack by holding his usual Sunday service with Livingstone's head on the mission altar.

His plan had been to trigger a mass of uprisings, but they either failed or didn't materialise, and his rebellion was short-lived and swiftly crushed by the colonial authorities. His church was destroyed, many supporters were imprisoned, and Chilembwe himself was executed in Mulanje. Today John Chilembwe is remembered as a national hero, with many streets named in his honour.

Transition & Independence

After WWI, the British began to introduce ways for the African population to become involved in the administration of the country. But these were half-hearted and things happened very slowly. It wasn't until the 1950s that Africans were actually allowed to enter the government. On the economic front, events also moved slowly. Nyasaland proved to be a relatively unproductive colony with no mineral wealth and only limited plantations. Human labour proved to be the only major export.

In 1953, in an attempt to boost economic development in the region, Nyasaland was joined to the Federation of Northern and Southern Rhodesia (today's Zambia and Zimbabwe). At the same time there was a growing disenchantment with colonial rule among the African population, and the recently formed pro-independence Nyasaland African Congress (NAC) opposed the Federation. The leading figure of this movement was Dr Hastings Banda, who had been living in exile since the 1920s – see the boxed text 'Hastings Banda – the early years'.

The NAC had been formed in 1944 and became the principal voice of opposition to colonial rule. Its strength and influence, however, remained limited until Banda took over leadership. It was felt that his qualifications and period of living overseas would give the movement a respectable front. Banda was so successful in gaining support for the movement that just one year after he took over, the colonial authorities declared a state of emergency. Banda and other leaders were thrown into jail and the authorities went on a rampage of suppression in which 52 Africans were killed.

Nevertheless, opposition to colonial rule continued, and in April 1960 Banda was

Hastings Banda – the Early Years

Details about the early life of Hastings Banda are confused. It is likely that he was born around 1898. Historians believe it unlikely that it was as late as 1906 – his official birth date. He was brought up in the town of Kasungu in the centre of the country and initially trained as a teacher at the Livingstonia Mission. It is unclear why he left there in 1915, but his travels then took him to Johannesburg (legend has it he walked all the way). While working as an interpreter for Chewa men in the South African mines, he came into contact with a group of American missionaries who arranged and paid for his training as a doctor in the USA. Following qualification in Ohio he moved to Britain, setting up a practice in Liverpool and later in London. Following his missionary education he remained a member of the Church of Scotland, and while in Britain he became an elder of the church. In the 1950s, as the rise of African nationalism grew, he became one of a group of prominent African nationalists based in London. His friends at the time included Jomo Kenyatta and Kwame Nkrumah. By the end of the 1950s he had moved to Ghana, and it was from here, after 40 years abroad, that he was to be invited home to lead the independence movement in Nyasaland.

released. He stepped back into his position as head of the NAC, now renamed as the Malawi Congress Party.

In 1961 the colonial authorities invited him to a constitutional conference in London. In the elections that followed, Banda's Malawi Congress Party (MCP) swept to victory. Shortly afterwards the Federation of Rhodesia and Nyasaland was dissolved and Malawi became independent in July 1964. Banda became prime minister and head of government while the former governor, Sir Glyn Jones, remained head of state for a transitional period. In July 1966, Malawi became a republic and Banda was made president.

The Banda Era

Within weeks of taking power, Banda was consolidating his position. When major political differences began to surface between him and his ministers, Banda demanded they declare their allegiance to him. Rather than do this, many ministers resigned and took to opposition. Drawing his support from the peasant majority, Banda was quickly able to defeat this move by driving the opposition leaders into hiding or exile.

With the opposition muzzled, Banda continued to strengthen his dictatorial powers by having himself declared 'President for Life' in 1971, periodically banning the foreign press, and waging vendettas against any group he regarded as a threat. His power was further increased by the

establishment of two companies: Press Holdings was his personal business, part of which was the countrywide chain of PTC supermarkets; Admarc was the state Agricultural Development and Marketing Corporation, to which all agricultural produce was sold at fixed rates. These two organisations between them controlled the country's economy, and through them Banda gained total economic control.

Alongside this move towards dictatorship, Banda remained politically conservative. He kept a distance between himself and the leaders of the newly independent African-governed socialist countries that were emerging around him in the region. He tended to encourage Europeans to remain in managerial positions, maintaining that they were better qualified for such roles. Most famously, he established diplomatic ties with South Africa, whereas the surrounding countries (the 'frontline states') all imposed sanctions against the Pretoria regime.

South Africa, concerned about the rise in socialism within the region and needing to defend its apartheid system, was delighted to have a sympathetic neighbour, and initially rewarded Malawi with aid and trade. South Africans were established in top positions in some of Malawi's most important companies. South African advisers were involved in training the Malawian security forces (others came from Israel and Taiwan). South Africa also provided the initial loan financing the building of Lilongwe, declared Malawi's new capital in 1975, and financed a new rail link from Malawi to Nacala in Mozambique (until then Malawi's only rail link with the sea was the line to Beira, originally built in 1908).

There was a cooling of relations between South Africa and Malawi in the mid-1970s (Lilongwe was actually completed with funds from other donor countries), but by the mid-1980s things picked up and there was an increase in trade between the two countries again, principally of imports into Malawi rather than exports to South Africa. Malawi also became a base for Renamo units making incursions into northern Mozambique. (Renamo was an alliance of South African–backed, trained and funded 'rebel' groups, specifically organised to oppose Mozambique's first post-colonial Marxist government. They destroyed roads, railways, schools and all other aspects of the country's infrastructure, and killed millions of people.)

Throughout the 1970s and '80s, the Organization of African Unity (OAU) was furious at Banda's refusal to ostracise the South African regime. It could be argued, however, that at least his approach was honest and avoided charges of hypocrisy. This was unlike several other African countries that had outwardly condemned South Africa while secretly maintaining trade links.

At home, Banda's increasingly repressive regime resulted in innumerable political prisoners and little observation of basic human rights. In a slight liberalisation in 1977 some 2000 detainees were released, but thousands more remained in jail.

In 1978, in the first general election to be held since independence, Banda personally vetted everyone who intended to stand as a candidate and demanded that each pass an English examination (thereby precluding 90% of the population). Even with these advantages, one Banda supporter lost his seat. He was simply reinstated.

Banda retained his grip on the country through the 1980s. The distinctions between the president, the party, the country, the government and Press Holdings became increasingly blurred. Quite simply, Banda

was Malawi. The phrase 'Malawi is a one-man-Banda' was coined. Prominent figures were expected to give total support to 'His Excellency'. If this support was not forthcoming, they were relieved of their posts, or worse. The secretary general of the MCP (who was also the managing director of Press Holdings) and two cabinet ministers were fired for 'disciplinary offences' after they questioned presidential directives. In 1983 three other ministers died in a mysterious car crash. There was a small exiled opposition movement, the Socialist League of Malawi, but this lost momentum when their leader was murdered in Zimbabwe. It wasn't only high-profile people who suffered; one newspaper reported the disappearance and murder of more than 250,000 people during the 30 years of Banda's rule.

Banda's Downfall

The 1990s brought increasing opposition to Banda's totalitarian one-party rule. The situation was also affected by the end of the Cold War era. As the strength and influence of the Soviet bloc withered, Europe, the USA and other Western powers had no further interest in propping up the leaders of 'friendly' countries such as Malawi (termed as such despite their distinctly unfriendly human rights records). Aid money and preferential trade deals were still up for grabs, but now there were conditions, namely 'good governance' – that is, the principles of free-market economics and democracy (in that order of importance, according to some cynics).

But there were changes inside the country too, and it was the Catholic bishops of Malawi who finally triggered Banda's downfall. In 1992 they issued a pastoral letter that was read in every Catholic church, condemning the regime and calling for change. This was a brave action, for even bishops in Malawi could not be guaranteed immunity from Banda's iron grip. Demonstrations throughout the country, both peaceful and violent, added weight to the bishops' move. As a final blow, donor countries cut off all non-humanitarian aid until Banda agreed to relinquish total control.

The Young Pioneers

Through the 1980s and early 1990s, members of the MCP youth organisation, the Young Pioneers, had been Banda's most ardent supporters – often with an enthusiasm bordering on the fanatical. Their activities ranged from organising spies and political informers to checking if market traders carried MCP party cards. They had become increasingly powerful and militarised and many were illegally armed, which caused considerable disquiet among senior figures in the army.

Prior to the general election, the Young Pioneers embarked on a program of intimidation against voters in an attempt to maintain the MCP's dominant position. In late 1993 tension between the Young Pioneers and the army peaked after an attack on some soldiers by a group of Young Pioneers in Mzuzu. The army retaliated by attacking Young Pioneers offices in the north of the country, followed by helicopter attacks on their headquarters in Lilongwe. Some Young Pioneers took refuge in the MCP headquarters, but this was attacked as well.

The country was ripe for an army takeover, but the generals ordered their troops back to barracks, and gave support to the new democratic order.

On 14 June 1993 a referendum was held in which the people of Malawi were asked to choose between a multiparty political system and Banda's autocratic rule. Over 80% of eligible voters took part. There was still a good deal of respect for the nonagenarian Dr Banda, but the desire for change was greater: the vote for a new system more than doubled the vote for the status quo. (It was reported that some Malawians thought they were voting for an organisation *called* Multi Party. This was understandable, as voting was a new thing in Malawi, and an organisation with a similar name had recently come to power in neighbouring Zambia.)

Banda accepted the vote, and constitutional changes were introduced to establish multiparty democracy in Malawi. The main political parties to emerge were the United Democratic Front (UDF), led by businessman Bakili Muluzi, and the Alliance for Democracy (AFORD), led by trade unionist Chakufwa Chihana. Banda's MCP also remained prominent. A general election was called for the following year.

Multiparty Democracy

Malawi's first full multiparty election was held on 17 May 1994. Essentially, it was a three-horse race between the MCP, the UDF and AFORD. All the parties' election promises were equally optimistic, so it was not surprising that voting was largely along ethnic and regional grounds: the MCP held in the centre of the country, and AFORD dominated the north, but support in the more heavily populated south of the country gave the UDF victory, although not an overall majority. Once again, Banda accepted the result. Bakili Muluzi thus became Malawi's second president.

Until winning the election President Muluzi was little known outside Malawi. He came from the south of the country and from a Muslim family. He was educated in England and Denmark. Although he rose through the MCP to become secretary-general in the early 1980s, he resigned from politics in 1982 to pursue business interests. It was not until the sanctioning of multiparty democracy that he returned to the political scene.

President Muluzi's first moves included the freeing of political prisoners, and offering ministerial posts to AFORD politicians in an attempt to form a coalition. This was rejected by AFORD leader Chakufwa Chihana, who later also questioned Muluzi's constitutional right to free prisoners without consultation with parliament or the judiciary. (At the time nobody had questioned the move – everyone was so used to the president acting alone.) AFORD and the MCP went on to form a combined opposition alliance.

Despite these misgivings, the new president went on to introduce several more changes: the political prisons were closed; freedom of speech and a free press were permitted; and free primary school education was to be provided for all Malawi's children. The unofficial night curfew that had existed during Banda's time was lifted. For tourists, the most tangible change was the repeal of Banda's notorious dress code that forbade women to wear trousers and men to have long hair.

The Muluzi government also made several economic reforms with the help of the World Bank and the International Monetary Fund, which had initiated a Structural Adjustment Programme (SAP) in 1993, during the last days of the Banda era. The kwacha (Malawi's unit of currency) had already been floated in February 1994, after many years of being pegged artificially high against foreign currencies. Effects of the SAP included the withdrawal of state subsidies and the liberalisation of foreign exchange laws. Further measures led to the closure of many private and state-owned businesses and a consequent rise in unemployment. A rationalisation of the civil service was also planned, which added to the job losses.

In September 1994, AFORD leader Chihana was made second vice-president and several other AFORD figures took seats in the cabinet. The UDF described the move as the formation of a coalition government. AFORD and MCP maintained that their opposition alliance also remained intact. Observers also pointed out that this situation was made all the more unclear because there was no provision in the country's constitution for a second vice-president. The obstacle was cleared with a bit of hasty rewriting.

Banda Back in the News

In April 1995, former president Banda was brought to trial (with five others, including his former second-in-command John Tembo) and accused of ordering the murder of the three government ministers who had died in a mysterious car accident in 1983. Banda's lawyers maintained he was too old and too ill to appear, but the trial went ahead in June.

In December 1995 the trial ended in his complete acquittal and the result was greeted with general approval, especially when Banda went on to apologise publicly for any suffering he might have 'unknowingly caused'.

By 1996 the UDF's honeymoon period was well and truly over. Running the country

was proving a tough job. Civil servants had gone on strike in mid-1995, following pay and job cuts. A scandal involving ministerial funds surfaced briefly, but was weathered. In April 1996, Chakufwa Chihana was sacked as second vice-president, and a month later pulled his AFORD party out of the coalition.

Outside the political arena, the effects of the post-election economic reforms, now optimistically named the Poverty Alleviation Programme, were hitting the average Malawian citizen very hard. Food prices soared as subsidies were reduced or withdrawn. The price of bread doubled, and the price of maize flour (the country's staple) rose eight-fold between mid-1994 and mid-1996. Unemployment was now officially recorded at 50%, but may have been higher. There were reports of increased malnutrition, especially among the young. Crime, particularly robbery, often at night, increased in urban areas. Matters were made worse by the sluggish pace of the resumption of international aid, after it had been frozen in the final years of Banda's rule.

In November 1997 Dr Banda finally died. His age was unknown, but he was certainly over 90, and probably almost 100. His death revived support for the MCP (now led by John Tembo), also helped in no small way by the continued poor performance by the UDF government. Unemployment and inflation remained high, while opposition politicians complained of corruption and mismanagement at the highest government levels. A United Nations report concluded that at least 70% of the population was nutritionally at risk.

Modern Times

Presidential and parliamentary elections were held in May 1999. President Muluzi won the race for the presidency, and his party, the UDF, retained its majority in parliament, despite the two main opposition parties (MCP and AFORD) forming an alliance. Before and during the election the opposition accused the UDF of manipulating the election process and falsifying the result, and afterwards took their complaints to an electoral commission and then to the

High Court – claiming that Muluzi holding the position of president was unconstitutional because of the vote-rigging.

While claims and counter-claims are bandied back and forth, the ordinary people of Malawi have become increasingly cynical and mistrustful of their politicians, and apathetic about the entire democratic process. Although many of the problems Malawi now faces were inherited from Banda's time, there is growing dissatisfaction around the country. After 30 years of totalitarianism, the country is now in a state of bewilderment.

Many Malawians we spoke to at the time of research ruefully admitted that the new freedom of speech was marvellous, but then politely pointed out that they now have no money and no food. When well-fed politicians are frequently seen in large cars and helicopters, or reported to be voting themselves increased salaries, this does little to alleviate resentment. Claims in the press of massive corruption and mismanagement of funds only adds fuel to the fire, and it hasn't escaped the attention of the newspapers that many of today's leading government figures are ex-MCP politicians anyway. The general feeling seems to be that little has changed since the old days. If anything, things are worse for the average Malawian. This comes at a time when the economy is under strain from weak commodity prices – poor rural people (that is, the vast majority of Malawi's population) feel the pinch even more.

As so often happens in Africa (and elsewhere), the improvements promised by new politicians have simply not materialised. In Malawi, many people are already starting to hanker for the old days, and say they'd be happy if a Banda-style strongman and the old style MCP took control again. Thirty years of enforced allegiance is taking time to wear off, and there's still considerable respect for the 'old statesman'.

The next elections are due in 2004. President Muluzi and the UDF have until then to make a significant change to the country they govern, and to satisfy the heightened expectations of the Malawian people.

GEOGRAPHY

Malawi is a small country compared with others in the region, and is wedged between Zambia, Tanzania and Mozambique, with no direct access to the sea. The country is roughly 900km long and between 80km and 150km wide, with an area of about 120,000 sq km.

The Great Rift Valley passes through Malawi, and the country's most obvious geographical feature – Lake Malawi – lies in a trough formed by the valley. This is the third-largest lake in Africa, covering almost a fifth of Malawi's total area. A strip of low ground runs along the western lake shore, sometimes 10km or more in width, sometimes so narrow there's only room for a precipitous footpath between the lake and the steep wall of the valley.

The lake shore is sandy in many places, with natural beaches, particularly in the south, where hotels and resorts have been built. Beyond the beaches and low plains, the Rift Valley wall rises steeply in a series of escarpments to high rolling plateaus that cover much of the country.

Lake Malawi's Weather

The weather on Lake Malawi is notoriously changeable, but the following patterns will give an outline. After the April/May rains, the winds are gentle and the water is generally calm and settled. June can be good too, although by July things can be a little more unsettled, with winds mostly from the south-east (called the *mwera*) combined with the generally cool climate. Through August and September winds start to drop and the waters get gradually calmer. By October the lake is very calm and the water is very clear – ideal for diving and snorkelling, although the weather is hot. These conditions can continue until the rains, which usually start in November and run until March/April. During the rainy season the lake weather is very unpredictable, with dramatic (and potentially dangerous) storms followed by crystal-clear air and spectacular views.

Malawi's main highland areas are the Nyika and Viphya Plateaus in the north, and Mount Mulanje (also called the Mulanje Massif) in the south. Malawi's highest point is the summit of Sapitwa (3001m) at the centre of Mount Mulanje. There are also several isolated hills and smaller mountains dotting the country. The largest is the Zomba Plateau, near the town of the same name.

As well as Lake Malawi, the country has three other lakes. The largest of these is Lake Chilwa, south-east of Lake Malawi. North of here is the remote Lake Chiuta, which spreads across the border into Mozambique. Less than 10km south of Lake Malawi is Lake Malombe.

Malawi's main river is the Shire; it flows out of the southern end of Lake Malawi, into and out of Lake Malombe and then southwards as the plateau gives way to an area of low ground called the Lower Shire Valley. The lowest point is a mere 37m above sea level. The Shire River flows out of Malawi near Chiromo and into the Zambezi River in Mozambique.

CLIMATE

Malawi has a single wet season, which runs from mid-October or early November to mid- or late April, and a dry season from May to October/November. During the wet season daytime temperatures are warm and conditions humid in low areas, although much less rain falls along the shores of Lake Malawi than in the highlands. The dry season is cool from May to August, with July being the coolest month. At the end of the dry season, during September and October, or until the rains start, it can become hot and humid at midday, especially in low areas.

Daily temperatures in the lower areas do not fluctuate much, with average daytime maximums around 21°C in July and 26°C in January, although dry season highs of 38°C have been recorded in the Lower Shire Valley. In the highland areas, average daytime temperatures in July are usually between 10°C and 15°C, while in September they get up to 20°C and above. Night temperatures on the highlands are low, sometimes dropping below freezing on clear nights in July.

ECOLOGY & ENVIRONMENT

The terms 'ecology' and 'environment' are used in such a variety of contexts that actual meanings often become vague. Generally speaking, however, environmental issues relevant to Malawi are similar to those faced by other parts of East and Southern Africa, and many countries elsewhere in the world. These include population growth, air and water degradation, industrial pollution, deforestation, soil erosion, urban encroachment, habitat and wildlife destruction and the conservation of resources.

When discussing any of these environmental issues it is important to realise that none can be addressed in isolation. They are all inter-related and linked to wider economic, social and political situations – on a national, regional and global scale. It is also important to realise

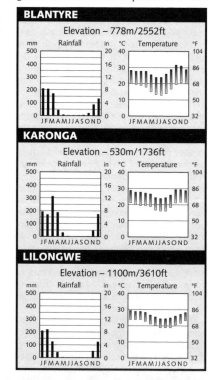

that environmental issues are never straightforward.

For example, in Malawi the population is growing rapidly. Malawi has more people than Zambia, Namibia and Botswana combined, and is far smaller than any one of them. Put even more starkly, Malawi's population is about the same as Mozambique's, but Malawi is one-tenth of the size, giving it one of the highest population densities in Africa. The ever-increasing human population puts great demands on the land and other natural resources. To conserve these resources, the rate of population growth needs to be lowered. But to suggest that the solution simply involves contraception or a change in cultural attitudes is a narrow view. Environmentalists with a broader perspective see rapid population growth closely linked to social issues such as unemployment, limited education and poor health care. Thus, conservation of natural resources must start with tackling the root of the problem – poverty.

Poverty & Resources

One strategy for the alleviation of poverty encourages poor (or Third World) countries to increase economic development to provide income for their citizens, which in turn will lead to a better standard of living, the lowering of birth rates and thus, eventually, an interest in conservation. Against this, economic development often involves industrialisation or large-scale farming – and this can cause its own environmental and social damage.

But even if the Third World's population growth rate was stabilised, and living standards were raised, this is not a solution on its own. With everybody on Earth enjoying the high standards (ie, high consumption) of the First World countries, the planet's finite resources couldn't support everyone anyway.

This point – that the First World uses more of the earth's resources than the Third World – is often overlooked, especially in areas like Southern Africa. Instead 'indigenous' situations are emphasised – eg, wood stoves create deforestation; over-grazing causes soil erosion. But an urban citizen of the UK, Aus-

tralia or the USA can consume 50 times more than a poor rural inhabitant of Malawi, and this global imbalance in the use of resources is a major environmental factor that cannot be ignored. It is ultimately related to all other environmental issues (such as those discussed below) in Malawi, throughout Southern Africa, and across the whole world.

Deforestation & Soil Erosion

The main environmental challenges facing Malawi are deforestation and soil erosion. In the mid-1970s Malawi's forest cover was 4.4 million hectares. It's now under two million, with 50,000 hectares being cleared each year, mostly for firewood. Cutting (or harvesting) trees is not necessarily an environmentally bad thing, although in Malawi's case the trees are being cut faster than they are being replaced, and that *is* detrimental. Although some replanting is taking place, at this current unsustainable rate the woodlands and forests of Malawi will eventually disappear.

As well as woodlands and forests being cut, throughout Malawi areas of grassland and scrubland (low bush) are also being cleared and the land used to cultivate crops. Much of this is marginal land (ie, with poor soil or on steep hillsides) which would previously have been ignored by farmers. Because the soil is exposed for part of the year it is often washed away by rain, and the problem is compounded by unreliable rainfall; some years there's no rain, so the crops fail and the bare soil is blown away by the wind. Even if the crops do grow, on the poor ground they tend to be stunted and low in nutrition. It's a grim scenario, and the end result is an increasing number of people living at starvation levels.

Overfishing

On Lake Malawi, even though people are less dependent on agriculture, things are also at a difficult stage. Traditionally, people living by the lake have enjoyed a better standard of living than people in the highlands because fish supplies were a good and plentiful source of protein. But once again, population growth means things have changed. The demand for fish has grown; more fish are caught every year, to such an extent that

The Ivory Debate

The conservation of elephants and the sale of ivory are constantly debated issues, especially in the countries of Southern Africa (including Malawi), where a number of strong and diverse views are held. The 'Ivory Debate' is also a good example of how environmental matters are never straightforward.

Basically, there are two sides to the argument. One side holds that elephant herds should be conserved (some say 'preserved') for their own sake or for aesthetic reasons; the other side argues that elephants must justify their existence on long-term economic grounds for the benefit of local people or for the country as a whole – 'sustainable utilisation' is the buzzword. The same arguments can be applied to most other animals and plants, but elephants and their ivory neatly illustrate the debate – and get most of the press!

Elephant poaching complicates the picture, and since the 1970s various factors have led to a massive increase in elephant poaching in many parts of Africa. By the late 1980s the price of one kilogram of ivory (US$300) was three times the *annual* income of over 60% of Africa's population. Naturally, the temptation was great, although the real money was made not by poachers – often desperately poor villagers – but by the dealers, in many countries acting with the full knowledge (and support) of senior government figures. In East Africa and some Southern African countries – notably Malawi, Mozambique and Zambia – elephant populations were reduced by up to 90% in about 15 years. But in some other countries of Southern Africa, where national parks or wildlife reserves were well managed – notably Zimbabwe, South Africa and Botswana – elephant populations were relatively unaffected.

In 1990, following a massive worldwide campaign from various conservation organisations, a world body called the Convention on International Trade in Endangered Species (Cites) banned the trade in ivory, and the global demand collapsed. At the same time there was an increase in funds for the protection of elephants. The improved law enforcement and closure of the trade were both seen as important steps in elephant protection.

But the issue does not stop there. Although elephant populations recovered in areas where they'd been previously ravaged, in the well-managed and protected parks of Southern Africa the populations continued to grow, and this created another problem. Elephants eat huge quantities of foliage, and a large herd remaining within an unnaturally small area (even though it may be hundreds of square kilometres) will quickly destroy its surroundings. In the past, the herd would have migrated, allowing time for vegetation regrowth, but with the increase in human population around national parks, this option is increasingly closed off.

So, by their successful protection of a species, the park authorities are now facing the problem of overpopulation. Solutions include relocation (where animals are taken to other areas) and a pioneering contraception project (where breeding females are injected with a 'pill' equivalent – so no jokes about jumbo condoms please). But the main solution is to cull elephants, sometimes in large numbers.

stocks are now taken from the lake at an unsustainable level. As demand increases, fishermen are using nets with smaller holes, so even the youngest fish are taken, which reduces next year's catch even more. Despite all this the amount of fish eaten by the average Malawian has fallen to half its mid-1970s level. And, once again, that means more people are living nearer starvation levels.

There is a glimmer of hope on the fishing front. Whereas fishing on Lake Malawi used to be controlled by an inefficient government department, in some areas decisions regarding net-sizes and closed seasons are now being taken by local communities. It's hoped that local people now have more incentive to protect their fish stocks and harvest them at sustainable rates.

Poaching

Poaching of wild animals from national parks in Malawi was a major environmental issue in the 1980s and early 1990s, despite lip service paid to conservation by the

The Ivory Debate

Killing elephants to conserve them seems a bizarre paradox, but illustrates the seriousness of the problem, and at present the other options remain experimental and limited in their effect.

In the late 1990s the countries that had protected their herds successfully were forced to deal with unsustainable numbers and argued for the ivory trade to be legalised again. Their argument was that funds raised from sales of ivory (including the tusks of culled animals) could go to conservation projects that benefit both animals and people. In this way the elephants would become a *resource* with a tangible value, giving governments and local people an incentive to ensure their survival.

Another aspect of this 'pay to stay' argument is the income raised by tourism. Put simply, it goes like this: If local people protect the animals, then foreigners pay money to come and see them, then some of the money can go back to the local people. Income is also generated by the employment that wildlife-tourism creates, such as wildlife rangers (often known locally as 'game scouts'), tour guides and jobs in the hotels, lodges and camps. Further spin-offs include the sale of crafts and curios – another way for local people to earn money direct from the tourists. But if there is no benefit, there is no incentive to conserve. Proponents of the 'pay to stay' argument go on to say that protected areas such as national parks are unlikely to succeed in the long term, and are in fact doomed, unless governments *and* local people can obtain real benefits from their presence.

All over the region there are moves to involve local people in wildlife conservation schemes. The best known is the pioneering Campfire (Communal Areas Management Programme for Indigenous Resources) in Zimbabwe, where local villagers 'own' the elephants and other animals that inhabit their traditional lands, and can generate funds from controlled hunting or photographic safaris that take place there. In Malawi the Wurcs (Wildlife Utilisation Raises Community Standards) scheme has been developed. Although it does not provide for hunting elephants, it does support locally based initiatives and encourages the sustainable harvesting of natural resources through projects such as plant nurseries, forestry projects and the husbandry of 'wild' animals like duikers and guineafowl.

Meanwhile, the ivory debate rages on. In March 1999 Namibia, Zimbabwe and Botswana were permitted by CITES to resume strictly controlled ivory exports. Despite these measures, opponents of the trade say that illegal ivory can now be laundered through the legal trade and, indeed, an increase in poaching through 1999 was reported Africa-wide – from countries as far apart as Kenya and Gabon. In Malawi, however, reports from several national parks and wildlife reserves indicate that more elephants have been seen in the last few years than at any time since the 1980s.

In April 2000 the countries in favour of the ivory trade agreed to a two-year moratorium and postponed sales until a foolproof system can be developed that allows only legal ivory to be traded. The debate continues, but as yet it is still too early to say if a resumed ivory trade will have an overall financial benefit for Malawi, or for any other countries in Africa where elephants still exist.

---

former government, and wildlife stocks were severely depleted, as they were in countries all over East and Southern Africa (see the boxed text 'The Ivory Debate'). Parks and reserves virtually empty of wildlife were hard to present as attractive to visitors, so this obviously affected Malawi's tourism industry, which was always a low-key affair at the best of times.

Following the elections of 1993 the new government promised to combat poaching, but a lack of resources and commitment meant little changed. However, since the mid-1990s several parks and reserves have received funds from donor countries or organisations, which should result in better anti-poaching measures, plus improved access roads, management, and staff morale. Part of the deal can be that accommodation is leased to private companies instead of being run by the Departments of National Parks and Wildlife. This attracts visitors from overseas, and will be better for Malawi. Ideally, in the future, park management will also be leased to private companies, and operated with the backing of (and for the benefit of) local communities, but this is still a long way off.

Tourism & the Environment

In Malawi, as in many other developing nations, tourism has become a major environmental issue. As one of the largest global industries, it is impossible to ignore. Tourism has been growing considerably in Southern Africa since the end of the apartheid government opened South Africa to foreign visitors, which has had a knock-on effect throughout the region.

In many cases international tourism is the only way in which wildlife species have a tangible value and thereby ensure their own survival. (See the boxed text 'The Ivory Debate' for the 'pay to stay' argument.)

It has become obvious since the early 1990s that without benefit for local people, there is absolutely no incentive to conserve wildlife. But in the last few years there has been another crucial shift in the argument. Now the benefit is central – it's the only justification for conserving wildlife. Saving animals because it's a nice thing to do simply isn't enough any more. Conservation for its own sake is a luxurious Western notion that the people of Africa simply cannot afford.

All over Southern Africa there are increased moves to involve local people in wildlife conservation schemes. In Malawi, examples include 'good neighbour' arrangements, where villagers on lands bordering national parks and wildlife reserves are allowed access to gather resources such as firewood and thatching grass.

For true success, a balance has to be struck between tourism growth and environmental destruction – in other words, all development has to be sustainable. The only reason for wildlife to be conserved is not for tourists to admire, but so local people can benefit. Wildlife is a resource like oil or copper, and (unlike those) infinitely sustainable, and possibly a lot more reliable.

Eco-Tourism

Although tourism can be an environmental saviour in some instances, it can also have

very negative effects. A problem arises when a destination cannot cope with the number of tourists attracted to it, which causes great damage to the natural and social environments.

Another issue, particularly relevant for visitors in Malawi and throughout Southern Africa, is the growth of so-called 'eco-tourism' – applied to any kind of activity with an environmental connection (however vague), or even if it's simply outdoors. The 'eco' tag is blatantly used to make the whole thing feel more wholesome. Even the slightly more specific term 'eco-friendly tourism' is now horribly overused. When choosing a holiday, tour or safari you shouldn't be fooled by travel companies blithely claiming to be eco-friendly. Activities such as camping, white-water rafting, wildlife viewing (by car, foot or balloon) or sightseeing trips to remote or fragile areas can be more environmentally or culturally harmful than a conventional hotel holiday in a specifically developed resort.

If you want to support tour companies with a genuinely good environmental record, you have to look beyond the glossy brochures and vague 'eco' claims and ask what they are really doing to protect or support the environment (and remember that includes local people, as well as animals and plants). See Responsible Tourism in the Facts for the Visitor chapter for more information.

FLORA & FAUNA

Malawi's wide range of vegetation and animal habitats in a relatively small area make the country ideal for those with any interest in natural history. Many visitors come to Malawi specifically to observe or search for the country's animal and plant species. Malawi also stands at a 'biological crossroads' between Southern, Central and East Africa, with species occurring from all these regions. Various field guides are listed in the Books section of the Facts for the Visitor chapter.

This section covers mainly the vegetation, mammals and fish of Malawi. Birds are covered in the special illustrated section 'Birds of Malawi'.

With the bridge gone, a temporary ferry shuttles passengers across the river near Dwangwa.

Early morning at Cape Maclear

Sunset at Senga Bay near Salima

Happy minding the boat, Nkhata Bay

A missionary house in Livingstonia

Cape Maclear: perfect for a bit of R and R

Cassava being pounded into flour

Boats ply up, down and across Lake Malawi.

An idyllic late afternoon on Lake Malawi

Fishing for dinner at the lake

Flora

Malawi's vegetation can be divided into several broad types or 'zones', each with characteristic plants (from tiny flowers to giant trees), as well as associated birds and animals. These zones are complex, and firm division lines are impossible to draw. There are considerable overlaps, pockets of one zone within another, and varying definitions among biologists. Though the list of major zones is not exhaustive and, by necessity, is greatly simplified, it will provide a useful overview.

Miombo This woodland is the dominant vegetation type in Malawi, originally covering 70% of the land, although much of it has now been cleared for farming or plantations. It occurs up to an altitude of about 1500m in areas where the rainfall is reliable. The relatively poor soil that covers much of Malawi encourages the growth of small-to-medium height, well-spaced trees that produce open-canopy woodland. Enough sunlight penetrates through this to the ground to allow the growth of grasses and shrubs. Good examples can be seen on the slopes of the Nyika Plateau and in Kasungu National Park. Apart from the diverse wildlife that miombo woodland supports, two of its most important functions are maintaining water catchment areas and preventing soil erosion. Thus several areas of this type of woodland are now protected. The dominant trees of the open canopy miombo are *Julbernadia globiflora* and several types of *Brachystegia*. The species of *Brachystegia* are so dominant that miombo woodland is often called *brachystegia* woodland.

In areas of high rainfall, including west of Nkhata Bay and south of Mount Mulanje, the trees tend to grow taller and closer together, producing a closed canopy. The tall *Brachystegia spiciformis* is often the dominant species of this type of miombo woodland.

Flowers of Malawi

Malawi has a great diversity of indigenous wild flowers. This is due to the wide range of habitats, from high mountains and plateaus to tropical evergreen forest and low-altitude woodlands. For visiting flower enthusiasts this range of habitats in such a small area means many species can be seen in a relatively short period of time. Malawi also stands at a 'biological crossroads' with species common to the Central, Southern and East African regions.

Malawi is particularly famous for its orchids and, despite its small size, contains one of the largest number of orchid species of any African country. The current figure is over 400; this includes over 280 terrestrial species, divided into about 30 genera, and over 120 epiphytic species, with about the same number of genera. Botanists believe that several more hidden 'specials' wait to be catalogued. The majority of terrestrial orchids flower in the rainy season, from November to early April, with a few species (mostly *Eulophia*) starting at the end of the dry season around October. The peak viewing time is January and February.

Good spots for flowers include the Nyika National Park, where montane grassland areas support many terrestrial orchid species and the patches of evergreen forest support epiphytes. Proteas and aloes are found on the lower slopes. Other highland areas include the Zomba Plateau and Mount Mulanje, where terrestrial and epiphyte orchids occur, as do proteas, aloes, stag's horn lily and various tree ferns, plus helichrysums (the dried effect of which gives them the name 'everlastings'). Kasungu National Park is also a good area; the miombo woodland is rich in tree species and the grassy dambos support orchids, gladioli, lilies and everlastings. Other forest areas supporting orchids include Dzalanyama, Dedza and Viphya. In miombo woodland areas, such as Liwonde and Majete, aloes also occur, plus the Sabi star (also called Impala lily). The lagoons in Liwonde are also noted for their water lilies and reed beds.

For keen botanists, several local field guides are available. Some are mentioned in the Books section of the Facts for the Visitor chapter. Others can be found at the Wildlife Society of Malawi bookshop in Limbe (see the Information section in the Blantyre & Limbe chapter).

The Baobab Tree

One of the great symbols of Africa, the baobab tree, with its bizarre appearance, is surrounded by myth and folklore, and has a multitude of uses for local people and for wildlife. In Malawi, baobabs are found principally on the lake shore, on Likoma Island, and in the areas along the Shire River.

Traditional stories have been passed down through the generations about how God, angry with the baobab, pulled it out and flung it back into the ground headfirst. With branches that look just like a root system when the tree is leafless, it is easy to see how this and many other similar stories came about. (Farther south, in Namibia and Botswana, San people [Bushmen] tell a story about God

SARAH JOLLY

giving all the animals a seed to plant. The hyaena, angry at being left until last, planted his allocated seed, the baobab, upside down.)

Baobabs live for a very long time – often for millennia. Research has shown that baobabs grow fast during the first 270 years, and then slow down. Trees with a circumference of over 30m could well be as much as 4000 years old. One of the largest in Southern Africa has been reported as having a circumference of over 46m, indicating a respectable age by any standard. Determining the age of these trees can prove very difficult, since growth rates vary enormously, and the trunk may even shrink during years of drought. Carbon dating is the only reliable method.

The wood of this tree is very light and almost spongy in appearance. When the tree dies, within a few months it will have rotted down to a mass of fibre. Baobabs produce big white flowers in October, each bloom only lasting 24 hours. These are pollinated by the fruit bat, and it's interesting to note that the distributions of fruit bats and baobabs throughout Africa are very similar. The flowers may also be pollinated by ants. Large oval fruit containing seeds are produced in April and May.

Uses of this tree seem endless. Although not suitable for hut construction, the very light fibrous wood can be used in the manufacture of paper and also as floats for fishing nets. The interior of the trunk frequently dies off, leaving a hollow shell – excellent for use as a water trap; a nesting site for birds and reptiles; a place of refuge for both humans and animals; and as a storage room. The fibrous bark makes a very strong thread, used for making nets, sacks, instrumental strings and even cloth.

All parts of the tree seem to have some nutritional value. The fruit is very rich in protein and vitamins, and is a favourite food of elephants and baboons. The seeds can be ground and roasted. The leaves can be eaten as a type of spinach. Animals eat the fruit, leaves, and flowers as well as young roots. Elephants strip and eat the bark. In times of drought they will also dig out and eat the inner wood, which has a water content of up to 40%. The baobab has medicinal uses too: the leaves are used to treat diarrhoea and fevers. The bark can also be used in the treatment of fevers, and was once sold commercially for this purpose.

More modern uses for the baobab include the WWI gun emplacement and ammunition store that was built in the branches of a tree at Karonga in Northern Malawi. Finally, we should not forget Major Trollip, who, while stationed at Katima Mulilo in Namibia, installed a flush toilet in his local hollow baobab. It remains there to this day.

Mopane This woodland occurs in hot lowland areas that have relatively low rainfall, including the middle parts of the Shire Valley and the plains along the southern shores of Lake Malawi and some of the smaller lakes. More than half of Liwonde National Park is covered by mopane woodland.

This vegetation zone derives its name from the mopane tree, a tall multi-stemmed tree that characteristically grows well on soils with high clay content. It has adapted well to the lack of rainfall and the heat in these areas; this is achieved through its shallow root system, which maximises water uptake and, through closing its distinctive butterfly shaped leaves together during the middle of the day, reduces water evaporation. When conditions are favourable these trees can reach up to 25m in height, although in poor soil they tend to grow as small shrubs. Other species in this zone include the broad-leafed shepherds tree and the small and large sour plum trees. Most easily recognised is the baobab tree, which favours the same dry conditions, and frequently occurs in mopane woodland areas (see the boxed text 'The Baobab Tree').

Evergreen Forest There isn't much forest left in Malawi (most has been cleared), but areas do exist that are thought to be remnants of the extensive evergreen forests that once grew all over the country, as well as in southern Tanzania, northern Zambia, and Mozambique. There are two main types – montane evergreen forest and semi-evergreen forest.

Pockets of montane evergreen forest occur in the highland areas of Malawi, such as the upper slopes of Mount Mulanje and the Zomba, Nyika and Viphya Plateaus. The variety of trees found in montane forest is enormous and the range of birds, animals and insects that they support is correspondingly great. Two notable, though uncommon, trees to be found in this type of forest are the Nyika juniper and the Mulanje cedar, both endemic to Malawi.

Semi-evergreen forest is more extensive than the montane forest. It is found on the lower and middle slopes of Zomba Plateau and Mount Mulanje, and in the Nkhata Bay area. It is also found along river courses. This type of forest overlaps closely with the closed-canopy miombo woodland mentioned previously.

Montane Grassland This type of vegetation occurs generally above 1800m and is predominantly found on the Nyika Plateau in northern Malawi, where the rolling hills are covered in grass. These grasslands are maintained by the annual fires, both natural and intentional, which sweep through and discourage the growth of shrubs and trees. On the Nyika Plateau, the land below 1800m (ie, valleys and on the escarpment edges) is covered in light open miombo woodland, and in between the two vegetation zones you can often see areas of large protea bushes.

Riverine & Wetlands Along the shores of the lakes and the banks of the rivers that flow into them, the natural vegetation consists of dense riverine woodland or long reeds and grasses. In various parts of Malawi, wide and marshy river courses where reeds and grasses grow are called *dambos*.

Plantation & Farmland Although this is not a natural vegetation, some naturalists refer to this as a separate zone because it covers most parts of Malawi. The vast majority of local people are subsistence or small scale farmers (see Economy later in this chapter). Plantation areas include the tea and fruit estates on the Thyolo Highlands between Limbe and Mulanje; rubber in the northern region; pine on the Viphya and Nyika Plateaus; and sugar near Dwangwa on the central lake shore.

Fauna

Most large mammals are found within the country's national parks and reserves, although there are a few non-protected areas where certain species also occur. This will give you the basics.

The country's main national park is Liwonde, noted for its herds of elephants and antelopes (including impalas, bushbucks and kudus). Liwonde is also a good place to see hippos and crocodiles, and the only park in the country where you might see rhinos. Elephants also occur in Kasungu National Park, as do buffaloes, zebras, hippos and several antelope species. Elephants are also regularly seen in Nkhotakota Wildlife Reserve, as are lions.

In the north is Nyika National Park, renowned for roan antelopes and the smaller reedbucks, as well as zebras, warthogs, elands, klipspringers, jackals, duikers and hartebeest. There's also a chance of seeing hyaenas and leopards. Nearby Vwaza Marsh Wildlife Reserve is renowned for its hippos, as well as elephants, buffaloes, waterbucks, elands, roans, sables, hartebeest, zebras, impalas and pukus. In southern Malawi, Lengwe National Park supports a population of nyalas – at the northern limit of its distribution in Africa. The park also contains bushbucks, impalas, duikers and kudus.

Because Malawi lacks vast herds of popular and easy-to-recognise animals it is not considered a major wildlife viewing country. However, for visitors less concerned with simply ticking off 'the big five', and those who enjoy seeking out unusual species in the quieter parts of Southern Africa, the parks and reserves of Malawi have plenty to offer.

Fish

Lake Malawi has more fish species than any other inland body of water in the world, with a total of more than 600, of which many are endemic (ie, found in this lake and nowhere else), and new species are continually being discovered. The fish of Lake Malawi are netted by local people for food, fished for sport by anglers, goggled at by snorkellers, or simply left alone by everyone.

The largest family of fish in the lake is the *Cichlidae* (cichlids), which includes the small, brilliantly coloured and remarkably varied *mbuna* species, which are trapped and exported to aquariums all over the world. (See the boxed text 'Cichlid Fish of Lake Malawi' in the Central Malawi chapter.) The mbuna are easy to spot around rocky shores, and are one of the reasons snorkelling and diving is so popular in Lake Malawi. In some areas, like Cape Maclear,

the fish are so accustomed to being fed that they flock towards any swimmer, and nibble anything that moves – including your toes. In other areas they are still a bit timid, or simply ignore passing humans.

Other fish families in the lake include the *usipa* (also called lake whitebait), a small fish that collects in large schools, and is netted by local people from dug-out canoes. Anglers go for *mpasa* (also called lake salmon), *ncheni* (lake tiger), *sungwa* (a type of perch), *kampango* or *vundu* (both catfish).

As well as the lake, Malawi has many rivers, streams, smaller lakes and dams, which are also habitats for a wide variety of fish. For example, rainbow trout can be fished for on the Zomba Plateau and Mount Mulanje, and tigerfish can be hooked in the Lower Shire River. See Fishing in the Activities section of the Facts for the Visitor chapter for more information.

National Parks & Wildlife Reserves

Malawi has five national parks. These are (from north to south) Nyika, Kasungu, Lake Malawi (around Cape Maclear), Liwonde and Lengwe. There are also four wildlife reserves (formerly called game reserves) – Vwaza Marsh, Nkhotakota, Mwabvi and Majete. Generally speaking, wildlife reserves are less developed for visitors than national parks, as they were originally established for conservation purposes rather than for tourism. Reserves have fewer accommodation options and a more limited network of roads and tracks (if any at all). Full details on the facilities of each park and reserve are given in the appropriate sections.

All national parks and reserves have accommodation; this ranges from simple camp sites and rustic resthouses to self-catering chalets and comfortable (even luxurious) lodges. Until the mid-1990s the lodges and camps in Malawi's national parks and reserves were not of a good quality, mainly because they were run by the Department of National Parks (now the Department of Wildlife & Tourism), and any money they did make simply disappeared into central government coffers (along with about 90%

National Park Maps

The maps of national parks and wildlife reserves in this book show main routes only. It is not possible to show all minor park tracks because many original tracks have become overgrown and simply disappeared, some tracks are lost after heavy rains and rebuilt in another position, and several new routes will be built as part of planned rehabilitation schemes.

of the revenue raised from national park entrance fees). There was very little reinvestment, and the poorly paid wildlife rangers and other staff had little incentive to improve standards or quality of service.

Despite lip service paid to wildlife conservation and management by the former government, poaching was rife through the 1980s and early 1990s, and game stocks in many parks and reserves were severely depleted. The new government promised to combat the poaching but a lack of resources and commitment meant little changed.

However, since the mid-1990s several parks and reserves have received development funds from international donor countries or organisations. The German government is assisting with development at Nyika National Park; the European Union is assisting at Kasungu National Park; Italian aid is received at Lake Malawi; South African aid is received at Liwonde; and aid from Japan is invested in Nkhotakota Wildlife Reserve. This injection of foreign aid has resulted in improvements to access roads, management, anti-poaching measures and staff morale. Part of the deal in most cases required accommodation to be leased out to private companies instead of being run by the Department of National Parks and Wildlife.

One of the first places to change was Mvuu Camp at Liwonde National Park, where the old park accommodation was completely renovated to comfortable standards and a separate luxury lodge built, now run by Central African Wilderness Safaris. This company also runs all tourism activities in the park such as wildlife viewing, bird-watching, bush walks and boat rides. Similarly, at Nyika National Park and Vwaza Marsh Wildlife Reserve, accommodation and tourism activities are now run by The Nyika Safari Company. Wherever such schemes have been introduced, accommodation and general park standards have definitely improved, although prices have also risen.

Accommodation In most parks and reserves, accommodation – lodges, chalets and camp sites – is run by private companies. In a few parks it's still run by the Department of Wildlife & Tourism, and you can get general information from the National Parks Information Office in Lilongwe, but reservations for privately run lodges and camps should be made directly or through an agent. Reservations for privately-run accommodation are recommended, but not essential. If you prefer not to stick to a rigid itinerary, you can try your luck and turn up without a booking. In popular parks this isn't recommended at weekends and during holiday times. Theoretically reservations can be made for Department of Wildlife & Tourism accommodation, but the system doesn't work very well, and the chances of these places being full anyway are extremely slight, so you might as well just turn up. It is not usually necessary to reserve camp sites in any national park or reserve, assuming you have your own tent. More details of accommodation options in each park and reserve are given in the relevant sections.

Entry Fees All parks and reserves (except Lake Malawi) cost US$5 per person per day (for a 24-hour period), plus US$2 per day per car. Citizens and residents pay less. Other costs are for optional services: fishing licence US$4; hire of a park ranger (locally called a 'scout') for guiding in your vehicle US$2. All fees are payable in kwacha. (Guiding fees are paid to the park, so it is usual to tip the rangers an extra US$2 or so.) Accommodation is additional to these fees.

Forest Reserves

As well as national parks and wildlife reserves, Malawi has almost 70 forest reserves across the country. Some forest reserves also have accommodation. These are usually log-cabin resthouses, simple and rustic (verging on tumbledown), but often quiet and cheap, with a pleasant atmosphere. The largest forest reserves, and the most famous for tourists, include Mount Mulanje and the Zomba Plateau. On Mulanje there's a series of huts especially for hikers and trekkers (for more details see the Mount Mulanje section in the Southern Malawi chapter).

There is usually no fee to enter a forest reserve, but a small fee is payable (around US$3) to use resthouses run by the Department of Forestry. These include: Dedza, between Lilongwe and Blantyre; Chintheche, on the northern lake shore; and Kasito, on the Viphya Plateau.

Some forest resthouses have been leased to private management, which means renovations and other improvements have been made. Prices at a privately managed resthouse range from US$10 to US$30 per person per night. These include: Dzalanyama, near Lilongwe; Luwawa on the Viphya Plateau; Senga Bay, on the central lake shore; Ntchisi, north-east of Lilongwe; and on the flanks of the Zomba Plateau.

GOVERNMENT & POLITICS

Until the elections of 1994, although a parliament existed, Malawi was effectively a dictatorship ruled by the President for Life, Dr Hastings Kamuzu Banda. There were elections for members of parliament, based on the British system, but all candidates came from the Malawi Congress Party – the only legal party in the country.

Following the move to multiparty politics, the parliamentary system of government is still the same. The big difference is that the people of Malawi now have representatives of different parties from which to choose. There are between eight and 15 parties at any given time. The main parties are the Malawi Congress Party (MCP), Banda's old party, traditionally strong in the centre of the country; the Alliance for Democracy (AFORD), traditionally strong in the north; and the United Democratic Front (UDF), drawing most of its support in the more heavily populated south of the country.

Elections are held every five years. Voters in each political constituency elect a representative to be their member of parliament. Separate presidential elections are held at the same time. There are no major ideological differences between the various parties, except that the MCP is considered more 'traditional' or 'conservative' (mainly because it's been around since independence, while the other parties are new on the scene). Party support is based on regional (and therefore ethnic) allegiances, and there is little genuine discussion on issues or policies. Although various matters are hotly debated in parliament, they often subside into personal accusations.

Malawi's current head of state is President Bakili Muluzi, the leader of the UDF. He holds this position for a five-year term, until the next elections (due in 2004).

Malawi is divided into three provinces. Northern Province, naturally, is in the north of the country, and the provincial capital is Mzuzu. The Central Province is in the centre of the country, and the provincial capital is Lilongwe (also the national capital). The Southern province is in the south of the country, and the provincial capital is Blantyre (effectively Malawi's commercial capital). Each province is of roughly equal size, although the Central and (particularly) Southern provinces are more heavily populated.

ECONOMY

Malawi's economy is dominated by agriculture. Around 85% of the population lives in rural areas and is engaged in agriculture; either as subsistence farmers or as workers on commercial farms and plantations. The main exports are tobacco, sugar and tea. Tobacco alone accounts for more than 70% of Malawi's export earnings (see the boxed text 'Tobacco' in the Lilongwe chapter). Tea and sugar make up another 20%. The main cash crops are usually grown on large plantations, but tobacco is also grown on smaller farms cultivated by a single family.

Most rural people cultivate their own plot of land to provide food for their needs. Any surplus is sold in markets or to the government-run agricultural cooperatives. Maize, millet and rice are staple food crops.

Until the 1970s Malawi was self-sufficient in food crops, and the economy was buoyant, but through the 1980s the economy suffered as a result of several factors. These included the general worldwide slump in trade following oil-price increases. There was also a fall in demand for tobacco and sugar, and an increase in international debt-servicing costs. Closer to home, the war in neighbouring Mozambique blocked land-locked Malawi's main access route to the sea (the railway line to the port of Nacala) so that imports and exports had to follow much longer and more expensive routes via Zimbabwe to South Africa, or through Tanzania. In the early 1990s there were also several years of bad drought, which hit agricultural output and also affected the rest of the manufacturing sector, itself largely agriculture-based. In early 1994 the flotation of the Malawian currency, the kwacha, caused it to plummet in value against international currencies, and inflation soared.

Since the mid-1990s there have been a few bright spots. There was an increase in investor confidence when the rule of President Banda ended and a free-market economic system was introduced. At around the same time the war in Mozambique ended, which once again gave Malawi access to Nacala (although it took another couple of years for the railway to be fully repaired). A resumption of foreign aid, after it had been frozen by many donors at the end of the Banda era, also helped boost the economy slightly, and in 1996 favourable weather conditions meant a bumper tobacco crop.

In the second-half of the 1990s the new government introduced other economic changes including a liberalisation of foreign exchange laws, an easing of border tariffs, and a drive to encourage the diversification

Economic Swings & Roundabouts

Former President Banda was undoubtedly a tyrant, but a policy that benefited Malawians to a certain extent was his determination to keep the economy agriculturally based. He encouraged most of the population to remain in villages as subsistence farmers, and avoided promoting industrial development (Malawi had little in the way of raw materials for industrialisation anyway).

'Cities breed poverty' Banda said, and compared with many other African countries the numbers of urban dwellers, particularly urban poor, was a small fraction of the population. Malawi also did not fall into the trap that caught other African countries: concentrating on industry and neglecting agriculture, only to spend export earnings on imported food. Throughout much of Banda's reign Malawi was self-sufficient in agricultural produce and staple foods were subsidised.

Following the political changes since 1994, the gradual drift from rural areas to urban areas has increased markedly. 'Informal settlements' or 'low-cost housing zones' (for which, read 'townships') around Malawi's main cities have grown, and crime has increased. There is no longer sufficient food produced to feed the country, and most food subsidies have been withdrawn.

Banda's policy of keeping most of the population in rural situations was not totally altruistic. In scattered settlements political opposition is harder to organise. Many Malawians also recall that Admarc, the government's agricultural purchasing department, bought goods from farmers at fixed (usually low) prices. These goods were then sold (also cheaply) to private companies within the Press Holdings group, an organisation almost wholly owned by Banda. Now, say observers, with the introduction of a free market economy, at least the farmers can get a fair price for the produce. The farmers agree, but go on to point out that now some of the locally produced food is more expensive, precisely because subsidies have been lifted.

of cash crops. An ambitious and far-reaching privatisation programme is underway, with more than 100 former state-owned businesses up for sale, including Air Malawi, the National Bank, plus various parts of Press Holdings, which was once more than 99% owned by former president Banda. Despite these reforms, after the 1999 election, political opponents of the UDF accused the ruling party of still having an unwarranted degree of control and influence in the Press group of companies. Investment in mining and manufacturing is also officially being encouraged, although critics say that in reality there is still too much government red tape and interference. Others point out that there is actually very little to mine.

Tourism is also seen as a great potential foreign currency generator. The tourism industry currently earns Malawi about US$5 million, and the government's official policy is to see this figure rise, ideally so that tourism is a (or even *the*) main earner of Malawi's foreign currency within a decade. A small number of international companies have invested in Malawi's tourism infrastructure (most notably the arrival in January 2000 of the Le Meridien hotel and resort group to manage several major hotels around the country).

Various other companies are poised to build new hotels and lodges on Lake Malawi and in national parks around the country, but industry observers report that despite the rhetoric there seems to be a lack of genuine will on the part of the government and its international advisers to positively encourage investment. These problems are not immediately apparent to visitors, but the observers in the tourism and aid industries have said it will have detrimental effects on the country as a whole unless government attitudes alter.

For the average Malawian, however, these economic changes and wranglings are irrelevant, as conditions for most people are extremely hard. By any yardstick, Malawi remains a poor country – among the 10 poorest – with a per capita annual income of US$180. By the purchasing power parity method of assessing income

(which works out how far the Malawian kwacha goes by comparing prices on basic consumer items) Malawians earn around US$750 per year (this is compared to an average of around US$20,000 in most industrialised Western countries).

In 1998 the kwacha was devalued by around 50%. This meant that prices for some items, including staple foods such as maize flour, went up by over 80%. This had a devastating effect on local people, but because exchange rates also increased it had little effect on visitors. Inflation increased from 20% to about 50% through 1998, and was unsteady in 1999, while economic mismanagement and political uncertainty have further hindered inward investment. Meanwhile, the national debt is reported to be around US$2 billion, with very little prospect of it being reduced. Unemployment is also alarmingly high. In January 1999 *Africa Today* magazine reported that of every 250,000 young people entering the job market in Malawi each year, only 16,000 to 20,000 would get jobs – far less than 10%.

Overall, the economy of Malawi is not good, and other socioeconomic indicators also paint a grim picture. Literacy rates are at about 50%, population growth is at around 4% a year, and infant mortality is at around 20%. Malawi has the second highest disparity between rich and poor in the world. Improvements are possible, but there's still a hell of a long way to go.

POPULATION & PEOPLE

Estimates in 1998 put the total population of Malawi at around 10 million. This is growing by around 3.5% a year. Around 15% of the population lives in towns and cities. The vast majority live in rural areas, in scattered villages and individual homesteads.

Malawi's main urban centres are Lilongwe, the political and administrative capital, in the centre of the country; Blantyre, the commercial capital (with its sister city, Limbe) in the south; Mzuzu, the main town in the north; and Zomba, a major trading centre and the former political capital, situated between Lilongwe and Blantyre. There are a few other small towns, mainly along

HIV/AIDS and the Population Hourglass

Although Africa continues to be a continent afflicted by wars, famines and natural disasters, the effect of AIDS is possibly the greatest problem it has ever faced. The personal, social and economic costs associated with the disease are already devastating: the US Census Bureau predicts that AIDS-related deaths will mean that by 2010, sub-Saharan Africa will have 71 million fewer people than it would otherwise.

The magnitude of HIV/AIDS infections in this region cannot be underestimated. Of the 30 million or so adults living with HIV/AIDS in the world, about 21 million live in sub-Saharan Africa. Half of the 16,000 new infections occurring daily are in Africa. Of every 10 children living with HIV/AIDS, nine live in sub-Saharan Africa.

AIDS has spread more quickly in Africa than in the West, due to inadequate screening of blood for transfusions, widespread ignorance as to the means of transmission, general poor health, the high incidence of venereal disease and limited use of contraception. In many African countries there is still a complete denial of the problem, particularly on the part of governments and some churches.

The inequities in health between rich and poor countries are starkly highlighted with AIDS. Drug treatments are available in the West to increase the lifespan of AIDS sufferers and reduce the risk of infection passing to the foetus in HIV-infected women. But these drugs are far too expensive for most people living in Africa.

Africa isn't uniformly affected by the epidemic. Although no country has escaped HIV/AIDS, some nations are more severely affected than others. Currently, North Africa has a fairly low infection rate, while many of the southern African nations have alarmingly high rates of infection: one in four are living with HIV/AIDS in Botswana and Zimbabwe, one in five in Namibia and Swaziland, and possibly as high as one in three in Malawi. Only a few sub-Saharan countries, such as Senegal and Uganda, have achieved significant success with programs aiming to slow the spread of AIDS, and the rate of new infections in these countries is finally starting to drop off.

In countries with high infection rates, the socioeconomic effects are overwhelming. Unlike many diseases that have more effect on the weak, HIV/AIDS predominantly hits the most productive members of society – young adults. It has a huge impact on family income, on food production and local economies. Africa faces the loss of a large proportion of whole generations of people. This is creating a population age profile in certain countries that resembles, rather than the usual pyramid, an hourglass.

These grim facts should not deter you from visiting Malawi, or indeed the region. They simply mean you should be aware of the problems for your personal safety (see the boxed text 'Aids in Malawi' in the Facts for the Visitor chapter), and as a way of understanding yet another challenge facing African countries today.

Hilary Rogers

the lake shore. In northern Malawi, where there's more high ground, the population is light and scattered. In the south and centre of the country the land is lower, densely populated and more intensively cultivated.

All the African people are of Bantu origin – the main ethnic groups ('tribes') are the Chewa, dominant in the central and southern parts of the country; the Yao, also in the south; and the Tumbuka in the north. Other groups include the Ngoni (also spelt Angoni), inhabiting parts of the Central and Northern Provinces; the Chipoka (or Phoka) in the central area; the Lambya; the Ngonde (also called the Nyakyusa) in the northern region; and the Tonga, mostly along the lake shore.

There are small populations of Asian and European people living mainly in the cities and involved in commerce, farming (mainly tea plantations) or tourism.

EDUCATION

Primary education in Malawi consists of eight years in school for pupils aged seven to 14. Officially, primary education is free of charge, but children must still provide books and materials, which their family must pay for, and are required to wear a uniform. The grades or classes are known as 'standards'. Thus a seven-year-old child starts school in standard one and goes on to finish in standard eight. There's an exam at the end of every year, and children who fail don't move up to the next standard. It is also common for children to take a year or longer out of schooling if they are needed at home or in the fields, or if the family simply cannot afford the necessary books. Thus it is not uncommon to find 15 year olds still in standard five. Some standard eight pupils are almost 20.

During the days of President Banda primary education was not compulsory, and the whole education system was neglected (some observers say this was a deliberate policy to ensure that the population remained docile). Even if every child had wanted to go to school, there was nowhere near enough – especially in rural areas. The result of this was the second-lowest literacy rate in Africa (after Mozambique, which suffered from the effects of war for almost 20 years). After the multiparty elections of 1994, the new UDF government announced plans to provide gen-

uinely free and universal primary education. Around 20,000 extra teachers were employed (some with just a few months of training) and one million kwacha (then about US$70,000) was allocated for books and materials. Primary school enrolment in 1996 was reported to have increased from under two million to over three million. Half of the standard one pupils were girls.

This was a great shock to the system, with up to 120 children in one classroom reported in many areas, but most Malawians generally saw the move as positive. Cynics noted that providing free education was actually quite easy, and not very expensive compared with other plans proposed by the new government. Others pointed out that the fact it was so cheap and easy meant that it should have been done years ago. Both sides agree, however, that providing secondary schools, or work for the school-leavers is a much tougher battle.

Children who reach standard eight take a Primary School Leaving Certificate. If they pass they can officially go on to secondary

Human Labour – Malawi's Greatest Export

Since the earliest colonial days, Malawi's greatest export has been manual labour, because there's never been sufficient employment to cater for the population, and vast numbers of young men have gone to find work in South Africa, mainly in mining or related businesses.

This process started at the end of the last century, when the British South Africa Company (BSAC) administered Nyasaland, and local men were encouraged to work in the mines of Rhodesia and South Africa, which were also owned by the BSAC. The former President Banda was one of many who went to South Africa (popular mythology had it he walked all the way), where he found work as a teacher and translator around 1915.

During much of the 20th century this pattern was repeated all over Southern Africa: Male workers from Namibia, Zimbabwe, Zambia, Mozambique, Lesotho and Swaziland, as well as Malawi, would aim for the mines around Johannesburg, and work in appalling conditions for low wages, either sending their pay home or returning for just a few weeks once per year to hand over saved money and to see wives and families. Sometimes they would stay away for a few years and come back with a lump sum. Sometimes they managed to spend half of it on the way home, and sometimes they never made it home at all. The terrible futility of this exodus is the subject of 'Coal Train', the haunting song by South African musician Hugh Masekela.

As you travel around Malawi today you'll undoubtedly meet men who have spent time in South Africa. Despite the social disruption caused by absent fathers and husbands in Malawi, the source of revenue was greatly needed. However, since the mid-1990s, the South African mining industry has hit hard times, and thousands of workers have been laid off or 'retrenched'. In many cases, it's the foreign workers (from Malawi and the other neighbouring countries) who are the first to go.

education. However, even after passing the exam, this move up is not guaranteed, as there are simply not enough secondary schools. Generally, this means only those with the highest marks are selected. For those who are selected, secondary education usually means travel away from home, as each school serves a vast area. Students must board at the school, or find accommodation with relatives who live nearby. Once again, money is a major factor, as fees must be paid, although a government ruling introduced in the late 1990s waived fees for girl pupils. For boys, fees in a state-run secondary school are about US$5 per term (or US$8 if it includes boarding), but even this is too much for some families, so even those who pass the exam may miss out on secondary education for financial reasons. In reality only about 20% of Malawi's school-age population completes secondary education.

Secondary education lasts for four years: the grades are known as 'forms'. After two years pupils take their Junior School Certificate; if they pass, this takes them into forms three and four. At the end of form four, pupils take their final exam: the Malawi Secondary Certificate of Education (MSCE). Ideally they are around 16 to 18 years old, but because of the 'years out' described above, many are in their early to mid-20s.

Since the mid-1990s about 30,000 to 40,000 secondary school students have taken MSCE exams each year, but only 20% to 30% pass. The worst year was 1998, when just 6000 out of 42,000 (16%) passed. The Ministry of Education attributed the poor results (perhaps not surprisingly) to inadequate resources, lack of qualified teachers, poor preparation on the part of the candidates and (more surprisingly) a tighter control on 'leakage' from the Malawi Examination Board, meaning pupils found it much harder to cheat.

Pupils unable to get into state-run secondary schools can go to a private school. There are several in Malawi, but fees in private schools start from around US$170 up to several thousand US dollars per year (in a country where average annual income for many people is less then US$100), so only the relatively better-off families can send their children here.

Tertiary education in Malawi consists of various colleges that make up the University of Malawi: Chancellor College, the School of Medicine, the Agricultural College and the Polytechnic. There are also three technical colleges – one in each province. University students are officially selected according to their secondary school performance, but once again fees are a considerable barrier for many. As part of the plans to expand tertiary education the government has announced plans to build a new 'university of the north' in Mzuzu.

ARTS
Visual Arts
The distinction between art and craft is often hard to determine, and this is the case in Malawi as elsewhere. All over the country, visitors will see hand-produced items for sale in curio shops, markets and roadside stalls. If you're looking for cheap souvenirs, there's plenty to choose from – animals carved from wood or soapstone, clay figures, mats and baskets, model cars and bicycles made from raffia or wire, and Malawi's famous chief's chairs (see Shopping in the Facts for the Visitor chapter). But in among the stuff that's hammered out in a hurry, you will also find works in wood and stone (and occasionally paintings) that have been created by artists of better-than-average talent. Salesmen often seem to make no distinction between works of good or mediocre quality, so it's always worth spending time to search the better pieces out.

Among places in Malawi where you can see artists in action, and buy their work, is Mua Mission (in Central Malawi, on the road between Salima and Balaka). A missionary named Father Boucher has established a school and studio here, providing the space and encouragement for local artists to explore and develop their own distinctive styles. Most of the artists work in wood, and while some of the work is strongly influenced by Western Christianity, other pieces are of traditional African design. Other pieces are impossible to classify in this simplistic way, and are the result of the artist's personal inspiration.

Malawian artists who have achieved recognition for their work inside the country and abroad include Kay Chirombo, Willie Nampeya, Cuthy Mede, Charley Bakari and Louis Dimpwa. Between them they represent various media, producing carvings in stone and wood, batiks and paintings, and many have exhibited outside Malawi. Cuthy Mede is also actively involved in the development and promotion of Malawian art, and in the late 1990s he opened Galerie Africaine (now sadly closed, although it may possibly reopen in a new position) in Lilongwe – the first high-profile art gallery in the country. Some critics and commentators have discussed the evolution of a distinct Malawi style or 'school', but others point out that influences from Europe or other parts of Africa have precluded this.

Several of the artists mentioned above also teach at the University of Malawi, where the department of Fine and Performing Arts at Chancellor College (Zomba) trains students to degree standard, under the guidance of Professor Berling Kaunda, an internationally recognised artist in his own right.

Places to see locally produced art include the exhibitions that are regularly held at the National Museum, and at the French Cultural Centre in Blantyre.

Traditional Music & Dance

Traditional music and dance in Malawi, as elsewhere in Africa, are closely linked and often form an important social function, beyond entertainment. In Malawi there are some country-wide traditions, and also some regional specialities where local tribes have their own tunes and dances.

Musical instruments are similar to those found in other parts of East and Southern Africa, with local names of special features. These include various drums, from the small hand-held *ulimba*, made from a gourd; to ceremonial giants carved from tree-trunks; and the *mambilira*, similar to the Western xylophone, with wooden keys, and sometimes played over hollow gourds to produce a more resonant sound. A single-string violin-type instrument called a *zeze* is sometimes played, and various rattles and shakers called a *maseche* are tied to dancers' legs and arms.

The most notable traditional dance in Malawi is the *Gule Wamkulu*, indigenous to the Chewa people (the largest and most dominant group in the country), but also enjoyed by some other tribes. The dance reflects traditional religious beliefs in spirits and is connected to the activities of secret societies. Leading dancers are dressed in ragged costumes of cloth and animal skins, usually wearing a mask, and occasionally on stilts.

Other groups have their own music and dance traditions. For example, among the Tumbuka, in northern Malawi, the *vimbuza* is a curative dance performed by traditional healers ('witchdoctors') to rid patients of sickness. Local anthropologists report that the demand for vimbuza dancers has increased significantly in recent years, and healers from other northern tribes, such as the Ngoni, have adapted the dance into their own curative ceremonies.

More secular in origin are the *beni* dances of the Yao people in southern Malawi. During colonial times many men from the traditionally war-like Yao served as *askaris* (from the Swahili word for guard) in a regiment called the King's African Rifles (KAR). *Beni* is believed to be a corruption of 'band', and the dance originally satirised what the African soldiers saw as the European military obsession with marching and parades, before developing into a more specific form of its own. Other tribes served in the KAR, as soldiers or porters, and similar dances are performed in other parts of Malawi. For example in the north, the style is called *mapilenga*. Today, dancers still wear a costume inspired by the colonial military uniform (which originated in India), which includes white tunics and red caps – often made from local materials such as sardine tins.

For visitors to Malawi, it is often difficult to witness genuine traditional music and dance. By their very nature, such dances are not advertised for public participation, and usually take place in rural areas. Displays are often performed in large hotels, or at cultural centres in Lilongwe and Blantyre, but these may often be simplified and shortened to suit Western tastes.

Contemporary Music

Modern homegrown contemporary music is not a major force in Malawi as it is in, say, Zimbabwe or South Africa. However, there are some significant local musicians; you can find their work on cassettes sold at roadside stalls and markets. Most influential and popular is Lucius Banda, who plays soft ('Malawian-style') reggae. He sometimes plays with his band Zembani, and sometimes with other musicians. Likewise, Zembani may perform without a frontman or with other lead musicians and singers. There's a lot of crossover in the modern Malawian music scene.

Lucius Banda also sometimes plays with the Alleluya Band, which was originally formed in the 1970s by his brother Paul Banda. Paul himself also plays reggae and is still going strong, and another reggae name to look out for is Billy Kaunda.

A band called Bubulezi plays a harder, more Jamaican-style reggae, while the Sapitwa Band tends towards Congo-style rhumba. Also very popular is Ethel Kamwendo, one of Malawi's leading female singers. Another name to look out for is Allan Namoko, who successfully combines traditional and modern themes; he sometimes plays with the Chimvu River Jazz Band.

Church music is also popular in Malawi, and features highly on local radio play-lists. This is sometimes called 'gospel music' (although it's not the same as American gospel) and usually features choirs singing hymns in local languages.

Literature

Like most other countries in Africa, Malawi has a rich tradition of oral literature. Collections of traditional stories that have been transcribed into print include *Land of Fire – Oral Literature from Malawi* by Scoffeleers and Roscoe.

Since independence, a new breed of Malawian writers has emerged. In the early years several confident poets and novelists wrote with an enthusiasm not permitted or encouraged under colonial rule. However, as the despotic President Banda became increasingly sensitive to criticism (real or imaginary) many writers found themselves under threat of imprisonment. Some abandoned their work, or continued in secret, while others were forced to leave the country. Until the mid-1990s many of Malawi's leading literary figures continued to live abroad for their own safety. Not surprisingly, common themes for many writers are oppression, corruption, deceit and the abuse of power.

Poetry is the most popular literary form, although the names of very few poets are known outside literary circles, either in Malawi or abroad. Most work is written in English, and nearly everything is published in English. If you want a taste of current literature, by well-known or new writers, try any of the short novels or poetry collections under the Malawi Writers Series imprint, available in good bookshops in Blantyre and Lilongwe. Most cost less than US$1.

Banda's Banned Books

Although many poets and novelists were jailed for their criticism of President Banda, it wasn't only works of literature that incurred his wrath. Several books on contemporary history were also banned, including, perhaps not surprisingly, *Malawi – the Politics of Despair*.

Newspapers from other countries and within Malawi itself were also frequently barred from circulation, especially if they were seen to be critical, but sometimes even if they weren't. Any form of pornography was also prohibited, but this included several medical textbooks, on the ground that the diagrams were indecent. Even guidebooks didn't escape; an early Lonely Planet book called *Africa on the Cheap* (forerunner of *Africa on a shoestring*) was critical of the regime in the Malawi chapter, and was promptly banned as well. Travellers with a low-budget appearance were often searched for the scurrilous tome, and getting across the Songwe border with the book intact was a notoriously difficult exercise.

Some anthologies that include Malawian writers are listed in the Books section of the Facts for the Visitor chapter.

Leading poets include Frank Chipasula, whose collections include *O Earth Wait for Me*, *Nightwatcher, Nightsong* and *Whispers in the Wings*. Another is Steve Chimombo, whose collections include *Napolo Poems*. His most highly acclaimed work is *The Rainmaker*, a complex poetic drama. But to many Malawians Chimombo is better known for his popular short stories, which appear in newspapers and magazines – a strange but vivid combination of traditional themes and harsh urban settings. He is also a lecturer, critic and commentator on the wider arts scene.

Another leading figure is Jack Mapanje, who studied in Britain before becoming a lecturer and Head of the Department of English at the University of Malawi. His first poetry collection *Of Chameleons and Gods* was published in 1981, but much of the symbolism (chameleons play an important role in traditional Malawian beliefs) is obscure for outsiders. Not too obscure for President Banda though – in 1987 Mapanje was arrested and imprisoned without charge. He was released in 1991, and two years later published his second book *The Chattering Wagtails of Mikuyu Prison*. The title refers to Malawi's notoriously harsh maximum security jail, where Mapanje was imprisoned.

David Rubadi, another literary figure, has studied and taught in Kenya, Uganda and Britain. He has compiled an anthology called *Poetry from East Africa*, which includes a section on Malawi, and also writes poetry himself. His novels include *No Bride Price*, which discusses the familiar themes of corruption and oppression.

Most critics agree that Malawi's leading novelists include Legson Kayira, whose semi-autobiographical works *I Will Try* and *The Looming Shadow*, based on his journey from Malawi through Africa and eventually to the USA, earned him critical acclaim in the 1970s. A later work, *The Detainee*, on the surface describes how one man is influenced and controlled by the state, but the title also refers to the country as a whole, oppressed

and imprisoned by a ruthless dictator. Also receiving high acclaim is James Ng'ombe, whose novel *Sugarcane with Salt* (1989) explores aspects of a changing African society.

Another more recently published writer is Sam Mpasu; his novel Nobody's Friend was ostensibly about a murder in a newly independent African country, but was also a comment on the secrecy of Malawian politics. Once again, this criticism did not go unchecked by President Banda and Mpasu was jailed for 2½ years. After his release he wrote Prisoner 3/75, about his imprisonment, and later became Minister for Education in the new UDF government. His comments on the time of Banda's rule sum up the situation for all writers, and the people of Malawi too: 'We had peace, but it was the peace of a cemetery. Our lips were sealed by fear.'.

SOCIETY & CONDUCT

During your trip to Malawi, although you will meet citizens and expatriates of European and Asian origin, the society and culture is predominantly African, and most of the advice here assumes you're in an African situation.

Behaviour

As in any part of the world, the best way to learn about a society's conduct is to watch or listen to the locals. The first thing to remember is not to worry: Malawians are generally very easy-going towards foreigners, and any social errors that you might make are unlikely to cause offence (although they may cause confusion or merriment). Having said that, there are a few things that are frowned upon wherever you go. These include public nudity, open displays of anger, open displays of affection (between people of the same or opposite sex), and vocal criticism of the government or country.

On top of these basics, a few straightforward courtesies may greatly improve your chances of acceptance by the local community, especially in rural areas. Pleasantries are taken quite seriously, and it's essential to greet someone entering or leaving a room. Learn the local words for 'hello' and 'goodbye' and use them unsparingly. For those out of earshot, it is customary to offer a smile and a pleasant wave, even if you're just passing in a vehicle.

Great emphasis is also placed on handshakes. There are various local variations, involving linked thumbs or fingers, or the left hand touching the right elbow, which you'll pick up by observation, but these are reserved for informal occasions (not greeting officials). A 'normal' Western handshake will be fine in most situations. Sometimes people who know each other continue to hold hands right through their conversation, or at least for a few minutes.

As in most traditional societies, older people are treated with deference. Teachers, doctors, and other professionals (usually men) often receive similar treatment. Likewise, people holding positions of authority – immigration officers, government officials, police, village chiefs (also usually men) – should be dealt with pragmatically. In Malawi, most officials are normally courteous and fairly efficient, sometimes even friendly. On your side, manners, patience and cooperation will get you through most situations. Even if you meet somebody awkward or unpleasant, the same rules apply. It is one thing to stand up for your rights, but undermining an official's authority or insulting an ego may only serve to waste time, tie you up in red tape and inspire closer scrutiny of future travellers.

At the other end of the spectrum, children rate very low on the social scale. They are expected to do as they're told without complaint and to defer to adults in all situations. Unfortunately for half the region's population, the status of women is only slightly higher than for children. For example, an African man on a bus might give his seat to an older man, but not normally to a woman, never mind that she is carrying a baby and luggage and minding two toddlers. In traditional rural areas, women are expected to dress and behave modestly, especially in the presence of chiefs or other esteemed persons. Visitors should act in the same way.

When visiting rural settlements, especially when away from areas normally

Photos from Home

Locals may regard single travellers in Malawi with bemused interest – women because they should be at home rearing families and men because they should be at home working. The interest turns to suspicion in some countries (rarely Malawi), where lone white foreigners recall the days of South African spies. Photos of home showing your family are good conversation openers and go some way to showing you are quite normal really. Some lone women travellers carry photos of handsome – but completely fictitious – husbands to ward off unwanted attention from potential suitors.

reached by tourists, it is a good idea to request to see the chief to announce your presence and request permission before setting up camp or wandering through a village. You will rarely be refused permission. Visitors should also ask permission before drawing water from a community well. Avoid letting water spill on the ground, especially in dry areas. If you want to wash your body or your clothing, fill a container with water and carry it elsewhere, and try to minimise the amount of water that you use.

Eating

Some visitors may have the opportunity to share a meal during their stay and will normally be given royal treatment and a seat of honour. Although concessions are sometimes made for foreigners, table manners are probably different from what you're accustomed to. Before eating, a member of the family may pass around a bowl of water, or jug and bowl, for washing hands. If it comes to you first as honoured guest and you're not sure of the routine, indicate that the bowl should be taken to the head of the family, then do what they do when it comes to you.

The African staple, maize meal (nsima), or sometimes sorghum meal, is the centre of nearly every meal. It is normally taken with the right hand from a communal pot, rolled into balls, dipped in some sort of sauce – meat gravy or vegetables – and eaten. As in most societies, it is considered impolite to

Malawian Dress Codes

There are no specific regulations regarding clothing or behaviour in Malawi, although in the days of President Banda all women (locals and visitors) were required by law to wear skirts that covered the knees, while men were required to have short hair and tidy beards. This law came about partly because many women travellers used to tour Malawi wearing shorts, which offended the locals (men and women), particularly in the mainly Muslim north, but also in the centre and south where most people are pretty conservative.

The law was dropped in 1994, and although you are now *allowed* to wear what you like, and have your hair as long as you like, it's still pretty insensitive to wander around with most of your legs showing (especially for women). Note that this mainly applies when you're in towns and villages – wearing shorts is usually no problem on the lake beaches, for hiking or for sports.

If showing disrespect for local sensibilities isn't reason enough, consider this: for women, if you wear shorts, you also make things harder for yourself – don't be surprised if kids laugh, adults (men and women) treat you disdainfully, and some young guns see you as easy prey. From a practical point of view, keeping reasonably covered with loose-fitting clothes also helps prevent sunstroke.

For men, what you wear is important too. Look around you; the only people wearing shorts or tatty clothes are kids, labourers or the poor. Ask yourself why some officials and other locals treat some bare-legged travellers with contempt.

scoff food; if you do, your hosts may feel that they haven't provided enough. In fact, for the same reason, it may be polite *not* to be the one who takes the last handful from the communal bowl. If your food is served on separate plates, and you can't finish your food, don't worry; again this shows your hosts that you have been satisfied. Often containers of water or home-brew beer may be passed around from person to person. However, it is not customary to share coffee, tea or bottled soft drinks.

Gifts

If you visit a remote community, please tread lightly and leave as little lasting evidence of your visit as possible. In some African societies it isn't considered impolite for people to ask others for items they may desire; but likewise it isn't rude to refuse. So if a local asks for your watch or camera, say 'no' politely, explaining it's the only one you've got, and all will be fine. If you start feeling guilty about your relative wealth and hand out all your belongings, you may be regarded as strange. Reciprocation of kindness is OK but indiscriminate distribution of gifts from outside, however well intentioned, tends to create a taste for items not locally available, erodes well-established values, robs people of their pride and in extreme cases, creates villages of dependent beggars.

On the other hand, when you're offered a gift, don't feel guilty about accepting it; to refuse it would bring shame on the giver. To politely receive a gift, local people may accept it with both hands and perhaps bow slightly, or they may receive it with the right hand while touching the left hand to your right elbow; this is the equivalent of saying 'thanks'. You can try this if you think it's appropriate. Spoken thanks aren't common so don't be upset if you aren't thanked verbally for a gift. In fact, Africans tend to think westerners say 'thank you' too often and too casually.

RELIGION

Most people in Malawi are Christian, usually members of one of the Protestant churches originally founded by the missionaries who came to Malawi in the late 19th century. There are also some Catholics, and many Malawians follow indigenous Christian faiths that have been established locally, ranging from small congregations meeting in a simple hut to large branches of the African Zion churches

DAVID ELSE

DAVID WALL

LEANNE LOGAN

DAVID ELSE

Discover the Malawian wilderness. **Clockwise from top:** hikers looking towards Chambe Peak, Mount Mulanje; colonial-style architecture on Mount Mulanje; horse riding on Nyika Plateau; Manchewe Falls, near Livingstonia

JULIET COOMBE

ANDREW MACCOLL

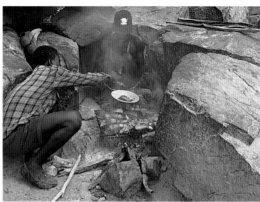

PAUL DYMOND

DENNIS JOHNSON

Different ways of spending the day. **Clockwise from top:** ready to plunge into the swimming pool again; enjoying a grilled fish meal; playing volleyball, Cape Maclear; selling an impressive array of carvings, Lilongwe

Witchcraft in Malawi

JENNY BOWMAN

A significant feature of the traditional religions of Malawi, and throughout much of Africa, is a belief in spells and magic, which is usually called witchcraft. This is a complex subject, hard for westerners to appreciate or understand, but in brief simplistic terms it goes like this: Physical or mental illnesses are often ascribed to a spell or curse having been put on the sufferer. Often, a relative or villager is suspected of being the 'witch' who placed the curse, usually for reasons of spite or jealousy. A traditional doctor, also called a diviner or witchdoctor, is then required to hunt out the witch and cure the victim. This is done in different ways in various parts of the country, and may involve the use of herbs, divining implements, prayers, chanting or dance. Services do not come free of charge, and many witchdoctors demand high payments – up to US$20, in a country where an average month's earnings is less than this.

Traditional doctors claim a high success rate when it comes to curing people of spells, but it's a sad fact that the 'witches' who are unearthed are frequently those who cannot defend themselves – the sick, the old or the very poorest members of society. There are even reports of very young children being accused by witchdoctors of harbouring evil spirits.

There has been a reported increase in the use of witchcraft in Malawi since the mid-1990s. This is thought to be due to the rapid population increase of recent years, combined with the falling standards of service in hospitals and clinics, and the growth of AIDS and other related illnesses.

Several medical relief organisations have described the use of and belief in witchcraft as a major impediment to their attempts to alter social behaviour, particularly in regard to the fight against AIDS, and even as a major hurdle in the development of the nation as a whole.

that are based in Zimbabwe and South Africa. Malawi also has a significant Muslim population, particularly in the north and along the lake – a legacy of the Swahili-Arab slave traders who once operated in this area.

Alongside the established churches many Malawians also follow traditional religions. As with traditional religions all over Africa, there are no great temples or written scriptures. For outsiders, beliefs can be complex (and to the Western mind strange), as can the rituals and ceremonies

that surround them. Most traditional religions are animist – based on the attribution of life or consciousness to natural objects or phenomena – and many accept the existence of a Supreme Being, with whom communication is possible through the intercession of ancestors. The principal function of ancestors is to protect the tribe or family, and they may on occasion show their pleasure (such as a good harvest) or displeasure (such as a member of the family becoming sick). Thus ancestors play a particularly strong role. Another aspect of traditional religions is the belief in the use of spells and magic (see the boxed text 'Witchcraft in Malawi').

LANGUAGE

All the different ethnic groups in Malawi have their own language or dialect. The Chewa are the dominant group and their language is called Chewa or Chichewa (sometimes written ChiChewa – the 'Chi' prefix simply signifies 'language of'.) It is the national language and is widely used throughout the country as a common tongue.

English is the official language and it is very widely spoken, particularly in the main towns. Even in remote rural areas it is usually possible to find people who speak English, but a few words of Chichewa will always be useful, and will also certainly raise interest, particularly in rural areas.

Other groups also have their own languages. Of these, Tumbuka, spoken by about 500,000 people, is dominant in the north, and Yao, spoken by about 600,000 people, is dominant in the south.

See the Language chapter later in this book for more information and some useful words and phrases in Chichewa, Tumbuka and Yao.

Facts for the Visitor

HIGHLIGHTS

This list of highlights includes all our favourites, plus those suggested by other travellers. After your visit, you'll no doubt have come up with your own highlights, but the following tips will at least give you a good starting point.

Malawi's number one attraction is **Lake Malawi**, a long, wonderfully beautiful and surprisingly varied stretch of water, lined with fishing villages, wooded escarpments and sandy beaches. Many visitors come for activities such as fishing, diving, snorkelling and boating, to enjoy some of Malawi's remarkable birdlife or simply to swim and lounge on the sand. All along the lake shore and on some of Lake Malawi's islands, there's a wide choice of places to stay, from budget beach huts to high-class hotels. The main centres are Nkhata Bay, the Chintheche Strip, Senga Bay, Cape Maclear, Likoma Island and the area north of Mangochi, but there are several other options – some are perfect hideaways.

One of the best ways to see and experience Lake Malawi is to take a **boat ride** on the *Ilala*, a venerable old passenger boat that steams up and down the lake each week. Cabins, comfortable deck space and more crowded 3rd-class options are all available. Other fine examples of Malawi's **colonial heritage** include the magnificent cathedrals at Blantyre and Likoma Island, and the time-warped missionary centre of Livingstonia.

If you're looking for **activities**, but prefer dry land, the best area in Malawi, and in this part of Africa, for **hiking** is Mount Mulanje. This massif rises high above the plains, with sheer cliffs, high peaks, endless views, fine hiking and good-value mountain huts. Also ideal for hiking is the Zomba Plateau and Nyika Plateau, and the four-day route from here down to Livingstonia and the lake shore is fast becoming a classic. The Nyika Plateau (the main feature of the Nyika National Park), with its wide open grassland, is also

one of the few places in Malawi where **horse riding** is available.

For another type of riding, the Nyika Plateau is also ideal for **mountain biking**, and you can hire bikes here. Bikes can also be hired at several other places (see the Activities section later in this chapter for more details).

If you prefer more relaxing pursuits, then Malawi is a top quality **bird-watching** destination. As well as Lake Malawi and several other smaller lakes, other good bird-watching areas include Liwonde National Park, Dzalanyama Forest, the Nyika Plateau and the Elephant Marsh in southern Malawi.

If you're looking for a **safari** and you prefer to watch the larger animals, especially African favourites like elephants, hippos and crocodiles, then Liwonde National Park should also be high on your list. The boat rides here are especially popular. Other excellent areas for viewing mammals include Nyika National Park and Vwaza Marsh Wildlife Reserve. The Nyika is also particularly renowned for its **wildflowers**. For a total wilderness experience, consider the reserves of Majete, Mwabvi or Nkhotakota.

To see what Malawians do with spare time or money, a visit to one of the country's large **markets** can be a major highlight. The City Market in Lilongwe is loud and lively, although it's good to travel very light here, while the town centre of Zomba is one big market with a much more laid-back ambience.

SUGGESTED ITINERARIES

Malawi is relatively compact, so where you go and what you do depends a lot on time and money. Another factor affecting the number of places you can reach will be your form of transport. Many visitors use buses and trains for their entire trip, and can get to most places this way at a fairly low cost, albeit sometimes quite slowly. A hired car reduces these delays, and is also near essential for getting into some national parks, but this option is more pricey. Some travellers combine public transport with a few days or weeks in a hire car, sometimes teaming up with others to split costs.

Whatever your transport, if you've got plenty of time, then naturally you can see a lot. If time is limited, then it would be far better to concentrate on visiting just one or two places rather than rushing around to fit everything in, and only skimming the surface.

Where you go will also depend on your own interests – see the Highlights boxes at the beginning of each chapter for some more ideas.

Two to Three Weeks

It's unlikely that visitors from Europe or farther afield will come to Malawi just for a week, but a two to three week tour might include the following: fly into Lilongwe, head for the lake shore (eg, Senga Bay, Cape Maclear or Club Makokola), continue to the pleasant town of Mangochi, then visit Liwonde National Park to enjoy the wildlife. From Liwonde go to Zomba, famous for its huge and lively market, and divert up the nearby Zomba Plateau, for good hiking. After that, head south to Blantyre, the commercial capital, then east through the tea plantations to Mount Mulanje (then go walking for a day or trekking for a week according to your inclination). Alternatively, head south down the escarpment to the Lower Shire area, taking in Lengwe, Majete and possibly Chiromo and the Elephant Marsh (if you're particularly keen on colonial history or birds). From there return to Blantyre and back to Lilongwe via Dedza.

One Month

With a month you could do the trip outlined above in more relaxed fashion, or include a loop through northern Malawi too. (If you only had two weeks you could still visit the north by cutting down on some of the places you go in the south – eg, missing out the Lower Shire or Mount Mulanje.) From Lilongwe, visit Kasungu National Park, or stop off on the Viphya Plateau. Then go to Mzuzu, from where you can reach Vwaza Marsh, the Nyika Plateau and Livingstonia, plus the beaches and quiet villages of the northern lake shore. Return to Mzuzu and then to the lake at the backpacker-friendly town of Nkhata Bay. From here you can take the historical *Ilala* lake steamer to the islands of Likoma and Chizumulu, only a stone's throw from the Mozambique mainland. Return to Nkhata Bay before following the lake shore road south as fast or as slow as you want (there are plenty of places to stay) to Nkhotakota or Senga Bay, from where you can reach Lilongwe to finish.

Another loop from Lilongwe becoming increasingly popular goes to South Luangwa National Park in neighbouring Zambia, for large-scale wilderness and sheer quantities of wildlife that Malawi simply does not have. You can join a trip in Lilongwe (see Organised Tours in the Getting Around chapter), or go independently. For more information see Eastern Zambia in the Central Malawi chapter of this book. For more details see Lonely Planet's *Southern Africa* guidebook.

Three Months

If you've got three months, you could travel at a very relaxed pace through Malawi and see every place described in the previous sections. You'd also begin to get an understanding of how the country ticks and still have time to laze on the beach. As well as the loop from Lilongwe to South Luangwa, some travellers venture deeper into Zambia (to Lusaka, Lake Kariba or the Lower Zambezi National Park). Another popular option from Malawi is to visit Mozambique – from southern Malawi you can reach the coastal town of Quelimane, or the fascinating Ilha de Moçambique. Many travellers also reach Mozambique via Likoma Island.

PLANNING

Lonely Planet's *Read This First: Africa* is an ideal place to begin your planning, especially if you have never travelled in this part of the world. It covers in more detail a lot of the general information (visas, equipment, health etc) included in this book, and also gives a country-by-country overview of Africa if you want to travel on from Malawi.

When to Go

Malawi's wet season runs from October/November to late April, and its dry season is from April/May to October/November (for more details see Climate in the Facts about Malawi chapter). The best time to visit Malawi is during the dry season. From May to July the landscape is green and lush, and conditions are cooler. July is the coolest time, then it gets increasingly warm towards September, when the landscape begins to dry out. It's positively hot in early October before the rains break.

When you go to Malawi will also be determined by your reason for coming. Late in the dry season is the best time for wildlife viewing as the vegetation is not so dense and animals converge at reliable watering holes, but the heat can be unpleasant – especially in the lowland areas. May to July is not so good for seeing wildlife, but the landscape itself is much more attractive and conditions less oppressive. August is a busy period, mainly because the weather is good, and also because it is school holiday time, both in Malawi and in South Africa, from where many visitors come. During the rainy season, wildlife viewing is usually not good, and it's also worth noting that in the rainy season or just afterwards, access roads in the parks (and other minor roads around the country) are often impassable unless you've got a rugged 4WD vehicle.

If you come to Malawi specifically for the birdlife, October/November is the best time, as European migrants are also present. However, at this time conditions are exceedingly hot or exceedingly wet (or both), so you have to be dedicated. The rest of the year is fine for most amateurs. If you've come for the angling, then see Fishing in the Activities section later in this chapter.

If you come only to take landscape photographs, the later months of the dry season may not be the best time as the views, especially from the highland areas (such as Livingstonia and the Nyika Plateau) can sometimes be obscured by haze and smoke from burning grass on the lower plains. Views are at their sharpest during the wet season (when it isn't actually raining) or in the first few months of the dry season.

The Total Eclipse in Southern Africa

A total solar eclipse (when the moon passes in front of the sun, obscuring it all and casting a shadow on a part of the earth's surface) will occur in Southern Africa on 21 June 2001. Eclipses of this sort happen less than once per year, but are sometimes in inaccessible areas or hidden by bad weather. In Southern Africa in June, the weather is likely to be very good, and this may be one of the best total eclipse viewing opportunities for many years anywhere in the world.

The 'path of totality' (the band formed as the shadow moves across the earth) passes through Angola, Zambia, the northern tip of Zimbabwe, and through Mozambique. The shadow will cross the African mainland between 12.35 and 13.25 GMT/UTC – 2.35 pm to 3.25 pm locally. The actual eclipse at any point along the path of totality between Zambia and Mozambique will last from four to 3½ minutes. (The time decreases as the shadow moves east.)

The path of totality passes just to the south of Malawi, at 13.20 GMT, so you won't be able to experience a 100% eclipse, although you will still get something like 95% if you're south of Blantyre, which would still be a spectacle worth watching. Note, however, that keen eclipse-watchers – and, yes, they do exist – believe that anyone who says they've seen an eclipse without getting the full 100% is like someone who stands outside a stadium listening to a rock band, then says they've seen the concert! To get the full effect you could always consider popping down to Mozambique, or over to Zambia, for a few days.

For more details on eclipses and how to see them, look at the following Web sites:
http://sunearth.gsfc.nasa.gov/eclipse/eclipse.html
www.holeinthesky.com

Although the views might be good, it's best not to consider hiking in the highlands during the wet season. Showers, which may be short on the lowlands, can last for longer on the higher ground, and stream crossings (particularly on Mount Mulanje) can be treacherous. Another factor to consider if you plan to visit southern Malawi, especially if you plan to visit Mount Mulanje, is a heavy mist called a *chiperone* (chip-er-**own**-ee), which occurs during the early months of the dry season, sometimes lasting up to five days at a time.

It's worth noting that the weather patterns all over Southern Africa have become less predictable in the last decade or so. Some years the rainy seasons have arrived later, some years they have finished earlier, and some years they have finished later. In addition, the chiperones in Malawi seem to be occurring less frequently.

What Kind of Trip

In Malawi *any* kind of trip is possible. If time is limited, you can visit for just two weeks and get a lot out of it. If time is of no consequence, there's enough to do to keep you going for two months at least. Some ideas are given in the Suggested Itineraries section earlier in this chapter.

If you're on a tight budget Malawi is ideal because distances are short, so travel is fairly cheap, and there are many accommodation options aimed specifically at backpackers. To give a rough idea, the cost of travel here is on a par with most parts of East and Southern Africa, noticeably more expensive than most parts of Asia, and a lot cheaper than Europe. What you get for your money is normally good value. If money is less of a problem, Malawi offers many possibilities. In the main towns and cities, and along the lake shore, are several mid-range and top-end hotels, while in some national parks there are very good quality lodges and safari camps.

Whatever your budget, Malawi is also a good place for first-time visitors in Africa, and for solo travellers. It provides a good introduction to travel in the region, without many of the more daunting aspects that some other countries present to first-timers.

Independent travel is fairly straightforward, since there are plenty of places to stay, English is widely spoken, the infrastructure (roads, phones, banks etc) is reasonably good, and the political climate is pretty stable. If you're considering wider travel in East or Southern Africa, Malawi can be a perfect gateway or place to find your feet.

Maps

Maps of Malawi suitable for general travelling are not widely available outside the country. The main choice is the *Malawi Travel Reference Map* (1:900,000) produced by ITM Publishing, which should be available from good specialist shops in your home country.

Malawi features on several regional maps of Southern Africa. The best is Lonely Planet's *Southern Africa Road Atlas*, covering Malawi along with Zambia and all other countries to the south.

The Michelin map *Africa Central & South* (Sheet 955) shows Malawi, and is good enough for general planning, especially if you're considering a visit to neighbouring countries. The detail is good, given the limitations of scale (1:4,000,000), and the map is regularly updated. It's the kind of map that lingers in bookshops for ages though, so make sure you buy a recent version. Even so, you should expect a few discrepancies between the map and reality, particularly with regard to roads, as old tracks get upgraded and once-smooth highways become potholed disasters. In South Africa, Struik publishes *Central & Southern Africa*, which covers a similar area.

Once in Malawi, you can easily buy maps of the country (see Information in the Lilongwe and the Blantyre & Limbe chapters for details). These include *Malawi* (1:1,000,000), which shows shaded relief features and most roads, although light red lines on a brown background makes map reading tricky. *Malawi Road & Tourist Map* (1:1,000,000) has one side showing all main roads and some minor roads, and national parks (but no relief details) plus street maps of the main towns. The other side contains some general information and another map of the country showing various features of interest to tourists. On both maps detail is not especially good, and the quality of roads is out of date, so you're probably better off using them together or using one of them alongside the Michelin 955 or the Lonely Planet road atlas.

For more detail, government survey maps (the most useful at scales of 1:50,000 and 1:250,000) are available from the Public Map Sales Offices in Blantyre and Lilongwe. In both places the staff are helpful, and most maps cost about US$2. Maps of popular areas, such as Mount Mulanje, are occasionally out of stock.

Specific maps and guidebooks on individual national parks and hiking areas are covered in the relevant sections.

What to Bring

Clothes Don't carry too many clothes; anything you don't have with you can easily be bought along the way. In cities and large towns, new clothes are comparably priced or cheaper than those in Europe, and in many markets you can find decent second-hand clothes.

In most places, especially cities, local people dress smartly if they can afford to, so

Second-hand Clothes

In the last few years, in Malawi and all over Africa, there has been a large increase in shops and market stalls selling second-hand clothes, mostly collected by charities and charity shops in Europe. You can also find factory overruns and items off-loaded by stores because they're out of fashion in Western countries. The clothes are good quality, and a fraction of what they'd cost new, which means local people can avoid forking out hard-earned money for fancy gear.

But there's a downside: The second-hand imports have wiped out any chance of the poorer countries of Africa (especially those like Malawi) ever having their own clothing industry. And all over the region, market and street tailors, who used to run up shirts and trousers from local material, are going out of business.

wearing some decent clothes will mean you get taken more seriously in 'official' situations. Generally, khaki or military-style clothing is not recommended, as you may be mistaken for a soldier, which can lead to extra questions at borders or checkpoints, or being met with a certain reserve by local people.

Equipment A tent and a set of camping gear will be useful if you plan to get right off the beaten track, and will also help you save money, especially in towns, cities and national parks. Malawi has some truly marvellous camping grounds, although on the lake shore there's hardly any price difference between camping and renting a beach hut.

Even if you're not into camping, a sleeping bag and sheet liner will be useful in budget hotels where bedding might not be provided.

Absolute essentials include a basic medical kit, a mosquito net, a water bottle, purifying solution and a water filter (see Health later in this chapter); a torch (flashlight) and spare good-quality batteries; and several passport-sized photos (for visa applications). Optional items include: a camera and film (see Photography & Video later in this chapter); binoculars (for wildlife viewing); a universal drain plug; a small padlock to secure the contents of your pack from opportunistic riflers; a travel alarm; a penknife; a clothes-drying line; and a sewing kit.

Don't forget things such as a wash kit and towel (although some travellers class this as optional too).

Hiking Extras If you plan to visit highland areas (eg, Mount Mulanje or the Nyika Plateau), remember they get cold at night even in warm months, so a jacket, a good sweatshirt, hat, gloves and some warm socks are worth taking. Thermal vests (T-shirt style) have good warmth-retaining capacity for their size and weight.

A tent is not essential on Mount Mulanje as there are mountain huts, but for multiday walks on Nyika they are a must. A camping stove is recommended on Mulanje (although there are fires and fireplaces you can use) and essential on Nyika, as fires are not allowed in many areas. One that runs on petrol will be the least hassle (don't rely on finding refined 'white gas' such as Shellite or Colemanfuel), but methylated spirits for Trangia-type stoves can usually be found in supermarkets, hardware shops or pharmacies.

Backpack To carry all your gear a backpack (rucksack) is most practical. Carry the sturdiest and best-made pack you can afford, paying special attention to the strength of zips and straps. Internal-frame packs are easier to handle, but some hikers prefer external-framed packs; they're cooler in hot conditions. Many travellers favour the type of travel-backpack that neatly turns into a normal-looking holdall. This is handy if you don't want to look like a backpacker, and particularly useful for keeping straps out of the way when your bag is loaded onto planes or bus roof racks. It's also wise to use plastic bags to protect the contents from moisture and dust.

Binoculars If you've got even the slightest interest in watching wild animals (and that's why many visitors come to Africa) you simply *must* bring a pair of binoculars. Some good cheap compact models are available, but if you can afford something larger and better you won't regret it. Many people say they don't need binoculars because they only want to look at big animals, like elephants or lions, and aren't interested in smaller animals or birds – but that's because they never see them properly in the first place. And even watching big animals is better through binoculars. Looking with your bare eyes or down a camera zoom lens just isn't the same. With binoculars you can observe behaviour or pick out markings, and simply get closer to the animals you've come so far to see. It's so much more rewarding than squinting at some vague brown beast in the distance.

RESPONSIBLE TOURISM

Tourism is one of the largest industries in the world, and the effects of tourists on destinations can be substantial. In some cases the effects of tourism can be positive (eg, throughout Africa tourists pay to visit areas with attractive landscape or interesting wildlife, and some of this money reaches local people, who then have an incentive to conserve the areas and the animals – see Ecology & Environment in the Facts for the Visitor chapter). But in other cases tourism can have a very negative effect. Across East and Southern Africa, including Malawi, there are many instances of indigenous people being excluded from their traditional lands to make way for wildlife reserves or tourist hotels.

In popular tourist areas, the sheer number of visitors can sometimes put a strain on the local environment (eg, big hotels can use valuable water and power resources or create problems of waste disposal to the detriment of local people, while large groups of tourists in vehicles compressed into a small wildlife area can disturb the very animals they've come to see). It's ironic that although tourism frequently relies on natural resources, such as healthy wildlife populations, pristine landscapes or rich cultural traditions, tourists and tour companies quite often do little to sustain them. From this point of view, it is fortunate that tourist numbers are low in Malawi compared to other countries in the region, and overbuilding or overcrowding in tourist areas have yet to become a big problem.

On your own trip through Malawi, the best way for you to make a positive contribution to the country is by carefully deciding where you want to spend your money. If you want to support tour companies with a good environmental record, you have to look beyond vague 'ecofriendly' claims and ask what they are really doing to protect or support the environment (and remember that includes local people too). Consider also the amount of money you pay during your holiday and ensure that as much as possible stays within the host country to the benefit of local people. Remember that overland truck passengers, independent backpackers and other budget travellers on a long trip contribute just as much to local economy as high-rolling tourists who come to a country on a short all-inclusive trip paid for overseas.

But tourism's effect is not just financial. It is also important for visitors to behave in a manner that limits their impact on the natural environment and the local inhabitants. Some ideas are listed in the following section. To be a responsible tourist you have to question some of your own actions and those of the tour companies you use. You also have to look closely at the actions of governments, both local and around the world. Being a responsible tourist doesn't mean you have to get depressed and spoil your holiday. In fact, by asking a few questions and getting a deeper insight, it can make your trip even more rewarding.

Guidelines for Responsible Tourism

Here are some guidelines for travellers who wish to minimise negative impacts on the countries they visit:

Save precious natural resources Try not to waste water. Switch off unneeded lights and air-conditioning. Avoid establishments that consume limited resources such as water and electricity at the expense of local residents.

Support local enterprise Use locally owned hotels and restaurants. Employ local guides. Support craft workers by buying locally made souvenirs, but avoid items made from natural material – wood, skin, ivory etc – unless they come from a sustainable source (although this is difficult to check).

Recognise land rights Indigenous peoples' ownership of land is recognised by international law. This should be acknowledged irrespective of whether the national government applies the law or not.

Ask before taking close-up photographs of people Don't worry if you don't speak the language. A smile and gesture will be understood and appreciated.

Don't give money, sweets or pens to children It's demeaning and encourages begging. A donation to a recognised project – a health centre or school – is more constructive and meaningful.

Respect local etiquette Politeness is a virtue in most parts of the world, but remember that different people have different ideas about what's polite. In many places, tight fitting wear, revealing shorts or skimpy tops are insensitive to local feelings. Loose lightweight clothing is preferable. Similarly, public displays of affection are often culturally inappropriate.

Don't be ignorant Learning something about the history and current affairs of a country helps you understand the idiosyncrasies of its people, and helps prevent misunderstandings and frustrations.

Be patient, friendly and sensitive Remember that you are a guest.

These guidelines are based on those issued by the British organisation Tourism Concern (☎ 020-7753 3330, fax 7753 3331, @ info@tourismconcern.org.uk), 277-281 Holloway Road, London N7 8HN. You can support its work by becoming a member – for information see the Web site: www.tourism concern.org.uk. Also from the UK is Action for Southern Africa (☎ 020-7833 3133, @ actsa@geo2.poptel.org.uk); it campaigns for – among other things – sustainable 'people- first' tourism throughout the region.

In the USA, the Rethinking Tourism Project (@ RTProject@aol.com), PO Box 581938, Minneapolis, MN55458, is similar.

TOURIST OFFICES
Local Tourist Offices

Malawi has tourist offices in Blantyre and Lilongwe (see Information in the Lilongwe and the Blantyre & Limbe chapters). At these tourist offices, information is usually limited to glossy brochures produced for Malawi by a PR firm (featuring beautiful models and optimistic text), plus a few leaflets on car hire and tour companies. However, the staff try to be helpful and can often assist with general inquiries on hotels, public transport, shops, hospitals etc, if you explain exactly what you want to do, and how much money you want to spend. Making inquiries over the phone is difficult.

Tourist Offices Abroad

Outside Malawi, tourism promotion is handled by the UK-based organisation Malawi Tourism (☎ 0115-982 1903, fax 9819418, @ enquiries@malawitourism.com), which responds to inquiries from all over the world. You can also get information from the Web site: www.malawitourism.com.

VISAS & DOCUMENTS
Passport
Your most important document is your passport. Some officials don't like passports near their expiry date, so it's better to have one that expires at least a few months after your trip ends.

Visas
For Malawi, visas are not required by citizens of Commonwealth countries, Luxembourg, Belgium, Denmark, Finland, Germany, Iceland, the Netherlands, Norway, Portugal, Ireland, South Africa, Sweden and the USA. Commonwealth citizens of Asian origin sometimes need visas that are not required by their compatriots of other races.

If you don't need a visa, you'll automatically be given a 30-day tourist pass when you enter Malawi at an airport or border unless you can prove you need longer (for example, an air ticket showing a return date), in which case getting up to three months is usually no problem. If you want even longer, you can easily extend your tourist pass (see Visa Extensions).

If you do need a tourist visa for Malawi, it can be issued by a Malawian embassy, consulate or high commission in another country, for a cost of around US$25 (or equivalent). Visas are usually issued in three days.

It is important to note that regulations are always subject to change, so it's best to check at a Malawian embassy or high commission in your own country before you leave (or in a neighbouring country as you're travelling). Otherwise you may arrive at the airport or border without a visa only to find that the rules have changed. The Lonely Planet Web site (see Internet Resources later in this chapter) includes links for up-to-date visa information.

Visa Extensions If you want to stay longer once you're inside Malawi you can get visa or tourist pass extensions at the immigration offices in Lilongwe or Blantyre, or at regional police stations. The process is straightforward and free, although some officials won't extend your visa or pass until the very day the existing one expires.

In Lilongwe, the Immigration Office (☎ 722995), is on Murray Rd, in Old Town; it is next to the Department of Wildlife & Tourism.

In Blantyre, the Immigration Office is in Building Society House, on the corner of Victoria Ave and Chilembwe Rd, open Monday to Friday from 7.30 am to noon, 1.30 to 4 pm and Saturday 7.30 am to noon.

Travel Insurance
A travel insurance policy to cover theft, loss and medical problems is highly recommended. There is a wide variety of policies available, so check the small print to see exactly what you're getting. Be especially sure that the policy covers ambulances (air and land) or an emergency flight home. Note also that some policies specifically exclude 'dangerous activities', which can include scuba diving, motorcycling and even hiking.

You may prefer a policy that pays doctors or hospitals directly rather than you having to pay on the spot and claim later. If you have to claim later make sure you keep all documentation. Some policies ask you to call back (reverse charges) to a centre in your home country where an immediate assessment of your problem is made.

The international travel policies handled by STA Travel, and other similar youth and student travel organisations, are usually good value, and not always restricted to the young or studious. Some companies specialise in flexible long-term policies that can be extended while you're travelling – ideal if you fall in love with (or in) Malawi and want to stay longer. In the UK this includes Worldwide Travel Insurance Services (☎ 01892-833338, fax 837744). You can also check out the Web site: www.worldwideinsure.com. In other countries similar specialist policies may take some searching out.

Other Documents
Other documents you may need include a vaccination certificate to show you've been jabbed for yellow fever, and possibly some other diseases (see Health later in this chapter); your driving licence and an Inter-

International Driving Permit

An International Driving Permit (IDP) is easily and cheaply issued by your national motoring association, and is very useful if you're driving in countries such as Malawi, where your own licence might not be recognised (officially or unofficially). It has the added advantage of being written in several languages, with a photo and lots of stamps, so it looks more impressive when presented to car rental clerks or police officers at roadblocks.

national Driving Permit; a student or young person's identity card (occasionally good for various discounts).

Copies

All important documents (plus your passport data page and visa page, credit cards, and air/bus/train tickets etc) should be photocopied before you leave home. Keep a copy with you, separate from the originals, and leave one copy with someone at home so it can be faxed to you in an emergency.

It's also a good idea to store details of your vital travel documents in Lonely Planet's free online Travel Vault – in case you lose the photocopies. Your password-protected Travel Vault is accessible online anywhere in the world – create it at www.ekno.lonelyplanet.com.

EMBASSIES & CONSULATES
Malawian Embassies & High Commissions

Countries with a Malawian embassy or high commission include Canada, France, the UK and the USA, but few other Western countries. Citizens of other countries should check in the phone directory of their capital city to see if there is a Malawian embassy. In some countries, such as Australia, Malawi is represented by a government department responsible for foreign affairs.

In Africa, Malawi has high commissions in Kenya, Mozambique, South Africa, Tanzania, Zambia and Zimbabwe. Generally, visa sections are open for applications in the morning only.

Malawian diplomatic representation abroad includes:

Australia
Malawi has no high commission in Australia, but as a Commonwealth country is represented by the Consular Office, Australian Department of Foreign Affairs and Trade (☎ 02-6261 3305), John McEwen Crescent, Barton, ACT 2600.
Canada
High Commission: (☎ 613-236 8932) 7 Clemow Ave, Ottawa, Ontario K1F 2A9
France
Embassy: (☎ 01 47 20 20 27) 20 Rue Euler, Paris 75008
Kenya
High Commission: (☎ 440569, fax 440568) Waiyaki Way, Westlands, Nairobi
Mozambique
High Commission: (☎ 01-492676) 75 Avenida Kenneth Kaunda, Maputo
South Africa
High Commission: (☎ 011-339 1569) Sable House, 41 De Korte St, Braamfontein, Johannesburg; *High Commission*: (☎ 012-342 0146, fax 342 0147) 770 Government Ave, Arcadia, Pretoria

Your Own Embassy

It's important to realise what your own embassy – the embassy of the country of which you are a citizen – can and can't do to help if you get into trouble while travelling.

Generally speaking, it won't help in emergencies if the trouble is remotely your own fault. Remember that you are bound by Malawi law. Your embassy will not be sympathetic if you end up in jail after committing a crime locally, even if such actions are legal in your own country.

In genuine emergencies you might get some assistance, but only if other channels have been exhausted. For example, if you need to get home urgently, a free ticket is exceedingly unlikely – the embassy would expect you to have insurance. If you have all your money and documents stolen, a new passport might be provided, but a loan for onward travel won't be. If you are ill, most embassies keep a list of selected local medical centres and can give you the relevant contact details, but that's all.

Tanzania
High Commission: (☎ 113240) 6th floor, Wing A, NIC Life House (Branch), Sokoine Dr, Dar es Salaam
UK
High Commission: (☎ 020-7491 4172) 33 Grosvenor St, London W1X 0DE
USA
Embassy: (☎ 202-797 1007) 2408 Massachusetts Ave, Washington DC 20008
Zambia
High Commission: (☎ 01-265765) Bishops Rd, Kabulonga, Lusaka
Zimbabwe
High Commission: (☎ 04-705611) 42/44 Harare St, Harare

Embassies & Consulates in Malawi

The following countries have embassies, consulates or high commissions in Malawi:
Germany
Embassy: (☎ 772555) Convention Dr, City Centre, Lilongwe
Mozambique
High Commission: (☎ 774100) Commercial Bank Bldg, African Unity Ave, City Centre, Lilongwe; *Consulate:* (☎ 643189) Kamuzu Highway, Limbe
South Africa
High Commission: (☎ 773722) off Convention Dr, City Centre, Lilongwe
UK
High Commission: (☎ 772400, 773036, 772123) off Convention Dr, City Centre, Lilongwe; *Consulate*: Hanover Ave, Blantyre
USA
Embassy: (☎ 773166) off Convention Dr, City Centre, Lilongwe
Zambia
High Commission: (☎ 772100, 772635) off Convention Dr, City Centre, Lilongwe
Zimbabwe
High Commission: (☎ 774988) off Independence Dr, City Centre, Lilongwe

Tanzania Be warned that there is no Tanzanian high commission in Malawi so if you need a visa it must be obtained elsewhere. Lusaka and Harare are the closest. If you're flying into Tanzania, you can get it at your airport of arrival. Also an increasing number of travellers have been issued visas on the spot at Tanzanian land borders, but this sometimes seems a vague process and may not be always reliable.

Visas for Onward Travel

If you need visas for neighbouring countries, these are the conditions. All embassies, consulates and high commissions are open from Monday to Friday.

Mozambique

Visas are available at the high commission in Lilongwe and the consulate in Limbe. Both are open from 8 am to noon. Transit visas cost US$5 (or US$10 for double transit) and are issued within 24 hours. One-month single-entry tourist visas cost US$10 and take a week to issue (four-day service costs US$15 and next day is US$20). A three-month multiple entry visa is US$30. All fees are payable in kwacha.

South Africa

Visas are free and take two days to issue. The high commission is open from 8 am to noon.

Zambia

Visas are issued on the same day if you get there early. Costs depend on your nationality: Britons pay US$60 for a single entry; all others pay US$25, except Norwegians (free). Payment in US dollars is preferred. Apply from 9 am to noon.

Zimbabwe

Single-entry visas for up to six months cost US$35 (payable in kwacha) and take a week to issue. Apply from 8 am to 12.30 pm. (Visas are also available at the border and are probably cheaper there.)

CUSTOMS

There are no customs restrictions on the amount of foreign ('hard') currency you can bring in or out of Malawi. You are not allowed to import or export more than about US$10 worth of Malawian kwacha, but a bit more than this is unlikely to be a problem. Currency declaration forms are no longer used. All entry regulations are liable to change, so contact your nearest Malawian embassy or tourist office for up-to-date information. Malawian immigration and customs officials are almost always polite and friendly, but they play strictly by the rules. If all your paperwork is in order there'll be no problems.

MONEY
Currency

The unit of currency is the Malawian kwacha (MK). This is divided into 100 tambala (t). Bank notes include MK200, MK100, MK50, MK20, MK10, MK5. Coins include MK1, 50t, 20t, 10t, 5t and 1t, although the small tambala coins are virtually worthless.

Inflation is high in Malawi, so quoting costs in MK is not helpful, as prices will have changed by the time you arrive. Therefore we have used US dollars (US$) throughout this book. At big hotels, and other places that actually quote in US dollars you can pay in hard currency or kwacha at the prevailing exchange rate.

Exchange Rates

In countries with high inflation and weak economies, such as Malawi, exchange rates are always liable to fluctuate. The exchange rates quoted here were correct as this book went to print.

country	unit		kwacha
Australia	A$1	=	MK27
Canada	C$1	=	MK32
euro	€1	=	MK43
France	10FF	=	MK7
Germany	DM1	=	MK22
Japan	¥100	=	MK45
New Zealand	NZ$1	=	MK20
South Africa	R1	=	MK7
UK	UK£1	=	MK70
USA	US$1	=	MK48

Although the actual exchange rate will have changed by the time you reach Malawi, the cost of things in US$ (or any other hard currency) will not have altered much.

Exchanging Money

Cash & Travellers Cheques The best way to carry money is as a mix of cash or travellers cheques. Cash is quicker to deal with and gets better exchange rates, but cannot be replaced if lost. If you lose your trav-

ellers cheques you get a refund. When you buy travellers cheques make sure you know what to do if the worst happens – most companies give a 24-hour international phone number to contact.

It's worth carrying a mixture of high and low denomination notes/bills and cheques. Thus, if you're about to leave Malawi, you can change for just a few days without having loads of spare cash to get rid of. Note also that, due to counterfeiting, old US$100 notes are not accepted at places that don't have a light machine for checking watermarks.

The most readily recognised international currency in Malawi (and all over Southern and East Africa) is the US dollar (US$). Other currencies that are easily accepted include UK pounds and German marks. South African rand are also quick and easy to deal with all over the region, but unless you're from South Africa it's not worth changing your own currency into rand to then change again into kwacha.

To exchange cash and travellers cheques, the banks where this is easiest are the National Bank of Malawi and the Commercial Bank of Malawi, which both have branches in cities and most towns all over the country. Rates and charges can vary, so it's worth going to branches of both banks if you can (in many towns they seem to be next to each other) to see which offers the best deal. For opening times of banks in cities see Business Hours later in this chapter. Banks in small towns may open only two or three mornings per week. You can still change money in smaller towns and rural areas, although usually no more than US$100 or US$200. The service here may be slow, but there's often less of a queue than in the city banks, so it works out about the same. If you arrive or leave by air at Lilongwe, the bank at the airport usually opens to coincide with international flights, but not always.

Bank charges for exchanging money are normally 1% of the value of the transaction, for cash or travellers cheques. To deal with travellers cheques the bank will want to see your passport and the original official purchase receipts (not just the till receipt from the place that sold you the cheques).

As well as banks, there are privately owned foreign exchange (forex) bureaus in cities and large towns. These usually offer a slightly better rate than the banks, make lower charges (or none at all), have longer opening hours (including weekends) and offer a faster service.

If you get stuck when banks and bureaus are closed, you might be able to exchange money at a large hotel, travel agent or tour company, although the rates are often poor – so only change enough to get you by. Alternatively, shops that sell imported items sometimes buy US dollars at around 5% to 10% more than bank or bureau rates. If you take this method, be discrete. Saying 'The banks are closed, do you know anyone who can help me...?' is better than 'Do you want to change money?'.

Credit & Debit Cards You can draw cash on a Visa card at branches of the Commercial Bank in Blantyre and Lilongwe. When you draw cash on a credit card, your card company will make a charge, and you have to make sure you've set up a system for paying your bill when it arrives, if you're away from home more than a month. If you use a debit card you don't have this problem – you simply load up your account and draw on it as you go along.

There are no reliable ATMs in which to use credit or debit cards, so you need to go inside the bank and deal with a bank clerk personally. Cash drawn on a card is payable in kwacha, which you can then reconvert to US dollars or another hard currency (if that's what you want), but reconfirm this before starting your transaction. The charge is US$2. The process sometimes takes several hours, but if you go in the morning before 9 am it can be quicker. Otherwise, leave your card and details, and come back later to pick up your cash. No card transactions are started after 1 pm.

To actually pay for goods or services you can use a Visa credit or debit card at some of the large hotels and top-end restaurants, but not all of them – and even those that accept cards often add an extra 5% to 10% surcharge to your bill. It seems even more difficult to use a MasterCard, although Diners Club card is accepted at a few places in Blantyre and Lilongwe. If you usually rely on plastic, you're probably better off using it to draw cash and paying with that.

International Transfers If you think your finances may need topping up while you're travelling, ask your bank about international bank-to-bank transfers. This is usually a complicated, time-consuming and expensive business. It is especially so when you get outside the major capitals, although if you're travelling for a long time it can save the worry (and sheer bulk) of carrying large wads of notes and cheques. It's probably better to consider using debit cards.

Black Market In various parts of the world, artificially fixed exchange rates in banks mean you can get more local money for your hard currency by changing outside, on the so-called black market. This is illegal, morally questionable and sometimes dangerous. However, in Malawi it's not an issue. Due to currency deregulation, exchange rates are not fixed. Thus, banks and forex bureaus can offer genuine rates, and the black market has virtually disappeared. You may be offered 5% or 10% more than bank or bureau rates by shady-looking characters on the street, but it's very likely to be a set-up. If they offer more than 10% you *know* it's a set-up. On top of this the chances of robberies or cons (plus fake US$100 and US$50 bills) make it definitely not worth the risk.

Moneychangers If all official methods of changing money are closed (eg, because it's a weekend or public holiday) you may be able to change at a shop selling imported items, as described in the earlier Exchanging Money section. Dealing with black market moneychangers is not worth the risk.

The only time that you might have to deal with moneychangers is at a border where there is no bank (this is usually the case at borders). Here customs and immigration officials tolerate moneychangers who change your Malawian kwacha into Tanzanian

'Sorry, No Change'

The lack of small coins and notes in shops and markets constantly frustrates visitors, who inevitably get large denomination notes when they change money in the banks and bureaus. Get and keep as much small change as you can, especially if you're going to Lake Malawi. Otherwise you'll end up with a pocket full of 'Cape Maclear currency' – little bits of cardboard saying 'I owe you 3 kwacha'.

shillings, Mozambican meticais, Zambian kwacha, Zimbabwean dollars or whatever. It's always important to be alert though, as these guys can pull all sorts of stunts with bad exchange rates or folded notes.

Security

To keep your money and other valuables (such as your passport and air ticket) safe from pickpockets, the best place is out of sight under a shirt or skirt, or inside your trousers. You can make or buy a pouch that goes around your neck or waist. Some travellers go for 'invisible pockets', money belts and other imaginative devices. Keep the bulk of your money here, and then use a separate wallet with just a little money in for day-to-day purchases. Avoid the mistake some travellers make of keeping their money carefully hidden but then exposing the lot when buying a ticket in a crowded bus station.

Costs

Very generally speaking, costs of consumer items in Malawi are around 50 to 75% of what they are in Europe, Australasia or North America. Obviously there are exceptions: locally produced goods (including food and beer) may be much cheaper, while imported things may be twice what they cost in Western countries.

Accommodation costs in Malawi range from less than US$1 per night for basic local resthouses to between US$3 and US$10 for camping, US$5 for hostel dorms, between US$25 and US$50 for mid-range hotels, and up to US$100 or US$200 for top-end establishments. Couples can save on accommodation costs, since double rooms are cheaper than two singles. Often couples can share a single.

Transport options are equally varied. You can hitch for free or go by chartered plane for something like US$10 per minute. Most people, however, travel by bus or train – this is cheap compared with Western prices. As a rule, buses charge between US$1.50 and US$2 per 100km, and express buses slightly more. (For more details see the Getting Around chapter.)

Other costs to consider when travelling in Malawi include the price of getting into some national parks, such as Liwonde, Nyika or Kasungu, which cannot be reached by public transport (see the relevant sections for more information). On the other hand, activities such as hiking, diving and kayaking are inexpensive compared with other countries in the region.

When working out your own costs you should also take into account extra items such as visa fees (if you're travelling on to Mozambique or other countries in the region), plus the cost of any organised tours or activities (such as a wildlife safari or sailing trip).

Taking all of this into account, budget travellers could scrape by on US$5 per day, although most will have a good time on US$10. For a bit more comfort, US$20 to US$25 per day is a reasonable budget for living expenses, plus whatever optional extras you decide on. For luxury travel, including car hire, top-end lodges, good food and wine, you could easily spend US$200 per day.

Tipping

Tipping can be a problem in Malawi because there are few clear rules applicable to all. Anyone staying in a fancy hotel would be expected to tip porters and other staff, but there would not be the same expectation from a backpacker in a budget resthouse.

At better restaurants, if service has been good, a tip is usually expected (from locals and foreigners); around 10% is normal. Check the bill closely to see if service is included. It frequently is – although you're not obliged to pay it if service has been bad. At more basic restaurants no tipping is expected from anyone. There's a grey area

The Fine Art of Bargaining

In some African countries, bargaining over prices – often for market goods – is a way of life. Visitors often have difficulty with this idea, and are used to things having a fixed value, whereas in Africa commodities are considered worth whatever their seller can get for them. It really is no different to the concept of an auction and should be treated as one more aspect of travel in Malawi, or wherever you go in Africa.

Basics

In markets selling basic items such as fruit and vegetables *some* sellers will invariably put their asking price high when they see you as a wealthy foreigner. If you pay this – whether out of ignorance or guilt about how much you have compared with locals – you may be considered foolish, but you'll also be doing fellow travellers a disservice by creating the impression that all foreigners are willing to pay any price named. You may also harm the local economy: By paying high prices you put some items out of reach from the locals. And who can blame the traders – why sell to locals when foreigners will pay twice as much? So in cases like this you may need to bargain over the price.

Having said that, many sellers will quote you the same price that locals pay, particularly away from cities or tourist areas. It is very important not to go around expecting *everybody* to charge high. It helps of course to know the price of things. After the first few days in a country (when you'll inevitably pay over the odds a few times) you'll soon get to learn the standard prices for basic items.

Remember that prices can change depending on where you buy. For example, a soft drink in a city may be one-third of the price you'll pay in a remote rural area, where transport costs have to be paid. Conversely, fruit and vegetables are cheaper in the areas where they're actually grown.

between these two classes of restaurants, where tipping is rarely expected from locals, but may be expected of foreigners.

Note however, that in Malawi only 4% of your total payment goes to the staff (see Taxes & Refunds later in this chapter), so if you normally work on the 10% rule of thumb, then a tip of about 6% on top of the 10% service charge added to your bill is appropriate here.

In privately hired taxis, tipping is not the rule among locals, but drivers expect well-heeled travellers to tip about 10%. In bigger cities with numerous foreigners, taxi drivers may still hope for a small tip, even from backpackers.

Some mountain huts and forest reserve resthouses are run by government departments and are staffed by caretakers who receive a very low wage. Although the price technically covers their services, in most cases it's reasonable to tip a small amount (the equivalent of US$1 is fine). The same applies to rangers (called 'scouts' locally) in national parks or wildlife reserves who may

guide you on walks or drives; the money you pay for their service goes to the national park, so if the service is good, an extra tip (around US$2 to US$3 per day) for them is reasonable.

At 'self-catering' camps and lodges in national parks or along the lake shore, the kitchen is often staffed by cooks and helpers. You can make your own food, but it's usual to give your stuff to the cook to prepare to your instructions. Even if you cook the food yourself, the helpers usually wash up your pots and pans. The fee you pay to stay in the lodge or camp officially covers their services, but once again a small tip (US$1 to US$3) is appreciated, and usually appropriate (most of them are pretty good cooks!).

Taxes & Refunds

All mid-range and top-end hotels and restaurants charge 10% service charge and 10% tourist tax. You should therefore add 20% to the cost shown on menus and tariff sheets. If in doubt, ask if the price is inclusive or not, as it can make quite a differ-

The Fine Art of Bargaining

Souvenirs

At craft and curio stalls, where items are specifically for tourists, bargaining is very much expected. The vendor's aim is to identify the highest price you're willing to pay. Your aim is to find the price below which the vendor will not sell. People have all sorts of formulae for this, but there are no hard-and-fast rules. Some vendors may initially ask a price four (or more) times higher than what they're prepared to accept, although it's usually lower than this. Decide what you want to pay or what others have told you they've paid; your first offer should be about half this. At this stage, the vendor may laugh or feign outrage, while you plead abject poverty. The vendor's price then starts to drop from the original quote to a more realistic level. When it does, you begin making better offers until you arrive at a mutually agreeable price.

And that's the crux – *mutually agreeable*. You hear travellers all the time moaning about how they got 'overcharged' by souvenir sellers. When things have no fixed price, nobody really gets overcharged. If you don't like the price, it's simple – don't pay it.

Some people prefer to conduct their bargaining in a stern manner, but the best results seem to come from a friendly and spirited exchange. There's no reason to lose your temper when bargaining. If the effort seems a waste of time, politely take your leave. Sometimes sellers will call you back. Very few will pass up the chance of making a sale, however thin the profit.

If sellers won't come down to a price you feel is fair (or you simply can't afford), it either means they really aren't making a profit, or that if you don't pay somebody else will. Remember – the sellers are under no more obligation to sell to you, than you are to buy from them. You can go elsewhere, or (if you want the item) accept the price. This is the raw edge of capitalism!

---

ence. Wherever possible in this book we have shown prices inclusive of taxes.

The 10% service charge officially means that tipping is not necessary, but this is not all it seems as hotels and restaurants making the 10% service charge have to pass on 60% of this to the Ministry of Tourism, for a general marketing fund. Thus staff actually receive only 4% of the total you pay for your room and meal.

It is not possible for foreign visitors to claim back any of the taxes they pay in Malawi.

POST & COMMUNICATIONS
Postal Rates

Post around, and in and out of, Malawi is a bit of a lottery. Some letters have been known to get from Lilongwe to London in three days, while others take three weeks. Mail from Cape Town to Lilongwe or Blantyre can often take a month. When letters eventually make it beyond the capital cities, the service is even more uncertain; it can be quick or slow – you just never know.

Letters (less then 10g) within Malawi cost the equivalent of about US$0.02. To other African destinations a letter costs US$0.10. To Europe, North America or Australasia it is US$0.20. It's quicker (and probably more reliable) to use the EMS Speedpost service at post offices. Letters up to 500g cost US$5 to Europe and US$7 to Australia and the USA.

Parcel rates used to be famously cheap in Malawi, allowing you to send home large wooden carvings at a very low price. However, it now costs about US$8 plus US$3 per kilogram to send stuff outside Africa.

Sending Mail

All towns (and many villages) in Malawi have post offices where you can buy stamps, and post letters, but the collection service is unreliable. In the larger towns, post offices often have long queues, so a useful tip is to buy your stamps at a quiet rural office, but post your letters in Blantyre or Lilongwe to give them more of a chance of getting home.

If you're posting a parcel, the maximum weight allowed is 10kg. Most chief's chairs (the favourite souvenir) are around 15kg, but fortunately they come in two sections, so you just send two parcels. However, there is a 1m maximum length restriction, so keep your purchase relatively small if you want to post it home.

Receiving Mail
The post offices in Blantyre and Lilongwe have poste restante services. See the Post & Communications sections in those chapters for more details.

Telephone & Fax
Telephone calls within Malawi are inexpensive and the network between main cities is reliable although the lines to outlying areas are often not working. Public phones (called 'booths' locally) take new 1MK coins only.

International calls (to destinations outside Africa) from public phone offices in main towns and cities cost around US$10 for three minutes – the minimum charge. Fax rates are the same. At hotels the service for phone calls and faxes may be quicker, but charges are around US$10 for calls within Africa, and between US$20 and US$25 for three minutes anywhere outside Africa.

Telephone Codes The international country code for Malawi, if phoning from abroad, is ☎ 265 (that is, ☎ 00 265 from the UK, ☎ 09 265 from South Africa etc).

To make an international call from Malawi, the international access code is ☎ 00. You then add the code for the country you want to call (eg, ☎ 00 61 for Australia) and then the number of the place you are calling, minus the 0 in the area or city code.

There are no area codes in Malawi, so wherever you dial within the country is just six digits. Numbers beginning with 7 are on the Lilongwe exchange; those starting with 6 are in Blantyre; 5 is around Zomba; 4 is the south of the country; 3 is the north; and 2 is the Salima area.

Numbers starting with 8 are to cell phones and are more expensive to call.

Phonecards There is no local phonecard available in Malawi. However, you could consider Lonely Planet's eKno Communication Card, which is aimed specifically at independent travellers and provides budget international calls, a range of messaging services, free email and travel information. Join online at www.ekno.lonelyplanet.com. Once you have joined, to use eKno phone services from Malawi, dial the international access number: 1-213-927-0100.

Telegrams
Telegrams can be sent from any post office, although those sent from Blantyre and Lilongwe will be faster. The cost for a telegram to Europe is US$1 per four words.

Email & Internet Access
Internet Bureaus & Cybercafes Email is a great way to stay in touch with the folks back home when you're travelling, and many people use Web-based email accounts, such as those offered by Hotmail, Yahoo and eKno, which allow the sending and receiving of email from any computer with Internet access. In Malawi there are Internet bureaus in the main cities of Lilongwe and Blantyre (see Email & Internet Access in the Lilongwe and Blantyre & Limbe chapters for details). One of the bureaus also sells drinks and chocolate bars, so calls itself a cybercafe, but that's pushing it! Most just provide desks, seats and terminals – which is all you want really. There is also an Internet bureau in Mzuzu (see Mzuzu in the Northern Malawi chapter). Elsewhere some hotels and lodges will let guests send or receive email for a nominal fee – details are given in the relevant sections.

For information on Lonely Planet's own free eKno Web-based email account, specially designed for travellers on the move, have a look online at www.ekno.lonely planet.com. For more information as to where you might find Internet access, check out www.netcafeguide.com.

Portable Computers Travelling with a portable computer that you can connect to a phone line is a great way to stay in touch with life back home, but unless you know what you're doing it's fraught with potential problems. If you plan to carry your notebook or palmtop computer with you, remember that the power supply voltage in the countries you visit may vary from that at home, risking damage to your equipment. The best investment is a universal AC adaptor for your appliance, which will enable you to plug it in anywhere without frying the innards. You'll also need a plug adaptor for each country you visit – often it's easiest to buy these before you leave home.

Also, your PC-card modem may or may not work once you leave your home country – and you won't know for sure until you try. The safest option is to buy a reputable 'global' modem before you leave home. Keep in mind that the telephone socket in each country you visit will probably be different from the one at home, so ensure that you have at least a US-standard RJ-11 telephone adaptor that works with your modem. You can almost always find an adaptor that will convert from RJ-11 to the local variety.

For more information on travelling with a portable computer, see www.teleadapt.com or www.warrior.com.

INTERNET RESOURCES

The World Wide Web is a rich resource for travellers. You can research your trip, hunt down bargain air fares, book hotels, check on weather conditions or chat with locals and other travellers about the best places to visit (or avoid!).

There's no better place to start your Web explorations than the Lonely Planet Web site (www.lonelyplanet.com). Here you'll find succinct summaries on travelling to most places on earth, postcards from other travellers and the Thorn Tree bulletin board, where you can ask questions before you go or dispense advice when you get back. You can also find travel news and updates to many of our most popular guidebooks, and the subWWWay section links you to useful travel resources elsewhere on the Web.

Other useful Web sites for travellers in Malawi and Southern Africa include:

Africa Insites A very good brochure-style site, concentrating on tourism in Southern Africa, with good links to other relevant sites. www.africa-insites.com

Africa Net A wide-ranging site on many different aspects of Africa, including tourism. www.africanet.com

African Travel & Tourism Organisation This site lists destinations, hotels and tour operators, with links to members' individual sites. www.goafrica.org

Backpack Africa A site for backpackers, with a Southern Africa bias, a list of around 400 travel-related companies, a live booking system and useful links to other sites. www.backpackafrica.com

Backpacking Aimed at budget travellers in East and Southern Africa, although South Africa biased, with hostel lists, details of Internet cafes, news, forums and links to other relevant sites. www.backpacking.co.za

Malawi Net A good home-grown site with links to sites of local newspapers and political parties, plus some basic information about the country, although little of direct use to tourists. www.malawi.net

Malawi Today The best of the Malawi-specific sites, with sections on news, tourism, magazine articles, business, development, environment and women's issues. www.malawi-today.com

Malawi Tourism The official site for Malawian tourism promotion, with news and updates on places to stay, things to see, events etc. www.malawitourism.com

BOOKS

The following books cover all aspects of Malawi, or cover East or Southern Africa with sections on Malawi. Some will give you a general sense of the country and are good to read before you go or while you are travelling. Others are detailed guidebooks and manuals if you're looking for deeper coverage on specific matters such as history or wildlife. Some larger books are too big to carry while travelling, but they make excellent souvenirs.

Most of the books listed here are available outside Malawi (most notably in the UK, USA and South Africa). Note that books may be published by different publishers in different countries – a hardcover rarity in one country may be a readily available paperback in another – so we have not included publishers in this list (unless particularly relevant). Fortunately, bookshops, libraries or mail order specialists search by title or author, so they are well placed to advise on availability.

Inside Malawi there are good bookshops in the main centres, especially in Blantyre and Lilongwe, which are well stocked with imported and locally produced books (see Bookshops under Information in the relevant chapters for details). Local publishers and imprints include Central Africana, with products including colourful coffee-table books and historical reprints; the Wildlife Society of Malawi, which produces natural history and national park guides; and the Kachere Series published by CLAIM, which produces a wide range of academic books about Malawi's religions, culture and society. The Kachere books are also available from the Church of Scotland Board of World Mission, 121 George St, Edinburgh, Scotland.

For information about literature by writers from Malawi (and information on the excellent publications in the Malawi Writers Series) see Arts in the Facts about Malawi chapter.

Lonely Planet

If you're travelling beyond Malawi, Lonely Planet has specific regional guidebooks on *Southern Africa* and *East Africa*, and country guides on *South Africa, Lesotho & Swaziland; Zimbabwe, Botswana & Namibia*; and *Kenya*. If you're heading even further afield, *Africa on a shoestring* will guide you across the continent. If you're a keen hiker, *Trekking in East Africa* has a good section on hikes and long-distance walks in Malawi, and also covers a wide range of routes in Kenya, Tanzania and Uganda.

Watching Wildlife East Africa and *Watching Wildlife Southern Africa* are perfect for travellers who want authoritative information but don't want to tote a field guide. They give advice on where, when and how best to view the region's wildlife and feature the top animal-watching destinations, with photos of more than 300 species.

Guidebooks

Trans-African Guidebooks If you're driving overland from Europe to Malawi in your own vehicle, or shipping a vehicle into South Africa and including Malawi in wider travels around the region, the following books will help with planning and route finding.

Adventure Motorbiking Handbook by Chris Scott. This manual covers the routes of the world 'where the tar ends', and contains lots of information on riding through Africa.

Africa by Road by Bob Swain & Paula Snyder. This book includes no-nonsense advice on everything from paperwork to driving techniques, and a complete country-by-country rundown.

Sahara Overland by Chris Scott. Another highly recommended tome from the well-respected desert expert, with 600 pages of information, including when to go, vehicles, routes, history, people and culture.

Local Guidebooks Malawi has a thriving home-based publishing industry, regularly turning out books on indigenous wildlife, local places to visit and so on.

Day Outings from Blantyre and *Day Outings from Lilongwe*, both published by the Wildlife Society of Malawi. These booklets are highly recommended if you're in the main centres for more than a few days. They contain suggestions on places to visit, things to see, local walks and so on, with an emphasis on wildlife. Well-written and well-researched, they cover a surprisingly wide area and are a good value investment. The only problem is they're aimed mostly at people with cars – thereby precluding many visitors and about 99% of Malawi's population.

Lake Malawi's Resorts by Ted Sneed. A good locally produced book covering every place to stay (more than 70) on the lake shore. It took so long to research that by the time Ted got to the south end, some new places had opened in the north!

Malawi's National Parks & Game Reserves by John Hough. This useful book is published by the Wildlife Society of Malawi, and covers all parks and reserves in the country, with full details of flora and fauna occurring in each.

Malawi Wildlife, Parks and Reserves by Judy Carter. A beautiful book (although quite dated now) with concise and useful information, and good coverage of all Malawi's protected areas, although its large size makes it difficult to carry around. This book is published by the Central Bookshop in Blantyre and is available there, if nowhere else.

Field Guides

Regional field guides to Southern Africa usually cover areas south of the Kunene, Okavango and Zambezi Rivers, and thus not Malawi, Zambia or northern Mozambique. However, many species found south of these rivers also occur to the north, so a Southern African guide is often useful for Malawi. Additionally, Malawi is also home to species more common to Central or East Africa, which are covered in guides to those regions. Books covering a larger area (ie, the entire continent) tend to be less detailed, although this is not a problem for most amateurs. What book you get depends on where you travel and how serious a naturalist you are.

Vegetation There are several good-quality books on Southern African flora available.

Flowers of Southern Africa by Auriol Batten. Highly recommended – a large-format book, more celebration than field guide, illustrated with superb and colourful paintings.

Southern African Trees – a photographic guide by Piet van Wyk. A more portable work perfectly adequate for amateurs.

Trees of Malawi by JS Pullinger & AM Kitchen. The best country-specific guide – a large format book with detailed colour illustrations.

Trees of Southern Africa by Keith Coates Palgrave. This is a classic volume, providing the most thorough coverage of the region's arboreal richness, with colour illustrations.

Mammals If you've come to Malawi for wildlife viewing then one of the following books could be useful.

Field Guide to the Mammals of Southern Africa by Chris & Tilde Stuart. This book is comprehensive and well-illustrated.

The Kingdon Field Guide to African Mammals by Jonathan Kingdon. An excellent and highly recommended book, covering more than 1000 species, with crisp design, accessible information, colour pictures and maps throughout, discussing ecology, evolutionary relationships and conservation status as well as the more usual notes on identification and distribution.

Land Mammals of Southern Africa by R Smithers. This book gives a brief rundown of 200 frequently observed species.

The Safari Companion by Richard Estes. A marvellous book for understanding animals – their courtship rituals, territorial displays and so on.

Southern, Central & East African Mammals by Chris & Tilde Stuart. A handy pocket guide.

Birds The following publications will be of interest to keen bird-watchers.

Birds of Southern Africa by KB Newman and *Roberts' Birds of South Africa* by GR McLachlan & GR Liversidge (popularly known simply as *Newman's* and *Roberts'*). The classic field guides to the region.

Birds of Southern Africa by Ian Sinclair. Another comprehensive tome.

Birds of Southern Africa – a photographic guide by Ian Sinclair. A slim and portable book, as is the similar *Birds of Central Africa* by the same author. These pocket-sized volumes include only the most commonly observed species, and it can be frustrating when whatever you spot in the field never seems to be in the book.

Bridging the Bird Gap by N Johnston-Stewart & J Heigham. This book describes the 64 species found in Malawi that don't get coverage in *Roberts' Birds of South Africa* and some of the other regional Southern Africa field guides, but this book is out of print now and hard to find outside Malawi.

Illustrated Guide to the Birds of Southern Africa by Ian Sinclair, Phil Hockey & Warwick Tarboton. An exhaustive, superbly illustrated publication covering all species likely to be found in the region. This is indispensable for any serious bird-watcher and one of the finest field guides you're likely to find anywhere.

Newman's Birds of Malawi by KB Newman. Covers all the species found in the country that are not listed in the main *Newman's* book and now does the job of 'bridging the bird gap' between species covered in most Southern and East African guides.

Fish Lake Malawi is home to a plethora of fish species.

Cichlids & Other Fishes of Lake Malawi by A Koning. This authoritative book is encyclopaedic in size and coverage.

Guide to the Fishes of Lake Malawi by L Digby. This book is much more portable, and is ideal for amateurs, although it was published in 1986 and is difficult to find now. It is sometimes called the 'WWF guide' as the organisation WWF-Malawi was the publisher.

Other Wildlife There are also several smaller books and leaflets devoted to more specialist subjects such as the orchids, snakes, and insects of Malawi. These can be found in the main bookshops in Lilongwe and Blantyre – see the relevant chapters for more information.

Travel
In Quest of Livingstone by Colum Wilson & Aisling Irwin. The story of two British travellers who followed the footsteps of David Livingstone, the great explorer, through Tanzania and Zambia combining contemporary observations with flashbacks to Livingstone's own journals. Although not directly about Malawi, this book provides great insights into the psychology of Livingstone. Wilson and Irwin travelled on mountain bikes, a choice of transport which may not have been ideal, but it was only through their discomfort that the authors got close to understanding Livingstone's own levels of suffering and doggedness.
The Ukimwi Road by Dervla Murphy. In which the famously eccentric Irish grandmother cycles from Kenya through Malawi, Zambia and Zimbabwe, along the way downing numerous beers and observing life at a human scale – most notably the harrowing effects of AIDS. In the sequel *South from the Limpopo*, her journey continues through South Africa.
Venture to the Interior by Laurens van der Post. The author (who went on to write many more books about Southern Africa) describes his 'exploration' of Mount Mulanje and the Nyika Plateau in the 1940s, although in reality this was hardly trail-blazing stuff. Descriptions of the landscape are poetic, but this book is most interesting for its description of the quaint workings of the British colonial administration of Nyasaland.

History & Politics
Africa by Phyllis Martin & Patrick O'Meara. This book is the nearest you'll get to a pocket library on Africa – with scholarly but accessible essays on a wide range of subjects including history, religion, colonialism, sociology, art, music, popular culture, law, literature, politics, economics and the development crisis.

Beggar Your Neighbours by Joseph Hanlon. An informative and accessible study of South Africa's policies towards other states in the region in the 1980s, which normally boiled down to encouraging economic dependence or promoting destabilisation.
Democratisation in Malawi: A Stocktaking by Ken Ross (ed). A collection of essays on political, economic, cultural, educational and constitutional dimensions of the democratic process, up until 1998. This is one of many books in the excellent Kachere Series published by CLAIM, available in Malawi bookshops.
The Early History of Malawi and *Malawi – the History of a Nation* by B Pachai. Two academic histories that cover the country from the Iron Age to colonial times, although both books were published in the 1970s they are hard to find.
Exploration of Africa by Anne Hugon. A fascinating and beautifully illustrated little book, with good coverage on the journeys of Livingstone et al in Malawi and the rest of East and Southern Africa.
From Nyassa to Tanganyika by James Stewart (edited by J Thompson). This book was originally written as a journal between 1876 and 1879, describing the author's journey in the lands that became Malawi and Tanzania. (This was the cousin of another James Stewart who helped to found the Livingstonia missions – see The Livingstonia Missionaries in the History section of the Facts about Malawi chapter.) It was reprinted in 1989.
History of Southern Africa by JD Omer-Cooper (published by James Currey). A wide-ranging book that covers mainly South Africa, but mentions all the other countries in the region, from earliest human times to the present.
Introduction to the History of Central Africa – Zambia, Malawi, and Zimbabwe by AJ Wills. This book has good coverage of Malawi and the other countries north of the Zambezi.
A Lady's Letters from Central Africa by Jane Moir. A collection of correspondence written in the 1890s by 'the first woman traveller in Central Africa', who came to Blantyre as the wife of Frederick Moir, co-founder of the African Lakes Corporation. It was reprinted 1991.
Let Us Die for Africa by DD Phiri. A new biography, with an African perspective, of John Chilembwe, Malawi's national hero. (For more details see Early Protest in the History section of the Facts about Malawi chapter.)
Livingstone by Tim Jeal. Often reckoned to be the best of the great explorer's biographies, this well-researched volume certainly avoids the adulatory nature of several others on Livingstone, present-

ing a complete picture of the great man, describing his obsessions, jealousies and weaknesses as well as his achievements.

Livingstone's Lake by Oliver Ransford. A classic volume about the history and events surrounding Lake Malawi. Published in the 1960s and now only available from specialist second-hand bookshops.

Masters of Illusion – The World Bank and the Poverty of Nations by Catherine Caufield. A hard-hitting discussion of the influence that the global development lending agency has had on poor countries around the world. The book's main observations – that the social and environmental effects of projects are inadequately analysed – are shocking, while the conclusions – that despite loans totalling billions of US dollars the people of the Third Word are worse off now than before – calls the whole institution seriously into question.

Nyasa – A Journal of Adventures by ED Young. Written in the 1870s, reprinted in 1984, this is a missionary's account of his journey to help establish the original Livingstonia mission at Cape Maclear.

The Nyika Experience by F Dorwood (ed). A collection of reminiscences from the chief ranger of Nyika National Park in colonial times, and six other people who were involved with establishing and running the Nyika – Malawi's first national park.

General

Large-Format Books Unlike some other countries in the region, Malawi has inspired only a few large-format pictorial books. These include:

Between the Cape and Cairo by Tony Grogan. A collection of sketches and paintings from all parts of Malawi. Coincidentally, an early European explorer and forebear of the artist called Ewart Grogan passed through Malawi (then Nyasaland), while becoming the first man to walk across Africa. He wrote a book about it called *From the Cape to Cairo* and in it said 'Nyasaland is an exceptionally beautiful country, awaiting only a good artist to capture its true magnificence.'. His descendant seems to have answered the call.

Legends of the African Lakes by Ann Walton & Gillian Mathew. A delightfully illustrated collection of traditional stories from Lake Malawi and the other Great Lakes of Africa.

Malawi – Lake of Stars by F Johnston & V Garland. A collection of fine photographs by Malawian-based photographer Frank Johnston, with text by local author Vera Garland.

Novels For information about literature by local Malawian writers see Arts in the Facts about Malawi chapter. There are very few novels based in Malawi by non-Malawian writers, but two are:

Elephant Song by Wilbur Smith. Good for reading on long bus rides, this is a ripping yarn based partly in Malawi, covering conservation and the ivory trade, with Europeans and Africans united against corrupt regimes. It follows a familiar formula with perfect heroes, evil villains and a bit of sex and violence thrown in for good measure.

Jungle Lovers by Paul Theroux. A light humorous work that neatly captures several aspects of life in Malawi for locals and foreigners, and also pokes fun at a head of state, who is remarkably similar to President Banda. Theroux was a Peace Corps Volunteer in Malawi in the 1960s. The book and the Peace Corps were later banned in Malawi by Banda.

Anthologies To place Malawi in a wider context, you may like to try a regional anthology. These include:

The Heinemann Book of African Poetry in English by A Maja-Pearce (ed)

The Penguin Book of Modern African Poetry by Moore & Beier (ed)

The Penguin Book of Southern African Stories by Stephen Gray (ed). This book collates stories from Malawi, Botswana, South Africa and several other countries in the region; some are thousands of years old and deliberately not classified by original language to show the similarities and common threads that exist in the various literary traditions.

The Traveller's Literary Companion – Africa by Oona Strathern (ed). This is by far the most useful and interesting book to carry on your travels. It contains more than 250 prose and poetry extracts from all over Africa, including a good section on Malawi, plus a list of 'literary landmarks' – real features that appear in novels written about these countries.

NEWSPAPERS & MAGAZINES
Foreign Press

For news on Malawi outside the country, your best option is one of the magazines that cover Africa. These include *Africa Now*, *Africa Today*, *Business Africa* and the BBC's *Focus on Africa* – the latter is usually available in large bookshops in Malawi.

Many foreign papers and magazines are available in bookshops in Malawi, including international titles like *Time* and *Newsweek*, various South African publications, and overseas editions of British and American papers like the *International Express* and the *International Herald Tribune*.

Regional magazines you might be interested in include *Getaway*, published in South Africa, with articles ranging from epic 4WD trips in Namibia, through to active and not-so-active package tours of Zimbabwe or Malawi, to reviews of timeshare developments in Cape Town. The advertisement section is a very useful source of ideas for places to go and things to do throughout the region. *Africa Environment & Wildlife* covers a wide range of environmental and conservation issues, mostly on Southern Africa, with quality and evenhandedness, plus excellent photography. Both magazines are available in main bookshops in Malawi.

Also look out for *Jungle*, a backpackers' freebie mag, full of information about fun places to visit, special events, tours and cheap transport deals all over Southern Africa. You can find it at hostels and other places where budget travellers lurk.

Malawian Press

For newspapers inside Malawi, there's a wide choice. During Banda's time there were just two papers, both staunchly pro-government. Officially there was no censorship, but the slightest hint of anything less than total support for the government or any of its ministries (which by extension meant a criticism of Banda) usually landed editors and journalists in jail. Journalists who may have followed the line in their writing still risked detention if they discussed 'antigovernment' matters in private conversation.When Banda fell from power, the number of newspapers blossomed as enthusiastic writers and editors

with access to paper and a printing press took advantage of the new-found freedom. Through much of the late 1990s there were sometimes up to 20 different newspapers – most with only four or six pages, and mostly full of gossip or other rubbish – available on the streets of Blantyre and Lilongwe. Most disappeared as quickly as they'd arrived. Today, the main papers include *The Malawi Times* and *The Daily News*, survivors from the old days, and still MCP supporters. Newcomers include *The Enquirer* and *The Nation*, blatantly pro-UDF, and *The Independent* and *Newsday* – not tied to any party.

RADIO & TV

Malawi's national radio station, produced by the Malawi Broadcasting Corporation, combines music, news and chat shows in English, Chichewa and some other local languages. International news is brief but wide ranging. There are commercial music stations in the large cities. At the time of research, our favourite was Radio 2 (91.5 FM), which is good for a sample of current trends – especially the Sunday afternoon Top 20 countdown. In Blantyre, Capital Radio (102.5 FM) plays a wide range of music and also broadcasts programs from the BBC World Service.

Until the mid-1990s Malawi was one of very few countries in Africa not to have a national TV station. In one of his wiser moves, Banda decreed it was not necessary. But with the former president-for-life gone, a fledgling service has recently been introduced, broadcasting in the evening and weekends, with local news in English, and imported programs. International satellite channels are available in most mid-range and top-end hotels.

PHOTOGRAPHY & VIDEO

In Malawi, film and camera spares are generally only available in Blantyre and Lilongwe, although you may find some items in other large towns. Some sample costs are: Fuji or Konika 100 ASA 36 exposure print film, US$4; developing and printing, US$6 for 12, US$12 to US$15 for 36. A set

Photography Hints

Timing
The best times to take photographs on sunny days are the first two hours after sunrise and two hours before sunset. This takes advantage of the colour-enhancing rays cast by a low sun. Filters (eg, ultraviolet, polarising or 'skylight') can also help produce good results; most camera shops will be able to give good advice.

Exposure
When photographing animals or people, take light readings on the subject and not the brilliant African background or your shots will turn out underexposed.

Camera Care
Factors that can spoil your camera or film include heat, humidity, very fine sand, salt water and sunlight. Take appropriate precautions.

Wildlife Photography
If you want to score excellent wildlife shots, a good lightweight 35mm SLR automatic camera with a lens between 210 and 300mm should do the trick. Videos with zoom facility may be able to get closer. If your subject is nothing but a speck in the distance, try to resist wasting film but keep the camera ready.

Restrictions
You should generally avoid taking pictures of bridges, dams, airports, barracks, government buildings and *anything* that could be considered strategic. If soldiers or police see you taking pictures of this type, you may be arrested or have your camera confiscated. Some countries – usually those with precarious military governments – are particularly hot on this. Malawi is fairly relaxed. But if in doubt, ask first.

Photographing People
Like people everywhere, some Africans may enjoy being photographed, but others do not. They may be superstitious about your camera, suspicious of your motives, or simply interested in whatever economic advantage they can gain from your desire to photograph them. To some people in poor areas, a foreigner with a camera is – understandably – simply seen as a chance to make money. If you want a picture, you have to pay, although doing this is a controversial issue. Other locals maintain their pride and never want to be photographed, money or not.

Some tourists go for discreet shots with long lenses, which is probably fine if you can get away with it, although it smacks a bit of voyeurism. Ideally, you should always ask permission first. If you get 'no' for an answer, accept it. Just snapping away is rude and unbelievably arrogant.

Local people may agree to be photographed if you give them a picture for themselves. If you don't carry a Polaroid camera, take their address and make it clear that you'll post the photo. Your promise will be taken seriously. Never say you'll send a photo, and then don't. Alternatively, just be honest and say that so many people ask you for photos that it's impossible to send to everyone.

Sacred Sites
Some local people are unhappy if you take pictures of their place of worship or a natural feature with traditional religious significance. In some instances, dress may be important. In mosques, for instance, wearing long trousers and removing your shoes may make it more likely that your hosts won't object.

of passport photos costs US$7. Tapes for video cameras are not available. For other photographic items your choice is often limited, so it's best to carry all you need with you when you come into the country. For places where you can buy film and the like see Shopping in the Lilongwe and Blantyre & Limbe chapters.

As well as your camera, useful photographic accessories might include a small flash, a cable release, filters and a cleaning kit. Also, remember to take spare batteries. If you're using a video camera you can recharge batteries in hotels as you go along, or in the cigarette-lighter socket of a bus or taxi (if you have a 12 volt adaptor, and if the ride's a long one).

Most people find 100 ASA perfectly adequate for most situations, and possibly 400 ASA for long-lens wildlife shots. If you think you might need something slower or faster, for more specialist situations, then you should consult a photographic manual.

There is a new Lonely Planet photography manual, *Travel Photography: A Guide to Taking Better Pictures*, written by internationally renowned travel photographer, Richard I'Anson. It's full colour throughout and designed to take on the road.

TIME

Malawi's time is GMT/UTC + 2. The country does not have daylight saving. When it's noon in Malawi, it's 2 am in Los Angeles, 5 am in New York, 10 am in London, 8 pm in Sydney and 10 pm in Auckland.

ELECTRICITY

Electricity in Malawi is 220V to 240V. Plugs are British-style three square pins.

WEIGHTS & MEASURES

The metric system is widely used throughout Malawi, especially in supermarkets, shops and petrol stations. If you're used to pounds and gallons, refer to the conversion chart at the back of this book. In markets, items like firewood, fruit and vegetables may be sold by the bundle or pile. You can always see exactly what you're getting.

LAUNDRY

There are no laundrettes (laundromats) in Malawi. However, finding someone to wash your clothes is fairly simple. The top-end and mid-range hotels charge per item (normally less than US$1 each), and in national parks it is often included in the overnight accommodation cost. At cheaper hotels, a staff member will do the job, or find you somebody else who can – the charge is also usually per item, and is often negotiable.

TOILETS

There are two main types of toilet in Africa: the Western style, with a toilet bowl and seat; and the African style, which is a hole in the floor, over which you squat. Standards of both can vary tremendously, from pristine to nauseating. Some travellers complain that African toilets are difficult to use, but it really only takes a little practice to accomplish a satisfactory and comfortable squatting technique.

In rural areas squat toilets are built over a deep hole in the ground. These are called 'long-drops', and the waste matter just fades away naturally, as long as the hole isn't filled with too much other rubbish (such as paper or synthetic materials, including tampons – these should be disposed of separately).

Some Western toilets are not plumbed in, but are just balanced over a long-drop, and sometimes seats are constructed to assist people who can't do their business unsupported. The lack of running water usually makes such cross-cultural mechanisms a disaster. A noncontact hole in the ground is much better to hover over than a filthy toilet bowl.

HEALTH

Travel health depends on your predeparture preparations, your daily health care while travelling, and how you handle any medical problem that does develop. While the potential dangers can seem quite frightening, in reality few travellers in Malawi experience anything more than an upset stomach.

Predeparture Planning

Immunisations You should seek medical advice at least six weeks before travel, and plan ahead for getting your vaccinations: some of them require more than one injection, while some vaccinations should not be given together. Note that some vaccinations should not be given during pregnancy or to people with allergies – discuss this with your doctor.

Be aware that children and pregnant women are often more prone to disease, and the effects can be more serious.

Discuss your requirements with your doctor, but vaccinations you should consider for a trip to Malawi or most other parts of sub-Saharan Africa include those listed following (for more details about the diseases themselves, see the following individual entries). Carry proof of your vaccinations, especially yellow fever. You may need to show certificates at the border or airport, or at borders of other countries if you're travelling further in the region.

Cholera Certificates showing proof of cholera vaccination are no longer required, as all countries and the World Health Organisation (WHO) have dropped cholera immunisation as a health requirement for entry.

Diphtheria & Tetanus Vaccinations for these two diseases are usually combined and are recommended for everyone. After an initial course of three injections (usually given in childhood), boosters are necessary every 10 years.

Hepatitis A Vaccinations provide long-term immunity (possibly more than 10 years) after an initial injection and a booster at six to 12 months. Alternatively, an injection of gamma globulin can provide short-term protection against hepatitis A – two to six months, depending on the dose given. It is not a vaccine, but a ready-made antibody collected from blood donations. It is reasonably effective and, unlike the vaccine, it is protective immediately, but because it is a blood product, there are current concerns about its long-term safety. A combined vaccine for hepatitis A and hepatitis B vaccine is also available. Three injections over a six-month period are required, the first two providing substantial protection against hepatitis A.

Hepatitis B Travellers who should consider vaccination against hepatitis B include those on a long trip, as well as those visiting countries where there are high levels of hepatitis B infection, where blood transfusions may not be adequately screened or where sexual contact or needle sharing is a possibility. Vaccination involves three injections, with a booster at 12 months. More rapid courses are available if necessary.

Meningococcal Meningitis Vaccination is recommended for travellers to certain parts of Africa. A single injection gives good protection against the major epidemic forms of the disease for three years. Protection may be less effective in children under two years.

Polio Everyone should keep up to date with this vaccination, which is normally given in childhood. A booster every 10 years maintains immunity.

Rabies Vaccination should be considered if you will spend a month or longer in Malawi in an area where rabies is common, if you are cycling (dogs love chasing bikes!) or handling animals. It is also recommended for children (who may not report a bite). Pretravel rabies vaccination involves having three injections over 21 to 28 days. If someone who has been vaccinated is bitten or scratched by an animal, they will require two booster injections of vaccine; those not vaccinated require more.

Tuberculosis The risk of TB to travellers is usually very low, unless you will be living with or closely associated with local people in high risk areas – which includes some parts of Southern Africa. Vaccination against TB (called a BCG) is recommended for children and young adults living in these areas for three months or more.

Typhoid Vaccination against typhoid may be required if you are travelling for more than a couple of weeks. It is now available either as an injection or as capsules to be taken orally.

Yellow Fever A yellow fever vaccine is now the only vaccine that is a legal requirement for surrounding African countries and parts of South America, usually only enforced when coming from an infected area. Vaccination is recommended for travel in areas where the disease is endemic (there is no yellow fever in Malawi). To get the vaccination you may have to go to a special health centre.

Malaria Medication Antimalarial drugs do not prevent you from being infected but kill the malaria parasites during a stage in their development and significantly reduce the risk of becoming very ill or dying. Expert advice on medication should be sought, as there are many factors to consider, including the area to be visited, the risk of exposure to malaria-carrying mosquitoes, the side effects of medication, your medical history and whether you are a child or an adult or pregnant. Travellers to isolated areas in high-risk countries may like to carry a treatment dose of medication for use if symptoms occur.

Health Insurance Make sure that you have adequate health insurance. See Travel Insurance under Visas & Documents earlier in this chapter for details.

Travel Health Guides If you are planning to be away or travelling in remote areas for a long period of time, you may like to consider taking a more detailed health guide.

CDC's Complete Guide to Healthy Travel. The US Centers for Disease Control & Prevention recommendations for international travel.
Healthy Travel Africa by Isabelle Young, Lonely Planet Publications. A handy pocket-size guide packed with useful information including pre-trip planning, emergency first aid, immunisation and disease information and what to do if you get sick on the road.
Staying Healthy in Asia, Africa & Latin America by Dirk Schroeder. Probably the best all-round guide to carry; it's detailed and well-organised.
Travellers' Health by Dr Richard Dawood. Comprehensive, easy to read, authoritative and highly recommended, although it's rather large to lug around.
Travel with Children by Maureen Wheeler, Lonely Planet Publications. Includes advice on travel health for younger children.
Where There Is No Doctor by David Werner. A very detailed guide intended for someone, such as a Peace Corps worker, going to work in an underdeveloped country.

There are also a number of excellent travel health sites on the Internet. There are links to the World Health Organization and the US Centers for Disease Control & Prevention on the Lonely Planet home page:
www.lonelyplanet.com/weblinks/wlheal.htm

Other Preparations Make sure you're healthy before you start travelling. If you are going on a long trip make sure your teeth are OK. If you wear glasses take a spare pair and your prescription.

If you require a particular medication you will need to take an adequate supply, as it may not be available locally. Take part of the packaging showing the generic name rather than the brand, which will make getting replacements easier. It's a good idea to have a legible prescription or letter from your doctor to show that you legally use the medication.

Basic Rules

Food There is an old adage that says: 'If you can cook it, boil it or peel it you can eat it...otherwise forget it'. Vegetables and fruit should be washed with purified water or peeled where possible. Beware of ice cream that is sold in the street or anywhere it might have been melted and refrozen; if there's any doubt (eg, a power cut in the last day or two), steer well clear.

Undercooked meat, particularly in the form of mince, and shellfish such as mussels, oysters and clams should be avoided. Steaming does not make shellfish safe for eating.

If a restaurant or food stall looks clean and well run and the vendor also looks clean and healthy, then the food is probably safe. In general, places that are packed with travellers or locals will be fine, while empty restaurants are questionable. The food in busy restaurants is cooked and eaten quite quickly with little standing around and is probably not reheated.

Water The number one rule is *be careful of the water* and especially ice. If you don't know for certain that the water is safe, assume the worst. Reputable brands of bottled water or soft drinks are generally fine, although in some places bottles may be refilled with tap water. Only use water from containers with a seal. Take care with fruit juice, particularly if water may have been added. Milk should be treated with suspicion as it is often unpasteurised, though boiled milk is fine if it is kept hygienically. Tea or coffee should also be OK, since the water should have been boiled.

Nutrition

If your diet is poor or limited in variety, if you're travelling hard and fast and therefore missing meals or if you simply lose your appetite, you can soon start to lose weight and place your health at risk.

Make sure your diet is well balanced. Cooked eggs, tofu, beans, lentils (dhal in India) and nuts are all safe ways to get protein. Fruit you can peel (bananas, oranges or mandarins, for example) is usually safe and a good source of vitamins. Melons can harbour bacteria in their flesh and are best avoided. Try to eat plenty of grains (including rice) and bread. Remember that although food is generally safer if it is cooked well, overcooked food loses much of its nutritional value. If your diet isn't well balanced or if your food intake is insufficient, it's a good idea to take vitamin and iron pills.

In hot climates make sure you drink enough – don't rely on feeling thirsty to indicate when you should drink. Not needing to urinate or voiding small amounts of very dark yellow urine is a danger sign. Always carry a water bottle with you on long trips. Excessive sweating can lead to loss of salt and therefore muscle cramping. Salt tablets are not a good idea as a preventative, but in places where salt is not used much, adding salt to food can help.

Water Purification The simplest way of purifying water is to boil it thoroughly. Vigorous boiling should be satisfactory; however, at high altitude water boils at a lower temperature, so germs are less likely to be killed. You must boil it for longer in these environments.

Consider purchasing a water filter for a long trip. There are two main kinds of filter. Total filters take out all parasites, bacteria and viruses and make water safe to drink. They are often expensive, but they can be more cost-effective than buying bottled water. Simple filters (eg, a fine-weave nylon mesh bag) take out dirt and larger foreign bodies from the water so that chemical solutions work much more effectively; if water is dirty, chemical solutions may not work at all. It's very important when buying a filter to read the specifications so that you know exactly what it removes from the water and what it doesn't. Remember also that to operate effectively a water filter must be properly maintained; a poorly maintained filter can be a breeding ground for germs.

Simple filtering will not remove all dangerous organisms, so if you cannot boil water it should be treated chemically. Chlorine tablets will kill many pathogens, but not certain parasites such as giardia and amoebic cysts.

Iodine is more effective in purifying water and is available in tablet form. Follow the directions carefully and remember that too much iodine can be harmful.

Medical Problems & Treatment

Self-diagnosis and treatment can be risky, so you should always seek medical help. An embassy, consulate or top-end hotel can usually recommend a good local doctor or clinic. Although we do give drug dosages in this section, they are for emergency use only. Correct diagnosis is vital.

Note that antibiotics particularly should ideally be administered only under medical supervision. For these drugs, take only the recommended dose at the prescribed intervals and use the entire course, even if the illness seems to be cured earlier. Stop immediately if there are any serious reactions and don't use the antibiotic at all if you are unsure it's correct.

In this section we have used generic names (not trade names) for medications – you can check with a pharmacist for brands available locally. Some people are allergic to commonly prescribed antibiotics such as penicillin; carry this information (eg, on a bracelet) when travelling.

For services in or near the two main cities, please see the Medical Services sections in the Lilongwe and Blantyre & Limbe chapters.

Environmental Hazards

Heat Exhaustion Dehydration and salt deficiency can cause heat exhaustion. Take time to acclimatise to high temperatures and make sure you drink sufficient liquids.

Salt deficiency is characterised by fatigue, lethargy, headaches, giddiness and muscle cramps; salt tablets may help, but adding extra salt to your food is better (and safer).

Heatstroke This serious, occasionally fatal, condition can occur if the body's heat-regulating mechanism breaks down and the body temperature rises to dangerous levels. Long, continuous periods of exposure to high temperatures and insufficient fluids can leave you vulnerable to heatstroke. The symptoms are feeling unwell, not sweating very much (or at all) and a high body temperature (39° to 41°C or 102° to 106°F). Where sweating has ceased, the skin becomes flushed and red. Severe throbbing headaches and lack of coordination will also occur, and the sufferer may be confused or aggressive, eventually becoming delirious or convulsive. Hospitalisation is essential, but in the interim get the sufferer out of the sun, remove their clothing, cover them with a wet sheet or towel and then fan continually. Give fluids if they are conscious.

Hypothermia Too much cold can be just as dangerous as too much heat, and hypothermia is a possibility in Malawi if you are hiking in the mountain areas of Mulanje and Nyika. Hypothermia occurs when the body loses heat faster than it can produce it and the core temperature of the body falls. It is surprisingly easy to progress from very cold to dangerously cold due to a combination of wind, wet clothing, fatigue and hunger, even if the air temperature is above freezing.

To avoid hypothermia it is best to dress in layers; silk, wool and some 'thermal' artificial fibres are all good insulating materials. A hat is important, as a lot of heat is lost through the head. A strong, waterproof outer layer is essential. Carry basic supplies, including food containing simple sugars to generate heat quickly and fluid to drink.

Symptoms of hypothermia are exhaustion, numb skin (particularly toes and fingers), shivering, slurred speech, irrational or violent behaviour, lethargy, stumbling, dizzy spells, muscle cramps and violent bursts of energy. Irrationality may take the form of sufferers claiming they are warm and trying to take off their clothes.

To treat mild hypothermia, first get the sufferer out of the wind and rain, remove their clothing if it's wet and replace it with dry, warm clothes. Give them hot liquids – not alcohol – and some high-energy, easily digestible food. Do not rub sufferers: instead, allow them to slowly warm themselves. This should be enough to treat the early stages of hypothermia. The early recognition and treatment of mild hypothermia is the only way to prevent severe hypothermia, which is a critical condition.

Jet Lag This is experienced when a person travels by air across more than three time zones (each time zone usually represents a one-hour time difference). It occurs because many of the functions of the human body (such as temperature, pulse rate and emptying of the bladder and bowels) are regulated by internal 24-hour cycles. When you travel long distances rapidly, your body takes time to adjust to the 'new time' of the destination, and you may experience fatigue, disorientation, insomnia, anxiety, impaired concentration and loss of appetite. These effects will usually be gone within three days of arrival, but to minimise the impact of jet lag follow these recommendations:

- Rest for a couple of days prior to departure.
- Try to select flight schedules that minimise sleep deprivation; arriving late in the day means you can go to sleep soon after you arrive. For very long flights, try to organise a stopover.
- Avoid excessive eating (which bloats the stomach) and alcohol (which causes dehydration) during the flight. Instead, drink plenty of noncarbonated, nonalcoholic drinks – or simply water.
- Avoid smoking.
- Make yourself comfortable by wearing loose-fitting clothes and perhaps bringing an eye mask and ear plugs to help you sleep.
- Try to sleep at the appropriate time for the time zone you are travelling to.

Motion Sickness Eating lightly before and during a trip will reduce the chances of motion sickness. If you are prone to motion sickness, try to find a place that minimises movement – near the wing on aircraft, close to midships on boats, near the centre on buses. Fresh air usually helps; reading and cigarette smoke don't. Anti-sickness preparations, which can cause drowsiness, have to be taken before the trip commences. Ginger (available in capsule form) and peppermint (including mint-flavoured sweets) are natural preventatives.

Prickly Heat This is an itchy rash caused by excessive perspiration trapped under the skin. It usually strikes people who have just arrived in a hot climate. Keeping cool, bathing often, drying the skin and using a mild talcum powder or prickly heat powder or resorting to air-conditioning may help combat this condition.

Sunburn You can get sunburnt surprisingly quickly, even through cloud. Use a sunscreen, a hat, and a barrier cream for your nose and lips. Protect your eyes with good quality sunglasses, particularly if you will be near water, sand or snow. Calamine lotion or an after sun preparation are good for relieving mild sunburn.

Infectious Diseases

Bilharzia Also known as schistosomiasis, this disease is transmitted by minute worms found in rivers, freshwater lakes and particularly behind dams. The worms enter through your skin and infect your intestines or bladder. Symptoms sometimes show immediately after infection – you may experience a general feeling of being unwell, fever, or a tingling and sometimes a light rash where a worm entered. Often the disease has to become well established (several months to years after exposure) before symptoms show. These include abdominal pain and blood in the urine. It's the long-term damage that is potentially more harmful, as damage to internal organs is irreversible.

You can avoid this disease by staying away from water where bilharzia may be

Everyday Health

Normal body temperature is up to 37°C (98.6°F); more than 2°C (4°F) higher indicates a high fever. The normal adult pulse rate is 60 to 100 per minute (children 80 to 100, babies 100 to 140). As a general rule the pulse increases about 20 beats per minute for each 1°C (2°F) rise in fever.

Respiration (breathing) rate is also an indicator of illness. Count the number of breaths per minute: Between 12 and 20 is normal for adults and older children (up to 30 for younger children, 40 for babies). People with a high fever or serious respiratory illness breathe more quickly than normal. More than 40 shallow breaths a minute may indicate pneumonia.

present. Highest risks are shallow or stagnant areas, near villages, and especially where reeds grow. The first move if you get unavoidably wet (eg, forced to wade a river) is to dry off quickly with brisk towelling and change wet clothes. If you swim in a lake (such as Lake Malawi, where swimming and watersports are very popular) it is absolutely essential to get a blood test (maybe combined with a stool or urine test) when you get home. You should get tested even for minor exposure.

You should note that many doctors and health centres have not heard of this disease, and may not be aware of appropriate tests and treatments, which may vary according to the strain of the disease. Note also that a blood test may not show positive until three months after exposure, and may occasionally show negative even if you are carrying the disease. Stool and urine tests may be intermittently positive. If you're in any doubt after the first test, take another test a few weeks later. If you have contracted bilharzia, the cure is a simple single dose of tablets. But don't let this easy treatment make you lower your guard. Bilharzia can be very serious indeed if not diagnosed early (see also the boxed text 'The Great Bilharzia Story' in the Central Malawi chapter).

Diarrhoea Simple things such as a change of water, food or climate can all cause a mild bout of diarrhoea, but a few rushed toilet trips with no other symptoms is not indicative of a major problem.

Dehydration is the main danger with any diarrhoea, particularly for children or the elderly, as dehydration can occur quite quickly. Under all circumstances *fluid replacement* (at least equal to the volume being lost) is the most important thing to remember – keep drinking small amounts often. Weak black tea with a little sugar, soda water, or soft drinks allowed to go flat and diluted 50% with clean water are all good. If you have severe diarrhoea a rehydrating solution will replace lost minerals and salts. Commercially available oral rehydration solution (ORS) are very useful; add them to boiled or bottled water. In an emergency, make up a solution of six teaspoons of sugar, a half teaspoon of salt and 1L of clean water.

You need to drink at least the same volume of fluid that you are losing in bowel movements and vomiting. Urine is the best guide to the adequacy of replacement – if you have small amounts of concentrated urine, you need to drink more. Stick to a bland diet as you recover.

Gut-paralysing drugs such as loperamide or diphenoxylate can be used to bring relief from the symptoms, although they do not actually cure the problem. Only use these drugs if you do not have access to toilets (eg, if you *must* travel). Note that these drugs are not recommended for children under 12 years.

Diarrhoea with blood or mucus (dysentery), any diarrhoea with fever, profuse watery diarrhoea, persistent diarrhoea or severe diarrhoea not improving after 48 hours all suggest a more serious underlying cause. In these situations, a stool test may be necessary to diagnose what bug is causing your diarrhoea and antibiotics may be required, so you should seek medical help urgently (and avoid gut-paralysing drugs).

Where this is not possible the recommended drugs for bacterial diarrhoea (the most likely cause of severe diarrhoea in travellers) are norfloxacin 400mg twice daily for three days or ciprofloxacin 500mg twice daily for three days. These are not recommended for children or pregnant women. The drug of choice for children would be co-trimoxazole with dosage dependent on weight. A five-day course is given. Ampicillin or amoxycillin may be given in pregnancy, but medical care is necessary.

Two other causes of persistent diarrhoea are giardiasis and amoebic dysentery. **Giardiasis** is caused by a common parasite, *Giardia lamblia.* Symptoms include stomach cramps, nausea, a bloated stomach, watery, foul-smelling diarrhoea and frequent gas. Giardiasis can appear several weeks after you have been exposed to the parasite. The symptoms may disappear for a few days and then return; this can go on for several weeks. **Amoebic dysentery**, caused by the protozoan *Entamoeba histolytica*, is characterised by a gradual onset of low-grade diarrhoea, often with blood and mucus. Cramping abdominal pain and vomiting are less likely than in other types of diarrhoea, and fever may not be present. It will persist until treated and can recur and cause other health problems. You should seek medical advice if you think you have giardiasis or amoebic dysentery, but where this is not possible, the recommended treatment is a 2g single dose of tinidazole or 250mg of metronidazole three times daily for five to 10 days.

Fungal Infections These infections occur more commonly in hot weather and are usually found on the scalp, between the toes (athlete's foot) or fingers, in the groin and on the body (ringworm). You get ringworm (which is a fungal infection, not a worm) from infected animals or other people. Moisture encourages these infections.

To prevent fungal infections wear loose, comfortable clothes, avoid artificial fibres, wash frequently and dry yourself carefully. If you do get an infection, wash the infected area at least daily with a disinfectant or medicated soap and water, and rinse and dry well. Apply an antifungal cream or powder such as tolnaftate. Try to expose the infected area to air or sunlight as much as possible and wash all towels and underwear in hot water, change them often and let them dry in the sun.

Hepatitis Hepatitis is a general term for inflammation of the liver. It is a common disease worldwide. There are several different viruses that cause hepatitis, and they differ in the way that they are transmitted. The symptoms are similar in all forms of the illness, and include fever, chills, headache, fatigue, feelings of weakness and aches and pains, followed by loss of appetite, nausea, vomiting, abdominal pain, dark urine, light-coloured faeces, jaundiced (yellow) skin and yellowing of the whites of the eyes.

Hepatitis A is transmitted by contaminated food and drinking water. If you get it, seek medical advice, but there is not much you can do apart from resting, drinking lots of fluids, eating lightly and avoiding fatty foods. **Hepatitis E** is transmitted in the same way as hepatitis A; it can be particularly serious in pregnant women.

Hepatitis B is spread through contact with infected blood, blood products or body fluids, for example through sexual contact, unsterilised needles and blood transfusions, or contact with blood via small breaks in the skin. Other risk situations include shaving and tattoo or body piercing with contaminated equipment. Early symptoms of hepatitis B may be more severe than those associated with type A and the disease can lead to long-term problems such as chronic liver damage, liver cancer or a long-term carrier state. **Hepatitis C** and **D** are spread in the same way as hepatitis B and can also lead to long-term complications.

There are vaccines against hepatitis A and B, but there are currently no vaccines against the other types of hepatitis. Following the basic rules about food and water (hepatitis A and E) and avoiding risk situations (hepatitis B, C and D) are important preventative measures. People who have had hepatitis should avoid alcohol for some time after the illness, as the liver needs time to recover.

HIV & AIDS Infection with the human immunodeficiency virus (HIV) may lead to acquired immune deficiency syndrome (AIDS), which is a fatal disease. Exposure to blood, blood products or body fluids puts you at risk. The disease is often transmitted through sexual contact – and Malawi along with other parts of Southern Africa has one of the highest populations of HIV/AIDS sufferers in the world (see the boxed text 'AIDS in Malawi') – so you should be careful in your choice of sexual partner, and particularly careful about protection. In new and short-term relationships, always use a condom. The disease can also be spread via dirty needles – vaccinations, acupuncture, tattooing and body piercing can be potentially as dangerous as intravenous drug use. Always make sure any needle you use is sterile. If you need an injection or blood test, make sure the needle and syringe is unwrapped in front of you, or carry a sterile kit (needle and syringe pack) in your medical kit for such emergencies.

HIV/AIDS can also be spread through infected blood transfusions, and unfortunately some developing countries cannot afford to screen blood used for transfusions. If possible, you should avoid blood transfusions, but if medical conditions are serious enough that you need one, the fear of HIV infection should never preclude treatment.

Intestinal Worms These parasites are most common in rural, tropical areas. The different worms have different ways of infecting people. Some (eg, tapeworms) may be ingested in food such as undercooked meat, and some (eg, hookworms) enter through your skin. Infestations may not show up for some time, and although they are generally not serious, if left untreated some can cause severe health problems later. Consider having a stool test when you return home to check for these and determine the appropriate treatment.

Meningococcal Meningitis This serious disease can be fatal and there are recurring epidemics in sub-Saharan Africa. The first symptoms are fever, severe headache, sensitivity to light and neck stiffness that prevents forward bending of the head. There may also be purple patches on the skin. Death can

AIDS in Malawi

In Malawi, and across Africa, the disease AIDS (acquired immune deficiency syndrome) is an increasingly pertinent issue. In fact, AIDS is possibly the greatest problem that Africa has ever faced, and for a continent not unused to wars, famines and natural disasters, that makes it very serious indeed.

Since the mid-1990s around 90% of the world's AIDS sufferers live in Africa, and AIDS has become the leading cause of death here. Figures released by the United Nations (UN) indicate that across the continent more than 30 million people will die of AIDS by 2020.

In Malawi, statistics are hard to pin down, because often AIDS or HIV-related deaths are recorded as something else. However, a report from the UN estimated that 30% of Malawi's urban population, and 15% of the rural population, was HIV positive. Other studies put the urban figure as high as 40%. Health workers also estimate that by 2005, almost half of Malawi's civil servants will have died of AIDS, and 25% of Malawi's children will be orphans.

The figures for the rest of Southern Africa also make grim reading: In Zimbabwe around 25% of the population, and up to 40% of pregnant women, are HIV positive. In Zambia the figures are even higher. Over the next few years around 60% of children in Botswana will die from AIDS. In South Africa 1500 people become infected every day.

AIDS is acquired more quickly and is more easily transmitted in Malawi, and in many other African countries, than in the West, due to a lack of nutrition and general poor health, the high incidence of venereal disease, limited awareness and limited precautions. In many Southern African countries there is still complete denial, particularly on the part of governments and some churches, that a problem exists. This does little to alter the attitudes of local people where AIDS (and, in many cases, sex) is a taboo subject at the best of times.

Some commentators have proposed that AIDS is a 'solution' to Africa's problems of high birth rates and overpopulation, but this shows a total lack of comprehension (not to mention a lack of compassion). Unlike 'normal' diseases, which have more affect on the very young and very old, AIDS tends to be a disease suffered by adults, and in Southern Africa particularly by those who are educated and have relatively high earnings or mobility. Thus, in some Southern African countries one in three teachers is HIV positive, and similar figures are estimated for civil service employees. This creates problems for government, for the economy, and eventually for democracy and peace. Treating sufferers is a great burden for already underfunded health services (in the late 1990s, Malawi was already spending 10% of its health budget on AIDS patents, and this is expected to rise to 50% in the next decade), while the increasing number of orphans whose parents die from AIDS puts even more strain on the state or on extended families.

The final problem is less tangible, but still important. During the research for this book, we spoke to many Malawian people, and almost all had experienced the recent death of a family member. Thus, in Malawi, as in many Southern African nations, the general morale of the people takes a plunge as the funerals of friends or loved ones become almost daily events.

---

occur within a few hours, so urgent medical treatment is required. Treatment is large doses of penicillin given intravenously, or chloramphenicol injections.

Sexually Transmitted Infections (STIs)

HIV/AIDS and hepatitis B can be transmitted through sexual contact (for more details see the relevant sections earlier). Other STIs include gonorrhoea, herpes and syphilis. Common symptoms are sores, blisters or rashes around the genitals and discharges or pain when urinating. In some STIs, such as wart virus or chlamydia, symptoms may be less marked or not observed at all, especially in women. Chlamydia infection can cause infertility in men and women before any symptoms have been noticed. Syphilis symptoms eventually disappear completely but the disease continues and can cause severe problems in later years. While abstinence from sexual contact is the only 100% way to prevent the disease, using condoms is also effective. The different STIs each require specific antibiotics for treatment. There is no known cure for HIV or herpes. If you do have a sexual relationship while in Malawi there is a good case for having a full screen for sexual infections when you return home, even if you don't have any symptoms.

Typhoid This fever is a dangerous gut infection caused by contaminated water and food. In its early stages sufferers may feel they have a bad cold or flu, as early symptoms are a headache, body aches and a fever that rises a little each day until it is around 40°C (104°F) or more. The pulse is often slow relative to the degree of fever present – unlike a normal fever where the pulse increases. There may also be vomiting, abdominal pain, diarrhoea or constipation. In the second week the high fever and slow pulse continue and a few pink spots may appear on the body; trembling, delirium, weakness, weight loss and dehydration may occur. Complications such as pneumonia, perforated bowel or meningitis may occur. If you contract this disease, medical help is essential.

Insect-Borne Diseases
Malaria This serious and potentially fatal disease is spread by mosquito bites. If you are travelling in endemic areas (which includes many parts of Malawi), it is extremely important to avoid mosquito bites and to take tablets to prevent this disease. Symptoms range from fever, chills and sweating, headache, diarrhoea and abdominal pains and joint pains to a vague feeling of ill-health. Seek medical help immediately if malaria is suspected. Without treatment malaria can rapidly become more serious and can be fatal.

If medical care is not available, malaria tablets can be used for treatment. You need to use a malaria tablet that is different from the one you were taking when you contracted the disease in the first place. The standard treatment dose of mefloquine is two 250mg tablets and a further two tablets six hours later. For Fansidar, it's a single dose of three tablets. If you were previously taking mefloquine and cannot obtain Fansidar, then other alternatives are Malarone (atovaquone-proguanil; four tablets once daily for three days), halofantrine (three doses of two 250mg tablets every six hours) or quinine sulphate (600mg every six hours). There is a greater risk of side effects with these dosages than in normal use if used with mefloquine, so medical advice is preferable. Be aware also that halofantrine is no longer recommended by the WHO as emergency standby treatment because of side effects, and should only be used if no other drugs are available.

Malaria is a serious disease and travellers are strongly advised to avoid the disease by preventing mosquito bites at all times. The main messages are:

- Wear long trousers and long-sleeved shirts, ideally light-coloured and treated with a repellent such as permethrin.
- Use mosquito repellents containing the compound DEET on exposed areas of skin (prolonged overuse of DEET may be harmful, especially to children, but its use is considered preferable to the effects of being bitten by disease-transmitting mosquitoes).
- Avoid perfumes or aftershave, which may attract mosquitoes.
- Sleep under a mosquito net – ideally impregnated with repellent (such as permethrin); it is well worth carrying your own.

Dengue Fever This viral disease is transmitted by mosquitoes and is fast becoming one of the top public health problems in the tropical world. Unlike the malaria mosquito, the mosquito that transmits the dengue virus *(Aedes aegypti)* is most active during the day, and is found mainly in urban areas in and around human dwellings.

Signs and symptoms of dengue fever include a sudden onset of high fever, headache, joint and muscle pains (hence its old name, 'breakbone fever') and nausea and vomiting. A rash of small red spots sometimes appears three to four days after the onset of fever. In the early phase of illness, dengue may be mistaken for other infectious diseases, including malaria and influenza. Minor bleeding such as nose bleeds may occur in the course of the illness.

The illness can progress to the potentially fatal dengue haemorrhagic fever (DHF), characterised by heavy bleeding, which is thought to be a result of second infection due to a different strain (there are four major strains) and usually affects residents of the country rather than travellers. Recovery even from simple dengue fever may be prolonged, with tiredness lasting for several weeks.

You should seek medical attention as soon as possible if you think you may be infected. A blood test can exclude malaria and indicate the possibility of dengue fever. There is no vaccine and no specific treatment for dengue. Aspirin should be avoided, as it increases the risk of haemorrhaging. The best prevention is to avoid mosquito bites at all times by covering up and by using insect repellents containing the compound DEET and mosquito nets (for more advice, see Malaria earlier in this section).

Cuts, Stings & Bites

Cuts If you cut your skin, wash the wound (however small) well and treat it with an antiseptic such as povidone-iodine. In tropical climates even the smallest cuts can be surprisingly slow to heal, and may become septic if ignored. Where possible avoid bandages and sticking plasters, which can keep wounds moist and hinder healing. Keep the wound clean though.

Stings Bee and wasp stings are usually painful rather than dangerous. Calamine lotion, sting relief spray or ice packs will reduce pain and swelling. However, in people who are allergic to stings severe breathing difficulties may occur and require urgent medical care. If you have a known allergy to bee or wasp stings, discuss your travel plans with your doctor. They may suggest you carry medication that can be self-administered in an emergency.

Scorpions often shelter in shoes or clothing and their stings are notoriously painful, so take care when camping in hot areas.

Bedbugs & Lice Lice cause itching and discomfort. They make themselves at home in your hair (head lice), your clothing (body lice) or in your pubic hair ('crabs'). You catch lice through direct contact with infected people or by sharing combs, clothing etc.

Powder or shampoo treatment will kill the lice, and infected clothing should be washed in very hot, soapy water and left in the sun to dry.

Leeches & Ticks Leeches may be present in damp rainforest conditions; they attach themselves to your skin to suck your blood. Hikers often get them on their legs or in their boots. Salt or a lighted cigarette end will make them fall off. Do not pull them off, as the bite is then more likely to become infected. Clean and apply pressure if the point of attachment is bleeding. An insect repellent may keep them away.

Bites from ticks can cause skin infections and other more serious diseases. You will recognise a tick by the way it has firmly attached itself to your skin. You should always check all over your body if you have been walking through a potentially tick-infested area – especially long grass where cattle or other animals graze. If a tick is found attached, press down around the tick's head with tweezers, grab the head and gently pull upwards. You can also try killing it first with a hot match. Avoid pulling the rear of the body as the tick may break, leaving the head under your skin. Squeezing too hard may force the tick's gut contents into your skin, increasing the risk of infection. Smearing chemicals on the tick will not make it let go and is not recommended.

Snake Bites To minimise your chances of being bitten, always wear boots, socks and long trousers when walking through undergrowth where snakes may be present. Don't put your hands into holes and crevices, and be careful when collecting firewood.

Snake bites do not cause instantaneous death, and antivenins are often available. If you or a companion is bitten, immediately wrap the bitten limb tightly, as you would for a sprained ankle, and then attach a splint to immobilise it. Keep the victim still and immediately seek medical help. Tourniquets and sucking out the poison are now comprehensively discredited.

Less Common Diseases

The following diseases pose a small risk to travellers, and so are only mentioned in passing. Seek medical advice if you think you may have any of these diseases.

Cholera This is the worst of the watery diarrhoeas, but cholera outbreaks are generally widely reported, so you can usually avoid problem areas. *Fluid replacement is the most vital treatment* – the risk of dehydration is severe as you may lose up to 20L of fluids a day. If there's a delay in getting to hospital, then begin taking tetracycline. The adult dose is 250mg four times daily. It is not recommended for children under nine years or for pregnant women.

Tetracycline may help shorten the illness, but adequate fluids are required to save lives.

Filariasis This is a mosquito-transmitted parasitic infection found in many parts of Africa, Asia, Central and South America and the Pacific. Possible symptoms include fever, pain and swelling of the lymph glands; inflammation of lymph drainage areas; swelling of a limb or the scrotum; skin rashes; and blindness. Treatment is available to eliminate the parasites from the body, but some of the damage already caused may not be reversible.

Leishmaniasis This is a group of parasitic diseases transmitted by sandflies, which are found in many parts of Africa, the Middle East, India, Central and South America and the Mediterranean. Cutaneous leishmaniasis affects the skin tissue, causing ulceration and disfigurement, and visceral leishmaniasis affects the internal organs. Laboratory testing is required for diagnosis and correct

Medical Kit Check List

Following is a list of items you should consider including in your medical kit – consult your pharmacist for brands available in your country.

- ☐ **Aspirin or paracetamol (acetaminophen in the USA)** – for pain or fever
- ☐ **Antihistamine** – for allergies, eg, hay fever; to ease the itch from insect bites or stings; and to prevent motion sickness
- ☐ **Cold and flu tablets, throat lozenges and nasal decongestant**
- ☐ **Multivitamins** – consider for long trips, when dietary vitamin intake may be inadequate
- ☐ **Antibiotics** – consider including these if you're travelling well off the beaten track; see your doctor, as they must be prescribed, and carry the prescription with you
- ☐ **Loperamide or diphenoxylate** –'blockers' for diarrhoea
- ☐ **Prochlorperazine or metaclopramide** – for nausea and vomiting
- ☐ **Rehydration mixture** – to prevent dehydration, which may occur, for example, during bouts of diarrhoea; particularly important when travelling with children
- ☐ **Insect repellent, sunscreen, lip balm and eye drops**
- ☐ **Calamine lotion, sting relief spray or aloe vera** – to ease irritation from sunburn and insect bites or stings
- ☐ **Antifungal cream or powder** – for fungal skin infections and thrush
- ☐ **Antiseptic (such as povidone-iodine)** – for cuts and grazes
- ☐ **Bandages, Band-Aids (plasters) and other wound dressings**
- ☐ **Water purification tablets or iodine**
- ☐ **Scissors, tweezers and a thermometer** – note that mercury thermometers are prohibited by airlines
- ☐ **Sterile kit (sealed medical kit containing syringes and needles)** – in case you need injections in a country with medical hygiene problems; discuss with your doctor

treatment. Avoiding sandfly bites is the best precaution. Bites are usually painless, though itchy, and are yet another reason to cover up and apply repellent.

Rabies This fatal viral infection is found in many countries, including Malawi. Many animals can be infected (such as dogs, cats, bats and monkeys) and it is their saliva that is infectious. Any bite, scratch or even lick from an animal should be cleaned immediately and thoroughly. Scrub with soap and running water, and then apply alcohol or iodine solution. Medical help should be sought promptly to receive a course of injections to prevent the onset of symptoms and death.

River Blindness This is found in many parts of Africa. Although it is best known as a cause of blindness, this disease actually causes more problems in the skin. It's a result of infection by a parasitic worm, spread via blackflies. The blackfly larvae spread under the skin and cause an intensely itchy reaction – so much so that it has been known to lead to suicide. With heavy repeated infections, larvae enter the eye, eventually leading to blindness. Treatment is with a drug called invermectin, which effectively sterilises the parasites, preventing them from producing larvae. Take measures to prevent insect bites and you should avoid camping close to rivers. You may get a mild infection, with some itchiness, but you are extremely unlikely to get any eye consequences. If you think you are infected, seek medical advice.

Sleeping Sickness In parts of tropical Africa, tsetse flies can carry trypanosomiasis, or sleeping sickness. The tsetse fly is about twice the size of a housefly and is recognisable by the scissor-like way it folds its wings when at rest. Only a small proportion of tsetse flies carry the disease, but it can be fatal without treatment. There is no vaccination – the only protection is avoiding the bites. Flies are attracted to large moving objects (such as safari buses), to perfume/aftershave and to dark colours – especially black and blue. Swelling at the site of the bite, five or more days later, is the first sign of infection; this is followed within two to three weeks by fever.

Tetanus This disease is caused by a germ that lives in soil and in the faeces of horses and other animals. It enters the body via breaks in the skin. The first symptom may be discomfort in swallowing, or stiffening of the jaw and neck; this is followed by painful convulsions of the jaw and entire body. The disease can be fatal. It is prevented by vaccination.

Tuberculosis (TB) This is a bacterial infection usually transmitted from person to person by coughing, but which may be transmitted through consumption of unpasteurised milk. Milk that has been boiled is safe to drink, and the souring of milk to make yoghurt or cheese also kills the bacilli. Travellers are usually not at great risk, as close household contact with the infected person is usually required before the disease is passed on. You may need to have a TB test before you travel as this can help diagnose the disease later if you become ill.

Typhus This disease is spread by ticks, mites or lice. It begins with fever, chills, headache and muscle pains followed a few days later by a body rash. There's often a large painful sore at the site of the bite and nearby lymph nodes are swollen and painful. Typhus can be treated under medical supervision. Seek local advice on areas where ticks pose a danger and always check your skin carefully for ticks after walking in a danger area (eg, a tropical forest). An insect repellent can help, and walkers in tick-infested areas should consider having their boots and trousers impregnated with benzyl benzoate and dibutylphthalate.

Yellow Fever There is no yellow fever in Malawi, but it is endemic in surrounding countries. This viral disease is transmitted by mosquitoes. The initial symptoms are fever, headache, abdominal pain and vomiting. The possibility of contracting yellow fever is another good reason to protect yourself against mosquito bites. If you think you have contracted the disease, seek medical care urgently and drink lots of fluids.

Women's Health

Gynaecological Problems Antibiotic use, synthetic underwear, sweating and contraceptive pills can lead to fungal vaginal infections, especially when travelling in hot climates. Fungal infections are characterised by a rash, itch and discharge and can be treated with a vinegar or lemon-juice douche, or with yoghurt. Nystatin, miconazole or clotrimazole pessaries or vaginal cream are the usual treatment. Maintaining good personal hygiene and wearing loose-fitting clothes and cotton underwear may help prevent these infections.

Sexually transmitted infections are a major cause of vaginal problems. Symptoms include a smelly discharge, painful intercourse and sometimes a burning sensation when urinating. Medical attention should be sought and sexual partners must also be treated. For more details, see Sexually Transmitted Infections earlier in this section. Besides abstinence, the best preventative is to practise safer sex using condoms.

Pregnancy Consult your doctor if you're planning to travel while pregnant, as some vaccinations that are normally used to prevent serious diseases are not advisable during pregnancy (eg, yellow fever). Also, some diseases (eg, malaria) are much more serious during pregnancy, and may increase the risk of a stillborn child.

Miscarriage is not uncommon and can occasionally lead to severe bleeding. Most miscarriages occur during the first three months of pregnancy. The last three months should also be spent within reasonable distance of good medical care. A baby born as early as 24 weeks stands a chance of survival, but only in a good modern hospital.

Pregnant women should avoid all unnecessary medication, although vaccinations and malarial prophylactics should still be taken where needed – talk to your doctor about what vaccinations are safe during pregnancy. Additional care should be taken to prevent illness and particular attention should be paid to diet and nutrition. Alcohol and nicotine, for example, should be avoided. Airlines will usually allow pregnant women to fly up to the 36th week of pregnancy, but the policies of individual airlines should be checked.

WOMEN TRAVELLERS

Generally speaking, women travellers in Malawi, whether travelling alone or with other women, will not encounter specific female problems (such as harassment from men) on a day-to-day basis any more than they might in other parts of the world. In fact, many women travellers report that, compared to North Africa, South America, and numerous Western countries, the entire Southern African region is relatively safe and unthreatening.

Southern Africa, including Malawi, is one of few places in the developing world where it is possible for women travellers to meet and communicate with local men – of any race – without their behaviour automatically being misconstrued. That's not to say the 'loose foreigner' stigma doesn't exist, nor that sexual harassment never happens (see Sexual Harassment later in this section), but local women of European descent – mostly South Africans, Namibians, Zambians and Zimbabweans – have done a lot to refute the image that female tourists are willing to hop into bed with the first taker.

Outright attack from thieves or muggers is another matter, and although much of Malawi is quite safe, there are a few hotspots where being attacked is a possibility. As anywhere, women (particularly lone women) are seen as easy targets, so it pays to keep away from potential problem areas, especially at night. Danger zones are listed in the individual chapters.

When it comes to evening entertainment, Malawi, along with much of East and Southern Africa, is very much a conservative, traditional, male-dominated society. There are some bars in Malawi which cater specifically for tourists (mostly on the lake shore), but elsewhere around the country bars are reserved for men only (by law of the establishment, or by the law of tradition), and even where women are 'allowed', cultural convention often dictates you don't go in without a male companion. Even if you do, it's worth being aware that accepting a drink from a local man is usually construed as a come-on. That's the situation, however distasteful it may be to liberated Westerners – and trying to buck the system will quite possibly lead to trouble. So, as an outsider, it's much better to go with the flow and only visit the places where women can go without attracting unwanted attention. Always try to get some local female advice first.

Because of these prevailing attitudes, it can be difficult to specifically meet and talk with local women while you're travelling. It may require being invited into a home, although because many women in Malawi have received little or no education, sometimes language barriers can be a problem. However, this is changing to some extent because in the last decade or so an increasing number of girls have had the opportunity to stay at school while the boys leave school to find work. Thus, many of the staff in tourist offices, government departments and so on are educated, young to middle-aged local women, and this can be as good a place as any to try striking up a conversation. In rural areas, a good starting point might be women teachers at a local school, or staff at a health centre.

When you're actually travelling, the best advice on what can and can't be undertaken safely will come from local Malawian women. Women of European descent living in Malawi are likely to be appalled at the idea of lone female travel and will do their best to discourage you with horrendous stories, often of dubious accuracy. Having said that, although Malawi and several other countries in this region are considerably safer than some parts of the world, hitching alone is not recommended. However, if you decide to thumb it, you should refuse a lift if the driver is drunk (sadly a common condition) or the car is chock-a-block with men (for example, military vehicles).

Wherever you travel and whatever you do, use common sense and things should go well.

Tampons & Sanitary Towels

Tampons and towels imported from Europe or South Africa are available from pharmacies or big supermarkets in Lilongwe and Blantyre (and less reliably in large towns such as Mzuzu). In tourist areas they are also available from shops at hotels.

Sexual Harassment

Despite sexual harassment being less of a problem for women travellers in Malawi and the rest of Southern Africa than it is in some other parts of the world, it is something that women have to occasionally deal with. Although unwanted interest is always unpleasant, it's worth remembering that although you may encounter a lewd border official, or an admirer who won't go away, real harm or rape is actually very unlikely.

Part of the reason for the interest shown in you arises from the fact that local women rarely travel long distances alone, and a single foreign female is a very unusual sight. Another reason is that, thanks to imported TV and Hollywood films, Western women are frequently viewed as being 'loose'.

What you wear may greatly influence how you're treated. African women dress conservatively, in traditional or Western clothes, so when a visitor wears something significantly different from the norm, she will draw attention. In the minds of some men this peculiar dressing will be seen as provocative. In general, look at what other women are wearing and follow suit. Keep most of your legs covered, at least below the knee, with trousers, skirt or culottes.

If you're alone in an uneasy situation, act prudish. Stick your nose in a book. Or invent an imaginary husband who will be arriving shortly – either in the country or at that particular spot. If you are travelling with a male companion, one of the best ways to avoid unwanted interest is to introduce him as your husband.

GAY & LESBIAN TRAVELLERS

Male and female homosexuality is illegal in Malawi. On top of this, the people of Malawi are conservative in their attitudes towards gays and lesbians, and gay sexual relationships are culturally taboo –

although some homosexual activity, especially among younger men, does occur. In most places, open displays of affection are generally frowned upon, whatever your orientation, and show insensitivity to local feelings.

Gay and lesbian travellers will find more information on the specific gay section of the Thorn Tree bulletin board on the Lonely Planet Web site (www.lonelyplanet.com), which also has links to other gay and lesbian travel sites. Alternatively, GayScape (www.gayscape.com) has links to other sites, including travel operators, who are based in (and mostly restricted to travel in) South Africa. However, some might be able to help with tours to Malawi: try Africa Outing (www.afouting.com).

DISABLED TRAVELLERS

People who don't walk will not have an easy time in Malawi. Even though there are more disabled people per head of population here than in the West, there are very few facilities. A few official buildings are constructed with ramps and lifts – but not many, and probably not the ones you want to visit. Some major hotels in the cities also have ramps and/or lifts, but again not many.

If you're travelling around the country with an able-bodied companion then Malawi does have some benefits: car hire is available, roads are generally quite good, distances are short, and at lodges in national parks or along the lake shore (which are usually single-storey) there are always willing staff able to help.

Before you leave, you might want to contact the national disability organisation in your home country (eg, Radar in the UK). Most produce leaflets on foreign travel and tour companies for disabled people, but it's unlikely that Malawi will get much coverage.

SENIOR TRAVELLERS

Malawi is generally good for senior travellers as facilities such as hotels and restaurants of a good or high standard are generally available. Many senior white South Africans tour Malawi independently – look out for the caravan convoys – or visit with organised package tours.

TRAVEL WITH CHILDREN

From a practical point of view, Malawi is a fairly good place to holiday with kids. There is a small domestic tourism industry, particularly on the lake shore, and many places are used to catering to families, although it's unlikely you'll come all the way here for the kind of beach holiday you could have at home. Horses, boats and bicycles can also be hired in many places. Large wild animals in the national parks are a major draw; even bored teenagers have been known to get a bit excited at the elephant herds in Liwonde. Snorkelling among the tropical fish of Lake Malawi is another attraction – although parents should read the advice about bilharzia in the Health section earlier in this chapter.

In hotels and lodges used to catering for tourists, family rooms and chalets are available for only slightly more than the price of a double. If this is not available, arranging an extra bed or two so that children can share a standard adult double is generally not a problem.

On local transport seats can be reserved on Express and Coachline buses (for more details see the Getting Around chapter), but not for children under five – even if you're prepared to pay. A useful tip from a travelling parent – lie about your child's age!

Whichever way you travel, Malawi is a relatively small country, so distances between 'sights' are not too long, although parents need to have a good supply of distractions to hand. ('Let's count how many black goats we can see...') Another advantage: compared with some other parts of the world, there's less in the way of nasty diseases here, and good (if expensive) medical services can generally be reached fairly quickly if you don't stray too far from the main centres.

Lonely Planet's *Travel with Children* by Maureen Wheeler provides more practical and sound advice, and several ideas for games on the bus.

DANGERS & ANNOYANCES
Robbery

It is very important not to make sweeping statements about personal safety in Malawi, or anywhere in East and Southern Africa. While there may be very great risk in some areas, other places are completely safe. Essentially, robbery with violence is much more prevalent in cities and towns, rather than in rural or wilderness areas. But even towns can differ, and there's more danger in places frequented by wealthy foreigners (such as beaches) than in places off the usual tourist track. Details of danger zones and where they exist are given in the individual chapters.

For travellers, Malawi used to be one of the safest countries in Africa – the national characteristics seemed to be friendliness, politeness and trustworthiness (possibly because Banda's iron grip on the country had created a cowed and subdued population). House breaking and theft from cars was a problem in cities, but muggings and violence were very rare. However, the changing political scene and ever-increasing levels of unemployment seem to have created a slightly different atmosphere. Reports now indicate that the levels of violent robberies against tourists are beginning to increase, particularly in the popular lake shore areas such as Cape Maclear and Nkhata Bay.

It seems more imaginative types of robbery are also on the rise. We've heard from backpackers, particularly about one of the cheaper hotels at Senga Bay, who were encouraged to keep their money in a safe for security, but some items went missing – usually just one or two notes or travellers cheques from a bundle in the hope they wouldn't be noticed. The owner and local police are reported to show a distinct lack of interest.

Whatever the reason, the situation should be put into perspective: Malawi is not dangerous; generally it's still much safer than many other parts of the Southern Africa region. As one traveller put it 'everywhere in Africa there's always a bit of danger, but it can always be avoided. Malawi has just caught up, that's all.'.

Animals

Other potential dangers include encountering a hippo or crocodile in Lake Malawi, but for tourists the chances of attack are extremely remote. Crocodiles tend to be very wary of humans and are generally only found in quiet vegetated areas around river mouths (although they may sometimes be washed into the lake by floodwater). Therefore you should be careful if you're walking along the lake shore and have to wade a river. Popular tourist beaches are safe although, just to be sure, you should seek local advice before diving in.

The most dangerous animals in Malawi are mosquitoes that transmit malaria, and the worms that carry bilharzia – see the Health section earlier in this chapter for more details.

Favourite Scams & Con Tricks

Annoyances in Malawi include con men and scam merchants. One trick to be aware of if you're buying curios are the eager young men who offer to wrap your purchase in paper and cardboard, without mentioning a price, then want more for this job than you paid for the carving. A variation of this is when they take it away to wrap it, and you don't find out until much later that they've switched your carving for a useless lump of wood. More games of this nature are described in the boxed text 'Scams & Con Tricks'.

Safety Tips

Some simple precautions will hopefully ensure you have a trouble-free journey. Remember, most travellers have no problems precisely because they were careful when required. The precautions suggested here

Scams & Con Tricks

The main annoyance you'll come across in Malawi, as in other parts of Africa, are the various hustlers, touts, con men and scam merchants that always see tourists as easy prey. Although these guys are not necessarily dangerous, they always want to get at your money. Some awareness and suitable precautions are advisable, and should help you deal with them effortlessly.

Remember Me?

A popular trick in the tourist areas is for a local lad to approach you in the street and say 'Hello, it's me, from the hotel, don't you recognise me?'. You're not sure. You don't really remember him, but then you don't want to seem rude either. So you stop for a chat. Can he walk with you for a while? Sure. Nice day. A few more pleasantries. Then comes the crunch: How about a visit to his brother's souvenir shop? Or do you wanna buy some grass? Need a taxi? A tour? By this time you're hooked, and you probably end up buying or arranging something.

The way to avoid the trap is to be polite but firm: You don't remember anyone, and you'd like to be alone. You could ask 'which hotel' after the first greeting, but the guy may *really* work there, or at least have noticed you coming out, and then perfectly calls your bluff.

Dud Sounds

You buy some cassettes from a booth in the market, or from the young guys who walk the streets selling from a box. When you get back to your hotel and open the box it's got a blank tape inside, or the music is by a completely different artist. Although often this is simply due to faulty technology than a deliberate trick, it's still annoying. Wherever you buy tapes, always try to listen to them first.

Phone Home

You give your address to a local kid who says he wants to write you letters. He asks for your phone number too, and you think 'no harm in that'. Until the folks back home start getting collect calls in the middle of the night.

A Nice Welcome

You may be invited to stay for free in someone's house, in exchange for buying them meals and drinks for a few days, but your new friend's appetite for food and beer may make this deal more expensive than staying at a hotel. More seriously, while you are out entertaining, someone else will be back at the house of your 'friend' going through your bag. (This scam is only likely to be tried in tourist areas – in remote or rural areas you'll quite often come across genuine hospitality.)

Change Money?

As the black market is now nonexistent, former moneychangers in Malawi have got a new scam. They ask you to break the US$100 bill they have into 10s and 20s. You are happy to help and hand over your small bills. Later on, when you come to change the US$100, you discover it's a fake.

Police & Thieves

If you're unwise enough to sample local narcotics, don't be surprised if dealers are in cahoots with the local police who then come to your hotel room and find you 'in possession'. Large bribes will be required to avoid arrest or imprisonment. The solution is easy – don't buy drugs from strangers.

are particularly relevant to cities, although some might apply to other places too.

On the streets, don't make yourself a target. Carry as little as possible. Consider leaving your day-pack and camera in your hotel – if it's safe; either in your room, or with the management. Even passports, travellers cheques and credit cards are sometimes safer left behind, if the hotel has a reliable security box. Don't wear jewellery or watches, however cheap they actually are.

Use a separate wallet for day-to-day purchases, and keep the bulk of your cash out of sight, hidden in a pouch under loose fitting clothing. Walk purposefully and confidently, and never look like you're lost (even if you are!). Don't obviously refer to this guidebook. Tear out the pages you need, or duck into a shop to have a look at the map and get your bearings. At night, don't walk in the back streets, or even some main streets; take a taxi – a dollar or two for the fare might save you a lot of pain and trouble.

To avoid the possibility of items being lifted from your wallet, even when it's in 'safekeeping' at a less reputable hotel, store your valuables in a pouch with a lockable zip, or in an envelope you can seal with tape.

Some travellers report stuff occasionally going missing from hotel rooms, and especially from shared hostel dorms. It might be the hostel staff, but sometimes you can hardly blame them when travellers leave their gear, including handy little items like penknives, films and jewellery, scattered all over the bed or floor. There are a few dishonest travellers around as well, some of whom are not averse to 'liberating' other peoples' possessions. The moral – keep your gear in your bag. Out of sight, out of mind.

If you're driving in Malawi, see Car & Motorcycle in the Getting Around chapter for more advice on avoiding potential dangers.

EMERGENCIES

The emergency phone number for the police and ambulance service is ☎ 199, but this works in Lilongwe and Blantyre only, and even then there's never enough vehicles, so if you do need assistance in the case of, say,

a robbery you'll probably have to go to the police station by taxi and bring an officer back to the scene of the crime. Once you've contacted the police, put aside several hours while a statement is laboriously taken.

If you have a serious injury (eg, from a car crash) don't waste time phoning an ambulance (unless you use the MRS service – see Medical Services in the Lilongwe chapter), get a taxi straight to the nearest hospital. The main hospitals and medical centres are listed in the Lilongwe and Blantyre & Limbe chapters.

LEGAL MATTERS

The most important legal matter for some tourists in Malawi concerns the use of marijuana or cannabis (also known as grass, hemp, dope, or locally as 'Malawi gold', 'Malawi black' or *chamba*). This drug is usually available in the 'grass' form (ie, dried leaves), and can be easily bought in many parts of Malawi, especially in some lake shore resorts frequented by younger travellers.

However, just because at Cape Maclear there's a lot of grass around, and plenty of stoned travellers, don't be fooled into thinking it is legal in Malawi. Buying, selling, possession and use are all serious offences. The usual penalty is a very high fine (several thousand dollars), and the maximum penalty can be life imprisonment. Tourists caught may be fined and then deported. Some dealers are police informers, and the police have been known to raid camp sites, arrest offenders, and then allow them to go free on payment of a large unofficial 'fine'. Either way it can be expensive and unpleasant. If you're a smoker, bear this in mind.

BUSINESS HOURS

Offices and shops in the main towns usually open from 7.30 or 8 am to 4 or 5 pm, with an hour for lunch between noon and 1 pm Monday to Friday. Many shops open Saturday morning also. In smaller towns, shops and stalls are open most days (including Sundays and public holidays), but keep informal hours.

Bank hours are usually from 8 am to 1 or 2 pm Monday to Friday. If you arrive or leave by air at Lilongwe or Blantyre, the airport banks usually open to coincide with international flights, but not always.

Post and telephone offices usually open from 7.30 or 8 am to 4.30 or 5 pm Monday to Friday. In Blantyre and Lilongwe they also open for shorter hours at weekends (see those chapters for details).

Note that all over Malawi, the official business hours of an office or shop are not always adhered to, as staff often have a more flexible attitude towards working times. Government officials are particular fans of long lunch breaks.

PUBLIC HOLIDAYS

Public holidays observed in Malawi include:

New Year's Day 1 January
John Chilembwe Day 16 January
Martyrs' Day 3 March
Easter March/April – Good Friday, Holy Saturday and Easter Monday
Labour Day 1 May
Freedom Day 14 June
Republic Day 6 July
Mother's Day 2nd Monday in October
National Tree Planting Day 2nd Monday in December
Christmas Day 25 December
Boxing Day 26 December

When one of these dates falls on a weekend, normally the following Monday is a public holiday. In northern Malawi and along the lake, many people are Muslim and observe Islamic festivals.

Government offices, banks and post offices in cities and big towns usually close on public holidays, but some shops open, and around the country smaller stalls and markets carry on as normal. In fact in rural areas shops and stalls might be busier on a public holiday than any other day. Public transport usually runs as normal.

ACTIVITIES

For those who like to be active, there's plenty to keep you occupied in Malawi. For those who like lounging on the beach, there's plenty to keep *you* happy too! This section provides a brief overview of what's available. More information is given in the relevant sections (eg, for hiking see the Mount Mulanje section, for diving see the Cape Maclear or Nkhata Bay sections, for fishing see the Nyika section).

Water Sports

As you might expect in a country dominated by a lake, there are plenty of water sports available in Malawi.

Scuba Diving & Snorkelling Lake Malawi's population of colourful fish attracts visitors for scuba diving, and the lake is reckoned by experts to be among the best freshwater diving areas in the world. (See Flora & Fauna in the Facts about Malawi chapter, and the boxed text 'Cichlid Fish of Lake Malawi' in the Central Malawi chapter.) The fresh water is warm (although thin wetsuits are still recommended) and

---

Diving Safety Guidelines

 Before embarking on a dive, carefully consider the following points to ensure a safe and enjoyable experience. Although aimed at divers worldwide, many of the following apply to Lake Malawi:

- Possess a current certification card from a recognised scuba diving instructional agency (unless of course you are learning to dive).
- Be sure you are healthy and feel comfortable diving.
- Obtain reliable information about physical and environmental conditions at the dive site.
- Be aware of local laws, regulations and etiquette about the local environment, fish etc.
- Dive only at sites within your experience, unless with a competent, trained dive instructor.
- Ask about the environmental characteristics that can affect your diving and how local trained divers deal with these considerations.

Considerations for Responsible Diving

The popularity of diving places immense pressure on many sites in Lake Malawi. Please consider the following tips to help preserve the ecology and the beauty of underwater areas:

- There are no coral reefs in Lake Malawi, and most diving is around rocky islets, but you should still ensure your anchor or fins do no damage.
- Avoid touching living organisms with your body or equipment.
- Be conscious of your fins. Even without contact the surge from heavy fin strokes can damage delicate organisms. When treading water in shallow areas, take care not to kick up clouds of sand. Settling sand can easily smother delicate organisms.
- Practise and maintain proper buoyancy control. Make sure you are correctly weighted and that your weight belt is positioned so that you stay horizontal. Be aware that buoyancy can change over the period of an extended trip: initially you may breathe harder and need more weight; a few days later you may breathe more easily and need less weight.
- Ensure that you take home all your rubbish and any litter you may find as well. Plastics, especially plastic bags that float, are a serious threat to lake life.
- Resist the temptation to feed fish. You may disturb their normal eating habits, encourage aggressive behaviour or be detrimental to their health.

generally clear (depending on season), and weather conditions usually favourable. Places where you can arrange diving include Nkhata Bay, the Chintheche Strip, Senga Bay, Cape Maclear and Club Makokola, on the stretch of lake shore between Monkey Bay and Mangochi. (For more information, see the relevant sections.) Some of these outfits also organise boat cruises on the lake, over several days, visiting various dive sites.

Instruction courses leading to internationally recognised certificates are also available, and very popular as Malawi is one of the cheapest places in the world to learn to dive. Remember if you are a diver that Lake Malawi is 475m above sea level, so your decompression calculations should be adjusted accordingly.

Even if you're not interested in diving, you can still enjoy Lake Malawi's underwater world. Gear for snorkelling can be hired from most dive centres, and from many hotels and camps along the lake shore.

Before plunging in, see the boxed texts 'Diving Safety Guidelines' and 'Considerations for Responsible Diving'.

Canoeing & Kayaking An increasingly popular activity on Lake Malawi is canoeing and kayaking. There are two main operators (Kayak Africa at Cape Maclear and Monkey Business at Nkhata Bay) where you can hire open Canadian canoes or touring kayaks, and go for a few hours or all day, or even longer. Many travellers highly rate the three- or four-day island-hopping trips that are organised.

Sailing You can go sailing for a few hours or longer on the catamarans based at Club Makakola, near Mangochi, and Chembe Lodge at Cape Maclear. Through Chembe Lodge you can even join a luxurious multiday 'sail safari'. For serious sailors, highlight of the year is the 'Malawi 500' Sailing Marathon – see the boxed text of the same name.

Other Water Sports Several places to stay along the lake also have sailboards (windsurfers) for hire. A few also have boats and equipment for water-skiing, notably Club Makakola, which as far as we know is also the only place in the country to offer wakeboarding.

Fishing

The fish species of Malawi that are of no interest to anglers are covered in Flora & Fauna in the Facts about Malawi chapter. These include the colourful cichlid species that attract snorkellers, and the various small fish that are netted by local people to eat or sell in markets. For rod and line anglers, the Malawi Tourism Department and the Angling Society of Malawi (PO Box 744, Blantyre) produce information on the following areas.

Lake Malawi Larger fish in Lake Malawi include *mpasa* (also called lake salmon), *ncheni* (or lake tiger) – well-known as a spectacular fighter, *sungwa* (a type of perch), plus *kampango* and *vundu* (both catfish). Light tackle is best; a 2kg sungwa gives good sport on a 1kg line. Most fish will take anything that moves and spinners of the Abu Flax or Droppen type are taken as readily as small Effzet spoons. In deeper water Abu's Pirk or Toby can be used.

Lake tigers are normally taken 1m to 2m below the surface in deep open water, and offer exciting angling. In the Senga Bay area, river mouths with heavy reed beds are good spots for the kampango or vundu. (There's little difficulty with snagging, but

Warning

If you dive or snorkel, or simply swim or partake in any water sport, be aware that a disease called bilharzia is present in Lake Malawi – see the Health section earlier in this chapter for more details.

a boat less than 5m is recommended.) For lake salmon the northern parts of the lake are better.

Popular destinations on the lake for visiting anglers include Nkopola Lodge and Club Makokola on the southern shore (see the Central Malawi chapter). Boats can be hired, although this should be arranged in advance if possible. From here, fishing spots to head for include Boadzulu Island and White Rock. Anglers with local knowledge launch their boats from Palm Beach near Mangochi or from Senga Bay, or from Sani Beach Resort near Nkhotakota, or at some of the places along the Chintheche Strip. These all might be useful places for visitors to meet local sport anglers, especially at weekends.

There is no season, and fishing is allowed at any time, although it's best between September and April.

The 'Malawi 500' Sailing Marathon

The 'Malawi 500' Sailing Marathon is a sailing race held every July on Lake Malawi. It's billed as the longest freshwater sailing competition in the world, with boats covering the 500km from Club Makakola, a large hotel near Mangochi, to Chiweta, a small village at the northern end of the lake, in eight days with overnight stops at designated beaches along the way. The race is held in July to take advantage of the *mwera* (southeasterly wind) that blows at this time of the year. Past events have hosted teams from Malawi, South Africa, the UK and several other countries. Most boats are Dart and Hobie catamarans, but the race is open to all classes with a Portsmouth rating of less than 1000, and it costs US$300 to US$500 per boat to enter.

You can get more information from:
🖂 quantum@malawi.net, texwise@mweb.co.za or windsport.international@btinternet.com

Messing About in Boats – Not Advised

If you take a boat out on Lake Malawi, for fishing, diving or just for a pleasure cruise, you should note that this is a large inland sea where the weather can change very quickly. Storms can be severe, and waves have been recorded more than 5m high – easily enough to swamp a small boat.

Even if the weather is calm, there's still an element of risk. Motor boats should ideally have a spare engine in case of breakdown. This is no idle warning: In 1999 three unfortunate tourists were adrift for 17 days, after their boat broke down at the southern end of the lake not far from Mangochi, and they were carried north by the wind. When they were missed, other boats and even planes searched for them for several days, but with no luck (that's how big the lake is). Eventually they were rescued by local fishermen near Likoma Island, several hundred kilometres away.

Visitors should always get local opinions before setting out on the lake, and leave details of plans (where you are going and for how long) with someone responsible.

Upper Shire River This river flows out of Lake Malawi, through Lake Malombe and then through various cataracts and waterfalls as it skirts to the west of the Shire Highlands. The sungwa is found here, although it's not as large as the ones in the lake.

Lower Shire River Below the last cataract – Kapichira Falls – the Lower Shire begins. The tiger fish here are relatively small (4kg to 7kg) but have a reputation as fierce fighters. Tackle should be upgraded accordingly. A popular combination is 5.5kg to 7kg line, wire trace and big silver lures or wooden plugs. Also in this area are vundus weighing up to 15kg and barbels up to 28kg. These fish have swum upstream from the Zambezi River, and heavy tackle is needed to land them. Fishing is usually from a boat. For visitors, this can be arranged at Majete Safari Lodge.

The fishing season here is May to November in the dry season, but no licences are required.

Zomba, Mulanje & Nyika For discerning anglers, the highland areas of the Zomba Plateau, Mount Mulanje and the Nyika Plateau offer good trout fishing. On Mulanje, rivers can be fished at the foot of the mountain or on the upper slopes around Chambe and Lichenya. The record for trout caught on the mountain is 1.5kg. The Zomba Plateau has many streams, plus Mlunguzi Dam. On the Nyika Plateau (which forms the main part of the Nyika National Park), three dams and several fast streams have been stocked with trout. Only fly fishing is allowed, and flies must be tied on single hooks.

The fishing season for Nyika, Mulanje and Zomba is September to May. Day licences are available. You should bring your own rod and tackle, but if you happen to run out of flies they can be bought in Zomba town, where there is a fishing-fly factory.

Wildlife Viewing & Bird-watching

Watching wildlife (often called 'game-viewing') is the most popular activity in Malawi's several national parks and wildlife reserves. You can see wild animals (from giants like hippos and elephants, to small antelopes like klipspringers and duikers) either from the comfort of a vehicle, from a boat, from horseback, or while on foot. For more details see National Parks & Wildlife Reserves in the Facts about Malawi chapter, and the individual sections on national parks and wildlife reserves throughout this book.

Malawi is a real draw for bird-watchers because there is a good range of habitats in a relatively small area, and species occur here from the Central, Southern and East African regions. More than 600 of Africa's 900-plus species have been recorded here, and a serious bird-watcher might well tick off a list of 250 or more in a two- to three-week trip around the country. For an idea of species that occur in Malawi, see Flora & Fauna in the Facts about Malawi chapter.

Cycling

Bicycles can be hired in Lilongwe (from Land & Lake Safaris – see Organised Tours in the Getting Around chapter) and from a few of the hotels along the lake shore. Bicycle rental is not a big thing in Malawi, which is a shame as the country lends itself very nicely to this type of travel. Roads are quite good, distances are short, and there are plenty of places along the way to stock up on food and water. Maybe getting around by bicycle will become more popular in the future.

Of the bicycles you can hire on the lake shore, these are mostly mountain bikes (usually the basic models), but you can also hire local style sit-up-and-beg steel roadsters. One of the best places in Malawi to explore by mountain bike is the Nyika National Park, and they can be hired here – see Nyika National Park in the Northern Malawi chapter for details.

Some information about bicycle tours and bringing your own bicycle to Malawi, and using that to travel around the country is given in the Getting Around chapter, which also lists some other places where mountain bike riding or general bicycle touring is possible.

Hiking

The main areas for hiking are the Nyika Plateau (the main part of the Nyika National Park, in the north of Malawi) and Mount Mulanje (in the south). Other areas include the Zomba Plateau, near the town of the same name, and various smaller peaks around Blantyre. These areas between them offer a range of routes and conditions, suitable for walkers of all standards. You can go hiking for a few hours, or trekking for several days. Full details are provided in the relevant sections.

The Mountain Club of Malawi is a disparate organisation mainly for Malawians and foreign residents. Occasional club nights and outings are arranged, but they don't normally cater for tourists. However, visitors (especially those who are members of other walking and climbing organisations), are welcome to join club activities – although it is not always possible to help with transport, equipment and so on. A newsletter is produced a few times per year and is available from the Tourist Office in Blantyre, or direct from the club (PO Box 240, Blantyre).

Before your trip, see the boxed texts 'Safety Guidelines for Hiking & Trekking in Malawi' and 'Considerations for Responsible Hiking & Trekking' later in this chapter.

Rock Climbing

Mount Mulanje is Malawi's main climbing area, with some spectacular routes (including the longest continuously roped climb in Africa). The *Guide to Mulanje Massif* describes many climbing routes – see Mount Mulanje in the Southern Malawi chapter. Local climbers also visit smaller crags and outcrops around the country.

Horse Riding

Most of Malawi is too low for horses to remain healthy due to the presence of tsetse flies. The main area for riding is the Nyika Plateau, where the vast open grassy landscape lends itself perfectly to exploration on horseback. You can go on morning and afternoon rides, or arrange longer horseback safaris. (For more details see the Nyika National Park section in the Northern Malawi chapter.)

Football (Soccer)

Soccer is Africa's most popular participation and spectator sport. Some details on where to watch a game are in the Lilongwe and Blantyre & Limbe chapters. If you want to play, the best places to find a good-quality game are university or college sports grounds, but outside every town in Malawi is a patch of ground where informal matches are played most evenings. (Along the lake shore, the beach is used.) The ball may be more suitable for tennis, or just a round bundle of rags, and each goal a couple of sticks, not necessarily opposite each other. You may have to deal with puddles, ditches and the odd goat or donkey wandering across the pitch, but the game itself

Considerations for Responsible Hiking

The popularity of hiking in some parts of Malawi is placing great pressure on the natural environment. Please consider the following tips to help preserve the ecology and beauty of Malawi's highland wilderness areas:

Rubbish

Burn your rubbish fully, or carry it out. If you've carried it in, you can carry it out. Empty packaging weighs very little anyway. Minimise the waste by taking minimal packaging. Don't overlook those easily forgotten items, such as silver paper, orange peel, cigarette butts and plastic wrappers. (You'd be surprised at how many people think silver foil will burn.) Make an effort to carry out rubbish left by others. Take a special bag of tough plastic especially to carry out all your rubbish.

Never bury your rubbish: Digging disturbs soil and encourages erosion, and the rubbish may be dug up by animals, who may be injured or poisoned. It may also take years to decompose, especially in cold conditions at relatively high altitudes.

Sanitary napkins, tampons and condoms should always be carried out, despite the inconvenience. They burn very poorly.

Human Waste Disposal

Contamination of water sources by human faeces can lead to the transmission of hepatitis, typhoid and several other diseases, causing severe health risks to members of your party, and to local residents and wildlife. Where there is a toilet, please use it. Where there is none, bury your waste. Dig a small hole 15cm (6 inches) deep and at least 100m (320 feet) from any watercourse. Consider carrying a lightweight trowel for this purpose. Cover the waste with soil and a rock. Use toilet paper sparingly and bury it with the waste. Alternatively, if possible, burn the used toilet paper, or carry it in a couple of strong plastic bags until it can be burnt properly. If you're using local guides and porters ask them to observe these guidelines too.

Washing

Don't use detergents or toothpaste in or near watercourses, even if they are biodegradable. All washing (personal or utensils) should be done at least 50m (160 feet) away from watercourses.

For personal washing, use biodegradable soap and a water container (a lightweight, portable basin, or even a strong plastic bag will do). Wash cooking utensils with a scourer or sand instead of detergent. Disperse waste water widely so it is filtered by the soil before going back to the watercourse.

Erosion

Hillsides and mountain slopes, especially at higher altitudes, are prone to erosion. It is important to stick to existing tracks and avoid short cuts. If you blaze a new trail straight down a slope, it will

---

is taken seriously. Play is fast and furious, with the ball played low, but foreigners are usually warmly welcomed and joining in a game is one of the best ways to meet the locals. If you bring along your own ball (which could be deflated for travelling) you'll be the hit of the day.

WORK

There are not many opportunities for finding casual work in Malawi, as the high unemployment rates means there's always a huge number of locals chasing every job. Of course if you had a skill or qualification that was in demand in Malawi (eg, computing, accounting, diving or safari guiding) you might be able to find temporary employment with a local company, but it would still probably be quite informal, as work permits for foreigners are hard to arrange. Having said that, some travellers with no special skills do find temporary positions as bar-

Considerations for Responsible Hiking

turn into a watercourse with the next heavy rainfall and eventually cause erosive soil loss and hill-side scarring.

In some areas you have to camp at designated areas. In others you can camp where you like, but along popular trails it's still better to set up camp in established sites to keep all the scars in one place.

Select a well-drained camp site so as to avoid having to dig trenches if it's raining, which just leads to more erosion. Avoid removing the plant life that keeps topsoil in place.

Fires & Low-Impact Cooking
Don't depend on open fires for cooking, except where there are good wood supplies, such as on Mount Mulanje. Elsewhere use a stove that runs on kerosene, meths or some other liquid fuel. Avoid stoves powered by disposable butane gas canisters, unless you're prepared to dispose of the canisters properly.

If you light a fire in the open, use an existing fireplace rather than creating a new one. Don't sur-round fires with rocks as this creates a visual scar. Use minimal wood, just what you need for cook-ing. Use only dead, fallen wood. Remember the adage 'the bigger the fool, the bigger the fire'.

Ensure that you fully extinguish a fire after use. Spread the embers and douse them with water. A fire is only truly safe to leave when you can comfortably place your hand in it.

Wildlife Conservation
Discourage the presence of wildlife around huts and camp sites by not leaving food scraps behind you. Do not use the rubbish pits provided by some huts, unless you are sure the rubbish will be buried quickly and not left to animals and birds to scavenge and possibly get injured.

Do not feed wildlife as this can lead to animals becoming dependent on hand-outs, to unbalanced populations and to disease.

Trekking in Populated Areas
Follow the social and cultural considerations outlined in the Society & Conduct section in the Facts about Malawi chapter when interacting with the local community.

Environmental Organisations
The Wildlife Society of Malawi (WSM) is an active conservation organisation, formerly called the National Fauna Preservation Society. It publishes several field guides to different parts of Malawi, has been involved in the establishing of several projects to the benefit of local wildlife and human populations, and has close links with the government departments responsible for national parks, forest reserves and other wildlife areas. For more information and a list of publications, you can con-tact the society's office (☎ 643428), PO Box 1429, Blantyre, or visit the WSM gift shop – both at the Heritage Centre in Limbe (see Information in the Blantyre & Limbe chapter for details).

tenders or cooks at some lodges and camps in Malawi, but again these tend to be very informal, and the 'pay' tends to be bed and board rather than actual money.

There are a few openings for ad hoc vol-unteer work. We've heard from visitors who have worked as volunteers in children's homes or wildlife areas. But there's no of-ficial system for this – people simply turn up and ask around. Organisations in these fields you might contact include SOS-Malawi (@ sosmalawi@malawi.net) and the Wildlife Action Group (@ safwag@malawi.net).

For more formalised volunteer work, organisations such as VSO (in the UK) and Peace Corps (in the USA) have programs in Malawi, where westerners with skills to offer (eg, teachers, health workers, envi-ronmentalists) stay for two years and work with local people. Schemes for 'gap-year' students who are filling the year between school and university (eg, Project Trust) are also available.

The following organisations can provide information about volunteering:

Australian Volunteers International (☎ 03-9279 1788, fax 9419 4280, ✉ ozvol@ozvol.org.au) PO Box 350, Fitzroy VIC 3065, Australia
Web site: www.ozvol.org.au

Co-ordinating Committee for International Voluntary Service (☎ 01 45 68 27 31, ✉ ccivs@ zcc.net) Unesco House, 1 rue Miollis, 75732 Paris Cedex, France
Web site: www.unesco.org/ccivs

Peace Corps of the USA (☎ 1800-424 8580, fax 202-6922201, ✉ webmaster@ peacecorps.gov) 1111 20th St NW, Washington DC 20526, USA
Web site: www.peacecorps.gov

Project Trust (☎ 01879-230444, fax 230357, ✉ info@projecttrust.org.uk) The Hebridean Centre, Isle of Coll, Argyll, Scotland, PA78 6TE
Web site: www.projecttrust.org.uk/

Voluntary Service Overseas, VSO (☎ 020-8780 7200, fax 8780 7370, ✉ enquiry@vso.org.uk) 317 Putney Bridge Rd, London SW15 2PN, UK
Web site: www.vso.org.uk

Volunteer Work Information Service, VWIS (☎ /fax 22-366 16 51, ✉ info@workingabroad .com) Case Postale 90, 1268 Begnins, Vaud, Switzerland
Web site: www.workingabroad.com

ACCOMMODATION

Malawi's choice and range of places to stay has expanded rapidly in the last few years. At the mid-range and top end of the market, several smart hotels and lodges have been built along the lake shore and in national parks. Additionally, former government-owned places have been privatised, and many have changed beyond recognition, with greatly improved facilities and services (although rates have gone up). This situation is still ongoing, and although we have tried to keep up with latest developments in this book, you should expect more changes by the time you arrive.

At the bottom end of the price range, in almost every town there is a council or government resthouse, or some other kind of cheap local-style hotel. Prices vary but can be as little as US$1, up to around US$5 a double, but conditions are generally spartan at best – and downright disgusting at worst.

Camping, with your own tent and camping gear, is available at many places, mostly in national parks and along the lake shore. Some camping grounds are pretty basic, while others have good facilities like hot showers, cooking shelters and security fences.

The last few years have also resulted in a dramatic rise in the number of backpackers hostels for independent budget travellers. Most of these are along the lake shore, but there are a few in the cities too. Prices range from US$1 for a dorm bed, up to about US$5 per person for a double. Camping is usually about US$1 to US$2 per person.

In the national parks and along the lake shore, there are many places offering self-catering chalets or cabins. 'Self-catering' in Malawi either means you get the use of a fully equipped kitchen, or the kitchen is staffed by cooks and helpers; you bring your food and they prepare it to your instructions (and wash up). The accommodation fee you pay (US$10 to US$25) covers this, although tips are always appreciated. Mid-range hotels range from about US$30 to US$100 per double, including taxes, usually with private (en suite) bathroom and breakfast. Quality of service at a smaller place, however, can be just as good or even better than at more pricey establishments.

Prices in top-end hotels or lodges generally range from US$100 to US$200 for a double room, with private bathroom and all facilities like TV, air-con and telephone, including taxes and breakfast. At the very top of the scale in Malawi you may pay US$200 per person per night, although in such places (eg, Mvuu Camp in Liwonde) this includes all meals and activities such as drives or boat rides to see wildlife.

Most places in the middle and upper brackets have two or three charge bands: visitors from overseas pay 'international' rates (that is, the full price); visitors from other Southern African countries pay about 25% less; Malawian residents get a 50% discount. Some places also give discounts in the low season. Where possible we have quoted international high season rates throughout this chapter.

Top-End Hotel Changes

In January 2000 the management of many mid-range and top-end hotels around Malawi was taken over by the international Le Meridien group. The Capital Hotel in Lilongwe and the Mount Soche Hotel in Blantyre had the Meridien tag added in mid-2000, after refurbishment. The same will happen to the Livingstonia Beach Hotel (Senga Bay), the Ku Chawe Inn (Zomba) and the Lilongwe Hotel (Lilongwe) in 2001. If you're planning to stay in one of these hotels, be prepared for the name changes, but also be ready for local people (such as taxi drivers) continuing to use the old names for some time to come.

Malawi's other top-end hotels include Ryall's Hotel in Blantyre and the Shire Highlands Hotel in Limbe. These hotels were taken over by the South Africa-based Protea group in early 2000. Major renovations (and possible price changes) are expected here too. A brand new Protea hotel in Lilongwe is also planned.

If you intend staying at mostly top-end hotels during your time in Malawi, it's well worth contacting a couple of travel agents in Malawi or in your own country to see if they can get prices cheaper than the standard 'rack rates'.

In most mid-range and top-end hotels (and even a few budget ones), the overnight cost includes breakfast. Breakfasts may be the full works, including eggs, sausage, cold meats etc, or a 'continental breakfast', which normally means tea and toast. Only in the top-end places should you expect croissants, pastries, marmalade and so on.

Definitions of single and double rooms are not always consistent. It may be determined by the number of beds rather than the size of the beds or the number of people. Therefore it is not unusual for two people to share a single room, paying either the single rate or something just a bit higher. If you want to save money it's always worth asking about this.

For more details on accommodation in national parks and wildlife reserves see Na-

tional Parks and Wildlife Reserves in the Facts about Malawi chapter.

FOOD

Your choice of food in Malawi is as broad as your choice of accommodation. Whatever your budget, there's plenty of tasty meals available, although it has to be said that Malawi's traditional food can sometimes be bland and boring, and will never rate against the cuisine of, say, India or South-East Asia.

Street Food & Food Stalls

For budget travellers, or anyone on the move, takeaway snacks ('street food') can be bought at roadsides, or in markets and bus stations. These include pieces of grilled meat, deep-fried potato or cassava chips, roasted corn cobs, boiled eggs, peanuts, biscuits, cakes and fried balls of flour-paste, which sometimes come close to tasting like doughnuts. Prices are always dirt cheap.

If you want something more substantial, but still cheap, aim for a food stall (sometimes called a 'tea stall' or a 'tea room'). These shacks, huts and other basic eating houses are usually found in markets, bus stations, or in any part of town which has low rents and a good passing trade (such as near factories – although tourists won't often visit such areas). At lunch time, food stalls may serve simple meals of *nsima* (cooked maize flour – see the boxed text 'The Joy of Nsima' later in this chapter), served with a sauce of beans or vegetables for about US$0.50. Sometimes you get rice instead of maize.

Meals at food stalls are served in a bowl, and although some locals prefer to eat with their hands, spoons are normally available. You may eat standing up, or a few rough chairs and table might be provided. The time for the main meal is around noon. Most of the very cheap places are closed in the evening. In the morning you can buy tea with milk for US$0.15 (without milk is cheaper) and a wedge of bread, maybe with margarine, or maybe a slightly sweetened bread-cake for US$0.03 to US$0.05.

Restaurants

Up a grade from the food stalls are the cheap restaurants that exist in cities and large towns, or in areas more used to tourists. These tend to be slightly larger, slightly cleaner and with slightly better facilities. You can buy traditional meals of rice or nsima and sauce for around US$1 to US$1.50, but also get food less unusual to Western tastes such as beef or chicken served with rice or chips (fries) for around $2. In places near lakes and rivers, fish may be available. *Chambo* is the most popular fish in Malawi.

Up another level from here are cheap to mid-range restaurants that have facilities such as tablecloths, waiters and menus, and where meals cost about US$3 to US$5, depending on the surroundings as much as the food itself, and if you eat in or takeaway.

These places serve traditional Malawian food and straightforward chicken-and-chips type meals, plus more elaborate options such as steaks, pies and fish in sauce. Some places in this bracket also serve meat or vegetable curry – in reality not very Indian but often a good spicy stew that goes well with rice. Another option often on the menu at this type of restaurant are Western-style foods such as burgers and pizzas, also around US$3 to US$5. Many restaurants in this bracket also serve cheaper snacks, such as sandwiches, omelettes, sausage rolls and – another Indian import – *samosas* or *sambusas* (parcels of meat or vegetables wrapped in pastry), all for US$1 to US$2. In cities there are also Western-style takeaway snack bars serving burgers, hot dogs, fried chicken, pizzas and so on.

Places that receive a lot of visitors, such as Cape Maclear or Nkhata Bay, have restaurants specifically catering for the tourist trade – where you can get all the goodies you miss from home, like a bacon sandwich or banana pancakes.

As you go further up the quality scale, most mid-range hotels and restaurants serve European-style food: steaks, chicken, fish, served with vegetables and chips or rice, plus pizzas, burgers and curries. The ingredients are more or less the same wherever

The Joy of Nsima

If you eat in local Malawian restaurants or are invited to eat in somebody's home, you will almost certainly be offered the regional staple called *nsima*, a thick dough-like substance made from maize flour (same as *ugali* in East Africa, or *nshima* and *mealie pap* further south). When fresh and cooked well, this is tasty and filling. It's usually eaten with a *relish* (sauce) that may be very basic, such as a few vegetable leaves, or a tasty stew of meat, beans or fish. What's in your relish is usually determined by the time of year, the availability of ingredients, or the type of place you are eating at. In some places you might be served *kondowole*, made from cassava flour, which is more rubbery and (to Western taste buds) less tasty than nsima.

you go; the price you pay is determined by the quality of cooking, presentation and service; usually between US$5 and US$10.

At top-end hotels and restaurants in cities and along the lake shore, you can find the straightforward standards mentioned earlier, plus more elaborate French, British or Italian cuisine. Blantyre and Lilongwe also have places serving genuine (or at least pretty close) Ethiopian, Lebanese, Indian, Chinese, Korean and Portuguese food. At top-end establishments, main courses range from around US$8 to US$15.

Note that in many smarter restaurants, taxes are added to the cost of your meal. For more details see Taxes & Refunds under Money earlier in this chapter.

Vegetarian

Although vegetarianism is rarely understood in Africa, and many locals think a meal is incomplete unless at least half of it once lived and breathed, you'll have a better chance in Malawi than in many other parts of the continent of finding a meal without meat. Many cheap restaurants serve meals without meat because it's all the locals can afford – although even the simplest (and seemingly innocuous) vegetable sauce may sometimes have a small bit of meat or animal fat added. You should note that in many places chicken is usually not regarded as 'real' meat, and might be served in a 'vegetarian' dish. If you eat fish, it's quite easy to find.

In the more straightforward upmarket establishments, vegan options do exist but are nearly always limited to omelettes or boiled vegetables. In cities and towns, you're much better off seeking out a Lebanese, Indian or Italian restaurant, which will offer more interesting meat-free choices.

Self-Catering

If you're self-catering, or just want a picnic, you'll find fresh fruit and vegetables for sale at shops, markets and roadside stalls all over Malawi. Depending on the season, these include bananas, pineapples, tomatoes, pawpaw (papaya), mangoes, avocados, carrots and potatoes. You can eat a lot of things raw (see Food under Health earlier in this chapter). Fresh bread can be bought in most towns. The 'PTC' and 'Kandodo' supermarket chains have branches all over Malawi, stocking locally produced and imported goods, much of it from South Africa or Europe and sold at similar prices. Malawian specials include guava jam, 'Tambala' peanut butter and Nando's extra hot piripiri sauce ('Friends, take care', it says on the label!).

DRINKS

You can buy tea and coffee in many places, from upmarket hotels and restaurants to the local eating house. International fizzy drinks, such as Coke and Pepsi, are widely available. As always, price reflects the standard of the establishment rather than the taste in your cup.

Traditional beer is made from maize, brewed in the villages and drunk from communal pots with great ceremony on special occasions, and with less fanfare in everyday situations. This product is also commercially brewed as Chibuku, and sold all over the country in large red and blue cartons. For most Europeans, the thick texture and bittersweet taste is not appealing.

> ## Epicurean Malawi
>
> Here's a few tasty local specialities we came across while researching this guidebook: fried mice on sticks, roasted caterpillars and 'patties' made from lake flies. Several local restaurants proudly offer fish gizzards on the menu. The best name of all was spotted at a place selling oven-ready ducks; they also sold the off-cuts, mainly heads and feet, neatly parcelled in a bag, and called 'walky-talky packs'!

Most visitors, and many Malawians, prefer beer produced by the Danish company Carlsberg in Blantyre – the company's only brewery in Africa. There are three main types of beer: 'green' (lager), 'brown' (more like a British ale) and 'gold' (a stronger brew). If you're a real beer fan, you can visit the Carlsberg brewery in Blantyre (see Things to See & Do in the Blantyre & Limbe chapter).

In towns and cities, most locals drink beer at a 'bottle store', which (despite the name) is not really a shop, but a very basic bar, where furniture may run to a few upturned crates or a bench, and sometimes there's music and dancing. Places that are actually called a 'bar' tend to be smarter, and the drinks a bit more expensive. They also tend to be more sedate. As one local told us – 'you can't dance in a bar, but you can do what you like in a bottle store!'.

ENTERTAINMENT

Most nightclubs, bars and sporting venues are in the main cities of Blantyre and Lilongwe, and are covered in the Lilongwe and Blantyre & Limbe chapters.

SHOPPING

For intrepid shoppers, Malawi offers a wide range of curios and souvenirs, including animals and figures carved from wood, ornaments such as bowls and chess-sets, and the very popular 'chief's chair', which is a three-legged stool made from two pieces of wood, with a high back decorated with pictures.

You can also find plenty of objects made from grass and palm leaves, such as baskets and boxes, or intricate models of cars and lorries, and even overland trucks! Contemporary soapstone carvings, paintings, clay pots and figures, and malachite jewellery is also available.

You can buy at roadside stalls or curio shops (mentioned throughout this book). But in among the stuff that's hammered out in a hurry, you will also find works in wood and stone (and occasionally paintings) that have been created by artists of better-than-average talent. Salesmen often seem to make no distinction between work of good or mediocre quality, so it's always worth spending time to search the better pieces out. Prices are usually not fixed, so you have to bargain (for more information see the boxed text 'The Fine Art of Bargaining' earlier in this chapter). However, if you prefer not to haggle there are some shops in Blantyre and Lilongwe that use price-tags.

In markets all over Malawi you can buy *chitenjas*, sheets of brightly coloured cloth that local women use as wraps, cloaks, scarves and baby carriers. They are also available at several shops along Glyn Johns Rd in Lilongwe and along Haile Selassie Rd in Blantyre. They make nice souvenirs and practical items for women travelling, especially if you're heading for the beach or rural areas where shorts are frowned upon.

Getting There & Away

AIR
Airports & Airlines

Malawi's main airport for international flights (from neighbouring countries in Africa, and from farther afield) is in Lilongwe. There is also an airport in Blantyre, served mostly by regional and domestic flights. International flights to Blantyre require a change to a domestic service in Lilongwe. This is also the case when flying out of Blantyre. All customs and immigration formalities are done in Lilongwe.

Lilongwe airport has a pharmacy, post office, bookshop, banks, car-rental outlets and tour-company desks, plus a restaurant and bar overlooking the runway, where you can use up the last of your kwacha before flying out (although beware of waiters overcharging). Blantyre has a small cafeteria, bookshop and Avis desk.

The main airlines serving Malawi from Europe are British Airways, KLM Royal Dutch Airlines and South African Airways. As well as long-haul flights to/from Europe, South African Airways has services between Malawi and other regional countries, including South Africa and Zimbabwe. Other regional airlines landing in Lilongwe or Blantyre include Air Zimbabwe and Kenya Airways, which both have services between Malawi and Europe and also between Malawi and other countries in East and Southern Africa. Kenya Airways has a code-share agreement with KLM and these two airlines combine to serve some routes. Ethiopian Airlines links Malawi to several other capitals all over Africa, and also has flights to/from Europe.

Air Malawi, the national carrier, has a network that links Lilongwe and Blantyre to several other East and Southern African cities. A new airline called Malawi Express flies between Malawi and South Africa, and has plans to expand to other routes within Africa and the Middle East.

Buying Tickets

Your first step, if you're flying to Malawi, is buying a plane ticket. This cuts a great slice out of anyone's budget, but you can reduce the cost by buying a discounted fare. Stiff competition has resulted in widespread discounting – good news for travellers! The only people likely to be paying full fare these days are those in 1st or business class. But unless you buy carefully, it is still possible to end up paying exorbitant amounts, especially for a relatively little-visited country like Malawi, so it's always worth taking time to research the market.

When you're looking for bargain air fares, go to a travel agent rather than directly to the airline. To find a suitable travel agent, look at advertisements in weekend newspapers, travel magazines or on the Internet. Once you've got a list of five or six, start phoning around.

Sometimes airlines have promotional fares and special offers that are better than travel agents' deals, but generally the airlines only sell fares at the official listed price. One exception is if you book on the Internet. Many airlines offer excellent fares to Web surfers, selling seats by auction or simply at cut prices to reflect the reduced cost of electronic selling. Many travel agents around the world also have Web sites, which can make the Internet a quick and easy way to compare prices, ideal for when you're ready to negotiate with your favourite travel agent. Online ticket sales work well if you are doing a simple one-way or return trip on specified dates. However, online superfast fare generators are no substitute for a travel agent who knows all about special deals, has strategies for avoiding unwanted stopovers, and can offer advice on things such as which airline has the best vegetarian food.

Buying a very cheap ticket used to be a risky business, but the days when some travel agents would fleece travellers by running off with their money are, happily, almost over. Paying by credit card generally offers protection, as most card issuers provide refunds if you prove you didn't get what you paid for. Similar protection can be obtained by buying a ticket from a 'bonded' agent, such as one covered by the Air Transport Operators License (ATOL) scheme in the UK, which guarantees to protect your money in case of problems.

Agents who only accept cash should hand over the tickets straight away and not tell you to 'come back tomorrow'. After you've made a booking or paid your deposit, call the airline and confirm that the booking was made. It's generally not advisable to send money (even cheques) through the post unless the agent is well established – some travellers have reported being ripped off this way by disreputable mail-order ticket agents.

You may decide to pay more than the rock-bottom fare by opting for the safety of a better-known travel agent. Firms such as STA Travel, which has offices worldwide, Council Travel in the USA and Usit Campus (formerly Campus Travel) in the UK are not going to disappear overnight and they do offer good prices to most destinations.

If you purchase a ticket and later want to make changes to your route or get a refund, you need to contact the original travel agent. Airlines only issue refunds to the purchaser of a ticket – usually the travel agent who bought the ticket on your behalf. Many travellers change their routes halfway through their trips, so think carefully before you buy a ticket that is not easily refunded.

Student & Youth Fares Full-time students and people under 26 have access to better deals than other travellers. The better deals may not always be cheaper fares but can include more flexibility to change flights and/or routes. You have to show a document proving your date of birth or a valid International Student Identity Card (ISIC) when buying your ticket and boarding the plane. There are plenty of places around the world where nonstudents can get fake student cards, but if you get caught using this you could have your ticket confiscated.

Travellers with Special Needs Most international airlines can cater to people with special needs – travellers with disabilities, people with young children and even children travelling alone.

Travellers with special dietary preferences (vegetarian, kosher etc) can request appropriate meals with advance notice.

If you are travelling in a wheelchair, most international airports can provide an escort from check-in desk to plane, and ramps, lifts etc are generally available.

Airlines usually allow babies up to two years of age to fly for free or 10% of the adult fare, although they don't get a seat. Reputable international airlines usually provide nappies (diapers) and all the other paraphernalia needed to keep babies clean, dry and half-happy. Children between the ages of two and 12 usually get a discount of between 25% and 50% on the full adult fare.

Departure Tax

For visitors flying out of Malawi, departure tax for international flights is payable at Lilongwe or Blantyre airports. This costs

US$20 and is only payable in US dollars (cash). No other currency is accepted. Unlike the situation at some other airports, this tax is not included in your ticket price – you must pay it on the spot.

USA & Canada

From North America, flights to Malawi go via Europe or South Africa. Although North Americans won't get the great deals available in London, there are a few discount agents. To give an idea, flights from New York to South Africa (usually Jo'burg) start at US$1050, from San Francisco at US$1300. From Jo'burg you can take a regional flight to Malawi for around US$200 more. It may be cheaper to fly on an economy hop from the USA to London, and then buy a discount ticket from there to Malawi. Canadians also will probably find the best deals travelling via London.

For more information, look in major weekend newspapers or travel magazines for agents' advertisements. Also worth checking are the student travel agents, although in the USA you must be a student or be under 26 to qualify for discounted fares. STA specialises in student travel, but also sells to nonstudents. To comply with regulations some agents are associated with specific travel clubs.

The following list of flight agents will get you started – some also sell tours and safaris. Likewise, some of the companies listed under Organised Tours later in this chapter also sell flights.

Ticket Planet is a leading ticket consolidator in the USA and is recommended. For more information visit the Web site at www.ticketplanet.com.

Council Travel (☎ 800-226-8624); offices nationwide; head office is at 205 E 42 St, New York, NY 10017
  Web site: www.counciltravel.com
Falcon Wings Travel (☎ 310-417 3590) 9841 Airport Blvd, Suite 822, Los Angeles, CA 90045
Flytime Tours & Travel (☎ 212-760 3737, fax 212-594 1082) 45 West 34th St, Suite 305, New York, NY 10001
Magical Holidays to Africa (☎ 800-223 7452) 501 Madison Ave, New York, NY 10022

Pan Express Travel (☎ 212-719 9292) 55 W 39th St, Suite 310, New York, NY 10018
Travel CUTS Offices nationwide throughout Canada
  Web site: www.travelcuts.com
STA Travel (☎ 800-781 4040); offices nationwide
  Web site: www.statravel.com
Uni Travel (☎ 314-569 2501) 11737 Administration Dr, Suite 120, St Louis, MO 63146

If you came to Malawi overland or on a one-way ticket and need to fly back home, a flight from Lilongwe to North America is around US$1100, via Europe or South Africa. It may be cheaper to go to Jo'burg, from where flights to New York cost from US$800. To LA is about US$1400, and to Toronto about US$900. From Cape Town it's usually a bit more.

Australia & New Zealand

To reach Malawi from Australasia, you'll probably have to go via South Africa or Zimbabwe. Many travellers also travel via Europe. Airlines flying between Australia and Southern Africa include Qantas, Air Zimbabwe and South African Airways. Between New Zealand and Southern Africa you must go via Australia.

To find an agent, start by looking at the ads in major weekend newspapers. Standard return flights between Australia and Southern Africa (usually Jo'burg, Cape Town or Harare) start at around A$1750. It usually costs an extra A$150 to A$250 to fly on to Malawi. For Australians and New Zealanders not pressed for time RTW tickets which include a stop in Southern Africa can be found for around A$2600. Another option is a RTW (Round the World) ticket or a return ticket to Europe with a stopover in Nairobi, from where Malawi can be reached by a regional flight or overland.

In Australasia two well-known agents for cheap fares are STA Travel and Flight Centre.

Australia

Flight Centre (☎ 131 600) 82 Elizabeth St, Sydney, NSW 2000 (main office)
  Web site: www.flightcentre.com.au

STA (☎ 131 776, 03-9349 2411) 224 Faraday St, Carlton, VIC 3053 (main office)
Web site: www.statravel.com.au

New Zealand
Flight Centre (☎ 09-309 6171) Shop 3B, National Bank Towers, 205-225 Queen St, Auckland 1001 (main office)
Web site: www.flightcentre.com/nz
STA Travel (☎ 09-309 0458) 10 High St, Auckland (main office)
Web site: www.sta.travel.com.au

Some of the companies listed under Organised Tours later in this chapter also sell flights.

The best one-way flights home are via Jo'burg (South Africa) or Harare (Zimbabwe). Jo'burg to Perth is around A$1050, Jo'burg to Sydney about A$1200.

The UK & Ireland
From the UK, airlines flying to Malawi include British Airways, Ethiopian Airlines, KLM, Kenya Airways, South African Airways and Air Zimbabwe. Some of these carriers also serve Ireland, or you may have to reach London on a separate flight. High season return fares from London to Lilongwe start at around UK£520 for airlines with long mid-flight connecting times, going up to around UK£730 for a direct flight. Low season fares are around UK£100 cheaper.

You can reach Malawi on flights via South Africa, which take longer but often work out cheaper than direct flights. Look out for the Virgin Atlantic flight from London to Johannesburg (Jo'burg) that ties in directly with the Air Malawi flight from Jo'burg to Lilongwe. British Airways also flies to Jo'burg and has a connecting flight to Lilongwe on its partner airline Comair.

There are many travel agents competing for your business. London is normally the best place to buy a ticket, and the following list of main players is a good starting point – although these days specialist travel agents outside the capital can be just as cheap and easier to deal with. To broaden your scope, you should check the ads in weekend newspapers and travel magazines. In London, the free listings magazines (often found outside train stations) all contain travel ads.

Bridge the World (☎ 020-7734 7447) 4 Regent Place, London W1R 5FB
Web site: www.b-t-w.co.uk
Flightbookers (☎ 020-7757 2000) 177-178 Tottenham Court Rd, London W1P 9LF
North-South Travel (☎ 01245-492882) Moulsham Mill Centre, Chelmsford CM2 7PX), an experienced agent where profits support development projects overseas
STA Travel (☎ 020-7361 6161) For students or travellers under 26, with offices at 86 Old Brompton Rd, London SW7 3LQ, and elsewhere in London and Manchester
Web site: www.statravel.co.uk
Trailfinders (☎ 020-7938 3939) 194 Kensington High St, London W8 7RG
Web site: www.trailfinders.co.uk
Usit Campus (☎ 0870-240 1010) 52 Grosvenor Gardens, London SW1W 0AG, has branches throughout the UK. Although these agents cater especially to young people and students, both deal with all travellers.
Web site: www.usitcampus.com

Some of the flight agents listed here also sell tours and safaris in Africa, and some of the companies listed under Organised Tours later in this chapter also sell flights.

If you come to Malawi overland or on a one-way ticket, and then need a ticket home, the cheapest fare to London will cost the equivalent of about UK£600. It might be cheaper to go to South Africa, and get a flight to London from there; flights start at about UK£500.

Continental Europe
Though London is the travel discount capital of Europe, there are several other cities in which you will find a range of good deals. Generally, there is not much variation in air fare prices for departures from the main European cities. All the major airlines are usually offering some sort of deal, and travel agents generally have a number of deals on offer, so shop around.

Denmark
Kilroy Travels (☎ 33 11 00 44) Skindergarde 28, Copenhagen
STA Travel (☎ 33 141 501) Fiolstraede 18, Copenhagen
Web site: www.sta-travel.com

France

OTU (☎ 01 40 29 12 12)
  Web site: www.otu.fr
Nouvelles Frontières (☎ 08 03 33 33 33)
  Web site: www.nouvelles-frontieres.fr
Wasteels (☎ 01 43 62 30 00)
  Web site: www.voyages-wasteels.fr

Germany

STA Travel (☎ 030-311 0950) Goethesttrasse
  73 Berlin

Italy

CTS Viaggi (☎ 06-462 0431) 16 Via Genova,
  Rome
Passagi (☎ 06-474 0923) Galleria Di Tesla,
  Stazione Termini FS, Rome

Netherlands

NBBS (☎ 020-627 1251) Rokin 34, Amsterdam
  is a Budget Air subsidiary
  Web site: www.nbbs.nl

Spain

Barcelo Viajes (☎ 91 559 1819) Princesa 3,
  Madrid
Nouvelles Frontières (☎ 91 547 42 00;) Plaza
  de España 18, Madrid
  Web site: www.nouvelles-frontieres.es
Usit Unlimited (☎ 902 25 25 75) 3 Plaza de
  Callao, Madrid
  Web site: www.unilimited.es

Asia

If you're going to Malawi from Asia, the main routes to/from Africa are from Mumbai/Bombay and Delhi (India) to Durban (South Africa) and Nairobi (Kenya), from where you can fly to Malawi or travel overland.

Although most Asian countries are now offering fairly competitive air fare deals, Bangkok, Singapore and Hong Kong are still the best places to shop around for discount tickets. Hong Kong's travel market can be unpredictable, but some excellent bargains are available if you are lucky.

Khao San Rd in Bangkok is the budget traveller's headquarters. Bangkok has a number of excellent travel agents, but there are also some suspect ones; ask the advice of other travellers before handing over your cash. STA Travel (☎ 02-236 0262), 33 Surawong Rd, is a good and reliable place to start. The Web address is www.sta travel.co.th.

Getting Home or Coming Back?

If you're already in Malawi and are looking for a flight back to Europe, North America or Australasia, the cheapest deals often go via Cape Town or Jo'burg in South Africa. Travel agents in Lilongwe and Blantyre where you can buy tickets home are listed under the chapters covering those cities.

Remember when buying tickets that standard one-way fares can often be more expensive than special deal 'excursion' return fares – so you might be better off buying a cheap return and simply not coming back. Though with an unused ticket in your pocket, maybe you will come back !

Singapore, like Bangkok, has hundreds of travel agents, so you can compare prices on flights. Chinatown Point shopping centre on New Bridge Rd has a good selection of travel agents. STA Travel (☎ 737 7188) at 33A Cuppage Rd offers competitive discount fares for Asian destinations and beyond. The Web site is www.statravel .com.sg.

Hong Kong has a number of excellent, reliable travel agencies and some not-so-reliable ones. A good way to check on a travel agent is to look it up in the phone book: fly-by-night operators don't usually stay around long enough to get listed. Many travellers use the Hong Kong Student Travel Bureau (☎ 2730 3269), 8th floor, Star House, Tsimshatsui or visit the Web site at www.hkst.com.hk.

West Africa

If you're travelling to Malawi from West Africa, you have to fly because the overland route is blocked by war in Congo (Zaïre). Travellers also tend to avoid Congo, Gabon, Cameroon and Nigeria. You can get flights out of Accra (Ghana) but the most popular flight is from Abidjan (Côte d'Ivoire) to either Jo'burg or Nairobi, from where you can reach Malawi by air or overland. To give an idea of fares, Ethiopian Airways has one-way flights from Abidjan to Nairobi for around US$600.

East & Southern Africa

If you're travelling to Malawi from other countries in East or Southern Africa (or going in the other direction), most regional flights go to/from Lilongwe, but some also serve Blantyre. One of the most popular flights for independent travellers is between Harare in Zimbabwe and Blantyre. All fares quoted here are one way. Returns are double, but excursion fares can be somewhat cheaper.

Air Malawi has a pretty good regional network, with flights to Harare (US$160) and Lusaka (US$170) both three times per week, and to Jo'burg weekly (US$400). Additionally, the following regional airlines serve Malawi, usually flying on the days Air Malawi doesn't (so you get a wider choice of flights), with fares mostly on a par: Air Zimbabwe, three times per week to/from Harare (with connections to Victoria Falls); South African Airways, twice per week

---

Air Travel Glossary

Cancellation Penalties If you have to cancel or change a discounted ticket, there are often heavy penalties involved. Some airlines impose penalties on regular tickets as well; insurance can sometimes be taken out against these penalties.

Fare Codes Airlines traditionally offer 1st class (coded F), business class (coded J) and economy class (coded Y) tickets.

Lost Tickets If you lose your ticket an airline will usually, after inquiries, issue you with another one. Legally, however, an airline is entitled to treat a ticket like cash: if you lose it then it's gone forever. So take good care of your tickets.

MCO Stands for Miscellaneous Charge Order – a voucher that looks like an airline ticket but carries no destination or date. Depending on its value (ie, what you pay for it) you can use it as full or part payment towards a ticket for a specific flight at any International Association of Travel Agents (IATA) airline. It's a useful alternative to an onward ticket in those countries that demand one, and is more flexible than an ordinary ticket if you're unsure of your route.

Open-Jaw Tickets These are return tickets where you fly out to one place but return from another, thus saving you backtracking to your arrival point.

Overbooking Since every flight has some passengers who fail to show up, airlines often book more passengers than they have seats. Usually excess passengers make up for the 'no-shows', but occasionally somebody gets 'bumped' onto the next available flight. Guess who it is most likely to be? The passengers who check in late.

Promotional Fares These are officially discounted fares, available from travel agents or direct from the airline.

Reconfirmation If you don't reconfirm your flight at least 72 hours prior to departure, the airline may delete your name from the passenger list. Even if the airline in your home country says reconfirmation isn't necessary, in Africa it is always worth reconfirming, either by phoning the airline or through a local travel agent.

Restrictions Discounted tickets often have various restrictions – such as incurring a penalty if altered, or having set minimum and maximum periods you must be away.

Round-the-World Tickets A RTW ticket gives you (usually) a year in which to circumnavigate the globe, via anywhere the carrying airlines go, without backtracking. The number of stopovers or total number of separate flights is decided before you set off.

Transferred Ticket An airline ticket cannot be transferred from one person to another.

Travel Periods Ticket prices vary with the time of year. There is a low (off-peak) season and a high (peak) season, and often a low-shoulder season and a high-shoulder season as well. Usually the fare depends on your outward flight – if you depart in the high season and return in the low season, you pay the high-season fare.

to/from Jo'burg (with connections to Durban, Cape Town etc); Kenya Airways, three times weekly to/from Nairobi (US$360).

If you're travelling between Malawi and Tanzania, you can fly between Lilongwe and Dar es Salaam, Kilimanjaro International Airport (KIA) or Zanzibar. Dar es Salaam to/from Lilongwe costs around US$200 one way or US$300 return, on either Air Malawi or Air Tanzania. If you're heading for Zanzibar, it's an extra US$40 from Dar. Dar to KIA is around US$80.

If you're heading for South Luangwa National Park in Zambia, there are regular flights between Lilongwe and Mfuwe. See Getting There & Away in the South Luangwa section of the Central Malawi chapter.

LAND
Border Crossings
Malawi shares borders with Tanzania, Zambia and Mozambique. The only land crossing to/from Tanzania is at Songwe, north of Kaporo, where a bridge crosses the Songwe River. (A new bridge is planned further upstream.) The main border crossing with Zambia is 30km south-east of Chipata, on the main road between Lusaka and Lilongwe. The four main crossing points to/from Mozambique are: between Mwanza and Zóbuè (**zob**-way), west of Blantyre; at Muloza, south-east of Blantyre; at Marka, south of Blantyre; and between Chiponde and Mandimba, east of Mangochi.

Malawi does not directly border Zimbabwe, but a lot of traffic between these two countries passes through a neck of Mozambican territory called the Tete Corridor.

All Malawi's border posts open from 6 am to 6 pm (possibly open later and shut earlier, but never the other way around).

If you're bringing a car into Malawi from another country without a carnet (eg, a South African registered car), a temporary import permit is US$3 (payable in Malawian kwacha or rand), and compulsory third-party insurance is US$9 for one month. When you leave Malawi, another US$3 permit handling fee is payable. Receipts are issued.

Mozambique
Bus If you're heading for the part of Mozambique south of the Zambezi, you should go from Blantyre via Mwanza and Zóbuè (the busiest and most popular border crossing) to Tete. The most direct way is by taking a bus between Blantyre and Harare (see the Zimbabwe section later in this chapter), which can drop you at Tete, from where buses go to Vilankulo, Beira and Maputo. You can also do the trip in stages by taking a local bus from Blantyre to the Malawian border post at Mwanza (3km west of Mwanza town), then walking, hitching or taking a share taxi 6km to the Mozambican border post at Zóbuè. From Zóbuè, get a bus or *chapa* (pick-up van or truck) to Tete. If you get stuck at the border, there are places to stay in Mwanza town, and plenty of moneychangers at both border posts, dealing in kwacha, Zimbabwean dollars, US dollars and meticais (Mozambique's currency), but rates are low.

Even if doing the trip in stages seems complicated, a single ride may not be heaven either. We heard from one traveller on this route who apparently went all the way from Vilankulo to Blantyre (around 1000km) in one bus ride:

'This was probably the scariest, most uncomfortable bus journey of my life. It was so crowded I stood the whole way, with barely enough room for one foot on the ground. There was so much luggage on the roof it was caving in. After the first few hours the roads got bad and when it stared to rain water came in everywhere.'

If you're heading for central Mozambique, there are several buses per day from Blantyre to Nsanje, or all the way to the Malawian border at Marka (pronounced maraka). It's a few kilometres between the border posts – walk or take a bicycle taxi. You can change money on the Mozambique side. From here chapas go to Mutarara, Nhamilabue and Vila de Sena, from where you can reach Caia.

To get to northern Mozambique, you can take the route between Blantyre and Mocuba. There are regular buses from Blantyre, via the town of Mulanje, to the Malawian border post at Muloza (US$3).

Mozambican Entry Taxes

If you are heading from Malawi into Mozambique, note that every foreigner entering Mozambique by land is subject to an official immigration tax of US$5 (or R10 rand – which, depending on exchange rates, is usually a cheaper way of doing things). Although you don't always get a receipt, this seems to be legitimate – there's a notice about it on every embassy wall. In remote border areas, the rate seems to be lower – around US$2.50 – maybe because regulations take a long time coming through.

Cars must also pay, but rates also seem to vary between borders. Drivers crossing between Mulanje and Milange have paid just US$5 or R10 for a temporary import permit, while others crossing between Mwanza and Zóbuè have paid at least double this. On top of this cost, drivers pay US$35 (or R100, which works out much cheaper) for one month's third-party insurance. If you're driving, check the current rates when you get your visa.

From here you walk 1km to the Mozambican border post at Milange, from where it's another few kilometres into Milange *vila* (town). Bicycle taxis cost US$1. There's a *pensão* (cheap hotel) and bank here. From Milange there's usually a chapa or truck about every other day in the dry season to Mocuba (US$4), where you can find transport on to Quelimane or Nampula. But if you're heading for Nampula anyway, you're better off going by train (see following section).

Your other option for northern Mozambique is the route between Mangochi and Cuamba. Minibuses run a few times per day between Mangochi and the last Malawian town of Namwera (US$2), where there are resthouses if you need one. Minibuses also sometimes go all the way to the Malawian border post at Chiponde (10km from Namwera) for US$2.50. If there's no transport between Namwera and Chiponde, you can walk, or take a local bicycle taxi for US$3. It's 6km to the Mozambican border post at Mandimba. You might be able to hitch, or

take a bicycle taxi (US$2). Mandimba has a couple of pensãos, and there's usually a daily chapa between here and Cuamba (US$4).

Yet another option on this route is to go by minibus from Liwonde to the Malawian border post at Nayuchi, along the dirt track running parallel to the railway. From the border you can get a train to Cuamba.

Train If you're heading to northern Mozambique, a passenger train departs from Balaka at 5 am every Monday, Wednesday and Friday, and goes via Liwonde to the border at Nayuchi (US$1.80). It arrives at the border around 10 am and comes back in the afternoon. You can also get on in Liwonde, but the train is crowded so there's less chance of getting a seat. From the Malawian border post at Nayuchi, walk to the Mozambican border post at Entre Lagos, where you catch a freight train to Cuamba (there's one most days). The fare is US$1.50, payable in meticais. There are moneychangers at Nayuchi. From Cuamba there are three passenger trains per week to Nampula and freight trains with a wagon for passengers most other days. Three separate train rides, none of which connect, plus a bad line between the border and Cuamba (especially in the rainy season), means this trip can take a day or a week, depending on your luck.

South Africa

If you need to get to South Africa quickly and cheaply, Intercape and Translux run direct luxury coaches from Blantyre to Jo'burg, five times a week between them, for about US$60. The coaches depart midmorning and arrive mid-afternoon next day.

Tanzania

Bus If you want to go the whole way between Lilongwe and Dar es Salaam, there are two companies which each run two buses per week. Both companies have their depot and ticket office on Devil Street in Lilongwe. These buses also pick up and drop off in Mzuzu and Mbeya, which is handy for going between northern Malawi and southern Tanzania. The journey should take

24 hours: Buses usually leave Lilongwe late afternoon, go through Mzuzu around midnight, cross the border at first light, go through Mbeya in the morning and get to Dar in the late afternoon. The fare is US$33 (or US$15 from Lilongwe to Mbeya), but – be warned – these buses may not depart at the advertised time. Instead they go when full – *really* full – and the journey can take 30 hours or more. (If you're travelling from the south, your first sight of a Tanzanian bus – like something from Mad Max or a fairground ghost train, complete with death-head decorations – may be quite a shock!)

If you're doing the trip in stages, a Stagecoach bus runs twice per day between Mzuzu and Karonga, via Chitimba, for US$4 (minibuses for US$5), but the journey takes a long time because the road between Chitimba and Karonga is bad. Minibuses and pick-ups run between Karonga and the Songwe border for around US$1. From the Malawian border post, it's a 200m walk across the bridge to the Tanzanian border post.

From the Tanzanian side, buses go to Mbeya (sometimes looping to Kyela – about 5km off the road between the border and Mbeya). If there's no transport around, you'll have to walk or hitch about 7km to the junction with the road between Kyela and Mbeya. Alternatively, bicycle taxis cost US$1. You can change money with the bicycle taxi drivers but beware of scams. From the junction, find a bus to Mbeya, from where buses and trains go to Dar es Salaam.

Coming from Tanzania to Malawi, if you get an early bus from Mbeya direct to the border, then cross quickly and get a good minibus to Karonga, you can change there and that evening be at Chitimba (US$2.50), or with luck and a following wind even Mzuzu (US$4).

There are plans to seal the roads between Karonga and Mpulungu (Zambia) via Chitipa and Nakonde (see the Grand Plans boxed text below). From Nakonde, the Tanzanian town of Tunduma is just across the border. In the next few years, if the road is completed, this may be an easier way to go between Malawi and Tanzania.

Zambia

Bus Direct buses run between Lilongwe and Lusaka three or four times per week, but they are slow, so it's better doing the trip in stages. Regular minibuses (US$2.50) run from Lilongwe to the Malawian border post, which is 2km west of the town of Mchinji, and 12km before the actual border, which is where the Zambian border post is sited. Local share taxis shuttle between the border posts for US$1.20 per person, or US$7 for a car. (A new Malawian border post is being built at the actual border, only a few metres from the Zambian post. When this is completed, minibuses will probably run straight to here from Lilongwe.)

From the Zambian border post, minibuses run to Chipata (30km north-west of the border) for US$1, from where you can get express buses to Lusaka (from around US$8) or local transport to South Luangwa National Park (see the South Luangwa section, in the Central Malawi chapter).

The other possible route to/from Zambia runs between Karonga and Tunduma, via Chitipa (in the far north-west of Malawi) and Nyala (the Zambian border post). This road is in very bad condition, rarely used by drivers, and has no buses. However, things may change (see the boxed text 'Grand Plans for the Karonga to Chitipa Road'). Until they do, if you need to get from northern Zambia to northern Malawi, you'll probably have to go through Tanzania, via Mbeya.

Zimbabwe

Although not a neighbouring country, many people go directly between Zimbabwe and Malawi, through a neck of Mozambique territory called the Tete Corridor.

When Mozambique was suffering from the effects of its horrendous civil war, traffic still used this road, although it was notoriously dangerous and known as the 'Gun Run'.

After the war the Tete Corridor route became safe, for drivers in their own cars and for buses, and many people now travel this way. Since the late 1990s, however, there have been incidents along this road in which armed bandits have held up and

Time & Trouble at the Tanzanian Border

Note that if you're going from Malawi to Tanzania, the border posts both close at 6 pm. However, Tanzania's time is an hour ahead of Malawi's, so the Malawian border officials will cheerfully stamp you through at 5.30 pm (their time) but once you cross the bridge it's 6.30 pm, and the Tanzanian border post is shut. You can either sleep on the spot (not advisable, as some fairly unsavoury characters frequent the area) or pay the guards 'overtime' to let you through. Better still, if it's getting late, stay in Karonga or somewhere else on the Malawian side and continue your journey next day.

When entering Malawi, also beware of a scam operated by the Malawian border guards involving imaginary 'errors' on your visa or passport that can only be sorted out for a US$20 fee. These guys probably haven't been paid for months, so it's hard to blame them for trying, but this kind of game just isn't on. Politely ask to see their commanding officer, or written regulations about the 'fee', and you'll find it swiftly waived.

stolen vehicles – nearly always fancy 4WDs. There seems to be no danger for people on buses, but if you're coming from Blantyre you can get the latest public transport safety information from Doogles backpackers lodge (listed in Places to Stay). Most popular with budget travellers is the daily Munorurama bus, which leaves Blantyre's main bus station (off 'old' Chileka Rd) at 6 am, and arrives in Harare by late afternoon. The service is good and costs US$16. Coming the other way costs the same, but is a much slower trip because local people bring in loads of Zimbabwean goods and there are long searches at the Mwanza border. Some travellers have been on the northbound bus for over two days! If you do get stuck at the border, you're better off abandoning the big bus, and getting a local minibus to Blantyre (US$2.50).

Luxury coaches operated by Trans-Zambezi Express and Translux go from Blantyre to Jo'burg via Harare a few times per week. You can get information or make reservations for these long distance buses at the Business Centre in the lobby of Le Meridien Mt Soche Hotel, or at the Stagecoach office which is attached to the same hotel.

East Africa

Many people visit Malawi as part of wider travels in East or Southern Africa, and by far the most popular starting-out point is Nairobi (Kenya).

From Nairobi, there are several options for reaching Malawi – the main route goes via Mombasa or Arusha to Dar es Salaam (Tanzania). From here, drivers follow the Great North Road, and those without wheels take the Tazara Railway; both lead through Mbeya in southern Tanzania, from where Malawi can be easily reached, via the border at Songwe.

Another route from Dar es Salaam takes you across the country to Kigoma on Lake Tanganyika, then by steamer to Mpulungu in northern Zambia, from where you can also reach Malawi.

Another, more esoteric but increasingly popular, option from Nairobi involves travelling to Dar es Salaam and then taking a boat or a bus southwards down the coast to Mtwara. From here you can take another boat, or go overland, to northern Mozambique, as far as Nampula, and then head inland, reaching Malawi either via the border between Namwera and Chiponde (50km from Mangochi) or via Lichinga and Cóbuè to reach Likoma Island and then Nkhata Bay (see the Mozambique section for more details).

Europe

A few hardy travellers come all the way to Malawi (and other countries in East and Southern Africa) overland from Europe, either by public transport or in their own vehicle. Describing the route is beyond the scope of this book, but Lonely Planet's *Africa on a shoestring*, or the regional guides to North Africa, West Africa or East Africa will be useful.

If you decide to try driving, the main points to be aware of include the incredibly long distances, the appalling condition of many roads, and the constant challenge of dealing with police or border officials. You should also be mechanically competent and carry a good collection of spare parts. You will need vehicle registration papers, liability insurance, a drivers licence and an International Drivers Permit. You may also need a carnet, effectively a passport for the vehicle and temporary waiver of import duty, designed to prevent car import rackets. Your local automobile association can provide details. For drivers, some manuals are listed in the Books section of the Regional Facts for the Visitor chapter. You might also want to check this Web site: www.sahara-overland.com.

LAKE
Mozambique

The Lake Malawi passenger boat *Ilala* (see the Boat section in the Getting Around chapter) stops at Likoma Island twice per week, and there's an immigration post in Chipyela (the main settlement on the island) where you must get stamped out. From here local boats go most days across to Cóbuè (**kob**-way) on the Mozambican mainland (US$2 by motor boat, US$0.50 under sail), where there's a Mozambican immigration post (you pay US$2.50 to enter) and a small friendly hotel if you get stuck (which is likely). The road to Lichinga is rough, virtually impassable where a bridge is down, and has hardly any traffic. So it's more reliable to go by boat from Cóbuè to Metangula (often the same boat which brought you over from Likoma). Boats usually leave Cóbuè the morning after the *Ilala* arrives at Likoma. Cóbuè to Metangula by motorboat costs about US$5 and takes six hours, a dhow costs US$2.50 and can take one to three days, so bring food. From Metangula there are trucks and chapas most days to Lichinga (US$4). You can use Malawian kwacha all the way to Lichinga, and change it into meticais in the market there. You must change US dollars in the bank. From Lichinga, there's hardly any traffic on the road heading east, but it's quite easy to go by chapa to Mandimba (on the Malawian border near Mangochi) or on to Cuamba.

It's possible to visit Cóbuè and the surrounding area in Mozambique for a few days, without needing a visa. You must

---

Grand Plans for the Karonga to Chitipa Road

If you're travelling in northern Malawi, or crossing into Tanzania or Zambia, note that there are plans to completely upgrade the road from Karonga (on the northern bank of Lake Malawi) to Chitipa in the far north-west of Malawi, near the border with Zambia) and then extend it through Nakonde and onwards all the way to Mpulungu on the southern tip of Lake Tanganyika.

These plans have been on the drawing board for many years, and have yet to be realised, but if they do eventuate, this will no doubt improve communications between Tanzania, Zambia and Malawi. Buses will start to run, and moving between northern Malawi and northern Zambia will become much easier. If you're going this way, ask around for the latest situation.

Ironically, this new road follows a route originally planned by the African Lakes Corporation over 100 years ago, to link Lakes Malawi (then Nyasa) and Tanganyika, forming a continuous 'highway' for many hundreds of miles through Central Africa. It was named the Stevenson Road, after one of the Glasgow businessmen who helped found the corporation in 1878, but the project was abandoned after the death of the senior engineer, one James Stewart. This was the cousin of another James Stewart who had earlier inspired and helped to found the Livingstonia missions (see History in the Facts about Malawi chapter). His journals were later published as a book *From Nyassa to Tanganyika*. If the new road is built, his plans will have finally been realised.

report to the immigration officials on the way out, and return the same way. The backpacker lodges in Nkhata Bay and on Likoma or Chizumulu Islands can advise you on this. This is particularly useful if you want to visit Manda Wilderness Area (as described in the Around Nkhata Bay section of the Northern Malawi chapter).

'From Cóbuè we caught a sailing dhow to Metangula as the motor boat was going later in the week. We left Cóbuè at 11 am and sailed until 4 pm when the wind dropped, after which the eight-metre dhow complete with 30 passengers, crew, children, chickens, maize etc was rowed for another four hours. After this the crew pulled it along the shore, through reeds and everything, for another hour or two! We then camped on an idyllic sandy beach until dawn and with the aid of a little wind and lots of rowing arrived in Metangula by 9.30 am. It was a great experience, especially as the sun set, with children singing and chickens running around. The crew, despite a few bottles of early morning Kachasu, were friendly and helpful. There is no shade on the boat so precautions need to be taken against the sun. From Metangula we got a lift to Lichinga and went on to Nampula. It is possible to get from Likoma to the coast in five days but it could take eight. The latter would be unlucky.'

Louse Kerbiriou and Stephen O'Conner (UK)

Tanzania

The *Ilala* passenger boat serves various ports on Lake Malawi (see the Getting Around chapter), and sometimes runs between Nkhata Bay and Mbamba Bay – a small town on the eastern (Tanzanian) side of the lake. From here you could reach the town of Songea, about 200km inland, but then your only real option is to go north, to Makambako (which is on the main road between Mbeya and Dar es Salaam, about 200km east of Mbeya). The road east from Songea towards the coast is in very bad condition, with very occasional trucks being the only form of transport.

The *Ilala* also occasionally steams up to the small Tanzanian town of Itungi, near Kyela, (which has regular transport links with Mbeya). However, the schedule is very vague, and this may involve a lot of waiting if you're coming from the north. Going from

Malawi to Tanzania, you can make inquiries at Nkhata Bay. If the boat doesn't go all the way to Itungi, simply get off at Chilumba, and continue to Tanzania by land.

At the northern end of the lake, a Tanzanian ship called the *Songea* operates between Itungi and Mbamba Bay, and there are apparently plans for it to start calling at Nkhata Bay (Malawi), but this service has been talked about for years.

ORGANISED TOURS

This section covers tours organised in your own home country. Tours that you can organise when in Malawi are covered in the Getting Around chapter.

There are two main ways of reaching Malawi (on its own or combined with other destinations in the region) on an organised tour. You can take an all-inclusive tour, which includes the flight from your home country, or you can come overland all the way (usually from Europe). The former is preferred by people with less free time, the latter is often an option for those with more time to spare. Another alternative, somewhere between the two, is to fly to a nearby country, such as Kenya, Zimbabwe or South Africa, and join an overland tour from there, either to or through Malawi. The tour can be anything from a few weeks to a few months.

Organised tours can be low-budget affairs, where you travel in an overland truck with about 15 to 30 other people, a couple of drivers/leaders, plus tents and other equipment, buying food along the way, and cooking together as a group.

At the other end of the spectrum are the 'tailor-made' or fully inclusive tours (FITs), arranged personally to your exact specifications. This is an increasingly popular option for visitors to Southern Africa, including Malawi. Although some companies offer highly exclusive and very expensive itineraries, others are reasonably priced and particularly attractive for individuals, families or a group of friends with specialist interests (such as bird-watching or fishing) who want to get away from larger organised groups.

In between the two extremes are the midrange tours, leaving on set dates and keeping to a set itinerary. You travel in a small group, probably in a minibus, staying in small hotels or maybe camping. The price includes transport and accommodation, and the services of a tour leader, but you may be able to arrange (and pay for) some meals or extra activities.

Some companies offer an option between all-inclusive tours and completely independent travel: they provide you with self-guided itineraries, including pre-booked flights, vehicle hire and accommodation where required, but let you decide exactly where and when you want to go.

Around the world there are many tour companies and agents featuring Malawi, usually along with other countries in East or Southern Africa, or elsewhere in the world. The best places to begin looking for ideas are the advertising sections in weekend newspapers and travel magazines. If you have specialist interests, look in specialist magazines. For example, companies organising wildlife tours advertise in nature magazines, or hiking tours in outdoor magazines. The following lists mention some companies that cover Malawi, to provide a few pointers. Some of the companies also sell flights, and some of the agents selling flights listed under Air earlier also sell tours. Contact them directly, ask for a brochure or Web site details, see what appeals, then take it from there.

USA & Canada

Africa Adventure Company (☎ 800-882 9453, 954-4918 877, fax 491-9060, ✉ noltingaac@ aol .com) 5353 N Federal Highway, Suite 300, Fort Lauderdale, FL 33308. Top safari specialists

Africa Travel Centre (☎ 800-631 5650, 732-542 9006, fax 800-542 9420, ✉ explorers@ monmouth.com) Explorers Travel Group, One Main St, Suite 304, Eatontown, NJ 07724. Flights, hotels, overland tours, safaris, tailor-made trips, plus visas and insurance

Bicycle Africa Tours (☎/fax 206-767 0848, ✉ ibike@ibike.org) 4887 Columbia Dr S, Seattle WA 98108-1919. Tours by bike all over Africa, including Malawi
Web site: www.ibike.org/bikeafrica

Born Free Safaris (☎ 800-372 3274, fax 818-753 1460, ✉ bornfreesafaris@att.net) 12504 River-

side Dr, North Hollywood, CA 91607. Safaris, trekking, cultural tours, flights

Bushtracks (☎ 800-995-8689, fax 650-463 0925, ✉ info@bushtracks.com) 845 Oak Grove Ave, Suite 204, Menlo Park, CA 94025. Expeditions, tours and safaris

Civilized Adventures (☎ 403-205 4120, 205 4121) 1228A 9th Ave SE, Calgary, Alberta T2G 0TI. Wide range of tours, including Malawi

Reservations Africa (☎ 888-891 5111, 250-386 1335, fax 250 386 3266, ✉ info@reservation safrica.com) 550-1070 Douglas St, Victoria BC V8W 2C4. Southern Africa specialists, offering tailor-made tours and safaris, plus flights

Safaricentre (☎ 800-223 6046, ✉ africa@safari centre.com) 3201 N Sepulveda Blvd, Manhattan Beach, CA 90266. Huge range of flights, camps, hotels, budget tours and luxury safaris

Spector Travel (☎ 800-879 2374, fax 800-338 0110, ✉ africa@spectortravel.com) 31 St James Ave, Boston, MA 02116. Budget tours all over Africa, plus discounted airfares

Voyagers (☎ 800-633 0299, ✉ explorer@ voyagers.com) PO Box 915, Ithaca NY. Photographic and wildlife-viewing safaris

Australia & New Zealand

Adventure World (☎ 02-9956 7766, fax 02-9956 7707, ✉ info@adventureworld.com.au) 73 Walker St, North Sydney, NSW 2060. Overland tours, safaris, car hire and hotel packages

Africa Travel Centre (☎ 02-9267 3048, fax 02-9267 3047, ✉ africa@travel.com.au) Level 11, 456 Kent St, Sydney, NSW 2000. Overland tours, hotels, custom safaris, plus flights

Africa Travel Centre (☎ 09-520 2000, fax 09-520 2001) 21 Remuera Rd, Newmarket, Auckland 3. Diving, overland tours, tailor-made safaris and trekking

African Wildlife Safaris (☎ 03-9696 2899, fax 03-9696 4937, ✉ office@africansafaris .com.au) 1st floor, 259 Coventry St, South Melbourne, Victoria 3205. Specialists mainly in safaris to Southern Africa

Peregrine Travel 2nd floor, 258 Lonsdale St, Melbourne, Victoria 3000 (☎ 03-9663 8611, fax 03-9663 8618, ✉ travelcentre@peregrine.net .au). Africa specialists, catering for all budgets

UK & Ireland

Acacia Expeditions (☎ 0207-706 4700, ✉ acacia@ afrika.demon.co.uk) 23a Craven Terrace, Lancaster Gate, London W2 3QH. Wide range of safaris, overland tours and camping trips in Africa for travellers on low and medium budgets

Dragoman (☎ 01728-861133, fax 01728-861127, @ info@dragoman.co.uk) Camp Green, Kenton Rd, Debenham, Stowmarket, Suffolk IP14 6LA. Smart end of the overland tour market, with short and long trips throughout Africa

Explore Worldwide (☎ 01252-760000, fax 01252-760001, @ info@explore.co.uk) 1 Frederick St, Aldershot, Hampshire GU11 1LQ. Good-value adventurous tours for small groups, including northern Malawi

Guerba (☎ 01373-858956, fax 01373-838351, @ info@guerba.co.uk) Wessex House, 40 Station Rd, Westbury, Wiltshire BA13 3JN. Short and long safaris on a budget by truck throughout Africa

Hartley's Safaris (☎ 01673-861600, fax 01673-861666, @ info@hartleys-safaris.co.uk) The Old Chapel, Chapel Lane, Hackthorn LN2 3PN. Tailor-made safaris in Africa for mid- and upper-range clients

Okavango Tours & Safaris (☎ 020-8343 3283, fax 020-8343 3287, @ info@okavango.com) Marlborough House, 298 Regents Park Rd, London N3 2TJ. Small specialist outfit with top-class tours in Malawi, Zambia and all over Southern Africa

Safari Drive (☎ 01488-681611, fax 01488-685055, @ safari_drive@compuserve.com) Wessex House, 127 High St, Hungerford RG17 0DL. Experienced and specialised, providing self-drive Land Rovers, plus privately guided tours and tailor-made safaris all over Southern Africa, including Malawi

Sunvil Discovery (☎ 020-8232 9777, fax 020-8568 8330, @ africa@sunvil.co.uk) Sunvil House, Upper Square, Old Isleworth TW7 7BJ. Imaginative, flexible and good-value tours or fly-drives in various parts of Southern Africa, including Malawi and Zambia

Travelbag Adventures (☎ 01420-541007, fax 01420-541022, @ info@travelbag-adventures .com) 15 Turk St, Alton, Hampshire GU34 1AG. Active and affordable small group tours around the world, including a combined Malawi and Zambia wildlife trip

Continental Europe

African Special Tours (☎ 061-01 58 30 53/4, @ ast-tours@t-online.de) Gronauer Weg 31, 61118 Bad Vilbel, Germany. Tours in many parts of Africa, including Malawi

All Over Tours (☎ 071-331 9034, 331 9156, @ info@allovertours.nl) Noordplein 19, 2371 DA Roelofarendsveen, Netherlands. Wide range of tours, including Malawi

Makila Voyages (☎ 01 42 96 80 00, fax 01 42 96 18 05) 4 Place de Valois, 75001 Paris, France. Upmarket company with tours and safaris all over East and Southern Africa, including Malawi and Zambia

NBBS Travel (☎ 071-568 8668, 522 6475) Schipholweg 101, 2316 XC Leiden, Netherlands

Getting Around

You can travel around Malawi by air, road, rail or boat. Compared with some African countries, such as South Africa or Zimbabwe, the infrastructure of Malawi is a little rough around the edges; but compared with other countries, such as Zambia or Tanzania, it's still pretty good – though deteriorating. Also compared with other countries in the region, distances between major centres are short, and generally roads and public transport systems are quite good, making independent travel fairly straightforward.

'I found Malawi one of the friendliest, easy-to-travel, inexpensive places that I have ever been to. No problem travelling alone, and hitching is easy. But get out there – there is more to Malawi than Cape Maclear, although you'd hardly know it by the number of tourists you see elsewhere!'

Joanna Rees, UK

AIR

Air Malawi, the national airline, has at least two flights a day between Lilongwe and Blantyre for around US$50 one way, and most days between Lilongwe and Mzuzu, also for US$50 one way.

Air Malawi also has flights from Lilongwe to Nyika National Park (US$72), and from Lilongwe or Blantyre to Club Makokola (US$45) on Lake Malawi – you don't have to be a guest to visit (from the airstrip you can reach other points on the lake).

Internal flights can be paid for in kwacha. Air Malawi's booking system is not always reliable, so be prepared for lost reservations or double bookings. For domestic flights, departure tax is $2.

Sefofane (represented by Central African Wilderness Safaris and Ulendo Safaris – see Organised Tours in this chapter and Travel Agencies in the Lilongwe chapter) is the only air charter company operating in Malawi, although others may start up as demand from the tourism trade increases. Sefofane operates two 'circuits' (one in the north of the country, one in the south) link-ing major towns and tourism centres around the country; the most popular route is between Lilongwe and Liwonde National Park (US$160 per person one way). There is no fixed timetable – planes fly on demand for two people or more.

If you want to charter a whole plane, fares vary according to the route and number of people in your group, so you should always get a quote through a travel agent in Lilongwe or Blantyre. As a guide, however, a five-seat plane from Lilongwe to Liwonde National Park costs US$650.

BUS

Most buses around Malawi are operated by a private company called Stagecoach. They come in several different types. Top of the range is Coachline, a daily luxury nonstop service between Blantyre and Lilongwe (370km, US$18) with air-conditioning, toilet, snacks, steward service and good drivers. Next comes Express or Speedlink services, fast buses between the main towns with limited stops and no standing passengers allowed. Intercity buses (often just called the Ordinary bus) cover long-distance routes but stop everywhere, so are slow. As a rule of thumb, Express buses charge between US$2 and US$2.50 per 100km, and Intercity buses slightly less. Stagecoach also runs local services that cover the quieter rural routes and tend to be very slow and crowded.

For Coachline and Express buses you can buy tickets in advance and have a reserved seat. Note that for the Coachline service in Lilongwe, you need to book at the Stagecoach bus depot (not the bus station) or at a large hotel or travel agent. In Blantyre you also need to book at a large hotel or travel agent. Express buses must be booked at the bus station in each city. The day before is usually sufficient for Express, but for Coachline a week's notice is sometimes required, particularly for Friday and Sunday services. Also note that seats cannot be reserved for children under five, even if you're prepared to pay. A tip from a travelling parent: lie about your child's age!

There are also many private buses and minibuses on the roads, either slotting in between Stagecoach services, or serving the routes Stagecoach won't. Fares are about the same as Stagecoach, or slightly more if the condition of the road is bad. There are also local minibus services around towns and to outlying villages, or along the roads that the big buses can't manage. In Malawi, a vehicle with about 30 seats is called a 'half-bus' to distinguish it from big buses or minibuses.

In rural areas, the frequency of buses and minibuses drops dramatically – sometimes to nothing. In cases like this, the 'bus' is often a truck or pick-up with people just piled in the back. In Malawi this is called a *matola*. Everyone pays a fare to the driver – normally a bit more than a bus would charge (ie, matolas charge around US$3 per 100km).

Travelling by bus can be a hair-raising experience.

If you take an overnight bus, when it arrives at its destination, you're normally allowed to stay on board until dawn.

Wherever you go by bus, be prepared for breakdowns and other delays. Buses nearly always run behind official timetables (where they exist). If you ask drivers or bus station staff how long a journey might take, remember that local people tend to give optimistic estimations, so it's always best to add at least a few hours to the time you are told.

TRAIN

The main railway line is centred on Blantyre, and passenger trains run daily Monday through Friday to/from Balaka (north-west of Zomba). The fare is US$1.50, but passengers rarely use the train because road transport on this route is quicker and cheaper.

The twice-weekly service between Limbe and Nsanje (US$2), in the south of Malawi, is used by passengers as the line reaches areas where road transport is limited. A bridge was washed away in 1998, and at the time of research trains were terminating at Makhanga.

The service of most use to travellers is between Balaka and Nayuchi (on the border with Mozambique) via Liwonde. For details see Mozambique in the Getting There & Away chapter. The line to Lilongwe from Blantyre via Salima (just west of the lake) no longer carries passenger trains.

CAR & MOTORCYCLE
Driving Regulations

If driving your own vehicle or a rented car, it is obligatory to carry your driving licence at all times, and you will need to show this and your insurance papers (and temporary import permit if applicable) to policemen, who will stop you at road blocks. An international driving permit is ideal – for more details see the boxed text 'International Driving Permit' in the Facts for the Visitor chapter. It is also obligatory to wear seatbelts in the front of a car if they are fitted.

Road Conditions

Most main roads in Malawi are well sealed, but in recent years several stretches have not

Driving in Malawi

Whether you drive a hire car or your own vehicle in Malawi (or beyond), you should be prepared for local attitudes towards motor vehicles. Generally speaking, driving standards are bad and drivers are unpredictable. Be ready for cars overtaking on blind corners and hills. Traffic officially drives on the left in Malawi – although you wouldn't always know it.

Other things to be prepared for include children playing on busy highways and cyclists on the wrong side of the road. You should also be vigilant about livestock. Goats run fast, but often go the wrong way, that is, *into* your path; cows have a better sense of direction, but are slower and make a hell of a dent in your paintwork. If you see kids with flags or sticks, it may mean they're leading a herd. Slow down, even if you can't see any cows – indeed, especially if you can't see any cows! If you see tree branches in the road, these are the local version of warning triangles; there's probably a broken-down vehicle on the road ahead.

All of these things become much harder to deal with in the dark, and it's simply not advisable to drive at night. You can't see children, cyclists and livestock, and the chances of an accident are high. There are also other vehicles to worry about; many have faulty lights – or none at all.

One last quirk to be ready for: If you're stuck behind a slow-moving truck or car, some local drivers use their right-side indicator to say it's OK for you to overtake. Other drivers use it to say the exact opposite – something is coming the other way. The moral of the tale is never overtake unless you can see that the road ahead is completely clear.

---

received maintenance and potholes are appearing. In some areas this has made driving slow, difficult and dangerous. Rural routes are not so good, and after heavy rain they are often impassable, sometimes for weeks.

Main roads are numbered. Major routes include the M1, from the northern tip of the country to the southern tip, through Karonga, Mzuzu, Kasungu, Lilongwe and Blantyre; the M3 from Blantyre, through Zomba and Mangochi to the Mozambique border at Chiponde; the M5 lake shore road between Nkhata Bay and Salima, which extends southwards to meet the M1 near Balaka; and the M10 along the southern lake shore between Mua and Mangochi.

Secondary roads are usually not sealed with tar, but made from a mix of dirt and gravel (these are called 'graded' roads in much of Africa). These also vary in condition; some are well maintained and easy to drive on in a normal car, others are very bad, especially after the rains, and slow even with 4WD.

Rental

If you need to rent a car, most hire companies are based in Blantyre and Lilongwe. Those with offices in more than one city can arrange pick-up-drop-off deals. International names include Avis, and there are several independent outfits. It's worth shopping around as companies often have special deals and some are prepared to negotiate. You can also hire a car through a travel agent – they may also have access to special deals. Rental cars are generally not up to Western standards. Check the tyres and anything else you can. If anything is worn or broken, demand a repair or a discount.

Self-drive rates for a small car start at US$30 per day, plus around US$0.30 per kilometre. Unlimited mileage (minimum seven days) costs from US$50 per day. To this add 20% government tax, plus another US$3 to US$7 a day for insurance. Land & Lake Safaris (see Organised Tours later in this chapter) offer car hire especially aimed at independent tourists, with saloon cars and 4WD vehicles available. Car rental companies in Malawi include the following.

Avis (Lilongwe ☎ 756105/3; Blantyre ☎ 623792), plus offices at Lilongwe and Blantyre airports and in some large hotels
Ceciliana Car Hire (Blantyre ☎ 641219, 822572; Lilongwe ☎ 756055)
Land & Lake Safaris (☎ 757120, fax 754560)
Sputnik Car Hire (Lilongwe ☎ 771013)

Fuel

The cost of fuel is fixed throughout the country: US$0.55 for petrol, US$0.50 for diesel. Supplies are usually reliable and distances between towns with filling stations are not great in Malawi, so you rarely need to worry about running dry. However, the quality of fuel is not excellent, in fact the 'blend' sold for cars in Malawi is a mixture of petrol and an ethanol by-product of the local sugar industry: you may notice surprisingly high fuel consumption rates and a tendency for the engine to stall more easily than normal.

BICYCLE

Cycling is a cheap, convenient, healthy, environmentally sound and, above all, fun way to travel. Not many people ride all the way *to* Malawi, but some tour companies based in Europe or the USA operate cycling tours (see Organised Tours in the Getting There & Away chapter). It is also possible to hire a bike once you arrive – for more details see Activities in the Facts for the Visitor chapter.

Another option is to take your own bike with you on the plane from your home country and cycle around Malawi when you arrive. You can dismantle the bike and put the pieces in a bag or box, but it's much easier simply to wheel your bike to the check-in desk. Also, if it's not dismantled, the baggage handlers see a bike and are unlikely to pile suitcases on top of it (although some travellers say that if your bike doesn't stand up to baggage handlers it won't last long in Africa anyway).

If you do go for the non-dismantle approach, you'll probably still have to remove the pedals, partly deflate the tyres and turn the handlebars sideways so that the bike takes up less space. Check this with the airline well in advance, preferably before you pay for your ticket. Some airlines don't charge to carry a bike (it counts as 'sporting equipment' along with golf clubs or surfboards), and don't even include it in the weight allowance. Others charge an extra handling fee of around US$50.

Once in Malawi, the country is very good for cycling. Distances between towns and places of interest are relatively short, and roads are mostly in reasonable condition for cyclists. (Even when they're badly potholed, it's less of a problem for bikes, as two wheels can weave between the bumps more easily.)

A worry on main roads are the trucks and buses that seem to take delight in getting as close as possible when overtaking. Keep your wits about you when the traffic is heavy and be prepared to take evasive action onto the verge as local cyclists frequently have to do. A rear-view mirror is useful in these situations, and cruising with a Walkman on is asking for trouble.

Malawi's rural roads are quieter and ideal for cycling – mountain bikes will cope easily with the dirt surfaces. Places where mountain-bike touring is particularly good include the area between Blantyre and Mount Mulanje (where you can do a marvellous circuit of the mountain, including a pass called the Fort Lister Gap); the road along the base of the Thyolo Escarpment south-east of Chikwawa; the 'old' road that runs across the plains between Phalombe (near Mount Mulanje) and Zomba; the road from Lilongwe to Lake Malawi, via Ntchisi and Nkhotakota Wildlife Reserve; the tracks and minor roads that run through the hills north-west of Nkhata Bay; the route from Mzimba to Rumphi, via Kazuni and Vwaza Marsh Wildlife Reserve; Dzalanyama Forest (which can be easily reached by bike from Lilongwe); and Nyika National Park.

Bikes in Malawi are generally straightforward machines. You'll have difficulty buying hi-tech European or American spares, so bring sufficient with you, and have a good idea of how to fit them. In particular, punctures will be frequent, so take at least four spare inner tubes. Consider the number of tube patches you might need, double it, double it again, and pack that many (plus tyre repair material and plenty of glue). A spare tyre is also worth carrying.

HITCHING

On the main routes in Malawi, especially between Mzuzu, Lilongwe, Zomba, Blantyre and the southern lake shore, hitching lifts in the Western fashion, (ie, for free, because you can't or don't want to pay) is fairly easy. At weekends, well-off residents and expatriates living in Blantyre and Lilongwe make a beeline for Salima, Cape Maclear and the southern lake shore, so it's easy to get a lift there on Friday (and on Sunday in the opposite direction).

Note, however, that just because we say hitching is possible, it doesn't mean we recommend it. Hitching is never entirely safe in any country in the world. Travellers who hitch should understand that they are taking a small but potentially serious risk. However, many people do hitch around Malawi and other countries in East and Southern Africa (using buses to avoid potential hot spots), and have no difficulties. If you're planning to hitch, heed advice from other hitchers (locals or travellers) first. Use common sense: hitching in pairs is obviously safer, while hitching through less salubrious suburbs and townships, especially at night, is asking for trouble. If possible, let someone know where you're planning to go.

Once you get off the main routes, hitching becomes very hard, simply because there are very few vehicles to give free lifts. The only vehicles you're likely to see are matolas, trucks or pick-ups, carrying goods and acting as an unofficial transport service for local people in rural areas – for more details see Bus earlier in this chapter. The distinction between hitching and public transport is blurred here, and while it cannot be proclaimed safe, problems are extremely unlikely. Anyway, in most cases it's your only choice.

All over the country you will see Malawian government cars (with MG number plates). These are of course always on important official business, although sometimes the drivers do stop to assist stranded travellers. Check whether a payment is expected in this case.

BOAT

A large passenger boat called the *Ilala* chugs up and down Lake Malawi, once per week in each direction, between Monkey Bay in the south and Chilumba in the north, stopping at about a dozen lakeside towns and villages. Many travellers rate this

Steamer Names

The *Ilala* (actually called the MV *Ilala II*) is named after a boat used by Scottish missionaries who founded a mission at Cape Maclear in the late 19th century. In turn this original boat was named after the place where the explorer David Livingstone died in 1873. The *Chauncey Maples* is named after one of the first bishops of Central Africa, who helped found the mission on Likoma Island, and drowned in Lake Malawi in 1895. *Mtendere* means 'freedom' in Chichewa.

journey as a highlight of the country, although there are occasionally nasty storms on the lake, so you should be ready for some pitching and rolling.

The whole trip, from one end of the line to the other, takes about three days. However, this boat is notoriously prone to delay. It can sometimes be a day late, especially towards the end of the schedule. See the Ferry Schedules table for the official and 'more likely' schedules (only main ports shown).

Note that the official schedule allows for the *Ilala* to make a leg from Nkhata Bay out to Mbamba Bay (Tanzania) and then back to Nkhata Bay. But sometimes the *Ilala* simply does not go to Mbamba Bay, and ties up at Nkhata Bay for most of Tuesday, or rolls in even later than usual from Usisya before departing for Chizumulu and Likoma.

The *Ilala* has three classes: cabin, which was once luxurious, and is still in reasonable condition; 1st-class deck – generally quite spacious, with seats, a small area of sunshade and a bar; and economy, which is the entire lower deck, and is dark and crowded, with engine fumes permeating from below.

All journeys to/from Mbamba Bay (Tanzania) must start/end in Nkhata Bay to comply with customs and immigration formalities.

The fare for cabin and 1st class includes food – served in the ship's restaurant. There's also a bar on the 1st-class deck. Economy fares don't include food. Food is served from a galley on the economy deck: beans, rice and vegetables cost under US$1.

Ferry Schedules

Northbound

port	arrival	departure
Monkey Bay	-	8 am Fri
Chipoka	8 pm	11.30 pm Fri
Nkhotakota	7 am	8.30 am Sat
Likoma Is	2.30 am	5.30 pm Sat
Chizumulu Is	7 pm	8 pm Sat
Nkhata Bay	11 pm Sat	4 am Sun
Chilumba	6 pm Sun	-

Southbound (official)

port	arrival	departure
Chilumba	-	3 am Mon
Usisya	11 am	1 pm Mon
Nkhata Bay	4.30 pm Mon	1 am Tue
Mbamba Bay	4.30 am	7.30 am Tue
Nkhata Bay	11 am	1 pm Tue
Chizumulu Is	4 pm	5.30 pm
Likoma Is	7 pm	10 pm Tue
Nkhotakota	3 am	4 am Wed
Chipoka	11.30 am	1.30 pm Wed
Monkey Bay	6 am Thu	-

Southbound (more likely)

port	arrival	departure
Chilumba	-	3 am Mon
Usisya	11 am	1 pm Mon
Nkhata Bay	10 pm Mon	3 am Tue
Mbamba Bay	6.30 am	10.30 am Tue
Nkhata Bay	4.30 pm	10 pm Tue
Chizumulu Is	2 am	5 am Wed
Likoma Is	8.30 am	11.30 am Wed
Nkhotakota	4.30 pm	5.30 pm Wed
Chipoka	1 am	3 am Thu
Monkey Bay	3 pm Thu	-

Reservations are usually required for the cabins and first class. This can sometimes be done in advance at the main *Ilala* ports (Monkey Bay, Nkhata Bay, Nkhotakota, Likoma and Chilumba) but not always – sometimes the ticket office simply doesn't open until a few hours before the boat is due. You can also reserve cabins and first class accommodation through Ulendo Safaris in Lilongwe (see Travel Agencies in the Lilongwe chapter).

For economy class, tickets are only sold at ports, and only when the *Ilala* is sighted.

Queuing tends to start about a day before it's due to arrive. On the other hand, there's no question of anyone being refused – it just keeps filling up! If you travel economy, you'll almost certainly be allowed onto the 1st-class deck to buy a beer, which you can then make last several hours. We've heard stories from economy travellers who bought the captain a few beers while they were in the bar, and were then allowed to use a 1st-class cabin.

When the *Ilala* stops at lakeside towns or villages, the water is too shallow for the boat to come close to shore. The lifeboat is used to ferry passengers ashore. Local village boats also carry people to the shore, for which there is a small charge. At the same time, traders come out in canoes and sell fruit, dried fish and other food.

Another boat called the MV *Mtendere* was out of service at the time of writing. There are rumours of a refit, so it may be relaunched, and have a schedule that fits in between the *Ilala* (so there would be a boat twice per week in each direction). An older boat, the *Chauncey Maples*, was also out of service at the time of research, but there's a vague possibility this boat may be brought back into service too. A voyage would be historically fascinating but possibly quite slow.

LOCAL TRANSPORT
Minibus

In cities and large towns, such as Lilongwe, Mzuzu, Zomba, Blantyre and Limbe, local routes are served by minibuses. Full details of routes and fares are given in the respective city/town section.

Ilala Sample Fares

destination	cabin	1st class	economy
Monkey Bay	41	26	5
Nkhotakota	15	13	3
Likoma	15	8	2
Chizumulu	-	6	1.50
Mbamba Bay	17	9	2.50
Chilumba	17.50	11.50	2.75

All fares from Nkhata Bay in US$

Taxi

Private hire taxis only operate in the main towns. You can find them outside bus stations, airports or large hotels. There are no meters, so rates are negotiable, particularly on airport runs. Clarify the price at the start of the journey. More details are given in individual citytown sections.

ORGANISED TOURS

Information about tour companies based outside Malawi (in the UK, the USA, Australia etc) can be found under Organised Tours in the Getting There & Away chapter.

In Malawi, several companies organise tours around the country, ranging from a few days to three weeks, with trips into Zambia or Mozambique also available (although Malawi's safari scene is much smaller than, say, South Africa's or Zimbabwe's).

Tours may be 'mobile' (ie, moving from camp to camp every few days), or based in just one place, with excursions each day. Most are vehicle-based although some outfits also organise walking trips, horseback safaris, or boating on the lake. Tours normally include transport, accommodation and food, but prices vary considerably according to standards – from budget to luxury.

Budget tours normally cost between US$50 and $70 per day. There are only a few budget options that can be arranged on the spot – most companies prefer advance bookings, although sometimes a couple of days is enough.

Most mid-range and top-end companies offering tailor-made trips charge from US$100 per person per day, some easily exceeding US$200 per day, and usually require bookings in advance (most of the clients come from agents overseas). However, if you're in Malawi and fancy joining a trip, it's always worth giving them a ring to see what they've got going. Alternatively, there are some tour and travel agents in Lilongwe and Blantyre (see Travel Agents under Information in the Lilongwe and the Blantyre & Limbe chapters for details) who can assist you with this.

Most tour operating companies that cover the whole country are based in Lilongwe, and are listed below.

Central African Wilderness Safaris (☎ 771153, ☎/fax 771397, ☏ wildsaf@ eomw.net or info@wilderness.malawi.net) Based at ADL House, in City Centre, Lilongwe, this is Malawi's leading mid-range to top-end safari operator. It is also a travel and tour booking agent, dealing in hotels, flights, air charter, tours, car hire and so on. This company also runs Chintheche Inn on the lake shore and two more places in Liwonde National Park.

Kiboko Safaris (☎ 828384, ☎/fax 754978, ☏ kiboko@malawi.net) This is a specialist budget tours outfit, based at Kiboko Camp (see Lilongwe, Places to Stay). Three weeks all round Malawi costs from US$1200, but the four-day safari to South Luangwa (US$250) is most popular. Other budget tours to Nyika, Vwaza, Mulanje, Liwonde and to Lake Malawi for canoeing tours are also available, and detailed on the Web site: www.kiboko-safaris.com

Land & Lake Safaris (☎ 757120, fax 754560, ☏ landlake@malawi.net) This company has a desk at the Bohemian Cafe on Mandala Rd, just west of the post office in Old Town, Lilongwe, and offers budget and mid-range safaris to South Luangwa and various parts of Malawi. Land & Lake also arranges car hire, rents Land Rovers, sells hiking equipment and runs the forest resthouses at Dzalanyama and Zomba.

Makomo Safaris (☎/fax 754584, 754695, ☏ makomo@malawi.net) Offering mid-range tours and budget camping trips, this company's office is on Mandala Rd, Old Town, Lilongwe, in the same building as the Bohemian Cafe and Land & Lake Safaris. Management also runs a lodge in Liwonde National Park, south of Lake Malombe, and operates tours to northern Malawi and southern Tanzania.

Tours around Malawi are also organised by some of the agents listed under Travel Agencies in the Information sections of the Lilongwe and Blantyre & Limbe chapters, and these are also worth checking.

Other, more specialist operators covering smaller areas, are listed in the relevant sections throughout the book.

Lilongwe

pop 450,000

Lilongwe is the political capital of Malawi, while Blantyre is the commercial capital. Originally a small village on the banks of the Lilongwe River, it became a British colonial administrative centre at the beginning of the 20th century, after its chief requested protection from war-like neighbours. Lilongwe grew into a settler town, and its location on the junction of the country's main north-south route and the road to Northern Rhodesia (later Zambia) meant that by the 1960s it was the second-largest urban area in Malawi.

In 1968 plans were announced to move the country's administration from Blantyre to the more central Lilongwe. The construction of the pleasantly landscaped but very sprawling new city, including wide boulevards and grand ministerial buildings, was largely funded by South Africa (for more details see History in the Facts about Malawi chapter), and the new capital was officially declared in 1975. Despite this, the parliament and several ministry buildings remained in the town of Zomba, which had been the political capital since British colonial times. In 1998 the parliament was moved from Zomba to Lilongwe, where it now occupies a modern grandiose palace originally built for former president Hastings Banda.

Orientation

Lilongwe has two centres. City Centre (which is also called New City or Capital City) has ministries, embassies, some smart hotels, a shopping centre, airline offices, travel agents and several restaurants and cafes. Old Town has a good range of places to stay (including cheapies and camping), the bus station, the main market, some more tour and travel companies, and a large number of shops. More importantly, City Centre is a surprisingly quiet and rather sterile place, whereas Old Town is more lively. The two centres are 3km apart and minibuses run between them.

Highlights

Lilongwe p128

Lilongwe Area 4 p135

- Wandering through the lively and colourful City Market, where everything is sold, from auto parts to dried locusts
- Exploring the Lilongwe Nature Sanctuary with its pleasant walking trails, surprisingly varied birdlife and nice open-air cafe
- Visiting the Tobacco Auction Floors – the vibrant heart of Malawi's major export industry
- Cycling, hiking or bird-watching in Dzalanyama & Dedza Forest Reserves, within easy reach of Lilongwe

City Centre The heart of City Centre (if this place can be said to have a heart) is Capital City Shopping Centre, a collection of office buildings and mini-malls around a circular car park reached from Independence Drive. There are several shops and travel agents, gift shops, some cafes and restaurants, a bank, a post office and the US Information Service. Nearby is a large supermarket called the PTC Hypermarket, the British Council Library and many embassies. Farther out are several ministries, more offices, a couple of smart hotels and the posh suburbs.

Old Town The heart of Old Town is the market on Malangalanga Rd. Just south of the market is the main Stagecoach bus station. Just to the north of the market is a narrow road lined with bars and cheap hotels. This road seems to have no official name but is called Devil St by most locals. Malangalanga Rd meets Glyn Jones Rd, the main road to/from Blantyre, lined with cheaper shops selling clothes, material, hardware and so on, running down to the bridge over the Lilongwe River. This part of Old Town used to be called the Asian Quarter; now the streets south of Glyn Jones Rd are called Area 1, and those to the north are called Area 2. On the other side of the bridge is a roundabout. This is Area 3. If you go right at the roundabout, you're on Kamuzu Procession Rd. This is the smart part of Old Town, with more expensive shops, restaurants, cafes and supermarkets, a shopping mall called the Nico Centre, the Lilongwe Hotel, banks, travel agents and so on.

Maps Street maps of Lilongwe, on a folded sheet that also shows maps of Blantyre, Limbe and Zomba, might be available at the Tourist Office in Old Town. They're supposed to be free, but a small charge might be made. You can also get government survey maps of Lilongwe, the surrounding area, and most other parts of Malawi at the Department of Surveys Public Map Office, about 500m south of the roundabout where Glyn Jones Rd meets Kamuzu Procession Rd. For more details on what might be available see the Maps section in the Facts for the Visitor chapter.

Information
Tourist Offices The Tourist Office is at the Department of Wildlife & Tourism (☎ 723566, 723676; PO Box 30131) on Murray Rd in Old Town. In the same building is the National Parks Information Office. (For more details about parks and reserves see the National Parks & Wildlife Reserves section in the Facts about Malawi chapter.)

The people in the tourist office and the park office are friendly but actual information is very limited. For details on tours, flights and hotels you're better off at a travel agent; several are listed under Travel Agencies in this chapter. If you need information about forest reserves (some of which have tourist resthouses), the Department of Forestry national office (☎ 781000) is in City Centre, opposite the Golden Dragon restaurant. For information on forest resthouses in the area around Lilongwe, go to the Department of Forestry regional office, which is off Chilambula Road in Old Town.

Money For exchanging money in Lilongwe there are branches of the National Bank of Malawi and the Commercial Bank of Malawi both on Kamuzu Procession Rd in Old Town. In the same area, in the Nico Centre, and on nearby Mandala Rd, are several exchange bureaus, generally offering better rates and quicker service. If you've got time, it takes about 10 minutes to shop around a selection of banks and bureaus in this area, and this might be worth doing as rates and commissions can vary considerably. Beware of moneychangers at the Golf Club gate and some other places – see the boxed text 'Scams and Con Tricks' in the Facts for the Visitor chapter.

Post Lilongwe has two main post offices: in Old Town at the junction of Mandala Rd and Kamuzu Procession Rd, and at Capital City Shopping Centre in City Centre. For details of postal rates etc, see Post & Communications in the Facts for the Visitor chapter. For details of opening hours see Business Hours in the Facts for the Visitor chapter.

If you're receiving post restante mail addressed to GPO Lilongwe, most letters or parcels go to Old Town, but some mysteriously land at City Centre, so the only way to avoid this is to have your letters addressed specifically to 'GPO, Old Town' or GPO, City Centre'.

If you're using American Express (AmEx) client's mail, the office is at Manica Travel, ADL House, City Centre.

LILONGWE

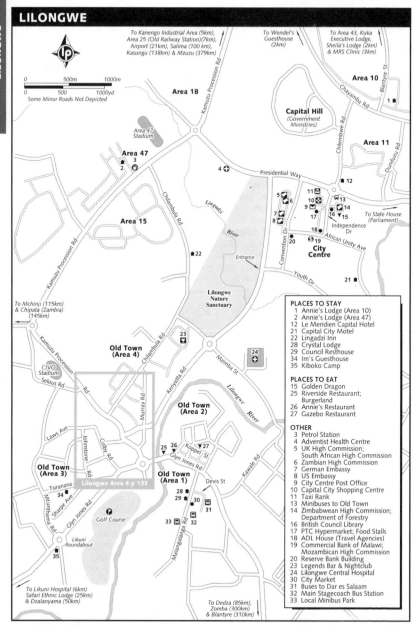

LILONGWE

0   500m   1000m

0   500   1000yd
Some Minor Roads Not Depicted

To Kanengo Industrial Area (5km),
Area 25 (Old Railway Station)(7km),
Airport (21km), Salima (100 km),
Kasungu (138km) & Mzuzu (379km)

To Wendel's
Guesthouse
(2km)

To Area 43, Kuka
Executive Lodge,
Sheila's Lodge (2km)
& MRS Clinic (3km)

Area 18

Area 10

Capital Hill
(Government
Ministries)

Area 11

Area 47
Stadium

Area 47

Presidential Way

To State House
(Parliament)

Area 15

Independence
Dr

City
Centre

Entrance

Lilongwe
Nature
Sanctuary

To Mchinji (115km)
& Chipata (Zambia)
(145km)

Old Town
(Area 4)

CIVO
Stadium

Selous Rd

Lilongwe Area 4 p 135

Old Town
(Area 2)

Old Town
(Area 3)

Old Town
(Area 1)

Devis St

Golf Course

Likuni
Roundabout

To Likuni Hospital (6km),
Safari Ethnic Lodge (25km)
& Dzalanyama (50km)

To Dedza (85km),
Zomba (300km)
& Blantyre (310km)

PLACES TO STAY
1 Annie's Lodge (Area 10)
2 Annie's Lodge (Area 47)
12 Le Meridien Capital Hotel
21 Capital City Motel
22 Lingadzi Inn
28 Crystal Lodge
29 Council Resthouse
34 Im's Guesthouse
35 Kiboko Camp

PLACES TO EAT
15 Golden Dragon
25 Riverside Restaurant;
   Burgerland
26 Annie's Restaurant
27 Gazebo Restaurant

OTHER
3 Petrol Station
4 Adventist Health Centre
5 UK High Commission;
   South African High Commission
6 Zambian High Commission
7 German Embassy
8 US Embassy
9 City Centre Post Office
10 Capital City Shopping Centre
11 Taxi Rank
13 Minibuses to Old Town
14 Zimbabwean High Commission;
   Department of Forestry
16 British Council Library
17 PTC Hypermarket; Food Stalls
18 ADL House (Travel Agencies)
19 Commercial Bank of Malawi;
   Mozambican High Commission
20 Reserve Bank Building
23 Legends Bar & Nightclub
24 Lilongwe Central Hospital
30 City Market
31 Buses to Dar es Salaam
32 Main Stagecoach Bus Station
33 Local Minibus Park

Telephone For phone calls and faxes, Lilongwe's only public office is in Capital City Shopping Centre, in the depths of Centre House Arcade. Calls cost US$9 for three minutes anywhere outside Africa, any time. You can also make international calls from any large hotel, but rates are more expensive; for details see the Post & Communications section in the Facts for the Visitor chapter.

Email & Internet Access Lilongwe's only full-on Internet bureau is Epsilon & Omega (☎ 773059) at ADL House, City Centre, where computers are available Monday to Thursday 9 am to 11.30 am, 1.30 pm to 4.30 pm, plus all day Friday and Saturday morning. Internet access is US$3 for the first 10 minutes, then US$0.20 per minute. For email (sending only) 15 minutes costs US$2. In City Centre you can also get Internet access at the British Council Library at US$1 for 15 minutes (but there's only one terminal and a long queue), and at the Business Centre in the Capital Hotel for US$10 for 20 minutes.

In Old Town, Kiboko Camp (see Places to Stay later in this chapter) offers Internet access for guests and non-guests from around US$1 for five minutes. Some travel and tour agents in Old Town also plan to offer Internet access soon, so check there too.

Travel Agencies In Old Town, travel agents selling flights include Midland Travel (☎ 756189, 753690) and Rainbow Travel (☎ 751556, 755760), both on Kamuzu Procession Rd. Ulendo Safaris (☎ 754926, 754950, fax 754717, @ info@ulendomalawi.net) is a switched-on company which sells air tickets and a range of tours and safaris, and often has special flight and accommodation deals to South Luangwa National Park (Zambia). It is also the agent for the *Ilala* ferry on Lake Malawi. The office is in The Old Town Mall, a new shopping centre off Chilambula Rd.

In Capital City Shopping Centre the main agencies selling flights include Air Tour & Travel (☎ 771053, 771362) and Soche Tours & Travel (☎ 772377, fax 771409) – the latter can also make hotel

reservations and assist with tours. Also in Capital City, in ADL House, are Manica Travel (☎ 773309), which sells flights, and Central African Wilderness Safaris (☎ 781393, 781153, fax 781397, @ wildsaf@eomw.net or info@wilderness.malawi.net), which is a very experienced travel and tour booking agent, dealing in hotels, flights, air charter, tours, car hire and so on, and also operating its own tours and safaris.

Some of the tour operators based in Lilongwe listed under Organised Tours in the Getting Around chapter also sell flights, arrange car hire and offer other tourism services, and are so also worth checking.

Bookshops In Old Town the TBS bookshop in the Nico Centre sells international and local newspapers and magazines, and a selection of paperback novels. The Maneno Bookshop on Mandala Rd has a better range. The Central Bookshop in Capital City Shopping Centre also sells magazines and paperbacks, plus a surprisingly good stock of African literature, local guidebooks and other books on Malawian subjects.

Libraries & Cultural Centres The main National Library is near the Zimbabwe Embassy just off Independence Drive in City Centre, open Monday to Friday from 8 am to 5 pm (Saturday to 3 pm). Nearby is the British Council Library (open 8.30 am to 4.30 pm Tuesday to Friday, plus Monday afternoons and Saturday morning). The US Information Service (USIS) library is in the Old Mutual building in Capital City Shopping Centre (open 8.30 am to 4.30 pm Monday to Friday, closed Wednesday afternoon). Both the British Council and the USIS allow non-members to read books and magazines in the library but not to take away. The USIS shows the previous day's CBS evening news at lunchtimes. Both places also show films on some afternoons and evenings. Check their noticeboards for details.

Medical Services If you have an embassy in Lilongwe and have time to contact it first, get advice there on recommended doctors and dentists who are used to dealing with tourists. If this is not possible, some suggested places are listed here.

For malaria blood tests, Medicare (☎ 742390) next to the Mobil station on Mandala Rd in Old Town charges US$2.50. On the same street, next to the Bohemian Cafe, Dr Tayoub is recommended for private consultations. The Adventist Health Centre (☎ 731049, 731819) in City Centre is also good for consultations, plus eye and dental problems. Another dentist is Dr Mazloum (☎ 780853) in ADL House, City Centre.

If things are serious, you might need hospitalisation. At Lilongwe Central Hospital off Mzimba St (☎ 753555, 756900) conditions and facilities are not good, but an 'expat bed' (a private ward) costs about US$50 per night. A better option if you have, for example, a bad dose of malaria or severe gastroenteritis is Likuni Mission Hospital (☎ 766574, 766140), 7km southwest of Old Town, with public wards, private rooms, and some expatriate European doctors on the staff. Fees for those who can afford it (you subsidise those who can't) start at US$100 per day. You can get there by minibus or taxi.

The best place for minor or major matters is the MRS Clinic (☎ 794967, 823590) off Ufulu Rd in Area 43. Fees are US$70 per consultation, US$110 after hours, US$100 for an overnight stay. MRS also has fully equipped ambulances with staff highly trained in emergency treatment. MRS will rescue you anywhere within 50km of Lilongwe, for US$160, but needs proof that you are insured or can pay. MRS is linked to Health International and MARS (Medical Air Rescue Service), which operate throughout the region and can arrange evacuation to Johannesburg if things get really serious.

For medicines and things like shampoo, tampons and condoms there are MPL pharmacies at the Nico Centre in Old Town and in Capital City Shopping Centre.

Emergency The emergency phone number for the police and ambulance service is ☎ 199 (in Lilongwe and Blantyre only). See the Emergencies section in the Facts for the Visitor chapter for more information.

Dangers & Annoyances We've had several reports from travellers who have had pockets picked or bags slashed as they pushed through the busy crowds on Malangalanga Rd in Old Town (Area 1) around the market and bus station, and a few unfortunate people have been violently robbed here. Be totally on your guard in this area. If you come into Lilongwe by bus during the day, and you're carrying a pack and feel a bit disorientated, leave Malangalanga Rd as quickly as possible. Once you leave Malangalanga Rd, things are OK and you can walk to Area 3 on the other side of the river. At night, however, Malangalanga Rd can be very dangerous and should be avoided, and even walking to Area 3 is not recommended. The bridge between Area 2 and Area 3 is a particularly favourite haunt for muggers. If you arrive on a bus after dark, take a minibus or taxi to the place you want to stay.

Another danger zone is the quiet stretch of Kenyatta Rd between Old Town and City Centre. Some travellers walking to the Lilongwe Nature Sanctuary have been mugged along here – in broad daylight! It's well worth taking a minibus or a taxi here as well.

But just to keep you on your toes, we've recently heard reports from travellers that a few fake taxis are operating in Lilongwe: The driver takes you via a quiet back street, and then stops and robs you at gunpoint. Note that official taxis have red on white number plates. If you're in any doubt, ask to see the driver's licence and ID.

Less worrying, but still annoying, is a con that travellers have reported being played in Lilongwe. Some local youths around town pose as bus ticket sellers; they promise a charter minibus service to Blantyre or Cape Maclear, farther south, and even issue phoney receipts. But when you go to the bus station the next day, of course no such bus exists. Some guys even promise that the bus will come to pick you up from your hotel – it never comes. You should not buy tickets anywhere except at the bus station itself.

Things to See & Do

Despite rumours to the contrary Lilongwe has enough to keep you occupied for a couple of days. The main **market** (see Shopping later in this chapter) is fun and frenetic, but for a total change of pace head for the

Lilongwe Nature Sanctuary – an incredibly peaceful area alongside the Lingadzi River just off Kenyatta Road. It covers over 150 hectares of indigenous woodland wilderness that escaped development when the capital city was moved to Lilongwe in

Tobacco

Tobacco is Malawi's most important cash crop, accounting for more than 70% of the country's export earnings, and Lilongwe is the main selling, buying and processing centre of this vital industry. Most activity takes place in Kanengo industrial area on the north side of Lilongwe, the site of several tobacco processing factories, and the huge and impressive tobacco auction rooms.

Tobacco was first grown in Malawi by a settler called John Buchanan, who planted the crop on his farm near Blantyre in the 1880s. Large-scale tobacco farming started in the area around Lilongwe in the 1920s and has grown steadily in importance ever since. Two types of tobacco are produced in Malawi: 'flue', which is a standard quality leaf; and 'burley', which is a higher quality leaf and much in demand from cigarette manufacturers around the world. Malawi is the world's largest producer of burley. The rainy season of 1999/2000 was erratic and bad for most crops, but good for tobacco. Production estimates for the 2000 harvest were put at around 140,000 tonnes.

Tobacco is grown on large plantations, or by individual farmers on small farms. The leaves are harvested and dried, either naturally in the sun or in a heated drying room, and then brought to Lilongwe for sale (in southern Malawi the crops go to auction in Limbe). In the auction room (called auction 'floors'), auctioneers sell tobacco on behalf of the growers. It is purchased by dealers who resell to the tobacco processors.

The tobacco comes onto the auction floors (the size of several large aircraft hangars) in large bales weighing between 80kg and 100kg, and is displayed in long lines. Moisture content determines the value of the leaves: if it's too dry the flavour is impaired; if it's too wet mould will set in and the bale is worthless.

Dealers have inspected the tobacco leaves in advance, employing a skilled eye, nose and 'feel'. They then move down the line in a small group with an auctioneer, pausing briefly at each bale to put in their bids, which are recorded by the auctioneer in a rapid-fire language completely unintelligible to outsiders. It takes an average of just six seconds to sell a bale, and the auctioneer and buyers hardly miss a step as they move swiftly down the line.

As soon as the dealers reach the end of the line, they move straight onto the next (there may be as many as 100 lines, each containing 100 bales) and the sale continues. Barrow boys whisk the sold tobacco off the floor, and within an hour a new line of bales is in place ready for the next group of auctioneers and dealers. The sold tobacco is taken to one of the nearby processing plants; some goes by truck, but a few processors are so close to the auction floors it simply goes on a conveyor belt.

A small proportion of tobacco gets made into cigarettes for the local market, but more than 90% gets processed in Malawi (the leaves are stripped of their 'core' and shredded into small pieces) before being exported for cigarettes abroad. Most processed tobacco goes by road to Durban in South Africa, to be shipped around the world, but an increasingly large amount goes by rail to the port of Nacala in Mozambique, and is shipped out from there.

The price for good quality tobacco is around US$2 per kg. Every day during the six-month harvesting and selling season, the auctions shift somewhere between 13,000 and 15,000 bales of tobacco. This raises a *daily* turnover of around US$2 million, and explains the rather sardonic sign on the wall of the main auction hall. It says 'Thank you for smoking'.

1972, with a signposted network of walking trails and an information centre that lists the birds and animals that may be seen. Mammals include duikers, vervet monkeys, porcupines and bushpigs, and the river contains crocodiles. Birds are surprisingly varied for such a small area, and many birdwatchers rate the sanctuary highly. Less pleasing are the caged hyaenas and leopards, but despite this the sanctuary is well worth a visit. It is open 8.30 am to 4 pm weekdays and Saturday mornings. The open-air cafe by the entrance is a good place to relax after your stroll.

Railway buffs may want to chug out to the **train station** (built in 1979, closed in 1992), where two Glasgow-made steam locomotives stand forgotten in a patch of rapidly growing grass and trees. Today the station buildings are used as a school. To get here by car or taxi, take the main road north (the continuation of Kamuzu Procession Rd towards the airport and Kasungu) until it crosses over the railway line on a bridge (about 5km from the Presidential Way roundabout). Turn at the next street on the left, towards Area 25, and continue for 3km. Then turn left again and travel for 500m to reach the station. By public transport it is quite straightforward – minibuses run from the market to Area 25, passing within 1km of the station.

For a view of Malawi's economic heart, go to the public gallery overlooking the **tobacco auction floors** at the vast Auction Holdings warehouse about 7km north of the city centre, in the Kanengo industrial area east of the main road (the M1) towards Kasungu and Mzuzu. It's best reached by taxi, although local minibuses serve the industrial area. Alternatively, you can arrange visits with a car and driver/guide through Ulendo Safaris and some of the other companies listed under Travel Agencies earlier and under Organised Tours in the Getting Around chapter. The auction season is May to October. See the boxed text 'Tobacco' for more on this vital commodity.

If you'd prefer a political view, Ulendo Safaris can also arrange visits to the **Parliament Building**, which moved from

Zomba in 1998 to the palace of former president Banda on the outskirts of Lilongwe. At least this obscenely grandiose monstrosity is being used now – during Banda's rule he only stayed one night here.

If you're the sporting type, **Lilongwe Golf Club** offers daily membership for US$7. This allows you to enter the club building, and use the bar or restaurant. To use the sports facilities there's a small extra charge: to swim in the pool, or play squash or tennis, is about US$1; 18 holes of golf with hired clubs costs US$7.

Places to Stay – Budget

All the budget places to stay in Lilongwe are in Old Town, and in easy reach of shops, the post office and most other facilities.

Camping A long-standing option for campers is *Lilongwe Golf Club*, which is comparatively expensive at US$8 per person, but for this price you get a clean, quiet site with hot showers and day membership of the club, so you can use the bar, restaurant, swimming pool and some of the sporting facilities. Camping is also possible at Kiboko Camp, listed under Backpackers in this section.

It might also be worth asking about *Safari Ethnic Lodge*, 25km west of Lilongwe, on the road towards Dzalanyama. This was closed at the time of research, but might reopen in 2001. You can get information from Safari Beach Lodge (see Places to Eat under Senga Bay in the Central Malawi chapter).

Resthouses If you're using public transport and you're short of cash, you could consider the *Council Resthouse* near the bus station. However, it's hard to find with its entrance behind a row of shops, and theft of gear from empty rooms, even when they're locked, seems to be a problem here. Basic double rooms in the old wing are US$2.50, and better ones in the new wing are US$4 (US$5.50 with bathroom). Three or four people can share a double for no extra charge. There's also a bar and restaurant.

Slightly nearer town on Devil St, next to the market, are several local resthouses, mostly a bit on the dingy side and doubling as brothels, so not at all for the fainthearted, and really only worth considering if you determinedly seek out local flavour or all the other budget places are full.

A better cheapie to consider is **Annie's Restaurant** (listed under Places to Eat), on Glyn Jones Rd in Area 2, which has a small dorm out the back with beds for US$3 per person, and camping for US$1.50, but this is another place where you should keep an eye on your gear. Even if you don't stay here, it's near the bus station and the route into town, and a safe place to sit down with a drink to get your bearings after getting off the bus.

Further west along Glyn Jones Rd is **St Peter's Guesthouse**. It's quiet and clean, charging US$4 a bed in doubles or triples, and US$7 for a private double, plus breakfast for US$1, but nearly always full. If you do get in here, remember it's a church place and behave accordingly.

Backpackers By far the most popular place for backpackers and overland drivers is the friendly **Kiboko Camp** (☎ 828384, ☎/fax 754978, @ kiboko@malawi.net), where camping costs US$2.50 per person, a bed in the dorm US$4, and a double room US$10. There's a good bar that closes at 10.30 pm and a restaurant serving lunch and evening meals. The people who run this place know Malawi well and can advise on buses, taxis, scams etc. They also offer Internet access. To get here from the bus station, take any minibus heading for Likuni, and get off at Likuni roundabout (the fare is US$0.25). Alternatively, a taxi (highly recommended at night) costs from US$4 to US$5.

Hotels Top of the range in the budget bracket is the **Golden Peacock Hotel** (☎ 756632), still known affectionately as the Golden Cockroach, but these days it's fairly clean, safe and good value, with standard doubles/triples for US$10/12, and doubles with bathroom for US$15. It's on the corner of Johnstone Rd and Lister Ave, in Area 3. Next door is the Korea Garden Restaurant, which is well signposted.

In the same part of town there are two other choices. The constantly expanding **Ivy Guesthouse** (☎ 753467) charges from US$15 for single and double rooms, and US$25 for triples, all with bathroom. Breakfast is an extra US$3. The small and basic **Im's Guesthouse** has just three rooms, each with bathroom, and costs US$5 per person. No meals are available, but there is a kitchen that guests can use.

Places to Stay – Mid-Range

All rooms at the hotels in this category have private bathroom, although some of the smaller lodges and guesthouses also offer rooms with shared facilities at cheaper rates. Breakfast is included in the price, unless otherwise stated.

The best place to stay in Old Town is the **Imperial Hotel** (☎ 753192, @ imperial@ malawi.net) on Mandala Rd, with friendly management and cool and airy single/ double rooms from US$48/78. The bar has a nice veranda, is a justifiably popular meeting place for visitors and well-off residents, and serves snacks from US$2. The restaurant has meals from around US$5.

On the southern edge of City Centre, the **Lingadzi Inn** (☎ 754143/31, fax 754129), on Chilambula Rd, is clean and friendly but uninspiring and a little frayed around the edges, with a nice large garden, an incredibly small restaurant, and rooms for US$72/94. Be ready for changes though, as this place has been taken over by a new management company and due for refurbishment in 2001.

Most other mid-range places to stay are converted villas in the suburbs. The cheapest is **Annie's Lodge (Area 47)** (☎ 762163), just off Kamuzu Procession Rd, where double rooms are US$30, and some smaller rooms with shared bathroom are US$23. The eponymous proprietor also has **Annie's Lodge (Area 10)** (☎ 795257), just off Blantyre St, a quiet place with restaurant, garden and pool, and double rooms for US$48 (US$40 with shared bathroom).

Kuka Executive Lodge (☎ 794763), off Blantyre St in Area 43, isn't quite as fancy as its name would suggest, but perfectly acceptable. There are just four rooms – singles/doubles with shared bathroom are US$60/65, and a double with private bathroom is US$85. Nearby is **Sheila's Lodge** (☎ 794010), also small, and low-key with a pleasant garden and rooms for US$72/87. Meals in the restaurant are US$4 to US$5.

Places to Stay – Top End

All rooms at the hotels in this category have private bathroom, and breakfast is included.

In Old Town, the **Lilongwe Hotel** (☎ 740488, fax 740505, central reservations ☎ 620588) on Kamuzu Procession Rd, is a low-rise building set around pleasant gardens, but is poor value with singles/doubles from US$175/210. Facilities include a travel desk, business centre, swimming pool, restaurant and bar (see Entertainment later in this section). Be ready for changes though, as this is one of several hotels in Malawi taken over by Le Meridien and due for refurbishment in 2001.

In City Centre, **Le Meridien Capital Hotel** (☎ 783388, fax 781273, central reservations ☎ 620588) is the smartest place to stay in Lilongwe – a full international-class hotel with all facilities, used mainly by top-end tourists, business travellers and diplomats, with rooms from around US$150/190. Facilities include a gift shop, bookshop, pharmacy, business centre, swimming pool, car hire and travel desks.

Places to Eat

Street Food In Old Town, around the market, and in the back streets off Kamuzu Procession Rd in Area 3, are **food stalls** selling deep fried cassava or potato chips and roasted meat, at very cheap prices. The Peace Corps' favourite **Chip Man** is on the street that runs behind the Nico Centre; he has clean plates, benches to sit on and also sells cold drinks.

In City Centre, **food stalls** around the PTC Hypermarket serve cheap eats at lunchtimes to local office workers. A plate of meat, vegetables and rice costs US$1.

Cafes & Fast Food For cheap sit-down food, a perennial favourite eatery is **Annie's**

Restaurant, in Area 2 of Old Town, where filling meals, such as chicken and chips or curry and rice are less than US$2. Coffee is US$0.50, and cold drinks are also available.

Near Annie's is the grandly named Riverside Shopping Mall, which contains **Burgerland**, doing burgers and snacks from around US$1, to eat in or take away, and the clean and tidy **Riverside Restaurant**, which also has an upstairs open-air terrace, providing snacks from US$1.20 and main meals with a Korean flavour from about US$4.

Also in this area is the clean, no frills **Gazebo Restaurant**, on Koppel St with good curries for around US$3, snacks from US$1 to US$2 and ice cream (but no alcohol).

In Area 3 on Kamuzu Procession Rd **Ali Baba's Snack Bar** is open every day until 10pm, serving pizzas from US$2.50, kebabs and burgers around US$1.50, Lebanese snacks, ice cream and coffee. Behind here is **The Summer Park**, a pleasant garden area, where ice creams are US$0.60, snacks from US$1 and full meals US$3. The nearby **Byee! Takeaway** does cheap local meals for around US$1, and has shady outdoor seating (admittedly in a car park).

On Mandala Rd, the popular European-style **Bohemian Cafe** (open 8 am to 4 pm Tuesday to Friday, plus Saturday morning) serves breakfasts, snacks and salads for US$1, big sandwiches for US$2, and other meals around US$3, plus good coffee and cakes. There are tables and chairs on the terrace outside or comfy sofas inside. This is also the base for Land & Lake Safaris (see Organised Tours in the Getting Around chapter). You can peruse brochures or camping kit while you're eating.

In Capital City Shopping Centre, facing the main car park near the post office, **Tasty Takeaway** has seats outside and is good for lunch, with local-style *nsima* (cooked maize flour) and sauce meals from US$1, burgers US$1.50, curries US$2, and chicken US$2.50. At the back of the same block is **Desiderata Restaurant** where the waiters go placidly but the food is OK, with local dishes for just over US$1, and other meals like fish or chicken and chips for US$2.

Also in Capital City Shopping Centre, above the Central Bookshop, *The Wild Side Cafe* caters for more well-to-do customers (as does the attached gift shop), but with an excellent selection of homemade sticky cakes and toasted sandwiches (all $1.50), plus good tea and coffee.

Restaurants In Old Town, *Don Brioni's Bistro* (☎ 826756), under the Imperial Hotel, is open every night and always has a good lively atmosphere, with 'mine host' (whose name is Brian) always paying great attention to his diners. Pizzas and pastas start at US$4, and Zimbabwean T-bone steaks at US$8. Groups can negotiate a special all-you-can-eat pasta, sauce and salad deal for US$10 per person.

Huts (☎ 752912), near the Lilongwe Hotel, has good Indian food and swift service, with three course meals working out around US$10 per person. Almost opposite is *Modi's* (☎ 751489), which also does curries, plus steaks, chicken and fish dishes. Locals report that quality here is varied; meals are always acceptable, and sometimes marvellous, with prices about the same as Huts.

The *Korea Garden*, next to the Golden Peacock Hotel on Johnstone Rd, has a slightly rustic outdoor setting with main courses from US$5 and a set menu of specialities for US$12.

In City Centre, the *Golden Dragon* (☎ 770414) serves large helpings of straightforward Chinese food; main dishes are US$2 to US$3, noodles US$1 to US$2, and specials US$7. Takeaways are the same price (but no tax). The *Restaurant Koreana* (☎ 771004) in Gemini House, Capital City Shopping Centre, has very good East Asian food, with main dishes from US$4 to US$7, and side orders US$1 to US$2 (closed Sundays). Nearby is the long-standing *Causerie* (☎ 773828) where steaks, fish and curries start at US$5, but quality is very varied.

Some restaurants are closed on Monday; phone first to check.

Hotel Restaurants Most of the middle and top-end hotels listed have restaurants open to nonresidents where standards and prices are on a par with the hotel. In Old Town, at the Imperial Hotel the *terrace restaurant* serves tasty kebabs and grills, from US$2 to US$5. The *Lilongwe Hotel* has an open-air terrace restaurant – a popular lunch spot and meeting place for business travellers and well-heeled tourists; light meals start at US$3.

In City Centre, at the Le Meridien Capital Hotel, the outside *Patio Restaurant* offers snacks from US$3 and meals for around US$6, while inside the *Greenery Restaurant* has starters for around US$3,

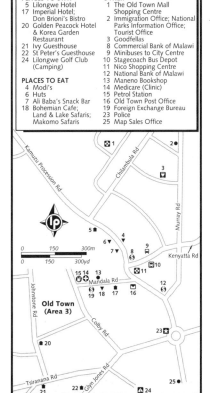

LILONGWE AREA 4

PLACES TO STAY
5 Lilongwe Hotel
17 Imperial Hotel;
   Don Brioni's Bistro
20 Golden Peacock Hotel
   & Korea Garden
   Restaurant
21 Ivy Guesthouse
22 St Peter's Guesthouse
24 Lilongwe Golf Club
   (Camping)

PLACES TO EAT
4 Modi's
6 Huts
7 Ali Baba's Snack Bar
18 Bohemian Cafe;
   Land & Lake Safaris;
   Makomo Safaris

OTHER
1 The Old Town Mall
   Shopping Centre
2 Immigration Office; National
   Parks Information Office;
   Tourist Office
3 Goodfellas
8 Commercial Bank of Malawi
9 Minibuses to City Centre
10 Stagecoach Bus Depot
11 Nico Shopping Centre
12 National Bank of Malawi
13 Maneno Bookshop
14 Medicare (Clinic)
15 Petrol Station
16 Old Town Post Office
19 Foreign Exchange Bureau
23 Police
25 Map Sales Office

and main courses from US$6 for vegetarian dishes, US$7 for steaks and up to US$20 for prawns.

Self-catering For information about Lilongwe's market and supermarkets see Shopping, later in this chapter.

Entertainment

Lilongwe's home-grown nightlife scene is not immediately obvious to outsiders, but if you dig beneath the surface a little there are some fine places to pass an hour or three in the evening.

Bars & Bottle Stores In Old Town, along the notorious Devil St, just off the equally notorious Malangalanga Rd, are several *bottle stores* and a couple of basic and disreputable *bars* that all play music loud and late. For the difference between a bar and a bottle store, see Drinks in the Facts for the Visitor chapter. Although this area has a very hard edge, and cannot be said to be completely safe, neither is it totally suicidal, and we've heard from a few brave travellers who have had good times with a local flavour here. They report most Malawians are friendly and happy to talk to strangers, especially (like anywhere else) after a few drinks. However, as an outsider, you should go to Devil St only with a streetwise friend, enough money for an evening's supply of beer and nothing else you can't afford to lose.

Also recommended for local flavour, but less daunting than Devil St, are the simple *bars and bottle stores* near the petrol station in Area 47, where most of the entertainment consists of talking, and sometimes listening, to other drinkers. To get here from Old Town or City Centre you'll ideally need a car. Otherwise you'll need to take a taxi.

At the *Lilongwe Hotel* (listed under Places to Stay), the *residents bar* is smart and open to non-guests, while the *nonresidents bar* is livelier, and the predominance of male business travellers and well-off locals attracts flocks of good time girls. There's a disco or live band on some evenings (cover charge US$2).

Harry's Bar at the Imperial Hotel is normally calm and relaxed, and very popular with expats (Friday evening happy hour can be busy). The music and the snacks are good, and you can watch the world go by from seats on the upstairs veranda.

Livelier is *Goodfellas Pub*, in the area between Chilambula and Kenyatta Rds, in Old Town, drawing mainly an expat crowd, with pool tables and draught beer, open from noon (lunches served) to 11 pm.

Nightclubs In Old Town, in the area between Chilambula and Kenyatta Rds, is *Legends*, a bar most evenings, and a nightclub at weekends, with a relaxed atmosphere and mixed crowd of young expats and well-to-do Malawians, and a fair blend of Western and African music.

For a more local feel, the *Zebra Disco* at the Lingadzi Inn near City Centre (see Places to Stay earlier in this chapter) plays mostly African music to a mostly Malawian clientele; it's open Friday and Saturday nights, with a cover charge of US$1.50.

Spectator Sports

Football matches are played at the CIVO Stadium, off Kamuzu Procession Rd, and at the stadium in Area 47. There is no set program – look out for posters, or ask local fans for information. To watch a local game costs around US$0.20. For international games you'll pay US$1 for a seat.

Shopping

Lilongwe's main market is the **City Market** on Malangalanga Rd, near the bus station in Old Town. It's worth a visit even if you don't want to buy anything. In the last few years this place has become considerably more crowded, mainly because at the 1996 election the United Democratic Front (UDF) promised vendors and stallholders freedom to trade (after they'd been hassled for years by members of the Malawi Congress Party's (MCP) Young Pioneers for not carrying party cards or not making political donations) and now any attempt to limit or control the number of traders is seen as a breach of that promise.

There's still just about enough room to walk between the stalls and it's always lively and colourful (although cameras are not appreciated here, especially in the metal-working section, which has a bit of a rough edge). But apart from dustbins and saucepans made from oil drums, you can tour the other parts of the market, where everything is sold – from car and bike parts, empty plastic containers, wood and charcoal to sugar, fruit, vegetables, toothpaste, batteries, dried fish and live chickens. Note also that pickpockets operate in the crowds, and some visitors with large bags have been violently robbed, so travel light here to avoid unwanted attention – another good reason not to bring your camera.

For a more peaceful shopping experience (although it depends on who's in charge of tapes in the muzak machine), the main supermarket is the PTC Hypermarket at a mall called the Nico Centre in Old Town. Opposite is a Kandodo supermarket where the stock is more limited but prices are a bit cheaper. The Nico Shopping Centre also has a bookshop, travel agent, pharmacy and several other shops.

For a range of imported food, and other imported goods like shampoo, disposable razors, tampons, batteries etc, Tutla's Supermarket on Mandala Rd and the 7-Eleven (which closes at 10pm) on Kamuzu Procession Rd, next to Ali Baba's Snack Bar, both have a good range, although they're more expensive than the PTC.

Capital City Shopping Centre, reached from Independence Drive, has shops, travel agents, restaurants, a bank and post office. Nearby is a large PTC Hypermarket, which has an in-store bakery and sells food and other goods, much of it imported from South Africa or Europe and sold at similar prices. You can buy CDs (US$28 to US$45) here.

If you're looking for souvenirs, there are several **craft stalls** outside the Old Town Post Office, where you can buy wooden carvings, basketware, jewellery, paintings, wire models and so on.

If you need film for your camera Central African Studio in Capital City Shopping Centre has a good stock of print film, and

Lilongwe's City Market is crowded and lively.

SARAH JOLLY

can take passport photos on the spot. Developing and printing is also available. In Old Town, Lee Photographic in the Nico Centre sells film, but a better place for developing and printing is Photo Plaza, next to Burgerland on Glyn Jones Rd in Area 2. See Photography & Video in the Facts for the Visitor chapter for an idea of prices.

Travellers with vehicles and large camping gas cylinders can get refills at the BOC depot in the Kanengo industrial area, about 5km north of the city centre, east of the main road towards the airport and Kasungu.

As we were researching this book, we heard that two new shopping centres are planned for Lilongwe. One of these is The Old Town Mall, just off Chilambula Rd, near the junction with Kamuzu Procession Rd, in Old Town, and will contain and will contain Ulendo Safaris, an Italian Restaurant, a furniture store, a large supermarket, some art, crafts, gift and jewellery shops, plus several other stores and food outlets. A new Shoprite supermarket is also planned.

Getting There & Away

Air Lilongwe international airport is on the north side of the city. See Getting Around in this chapter for details of travel to and from the airport. For details on domestic flights from Lilongwe to other cities in Malawi, and on international flights between Lilongwe and the rest of the world, see the Getting Around and Getting There & Away chapters. If you need to fly out of Lilongwe, the following airlines have offices in the city:

Air Malawi (☎ 753181, 750747) New Building Society House, Mandala Rd, Old Town, opposite the Imperial Hotel; (☎ 772132, 773680/10) Le Meridien Capital Hotel, City Centre

Air Tanzania (☎ 773636); Capital City Shopping Centre

KLM & Kenya Airways (☎ 771330); at Le Meridien Capital Hotel

South African Airways (☎ 772242); at Le Meridien Capital Hotel

If you're buying a ticket, it's also well worth trying an agent (see Travel Agencies under Information earlier in this chapter) as they offer a wider range of options, charge the same rate as the airlines, and sometimes have special deals.

Bus & Minibus The Stagecoach bus company runs a luxury express Coachline service four times per day between Lilongwe and Blantyre (US$18). The journey takes four hours. You can make reservations at Le Meridien Capital Hotel in City Centre or at the Stagecoach depot (☎ 753226, 756231), on Kenyatta Rd near the Nico Centre in Old Town, where you can also make general inquiries about long-distance buses. It is important to note that the Coachline service does *not* go to/from the main Stagecoach bus station near the City Market; it picks up and drops off passengers at Le Meridien Capital Hotel in City Centre or at the Stagecoach depot near the Nico Centre in Old Town.

Stagecoach also runs five Express buses each day between Lilongwe and Blantyre: two go direct via Zalewa (the junction with the Mwanza road), which takes five hours (US$5); and three go via Zomba (seven hours, US$6). Lilongwe to Zomba is US$4.50. Express buses go twice daily to Mzuzu (US$6) via Kasungu (US$2.50). All Express buses go to/from the Stagecoach bus station near the market in Old Town, which is also where you can buy advance tickets for this service.

All other buses are ordinary (ie, slow). Services from Lilongwe include hourly to Mchinji (US$1.50) and twice daily to Nkhotakota via Salima (US$3). Getting to Monkey Bay can be a nightmare – see Monkey Bay in the Central Malawi chapter for more information.

Minibuses to nearby destinations such as Salima, Mchinji and Dedza (fares for all destinations are around US$1.50) leave from the street outside the Stagecoach bus station on Kenyatta Rd.

Getting Around

Getting around Lilongwe can be tiresome, especially if you don't have your own transport, as the city is very spread out. It's also confusing for newcomers as a lot of the main avenues look the same. Most visitors, however, will probably stay in the compact Old Town where getting around is easy, only having to head for City Centre to buy a visa or search for long-lost letters at the poste restante.

To/From the Airport Lilongwe international airport is 24km north of the city centre. A taxi will cost about US$10 if you're going from the airport to town, but less the other way. The fare is negotiable, but drivers will expect a tip of 10%.

At the airport look out for the Air Tours & Travel shuttle minibus that will drop you by any of the main hotels in town for US$4. Going the other way, ask at any main hotel.

If you're short of cash, local buses and minibuses run from Old Town to the commercial part of the airport (about 200m from the passenger terminal) for just US$1, or you can get any minibus running along the main road (the M1) towards Kasungu, and get off at the airport junction, from where it's 3km to the airport.

Coming from the airport, if there's no bus and you don't want to pay for a taxi, you can try hitching (walk 500m to the last turnoff after the commercial area), or hoof it from the terminal to the main road (3km), where minibuses run to Lilongwe. See Hitching in the Facts for the Visitor chapter for more information.

LILONGWE

Minibus There are minibus routes all over Lilongwe, linking the centre with the outer suburbs. The most useful local minibus service for visitors is between Old Town and City Centre. Minibuses leave from the bus park opposite the market in Old Town, go southwards along Malangalanga Rd (which is a one-way street) then round the block, turning left and left again, to go west along Glyn Jones and Kamuzu Procession Rds, then turn right at the junction near the post office, into Kenyatta Rd. There's a bus stop at the western end of Kenyatta Rd (opposite the Nico Centre). Buses then go north up Kenyatta Rd, via Youth Dr and Convention Dr or via Independence Dr to reach City Centre. From City Centre back to Old Town, the bus stop for the return journey is at the north end of Independence Dr. Either way the fare is US$0.30.

Taxi The best place to find private hire taxis is at the main hotels. There's also a rank on Presidential Way, just north of Capital City Shopping Centre. Between Old Town and City Centre by private taxi is about US$5. From City Centre to any of the hotels in the suburbs costs about US$4; from Old Town it's US$6. For fares to/from the airport see the To/From the Airport section, earlier.

Around Lilongwe

DZALANYAMA

Dzalanyama is a beautiful forest reserve in a range of hills about 50km by road south-west of Lilongwe. The hills run in a roughly north-west to south-east line, and their watershed forms the border between Malawi and Mozambique. The highest point is a peak called Silamwezi (1713m). The hills are covered in miombo forest, and the region is protected because the rainwater collected here is the water supply for all of Lilongwe.

The name Dzalanyama means 'place of meat', from the plentiful supply of animals that used to live in the forest. Numbers have been hunted down to almost nothing over the years, although there are still small

antelopes, and even leopards and hyaenas, but these are rarely seen. There are, however, several good walks in the forest, which is particularly rich in birdlife. It might be interesting to walk up to the watershed; the views over Malawi and Mozambique are reported to be splendid, but you should ask locally about the presence of mines in the border area. Other walks in this area are covered in *Day Outings from Lilongwe* (see Local Guidebooks under Books in the Facts for the Visitor chapter).

Places to Stay

The delightful and recently renovated log-cabin-style *Dzalanyama Forest Lodge* (formerly Dzalanyama Resthouse) is run by Land & Lake Safaris (see Organised Tours in the Getting Around chapter), and should be booked in advance at their Lilongwe office. The lodge has three twin bedrooms and one double bedroom, sleeping a total of eight people, for US$12 per person if you're sharing or US$18 if you want a room to yourself. The bathrooms are shared, and lighting is by kerosene lamps. The kitchen is fully equipped for self catering – you just need to bring your food and drink. Land & Lake offers walking trails, mountain biking and bird-watching, but this is also an ideal spot for simply relaxing.

Getting There & Away

There's no public transport to Dzalanyama, but Land & Lake Safaris arranges lifts to the forest for US$22 per person, so check when you book accommodation. Alternatively you could hire a car, or (if you're feeling fit and adventurous) hire a mountain bike from Land & Lake's Lilongwe office and ride to the lodge.

By car or bike, to reach Dzalanyama from the centre of Lilongwe's Old Town take Glyn Jones Rd west past Likuni Roundabout by Kiboko Camp. From here continue south-west through the outer suburb of Likuni, past Lilongwe Dam (formerly Kamuzu Dam) to reach the forest gate (32km from Lilongwe), where you have to sign the book. There's no fee. From here it's about another 20km to 25km through the forest. There are a couple of junctions but the lodge is signposted. If the road feels rough or you get a bit pedal-weary, remember that local men cover the route on their heavy steel bicycles with huge piles of firewood on their backs.

DEDZA

Dedza is a small town 85km south of Lilongwe, on the border with Mozambique, just off the main road (the M1) between Lilongwe and Blantyre. The many trees give the town a foresty feel, and there are some good walks and spectacular views in the nearby Dedza Mountain Forest Reserve.

Hiking

You can walk to the summit of Dedza Mountain (2198m) in two to three hours. The path starts near the golf club and heads towards a large communications aerial. Beyond here there's a maze of paths, but a reasonable sense of direction will take you to the top. The vegetation is mostly pine plantation but there are patches of indigenous forest on the higher slopes. More walks are described in *Day Outings from Lilongwe* mentioned under Local Guidebooks in the Facts for the Visitor section.

Places to Stay & Eat

You can camp at the dreary *Golf Club* for an outlandish US$10 per tent. This place also seems to be a resthouse but the rooms are most unappealing. You're much better off at one of the cheapie resthouses on the main street. The *Rainbow Resthouse & Restaurant* is clean and friendly with doubles for US$2.50, with bathroom. Also on the main street are some local *restaurants* and *bars*, and a supermarket.

On the northern outskirts is Dedza Pottery, with ceramic products aimed squarely at the expat and tourist market, and a pleasant *coffee shop*; try the fresh scones and jam for US$1.50.

Getting There & Away

All buses between Lilongwe and Blantyre or Zomba stop on the main road, from where you have to walk about 2km into Dedza town. The Express bus fare to Dedza from Lilongwe is US$2; from Blantyre it's US$5.

NTCHISI FOREST RESERVE

This small and rarely visited forest reserve is about 80km north of Lilongwe, near the large village of Ntchisi ('nchee-see'). At the centre of the reserve is Ntchisi Mountain, which offers splendid views of the surrounding area. The vegetation on the higher slopes is mainly evergreen forest – reckoned to be one of the best examples in the country – with large buttressed trees. The lower slopes consist of miombo forest. Birdlife is varied, and mammals that occur here include blue monkeys, baboons, bushpigs and duikers. Elephants were once recorded, and a few are thought to have escaped the rise in poaching during the 1980s and '90s, but these are very unlikely to be seen.

The place to aim for is the resthouse (see Places to Stay and Eat), which was originally built as a 'hill station' for the colonial district commissioner who came here to escape the heat of his normal base in Nkhotakota. There are truly excellent views from the resthouse to the east, across Lake Malawi (sometimes as far as Likoma Island and Cape Maclear).

From the resthouse, you can walk to the summit of Ntchisi Mountain by following a track and various paths through the forest. From the resthouse the peak is about 4km, so allow about three hours for a return walk, more if you enjoy bird-watching.

Places to Stay & Eat

Ntchisi Forest Reserve Resthouse used to be run by the Department of Forestry, but it has now been privatised. There are four bedrooms, a lounge and a kitchen, staffed by a helpful cook who will prepare any food you bring. To stay costs US$15 per person. If you want meals provided, dinner, bed and breakfast costs US$30, but this must be arranged in advance. You can make bookings or get information from Makomo Safaris, listed under Organised Tours in the Getting Around chapter.

Getting There & Away

The main settlement of any size is Ntchisi village, on the dirt road between Lilongwe and Nkhotakota (which also passes through Nkhotakota Wildlife Reserve). To get here from Lilongwe, aim north on the main road towards Kasungu, and turn right (east) towards the village of Dowa, then left (north) at a junction to Ntchisi village. About 18km north of this junction (12km south of Ntchisi village), a dirt road turns right (east) to the forest reserve; there is a signpost. It's another 16km along here, through a village called Chindembwe, to the reserve entrance and resthouse. There is public transport between Lilongwe and Nkhotakota (via Ntchisi village and the turn-off to the forest reserve junction), but none to the resthouse itself, so a trip here is only really possible for keen hikers or those with wheels.

Northern Malawi

Malawi's Northern Province, with the provincial capital Mzuzu roughly at its centre, runs from the northern tip of the country down to the Viphya Plateau. This chapter covers most parts of the Northern Province, and includes coverage of Nkhata Bay and many other villages and beaches on the lake shore, plus highlights such as Nyika National Park, Vwaza Marsh Wildlife Reserve and Likoma Island. The Viphya Plateau is covered in the Central Malawi chapter. For details see the boxed text 'Lake Malawi' at the end of this chapter. Places are described roughly north to south.

KARONGA

Karonga is the first or last town you reach if you're travelling on the road between Mzuzu and Malawi's border with Tanzania at Songwe (for more information see the Getting There & Away chapter). Facilities in Karonga include the only bank north of Mzuzu (although it doesn't accept Tanzanian shillings).

The town is spread out for about 2km along the main street between a roundabout on the main north-south road and the lake shore. Near the roundabout, the *Mukumbukeghe Resthouse* has double rooms for US$3. Next door, the *Fukafuka Resthouse* is cheaper. Down by the lake, *Mufwa Lakeside Centre* has clean rooms for US$2.50 per person, shady camping for US$1, and a bar with cold beer – well worth the long, hot walk from the roundabout. The nearby *Club Marina* has chalets with bathrooms for US$10 per person. Both places can advise on places to change money (including Tanzanian shillings).

CHITIPA

You'll pass through this frontier town if you're travelling between the extreme north of Malawi and Zambia. If you need a place to stay, there's a couple of local *resthouses*. Due to the lack of transport,

Highlights

- Exploring the Nyika Plateau's unique montane grassland, beautiful wildflowers and skyline-posing zebras

- Wandering around Livingstonia, a missionary centre with a time-warp atmosphere

- Hiking the marvellous Livingstonia Trail from Nyika to Livingstonia and Lake Malawi

- Checking out Vwaza Marsh's frequently overlooked but good wildlife viewing

- Discovering Nkhata Bay, an up-and-coming travellers haunt with a local feel and a fine selection of restaurants

- Escaping to Likoma & Chizumulu Islands with their remote atmosphere and good beaches

- Relaxing on the Chintheche Strip's 40km of beautiful beaches

few people travel this way, but a new road may be built in the future – see the boxed text 'Grand Plans for the Karonga to Chitipa Road' in the Getting There & Away chapter.

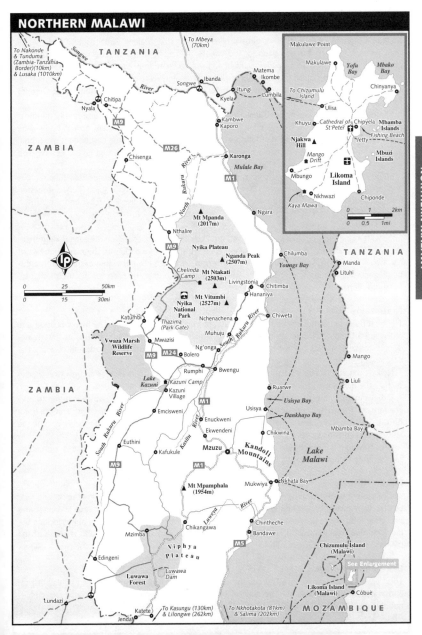

NORTHERN MALAWI

NORTHERN MALAWI

Birds of Malawi

Malawi is a popular destination for bird-watchers. For its size, Malawi contains more bird species than most African countries, reflecting the variety of natural habitats, ranging from mountain plateaus to lake shores. Some 645 species have been recorded in Malawi, and about 530 species probably breed here. Those that don't breed here are mainly long-distance migrants from Europe or Asia (mostly present in Malawi either just before or during the rainy season from about October to April).

Some of Malawi's breeding birds leave the region during the dry season, so probably the most productive time of year for bird-watching is November and December, but any time is likely to be very rewarding. There are many good places for bird-watching, some of the best being the national parks of Liwonde, Kasungu, Lengwe and the Nyika Plateau, and Dzalanyama Forest Reserve and Lilongwe Nature Sanctuary.

Some indication of the bird-watching opportunities in Malawi can be gleaned from the number and beauty of birds that you may well see in the gardens of the towns and cities. The lilac-breasted roller, little bee-eater, green loerie, a number of sunbirds, the paradise flycatcher and the African hoopoe are just a few of the parade of birds that you may see in the gardens of Le Meridien Capital Hotel for instance.

As with anywhere, the species of birds you are likely to see will depend on the surrounding habitat. Main vegetation zones are listed above. Below are some more details on the major habitats of Malawi, with a brief overview of the great variety of birds to be found within each. For more detail, a good field guide is recommended. (See the Books section in the Facts for the Visitor chapter for suggestions.)

Mountains

The high open grasslands of the Nyika Plateau are home to wattled crane, Denham's bustard and red-winged francolin. Flowering plants in the grasslands may attract sunbirds such as the greater double-collared sunbird and the red-tufted malachite sunbird. Mountain cisticola and churring cisticola can be found in the bracken belts around the areas of forest.

Nyika's patches of evergreen forest can be rewarding for bird-watchers, with beautiful species such as the bar-tailed trogon, starred robin and the cinnamon dove often seen.

Other mountain areas include Thyolo Mountain, to the east of Blantyre, which is home to several rare and threatened species such as the green-headed oriole, bronze-naped thrush and the Natal thrush. The forest on Zomba Plateau is also a good spot; species found include the Thyolo alethe and the black-headed apalis.

Ntchisi Mountain, north-east of Lilongwe, is topped with evergreen forest, which is a breeding site for birds such as the narina trogon.

Rocky Hills

Rocky hills are scattered throughout Malawi, particularly in the area around Cape Maclear and near Dedza. They provide good vantage points from which to watch birds of prey such as lanner and peregrine falcons and black eagles. Other birds that may be seen in this type of habitat include the mocking chat, rock cisticola, large striped pipit and black stork. On rocky hills in the south of the country, you may see cape bunting.

Lake Shore Forest

The Kalwe Forest near Nkhata Bay closely resembles the coastal evergreen forests of East Africa. Bird-watching here is excellent – you may see birds such as the green coucal, red-capped robin, blue-mantled crested flycatcher and the local speciality, Cunning's akalat.

African fish eagle

Pygmy goose

Southern yellow-billed hornbill

Lesser masked weaver

Pied kingfisher

White-breasted cormorants

ANDREW MACCOLL

Giant eagle owl

DAVID WALL

Southern crowned crane

ROB DRUMMOND

DEANNA SWANEY

A small flock of carmine bee-eaters nesting on the cliffs

Paradise flycatcher

DAVID TIPLING

Cattle egret

DAVID TIPLING

Lilac-breasted roller

DAVID TIPLING

Great white egret

Birds of Malawi

Miombo Woodland
Miombo or brachystegia woodland occurs in several parts of Malawi, including on the lower slopes of the Nyika Plateau and Ntchisi Mountain, but probably the best examples are at Dzalanyama Forest Reserve and Kasungu National Park. Nearly every miombo bird species can be found in Dzalanyama, including such rarities as olive-headed weaver and Stierling's woodpecker. Other more common species that are frequently seen include wood hoopoes and helmet shrikes.

Mopane Woodland
The best example of mopane woodland is found in Liwonde National Park. Birds typical of this habitat include the red-billed and crowned hornbill, long-tailed starling and white-browed sparrow-weaver. In Liwonde you will also find Malawi's only population of Lilian's lovebird, and get your best chance to see Pel's fishing owl. There is also a good chance of seeing nightjars here, for example the fiery-necked nightjar and Mozambique nightjar.

Thicket
Dense deciduous thickets, most notably in Lengwe National Park, are yet another haven for ornithologists. Here you may find crested guineafowl, barred long-tailed cuckoos, black-and-white flycatchers and gorgeous bush-shrikes, birds unlikely to be seen elsewhere in Malawi. You may also see African broadbills and the beautiful Boehm's bee-eater.

Mixed & Acacia Woodland
Two of the best areas for bird-watching in this type of habitat are Lengwe National Park and Lilongwe Nature Sanctuary. The yellow-billed hornbill is confined to this habitat, and other birds that may be seen include the red-winged warbler and the spectacular giant eagle owl.

Lake Malawi
The southern end of Lake Malawi is home to enormous numbers of the African fish eagle. The sound of its plaintive call and the sight of one of these magnificent birds perched in a tree overlooking the lake is for many one of the most enduring impressions of Malawi. The lake is also home to several large breeding colonies of white-breasted cormorants which nest offshore. Reedbeds along the shore support colonies of golden and brown-throated weavers. Other birds that are often seen include the palm swift and the collared palm thrush.

Rivers & Wetlands
There are several rivers in Malawi which are excellent for bird-watching. The Upper Shire River in Liwonde National Park is home to an enormous variety of birds, including several species of kingfisher, such as the pied, malachite and giant kingfisher, and a number of herons, including the white-backed night heron, and egrets and ducks. Further south, on the Lower Shire, near Chikwawa, are several large colonies of beautiful carmine bee-eaters which nest in the sandcliffs during the dry season. Mpatamanga Gorge and Kapichira Falls can also be rewarding; birds often seen include the rock pratincole and Livingstone's flycatcher. The Bua River in the Nkhotakota Game Reserve is another good spot.

Wetland areas support a great variety of waterfowl, and during the months of August to November they are often visited by a number of migrating Eurasian shore birds. Some of the best wetland areas in Malawi include Lake Kazuni in Vwaza Marsh Game Reserve and Lake Chilwa, near Zomba. In the far south of Malawi, the little-visited Elephant Marsh is an excellent bird-watching area; African skimmer and pygmy goose can be seen here, plus herons, storks and kingfishers.

CHITIMBA

This village is where you turn off the main north-south road to reach Livingstonia. The nearby long, white beaches and clear waters of Lake Malawi make it a good place to relax, especially if you've just travelled down from Tanzania.

There are three places to stay at the junction: the *Florence Bay Resthouse*, *Lusekero Nyabweka Resthouse* and *Brothers Inn Arms* – all much of a muchness, and all very reasonable. They can store your gear and arrange a guide if you want to walk up to Livingstonia. (We heard from a traveller who had some items taken from his bag, which he'd left at one of these places, so it is worth making sure your gear is under lock and key, not just dumped in a corner somewhere.)

About 1km north of the Livingstonia turn-off, on the beach, *Chitimba Campsite* is very popular with overland trucks, and provides camping or a bed in the dorm for US$2, simple cabins for US$3 or doubles with bathroom for US$20. Food is available and the bar rocks until late if there's a couple of trucks in.

About 5km north of Chitimba (90km south of Karonga) is *Mdokera's Beach Campsite*, close to the road and the beach and run by a friendly Malawian couple. Camping is US$1.50, and huts are US$3 per person. Our favourite was the bed in the tree! Meals in the simple but clean local-style restaurant range from US$0.50 to US$2.50, and there's a visitors book of hints and comments.

If you want something a bit smarter, about 5km south of Chitimba is *Namiashi Resort* with pleasant singles/doubles, both with bathroom, for US$10/15 with breakfast, camping for US$3 and a good menu of European and Malawian dishes.

A minibus or *matola* (pick-up) between Chitimba and Mzuzu or Karonga costs around US$2.50.

LIVINGSTONIA

Livingstonia is a small town, based around a mission station built on the high escarpment overlooking the lake, to the west of the main north-south road between the bor-

der and Mzuzu. It's a fascinating place, like a small piece of Scotland transported to the heart of Africa. Although not easy to reach, it's well worth making an effort to get here. The town is quiet and restful, and an ideal place to base yourself for a day or two to recover from hard travel in Tanzania or the rigours of beach life on Lake Malawi.

History

The death of famous explorer David Livingstone in 1873 rekindled British missionary zeal and support for missions in Central Africa. In 1875 a group of missionaries from the Free Church of Scotland arrived at Lake Malawi and built a new mission on the lake shore at Cape Maclear, which they named Livingstonia after the great man himself. Their early mission site was malarial and unsuccessful, so it was moved north along the shore to a place called Bandawe. Again, conditions were not ideal so in 1894 the Livingstonia Mission, led by the inde-

The bell at Livingstonia is a memorial to the Laws family, who worked there as missionaries.

Ephesians 2:14

In February 1959, as colonial rule was coming to an end in Malawi (then called Nyasaland), various pro-independence movements were active in the north and violence had escalated in the Karonga and Rumphi districts surrounding Livingstonia. The missionaries were thought to be in danger, so the colonial government sent a small plane over the town to drop a message saying that the European missionaries could be evacuated if necessary. The missionaries were instructed to display a large symbol on the grass outside the church: 'V' if in danger and 'I' if they were safe, which a plane returning next day would be able to see.

The missionaries decided against evacuation, but also wanted to tell the outside world that, despite extreme racial tension in Malawi, they were living in peace and harmony with their African neighbours. Using bricks they spelt out *Ephesians 2:14* in large letters that could be clearly seen from the air.

Back at base, the government officials presumably turned to the appropriate page in the Bible and read: 'For He is our peace who hath made both one, and hath broken down the middle wall of partition between us.'

The bricks were later relaid outside the Stone House and whitewashed, where they remain to this day. They haven't been painted for a while and are becoming overgrown, so anyone in a plane flying over the site these days may have to look quite hard to spot the message.

---

fatigable Dr Laws, was moved to an area of high ground between the eastern escarpment of the Nyika Plateau and Lake Malawi. This site was successful and the mission station flourished and developed into a small town, which is still thriving today. (For more details see the History section in the Facts about Malawi chapter.)

Information

Facilities at Livingstonia include a post office (where you can make phone calls), hospital, market and some local-style stores, including the delightfully old-fashioned Overtoun Grocery. There's also the Khondowe Craft Shop selling carvings and clothing made by local people. (Khondowe was the original name of this area, before it was changed to Livingstonia.)

Things to See & Do

Anyone keen on history will find the **museum** in the Stone House fascinating. It's open from 8 am to noon and 2 to 5 pm Monday to Saturday and Sunday afternoons. The entry fee is US$0.30. The exhibits tell the story of early European exploration and missionary work in Malawi. Many original items that once belonged to Livingstone and the Livingstonia Missionaries are still here, including a collection of magic lantern slides.

Near the Stone House is the **church** dating from 1894 and built in Scottish style. It has a beautiful stained-glass window of David Livingstone and his two companions, Juma and Guze (sometimes spelt Chuma and Suzi), his sextant and medicine chest, and Lake Malawi in the background. The church is often locked, but the keys are held at the museum or by the Head of Station, who lives nearby (ask for directions at the museum).

Other places of interest include the **secondary school** complete with Victorian facade and the **clock tower** at the old post office, now a small bookshop. The nearby **industrial block** built by the early missionaries as a training centre is now a technical college. Outside is a huge **bell** on a pedestal – now a memorial to the Laws family.

Down the road from here is the **David Gordon Memorial Hospital**, once the biggest hospital in Central Africa, and the **stone cairn** marking the place where Dr Laws and his African companion Uriah Chirwa camped in 1894 when they decided to build the mission here. Also nearby is **House No 1**, the original home of Dr Laws before he moved into the Stone House.

Outside the Stone House you might notice some huge letters almost hidden by the grass, designed to be read by anyone who happens to be flying overhead in a small plane. They

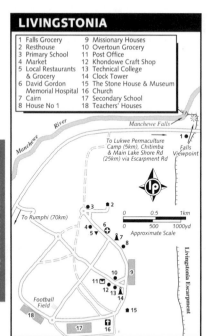

LIVINGSTONIA

1 Falls Grocery	9 Missionary Houses
2 Resthouse	10 Overtoun Grocery
3 Primary School	11 Post Office
4 Market	12 Khondowe Craft Shop
5 Local Restaurants	13 Technical College
& Grocery	14 Clock Tower
6 David Gordon	15 The Stone House & Museum
Memorial Hospital	16 Church
7 Cairn	17 Secondary School
8 House No 1	18 Teachers' Houses

River Manchewe

Manchewe Falls

To Lukwe Permaculture
Camp (5km), Chitimba
& Main Lake Shore Rd
(25km) via Escarpment Rd

Falls
Viewpoint

To Rumphi (70km)

0   0.5   1km

0   500   1000yd

Approximate Scale

Livingstonia Escarpment

Football
Field

read *Ephesians 2:14*. For an explanation – see the boxed text 'Ephesians 2:14'.

Manchewe Falls, about 4km from the town, is a spectacular waterfall, about 50m high, with a cave behind it where local people hid from slave traders some 100 years ago. Allow one hour going down and 1½ hours back up. There are several paths leading to the falls, and several young boys hanging around the resthouse who will show you the way for a small fee. Alternatively, if you're walking to/from Chitimba, you can take a short side trip to visit the falls. The viewpoint is just 500m off the escarpment road, reached by a clear footpath. The friendly people at Lukwe Permaculture Camp (see Places to Stay & Eat later in this section) have plenty more hiking suggestions.

Places to Stay & Eat

The **Stone House** (☎ 368223) on the south-eastern side of town was built by missionaries early in the 20th century, and still contains its original furniture, but unfortunately it's seen little maintenance and is getting tatty round the edges. (Dr Laws must be turning in his grave.) However, it's still quite atmospheric, with superb views, and good value: a private room for up to four people is US$7, and a bed in a shared room is US$2. There's a friendly caretaker, clean bathrooms and occasional hot water. Meals of soup, followed by beans, vegetables or meat with rice, plus tea, are around US$2 (you need to order a few hours in advance). For an extra fee the kitchen staff can buy and prepare a chicken for you, but make sure they don't 'forget' to serve half of it and tuck in themselves! Breakfast of tea and pancakes (US$0.50) is also available. Alternatively, you can provide your own food for the cook to prepare, or simply use the kitchen yourself. Camping on the lawn costs US$1, and use of the kitchen for campers is US$0.50.

Another option is the **Resthouse** on the north-eastern side of town, which you reach about 15 minutes before the Stone House if you have just staggered up the escarpment road from Chitimba. The cost is US$1 per person in bedrooms with two to six beds, although facilities are more basic than the Stone House. Camping, meals and use of the kitchen are the same price as the Stone House. From the garden you can see down to Lake Malawi, and the beautiful curved spit of land on the northern side of the bay that appears in the picture in the church window.

If you're self-catering at either the Stone House or the Resthouse at either end of town, there's a market and some shops on the road near the hospital.

On the escarpment road, you can camp at **Falls Grocery** opposite the path to Manchewe Falls, where the friendly shopkeeper, Mr Edwin, lets you pitch a tent for US$0.70. There is a basic toilet, and water comes from the stream nearby, but the shop is very well stocked with food and drink (including beer).

On the north side of the escarpment road, is the restful **Lukwe Permaculture Camp** (✉ ecologique2000@hotmail.com), it is above the steep zigzags, an hour's walk east (down) from Livingstonia, or about 20km from Chitimba if you're coming up. It is a beautiful, shady place, with stunning views and a friendly atmosphere, and it's highly recommended. Camping costs US$3 per person, and simple cabins (sleeping two people) cost between US$10 and US$20. Hot showers and clean compost toilets complete this sustainable paradise. All food comes from the garden, with meals around US$1.50 to US$3. Hikes, with or without local guides, can be arranged to surrounding hills and peaks. Guides can also hired here for the walk down to the lake shore at Chitimba (this village is covered earlier in this chapter). You can hike down either by the escarpment road or via an alternative path, but please see the warning in the Getting There & Away section following. More information about this wonderful place to stay is available on the Web site: www.malawi-today.com/lukwe

Getting There & Away

From the main north-south road between Karonga and Mzuzu the road to Livingstonia turns off at Chitimba, forcing its way up the escarpment in a series of acute hairpin bends (20 to be precise – they're numbered) with a bad road surface, steep gradients, and pretty frightening drops to add to the fun. If you're driving it starts off well, but the wide dirt road soon becomes a steep rutted track, only just passable even with a 4WD. Even after you get past bend 20, there's still 5km or so of uphill driving until you reach Livingstonia. There's no bus, and you'll wait a very long time if you're hitching.

Your alternative is to walk up: this is about 25km, and steep in places, so it takes about five hours from Chitimba if you follow the road. There are short cuts that reduce it to about four hours, but these are even steeper. Going down the escarpment road is obviously easier on foot; it takes three to four hours. We met a gang from an overland truck who jogged up *and* down in five hours, and we've heard from other travellers who started before dawn and walked more gently in the cool of the morning,

Warning

Take great care if you decide to walk up or down the escarpment road between Chitimba and Livingstonia. We have heard from several travellers who have been mugged or robbed on this road. Most worryingly, even a few travellers who hire a local guide (as protection as much as to show the way) have also been attacked. These may have been isolated incidents – probably hundreds of travellers walk up here every year – but incidents do seem to be on the increase, and you are strongly advised to check the latest security situation before you set off, by asking at one of the reliable places to stay at Chitimba if you're going up (or in Livingstonia if you're coming down).

stopping off at Manchewe Falls on the way. If you want to make things easier, local boys who wait around the resthouses near the junction in Chitimba will offer to carry your pack for about US$2. Unfortunately, this walk is not the breeze it used to be: please see the Warning boxed text.

The other way to reach Livingstonia, especially if you're coming from the south, is to go to Rumphi and catch a minibus or matola up the scenic 'old road' (west of the main north-south road) to Livingstonia. Sometimes the public transport only goes as far as Nchenachena or Hananiya, from where you'll have to walk 17km or 7km respectively to Livingstonia. The fare is US$1 to US$3, depending on the state of the road.

A final option is to walk to Livingstonia from the Nyika Plateau. See Nyika National Park later in this chapter for more details.

If you're in Livingstonia and looking for a lift out, ask at the shops (the owners sometimes go to Mzuzu for supplies), or ask one of the young boys who hang around the resthouses to look for you – they normally know what's going on. A small tip (around US$0.25) might be expected by your fixer. A lift in a pick-up costs US$1 to US$5. If there's nothing going when you want it, you

Mr Ngoma's House

South of Chitimba and about 20km north of the junction where the Rumphi road turns west off the main north-south road, you pass (on your right, if heading south) a remarkable two-storey building, constructed of scrap metal, old car parts, brightly painted wood, ancient beds and disused road signs. This is the house of Mr SS Ngoma, one of Africa's great eccentrics, who spends most of his time sitting on his front porch watching the world go by. Mr Ngoma, in the nicest possible way, is obsessed with his forthcoming death, and has already built his coffin, grave and tombstone. He wel-

DAVID ELSE

comes visitors, and will happily show you around his bizarre house. (It was once a shop, and the sign still says 'Grocery', but the shelves have been empty for years.) It has several bedrooms which he seems to use in rotation, a 'mortuary', a 'hospital', a chapel (complete with ancient record player with a speaker wired to the veranda so that hymns can be played to the local inhabitants), an intriguing upstairs toilet, a couple of bells, plus hundreds of letters, cards and photos from admirers all over the world. Mr Ngoma used to have a red telephone by his graveside, which he said was linked directly to God and other friends who have already gone to heaven. But times change, and now he's got a mobile phone hanging round his neck at all times. Mr Ngoma is weird but likeable and a visit to his house will never be forgotten. On leaving you should sign the visitors book (he's on his sixth) and make a small donation to his long-suffering daughter.

could hire the whole pick-up to take you to the foot of the escarpment. This costs from about US$10 – and, once again, the local fixers will help you sort this out.

The Nyika Plateau Area

RUMPHI

Rumphi (**rum**-pee) is a small town about 70km north of Mzuzu, west of the main road (the M1) between Mzuzu and Karonga. Most people pass through here on their way to Vwaza Marsh or the Nyika Plateau, but from Rumphi you can also get to Livingstonia and to the northern outpost of Chitipa (from where you can enter Zambia and Tanzania – see the Getting There & Away chapter for details).

Places to Stay & Eat

The *Happy Landing Motel* between the petrol station and the Stagecoach bus stop has basic rooms at US$3, but get one with a private bathroom, because the shared facilities are dirty. The *Lunyina Guesthouse* opposite is better, with simple rooms at US$1, and 'executive' rooms at US$2/3 for a single/double.

On the edge of town, as you come in from Mzuzu, try the friendly and good-value *Simphakawa Inn*. It was being renovated when we passed through, but when the work is finished double rooms should cost around $4.

Getting There & Away

Buses between Mzuzu and Karonga stop at Rumphi. To/from Mzuzu is about $1. A minibus between Mzuzu and Rumphi is also US$1.

NORTHERN MALAWI

Matolas from Rumphi to Nyika and Vwaza go from opposite the PTC supermarket. You can also ask here about matolas to Nchenachena or Hananiya (for Livingstonia), or to Chitipa.

NYIKA NATIONAL PARK

The Nyika National Park was established in 1965, making it Malawi's oldest, and it has also been extended since then, so that it is now the largest in the country. (More details are given in the boxed text 'History of Nyika'.) The plateau is roughly oval in shape, about 80km long and almost 50km across at its widest points, covering some 3000 sq km as well as an area in Zambian territory. The main feature of the park is the Nyika Plateau, with a landscape and climate that is unique in Malawi, and unusual in Africa – a vast range of high rolling hills, covered in montane grassland, where the air is cool and crisp, and the views (on clear days) endless.

The wild, open nature of the Nyika Plateau attracts visitors who come to drive or ride around the park's vast network of wildlife-viewing tracks, to admire the birds and animals, take a horseback safari, study the flowers, try a spot of fishing, or simply sit in the sun and absorb the magnificent scenery. Some of the park's main attractions are the series of short walks and longer hikes or treks.

Much of the Nyika is above 1800m and, although it's called a plateau, it's by no means flat. The landscape consists mainly of rolling grassy hills split by forested valleys and surrounded by steep escarpments. There are several peaks on the western, northern and eastern sides that rise above 2000m, with great views over the surrounding valleys and plains. The highest point on the Nyika is Nganda Peak (2607m), which overlooks the northern section of the plateau and from where you can see the plains of Zambia in one direction and the distant mountains of Tanzania in the other, as well as the waters of Lake Malawi shining in the distance.

Entry fees must be paid. For details see under National Parks & Wildlife Reserves

in the Facts about Malawi chapter. All accommodation and tourist activities (such as hiking and horse riding) are operated by The Nyika Safari Company, based at Chelinda Camp in the centre of the plateau. It also has a central office in Lilongwe (☎/fax 757316, 752379, @ nyika-safaries@ malawi.net), based at Ulendo Safaris in The Old Town Mall (see Travel Agencies in the Lilongwe chapter).

Flora & Fauna

The vegetation on the Nyika is unique in Malawi (and unusual in Africa) and worthy of special attention. About 1800m above sea level, most of the Nyika is covered in rolling hills of montane grassland. The land below this altitude, in valleys and on the escarpment edges, is covered in light open miombo woodland, and in between the two vegetation zones you can often see areas of large protea bushes. Other areas are covered in dense evergreen forests, which are thought to be remnants of the extensive forests that once grew all over Malawi, as well as southern Tanzania, northern Zambia, and Mozambique. The plateau also contains small areas of damp grassy bog.

This range of flora attracts a varied selection of wildlife, and a major feature of a visit to the Nyika is the number of birds and animals you are likely to see. Because of the general lack of trees and bushes, spotting is easy too. (In fact, many animals seem to deliberately pose on the skyline for that classic wildlife shot.) Most common is the large roan antelope (numerous here, but rare elsewhere), and the smaller reedbuck, which moves about through the grassland in herds. From a car or on foot, you'll also see zebras, warthogs and elands (although, because they are a favourite target for poachers, these are very shy). Walking quietly, and crossing hilltops slowly, you might also see klipspringers, jackals, duikers and hartebeest. You might even catch a glimpse of hyaenas and leopards, but you'll be more likely to see their footprints and droppings. In the woodland areas, you may see blue monkeys. More than 400 species of birds have been recorded in the park.

History of Nyika

The word 'nyika' means wilderness, and this particular expanse of high open wilderness has probably existed in its current form for many centuries. A small population of hunter-gatherers is believed to have inhabited the area more than 3000 years ago, and ancient rock paintings have been found at Fingira Cave, at the southern end of the plateau. When the Bantu-speaking people arrived in northern Malawi, most stayed on the plains below the Nyika. The plateau was a place to hunt and smelt iron, but it was never settled in a big way.

The first Europeans to see the Nyika were probably Scottish missionaries, who reached this area in 1894 after it was brought to the attention of the British government by explorer David Livingstone (see the History section in the Facts about Malawi chapter), although it's quite possible that it was seen by Portuguese explorers who were active in the area long before Livingstone came through. The mission station built by the Scottish missionaries, between the Nyika's eastern edge and Lake Malawi, was named Livingstonia, and is still a thriving centre today.

Scientists and naturalists who visited the Nyika in the early 20th century recognised the biological importance of the area, and in 1933 measures were taken to protect the stands of juniper trees on the southern part of the plateau from bushfires. In 1948 this section was made into a forest reserve, and at the same time pine plantations were established around Chelinda, near the centre of the plateau.

There were later plans to extend the plantations and develop the area as a source of wood for a proposed pulp mill on Lake Malawi, but access for logging vehicles proved difficult and the scheme was abandoned. Plantations were, however, established on the Viphya Plateau (see the Central Malawi chapter), and plans for a Lake Malawi mill were shelved, although still occasionally discussed, even as late as the 1990s.

In 1965 the entire upper Nyika Plateau was made a national park, and in 1976 this area was extended further to include the lower slopes of the plateau – an important water catchment area. This most recent boundary extension included several small settlements, and the people living here were relocated to areas outside the park. When they moved they took the names of their villages with them and now, in the area bordering the park, there are several settlements that share names with valleys and other features inside the park itself.

The Nyika is also famous for its wildflowers. The best time is during and just after the wet season (September to April), when the grassland is covered in colour and small outcrops turn into veritable rock gardens. More than 200 species of orchid alone grow on the plateau.

Lake Kaulime is the only natural lake on the Nyika Plateau and is the subject of many stories and beliefs of the local people. In the days before the Nyika was a park, local people came here to pray for rain, or to throw in white beads as a sign of respect for their ancestors. If you listen hard you're supposed to be able to hear the sound of doves calling, or women pounding maize. The lake was thought to be bottomless, and on a misty day it does have a certain air of mystery about it, but it's actually not that deep: you can often see roan antelopes wading through the water, eating reed shoots.

Information

The national park produces a small booklet with good background information on the Nyika's wildlife and vegetation. There are also leaflets and displays in the information centre at Chelinda Camp. *A Visitor's Guide to Nyika National Park* by Sigrid Johnson is available here and in Blantyre and Lilongwe bookshops, and is a good investment if you plan more than a cursory visit.

The map we provide in this book will be enough to guide you around the park's network of tracks if you're touring on two or four wheels, or if you're walking. If you want a more detailed map, the entire Nyika Plateau is covered by the government survey 1:250,000 map sheet 2, but many of the park tracks are not shown. The plateau is also covered by 12 1:50,000 maps: 1033 B1 to B4, 1033 D1 to D4, 1034 A1 and A3, 1034 C1 and C3. (Chelinda Camp area is covered by 1033 D2.) These have excellent topographical detail but, once again, do not show all the park tracks.

A chapter on long walks in Malawi is included in Lonely Planet's *Trekking in East Africa*, covering several routes on the Nyika, plus Mulanje, Zomba and some other areas.

Wildlife Watching

To appreciate the animals and flowers on the Nyika, you can tour the network of park tracks in your own car, or arrange a guided wildlife-viewing drive (called a 'game drive' by the park staff) from Chelinda Camp. Most leave in the morning or evening, but you can also go all day, or at night, when the guide uses a spotlight to pick out animals. Wildlife viewing is good all year, although in July and August the cold weather means the animals move to lower areas. Bird-watching is particularly good from October to April, when migrants are on the move

Horse Riding

The wide open Nyika landscape lends itself perfectly to horse riding, and this is by far the most enjoyable and exhilarating way to experience the plateau. At Chelinda Camp you can hire good quality horses suitable for beginners and experts. Rates are US$10 per hour or US$50 all day. Horses easily cross the tussock grass and boggy valley bottoms that can tire hikers, and the extra height means views are excellent. You can also get much closer to animals like zebras, elands and roan antelopes when on horseback. A long but excellent day ride is from Chelinda to the viewpoints on the western escarpment.

Also available are horse safaris, which last from two to 10 days, according to your time, budget or hardiness. These are based at Chelinda Lodge, about 1km from Chelinda Camp, or they use luxury tents and explore the remote parts of the plateau. The cost is US$200 per person per night all inclusive.

Walking

Although you can't enter the park on foot, once inside walking is allowed. There are several spots where you leave your car and walk for an hour or all day; staff at Chelinda Camp can advise you on which routes to take.

One of the most popular options is to park at the Jalawe Roadhead, about 35km from Chelinda Camp, then follow the path to Jalawe Peak. Beyond the summit is a rocky outcrop overlooking the Chipome Valley, about 1000m below. You can sometimes spot elephants here. Beyond the Chipome Valley, the land rises steeply again to the peak of Kawozia (also called Kamozya) and beyond to the twin peaks of Mpanda, the northernmost summit in the Nyika National Park.

For longer walks (although not longer than all day) you can walk alone or hire a park ranger (called a 'scout') to guide you. If you've come without a car, around Chelinda Camp various paths and tracks wind through the plantation woodland, or across the grassland to nearby small lakes, and these can be followed for several hours without the need of a guide.

You can't really get lost as a large dirt road circles the woodland area, so if you keep going you'll eventually come across it, and can follow it back to the camp. Alternatively, you can go south of the camp on the park track towards Chelinda Bridge, which passes two small lakes called Dam 2 and Dam 3. These are pleasant spots for bird-watching, and if you're patient you'll probably see roan antelope and other animals coming to drink.

From Dam 3 a footpath (indistinct in places) follows the small Chelinda River upstream back towards Chelinda Camp. If the path is unclear, keep left to avoid boggy sections. Alternatively, if you feel energetic, from Dam 3 you can head south then west on the park track, which eventually loops round to meet the main access road between Chelinda Camp and Thazima near Lake Kaulime. Heading back to Chelinda Camp from here makes a 20km circuit.

For longer walks of more than a day, see the following Hiking section and 'The Nyika Highlights Route' boxed text.

The Nyika Highlights Route

This trekking route follows paths and tracks for much of the way, rather than cutting across open country, and takes in many of the Nyika's main attractions, including Lake Kaulime, the Zovo-Chipolo Forest, Chisanga Falls, Domwe Peak, the western escarpment and Nganda Peak, the highest point on the plateau. This trek starts and finishes at Chelinda Camp and takes four days, although you could do it in three at a push. It can be done in either direction. The daily distances are quite long, although there are no major gradients to contend with. Alternatively you could stretch it over five days, or turn the route into something less demanding by taking short cuts.

Stage 1: Chelinda Camp to Chisanga Falls

(29km, 7 to 8 hours) From the start at Chelinda, the route passes Lake Kaulime then cuts through the grassland to Zambian Resthouse junction and passes Zovo-Chipolo Forest, where there's a nature trail. It then follows the border track between Malawi and Zambia until you reach a path going down through woodland to reach Chisanga Falls. There is a good place to camp above the falls.

Stage 2: Chisanga Falls to Domwe Peak

(17km, 6 to 7 hours) From Chisanga Falls, the route gains the edge of the western escarpment with splendid views over the North Rukuru Valley and into Zambia. Domwe Peak (2340m) is the highest point on the western escarpment and a particularly good viewpoint.

Stage 3: Domwe Peak to Lower Mondwe Stream

(17km, 5 to 6 hours) From Domwe Peak, the route strikes out across the heart of the plateau, through classic montane grassland scenery to reach to Lower Mondwe Stream, below Nganda Peak, where there's a choice of camp sites, all of them slightly damp. You can finish for the day here, or take another two to three hours to go up and down Nganda Peak (2607m), the highest point on the Nyika Plateau. From the summit, the entire rolling expanse of the plateau spreads away towards the south, and to the north-east you can often see the glistening waters of Lake Malawi.

Stage 4: Lower Mondwe Stream to Chelinda Camp

(20km, 6 to 7 hours) If you chose to finish yesterday without going up and down Nganda Peak (as described in Stage 3), you can do it at the start of this stage before heading home. Your return route is long but straightforward. It cuts across the top of the North Rumphi Valley then aims south all the way back to Chelinda Camp.

Hiking

A good range of long-distance routes (sometimes called 'wilderness trails') are available on the Nyika, and all hiking is now efficiently organised by The Nyika Safari Company at Chelinda Camp. For hikes and treks of more than one day (ie, which involve camping overnight in the park) you have to be accompanied by a ranger who acts as guide. The fee you pay covers the guide's services – described at the end of this section. You must provide all the equipment and food you need. Guides and porters have their own sleeping bags, tent and cooking pots, and food.

Generally, there are no set routes in the park. You either follow the park tracks, paths and wildlife trails or simply walk across the trackless grassland, but some routes are more popular than others – especially to the peaks and view points on the western and northern escarpments. There are no set camp sites either.

The wilderness trails are not designed so you can stalk wildlife to get better photos, but rather to show you the animals as part of the wider environment, and help you enjoy the splendid feeling of space that walking on the Nyika provides. If you dis-

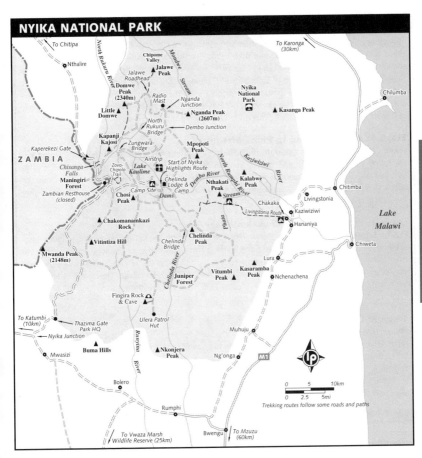

NYIKA NATIONAL PARK

To Chitipa

Nthalire

To Karonga
(30km)

Chilumba

North Rukuru River

Chipome
Valley

Jalawe
Roadhead

Jalawe
Peak

Monkhe Stream

Nyika
National
Park

Kasanga Peak

Domwe
Peak
(2340m)

Radio
Mast

Nganda
Junction

Little
Domwe

Nganda Peak
(2607m)

North
Rukuru
Bridge

Dembo Junction

Kapanji
Kajosi

Zungwara
Bridge

Mpopoti
Peak

Kaziwiziwi River

Kaperekezi Gate

Airstrip

Start of Nyika
Highlights Route

North Rumphi River

ZAMBIA

Chisanga
Falls

Zovo-
Chipolo
Trail

Lake
Kaulime

Chelinda
Lodge &
Camp

Nthakati
Peak

Kalabwe
Peak

Chitimba

Maningiri
Forest

Camp Site

Dembo River

Dams

Stream

Chakaka

Livingstonia

Zambian Resthouse
(closed)

Chosi
Peak

Kaziwiziwi

Lake
Malawi

Livingstonia Route

Hananiya

Chakomanamkazi
Rock

Phoka

Chiweta

Vitintiza Hill

Chelinda
Bridge

Chelinda
Peak

Chelinda River

Lura

Mwanda Peak
(2148m)

Juniper
Forest

Vitumbi
Peak

Kasaramba
Peak

Nchenachena

Fingira Rock
& Cave

To Katumbi
(10km)

Thazima Gate
Park HQ

Ulera Patrol
Hut

Muhuju

Nyika Junction

Ruryina River

Mwasizi

Buma Hills

Nkonjera
Peak

Ng'onga

M1

Bolero

Rumphi

To Vwaza Marsh
Wildlife Reserve (25km)

Bwengu

To Mzuzu
(60km)

0   5   10km
0   2.5   5mi
Trekking routes follow some roads and paths

NORTHERN MALAWI

cuss your interests with the staff at Chelinda Camp they can advise on a suitable route.

The only set route on the Nyika – and by far the most popular – is The Livingstonia Route which, as the name implies, goes from Chelinda Camp to Livingstonia, a spectacular and hugely rewarding walk, crossing the high grassland, then dropping steeply through the wooded escarpment and passing through villages and farmland to reach the old mission station at Livingstonia. This route takes three days. The third night is spent in Livingstonia, and you can walk down to the lake shore at Chitimba on the fourth day.

Another option, if you want to start and finish at Chelinda Camp, is the Nyika Highlights Route. (For details see the boxed texts 'The Livingstonia Route' and 'The Nyika Highlights Route'). For more ideas, a chapter on long walks in Malawi is included in Lonely Planet's *Trekking in East Africa*.

Walking trails can usually run with a day or two's notice. Advance warning (through The Nyika Safari Company's office in Lilongwe) is preferred. The Livingstonia Route is proving so popular that it may soon run on set days only – probably with departures from Chelinda Camp twice per week.

The Livingstonia Route

This route follows tracks and paths for its entire length. From Chelinda Camp the route goes through the rolling grasslands of the park, and then drops dramatically down the wooded escarpment on the eastern edge of the plateau. It leaves the park and goes via the village of Chakaka and Hananiya to reach the old mission station of Livingstonia. Daily distances are not long, and most of the route is downhill. It takes three days to reach Livingstonia, with the probability of a fourth to go from Livingstonia to the lake shore. If you're short of time, and feeling fit, the first two stages can be done in one day, but it's long and hard. This route cannot be done in reverse.

Stage 1: Chelinda Camp to Phata Stream

(18km, 6 to 7 hours) From the start at Chelinda Camp the route goes south then east from Chelinda, across fine rolling grassland, passing south of Nthakati Peak, and crossing several small streams to reach the larger Phata Stream, which makes a good camp site. Some people prefer to trek up the valley side beyond the stream and camp higher up, as this gives better views and avoids starting the next day's walk with an uphill section!

Stage 2: Phata Stream to Chakaka Village

(12km, 5 to 6 hours) From Phata Stream, the route climbs up the valley side, then continues eastwards over the crest of a large broad ridge marking the eastern edge of the escarpment. The route then follows a secondary ridge through forest, bush and long grass to leave the park and descend very steeply to eventually reach the huts and small fields of Chakaka village. The people at The Nyika Safari Company, who run the treks, have plans to build a small resthouse here that will be run by locals for the benefit of the surrounding community.

Stage 3: Chakaka to Livingstonia

(16km, 5 to 6 hours) From Chakaka village, a small dirt road winds down the valley beside the large North Rumphi River to reach the main dirt road between Livingstonia and Rumphi at a small village called Hananiya (which is also marked on some maps as Phoka Court). Some sweaty uphill sections and some final switchbacks over steep ridges lead you to Livingstonia. In Livingstonia there are several things to see and a good selection of places to stay. (For full details, see Livingstonia earlier in this chapter, which also contains some advice about how to travel on to the lake shore.)

Two-day (one-night) trails cost US$30 per person for two hikers (three days US$50, five days US$90), plus US$5 for each extra hiker. The Livingstonia Trail (three days, two nights) costs US$80 per person for two, plus US$10 per extra person. The fees you pay cover the guide and all his costs. Porters are also available, if required.

All the guides speak English, and are generally very pleasant, quite knowledgeable about the birds and wildlife, and good company on a long trek. A tip (of around US$1 or US$2 per day) at the end of your trek is appropriate if the service has been good.

Fishing

The Nyika is reckoned by anglers to offer some of the best **rainbow trout** fishing in Malawi. The best time of year is October and November. Fishing is allowed in the dams near Chelinda Camp and in the nearby streams. A daily licence costs US$4. Rods can be hired. Only fly fishing is permitted.

Mountain Biking

The Nyika's dirt roads are ideal – base yourself at Chelinda Camp and go for day rides in various directions, or camp overnight. Hardy cyclists could bring their own mountain bike and the people at Chelinda Camp also plan to offer mountain bike hire in the future.

Places to Stay & Eat

All accommodation (the camp, the camp site and the lodge) in the national park is run by The Nyika Safari Company (☎/fax *757316, 752379 in Lilongwe,* ❷ *nyika-safaries@malawi.net). Chelinda Camp* has chalets with two bedrooms, each with two beds, bathroom, lounge and fully equipped kitchen; they cost US$100 per night for four people. You provide your own food and each chalet has a cook who will prepare meals for you. Chalet guests can also order meals in the restaurant.

Alternatively you can stay in a double room with private bathroom, which costs US$60 per person, including all meals – which are filling and wholesome, and served in the small and cosy restaurant. Chelinda Camp also has a bar, information room and shop. This place got very run-down when operated by the national park, but since The Nyika Safari Company took over it's been nicely spruced up, without losing any of the cosy atmosphere for which Chelinda Camp was famous. A beer by the roaring fire, after a long day's walk on the hills, is one of Malawi's great pleasures.

About 2km from the main camp is a *camp site* with clean toilets, hot showers, endless firewood and shelters for cooking and eating. It costs US$5 per person. If you don't have your own tent, you can hire one for US$10 (fits two people).

New on the scene is *Chelinda Lodge* about 1km from the camp where luxury log cabins perched on a hillside with stunning views over the plateau cost US$200 per person per night, including all meals, wildlife-viewing drives and walks.

Getting There & Away

Despite most maps showing otherwise, there is no road of any sort between Chelinda Camp and Livingstonia or any other town on the east side of the plateau.

Air The quickest way to reach the Nyika is by the twice-weekly Air Malawi flight from Lilongwe (US$72), or from Mzuzu (a bargain at US$35) to the airstrip at Chelinda. You can get details from travel agencies in Lilongwe, or from the Air Malawi office in Mzuzu. Alternatively, from June to October, an air charter company called Sefofane runs flights from Mzuzu to Chelinda for US$83 per person one way. This plane ties in with the daily Air Malawi service running between Lilongwe and Mzuzu. You can get more information from Ulendo Safaris or Central African Wilderness Safaris (see Travel Agencies in the Lilongwe chapter). Note that planes won't land at Chelinda in bad weather, and there may be limits on the amount of baggage you can carry.

Bus & Matola There is no public bus into the park. The nearest you can get is Rumphi (reached from Mzuzu by bus or minibus for US$1). You might be lucky and find a matola in Rumphi heading for Nthalire, which goes through the park via Zambian Resthouse junction (the Zambian Resthouse is now closed), about 12km from Chelinda. From Zambian Resthouse junction you'll have to walk or hitch to Chelinda. Alternatively, matolas and minibuses run from Rumphi once or twice per day to Katumbi, via Nyika Junction (8km from Thazima Gate). You can try hitching at Nyika Junction or at Thazima Gate – it's what the staff that work at Chelinda Camp do – but be prepared for a long wait.

Car The main Thazima Gate (also spelt, and pronounced, Tazima) is 54km from Rumphi and it's another 55km to Chelinda Camp. The road is dirt after Rumphi, and in fair condition as far as Thazima Gate. In the park it's rough in a few places but easily passable with high clearance (4WD not required). Kaperekezi Gate, passed on the road to/from Chitipa and Nthalire, is rarely used by visitors. Fuel is available at Chelinda.

Private Taxi You can hire a taxi or matola in Mzuzu and Rumphi to take you all the way to Chelinda Camp. This costs around US$100 (less from Rumphi) – not too bad if you get a few people together. The road is just about passable in the dry season in standard 2WD taxis, although a high-clearance matola pick-up would be better. Of course,

Being Prepared on the Nyika

It can get surprisingly cold on the Nyika, especially at night from June to August, when frost is not uncommon. Log fires are provided in the chalets and rooms, but bring a warm sleeping bag if you're camping.

Most days are warm, but because of the high latitude some can feel chilly. Either way, don't be fooled into thinking the sun isn't strong. Many hikers and horse riders are surprised at how sunburnt they get, even in the apparently mild climate.

During dry periods, sectors of the park are burnt to prevent larger fires later in the season. Before setting off for drives or walks, inquire at the park office and avoid the burning areas.

if the taxi has to wait around for a few days to take you out again this will be more expensive, but we've heard from several travellers who have used this method to reach Chelinda Camp then hitched out a few days later, or walked out via the Livingstonia Route. If you come by taxi it's essential to leave early in the morning, so your driver has time to get back to Rumphi or Mzuzu.

Bicycle Although cycling is allowed in the park (see Mountain Biking under Activities earlier in this chapter) regulations seem uncertain about whether you can enter the park by bike. We heard of a hardy Norwegian traveller who flew with his bike on Air Malawi to Chelinda, then rode eastwards, finally carrying his bike down the precipitous path to Livingstonia (an option only for the truly mad). Flying in to Chelinda Camp and then riding out to Rumphi would be a better option – cycling this way is mostly (but not all) downhill.

VWAZA MARSH WILDLIFE RESERVE

This beautiful and all-too-frequently overlooked reserve is well worth visiting. Access by car is easy, and it's also pretty straightforward by public transport, making Vwaza an ideal destination for those without wheels. The best way to get around is on foot, and a lot of wildlife can be seen from the main camp.

There's a range of vegetation and habitats in the reserve. In the north is Vwaza Marsh itself and a large area of swamp surrounded by miombo woodland. There are also smaller areas of mopane and acacia woodland. Draining the marshland, the Luwewe River runs through the reserve, joining the South Rukuru River (the reserve's southern border), which flows into Lake Kazuni. The two places to stay are both at the lake, and the main gate is nearby.

Several hundred elephants inhabit the reserve, and can often be seen around Lake Kazuni. Other mammals include buffaloes (rumoured to be particularly aggressive here), waterbucks, elands, roan antelopes, sables, zebras, hartebeest, impalas and pukus, all surprisingly easy to see from the area around the lake, which also supports a good population of hippos. The birdwatching is excellent – this is one of the best places in Malawi for waders.

There are several driveable tracks in the reserve, but these are suitable only for high-clearance vehicles, and not really designed for wildlife-viewing anyway. The best route for a drive is along the southern edge of the reserve, parallel to the river, to Zoro Pools. Construction of proper wildlife-viewing tracks is planned, but meanwhile you're better off walking – either around Lake Kazuni or on a longer wilderness trail. (For either, a ranger must accompany you at all times – for details of costs see National Parks & Wildlife Reserves in the Facts about Malawi chapter.)

All tourist activities and all places to stay are operated by The Nyika Safari Company (see under Nyika National Park earlier in this chapter for details) and have improved considerably since they were taken over from the national park authority.

Places to Stay & Eat

Kazuni Camp has simple rustic chalets with beds, clean sheets, nets and shared bathrooms for US$10 per person. Camping is US$3. You must bring food and the very friendly staff will cook for you if required. Basic supplies can be bought in Kazuni village – a few kilometres outside the park gate. The smarter *Kazuni Safari Camp* has stylish chalets overlooking the lake, and costs US$140 per person full board, which includes drives and walks, but if you don't want the entire package, cheaper rates may be available.

Getting There & Away
First get to Rumphi (reached from Mzuzu by bus or minibus for US$1). From here fairly frequent matolas and minibuses run to Kazuni village for US$2. By car, head west from Rumphi. Turn left after 10km (Vwaza is signposted), and continue for about 20km. Where the road swings left over a bridge, go straight on to reach the park gate and camp after 1km.

Mzuzu & the Northern Lake Shore

MZUZU
pop 90,000
Mzuzu – often dubbed 'the Capital of the North' – is a large town with banks, shops, a post office, a supermarket, a pharmacy, petrol stations and other facilities. Officially classed as a city (if only by Malawian standards), this place may be your first taste of 'civilisation' for quite a while, especially if you've come from Tanzania. Most visitors find themselves staying for at least one night, as a stopover on the north-south route, or a jumping-off point for Vwaza, Viphya, Nyika or Nkhata Bay.

The **museum** on M'Mbelwa Rd, just off the main street, has good displays on the history of African and European peoples in northern Malawi, and a section on indigenous plants and wildlife. It's open from 7 am to noon and 1 to 5 pm daily. Entry and guided tours are free, but a small donation to the curator (always around to answer questions) may be appropriate.

Information
There is a small tourist office opposite the Kandodo supermarket, near the bus station, but the best place for information is the switched-on Tonga Tours (☎ 334694, ✆ tongatours@malawi.net, easymail@ sdnp.org.mw), on the second floor of the Bazaar Building next to the large PTC supermarket on the main street. This company sells tickets for buses within Malawi or to Tanzania, makes accommodation reservations, arranges flights by charter plane to Nyika National Park and Likoma Island, and can set up tours or safaris anywhere in Malawi. Even if you don't buy anything the staff here are happy to help with advice on public transport, places to stay and so on. If you need Internet access, in the same office is the Easy Mail Internet bureau. It costs about US$1 to send an email, and about US$0.50 to receive. Internet access is about US$1 per four minutes. Tonga Tours has another office in Nkhata Bay, offering a good choice of activities, many aimed at backpackers – see Nkhata Bay later in this chapter.

If you need to exchange money in Mzuzu, there are also two banks on the main street. If the banks are closed, or you're heading for Nkhata Bay, you can also exchange at the Easy Money bureau in Nkhata Bay – see the next section for details.

Places to Stay
If you're really short of cash, the *Council Resthouse* near the small market has basic rooms for US$1.50 per person. Most budget travellers head for the *CCAP Resthouse* (also called the William Koyi Resthouse) north-east of the bus station. It costs US$4 per person in rooms with two, three or four beds, but some travellers have reported that items have gone missing while they were out. So try the nearby *Chiwanja City Resthouse*, where straightforward rooms with shared bathroom cost US$3/5 a single/double. Travellers have also recommended the similarly priced *Mphatso Guesthouse*, also nearby.

Better still is the homely *Flame Tree Guesthouse*, offering B&B for US$7/9. This place is a little gem (there are only

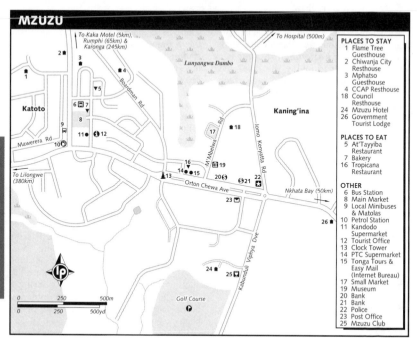

MZUZU

PLACES TO STAY
1 Flame Tree Guesthouse
2 Chiwanja City Resthouse
3 Mphatso Guesthouse
4 CCAP Resthouse
18 Council Resthouse
24 Mzuzu Hotel
26 Government Tourist Lodge

PLACES TO EAT
5 At'Tayyiba Restaurant
7 Bakery
16 Tropicana Restaurant

OTHER
6 Bus Station
8 Main Market
9 Local Minibuses & Matolas
10 Petrol Station
11 Kandodo Supermarket
12 Tourist Office
13 Clock Tower
14 PTC Supermarket
15 Tonga Tours & Easy Mail (Internet Bureau)
17 Small Market
19 Museum
20 Bank
21 Bank
22 Police
23 Post Office
25 Mzuzu Club

three bedrooms, with two beds each, and you share the rest of the house with the family) but unfortunately it's often full, although always worth trying. Camping is allowed in the garden. The nearby *Katoto Guesthouse* is simple, but friendly and clean, charging US$4 per person, with breakfast.

About 5km north of town, on the road towards Rumphi and Karonga, the *Kaka Motel* has comfortable rooms with bathroom from US$7/9, including a cooked breakfast. There's safe parking but no camping allowed.

The *Government Tourist Lodge* is about 1km from the town centre, on the Nkhata Bay road. Formerly the plain old Government Resthouse, it has been revamped by the Hotel Training School and offers (as its signboard proudly states) 'accommodation, meals and an assortment of drinks and camping services'. Clean and comfortable rooms with a colonial feel and shared bathroom cost from US$25/35, including break-

fast. Camping on a fenced grassy site is US$4, or US$5 if you want hot showers. Evening meals are around US$3.

Top of the range is the *Mzuzu Hotel* (☎ 332622, 620588 for central reservations) a large modern block with 60 rooms on the east side of town, overlooking the golf course. Double rooms cost US$130 with private bathroom, air-con, phone and full buffet breakfast. In the restaurant, starters cost around US$3 and main courses are US$5 to US$10. There is a quiet residents' bar, while the non-residents' Choma Bar provides evening entertainment with a loud local flavour.

Places to Eat

Most of the places to stay have restaurants. Added to these, there's *street food* around the market, a supermarket opposite the tourist office, and several shops and a *bakery* by the bus station.

The *Tropicana Restaurant* is recommended for excellent cheap meals, with large portions, and a nice veranda giving it a vaguely Mediterranean feel. Snacks cost from US$1, local-style meals cost US$1.50, and chicken and chips costs US$2. There's a bar inside the restaurant.

There isn't any beer at the Muslim-run **At'Tayyiba Restaurant** (the name means something like 'goodly sustenance'), but it's clean and friendly and the food is very fine: fish and chips, beef and rice or *nsima* (cooked maize flour) cost around US$1.50.

For more stylish surroundings, the bar and restaurant at **Mzuzu Club** next to the Mzuzu Hotel, is usually open to nonmembers, offering cold beers, various other drinks, plus Malawian and Western food, including good-value steaks from US$2.50.

Getting There & Away

Stagecoach Express buses run to Lilongwe for US$6 (via Kasungu US$3.50), and ordinary buses go to Rumphi for US$1 and Nkhata Bay for US$0.75. Rumphi and Nkhata Bay are also served by minibus (same fare as the bus). To Chitimba is US$2.50, and to Karonga is US$4 by bus and US$5 by minibus.

If you're heading for Tanzania, two international buses go between Lilongwe and Dar es Salaam, via Mzuzu, each twice weekly in each direction. The buses should come through Mzuzu around midnight, cross the border at first light, go through Mbeya in the morning and get to Dar in the late afternoon. The fare from Mzuzu to Dar is around US$18, and from Mzuzu to Mbeya is around US$10. Note, however, that despite their 'international' status these buses can be crowded and uncomfortable, and may not depart anywhere near the advertised time. We've heard from travellers who waited until dawn at Mzuzu, and got into Dar almost a day later than expected. You can get details or arrange tickets at Tonga Tours (listed in the Information section earlier).

NKHATA BAY

Nkhata Bay is situated beside Lake Malawi about 50km east of Mzuzu. This is probably the most scenic of Malawi's lake shore

towns, and a few travellers have even described it as 'Caribbean'. That may be a touch too fanciful, although at sunrise and sunset it does become quite picturesque. It's busy too. The *Ilala* passenger boat docks here on its voyage up and down the lake, and buses go regularly to/from Mzuzu and Salima.

In the last few years, Nkhata Bay has started to rival Cape Maclear as a budget travellers' destination; there are several good places to stay, and lots to do. You can get more information from Nkhata Bay's own tourist Web site: www.malawi-today.com/nkhatabay

Despite such modern touches, and the influx of foreigners, Nkhata Bay retains its strong Malawian feel, especially around the large and lively market.

Information

You can exchange cash or travellers cheques for kwacha, buy US dollars cash, or get cash on a Visa or MasterCard at the appropriately titled Easy Money change bureau, on the edge of town, opposite the police station. Next door, Tonga Tours (☎ 352341, **@** tongatours@malawi.net) organises tours and safaris (see Activities following). The helpful staff also organise flight confirmations, dive courses and boat charters, and provide assistance or insurance liaison in case of emergency. For long-distance travellers, Tonga Tours can arrange tickets for the international bus between Lilongwe and Dar es Salaam (Tanzania), which you can join in Mzuzu.

Dangers & Annoyances Unfortunately, security has become a bit of a problem in Nkhata Bay. Travellers have been attacked and robbed when walking outside the town centre (especially to/from Chikale Beach and the places to stay nearby), and a few people had bags snatched near the bus stand (thieves love new arrivals). These are isolated incidents, but to combat the problem, the hotels, lodges, restaurants and Aqua Africa have teamed up and will 'lend' their watchman free of charge to anyone walking outside the town centre. Use this service and you'll have no worries.

As at most places along the lake shore, the disease bilharzia exists here, and can be very dangerous (see Health in the Facts for the Visitor chapter, and the boxed text 'The Great Bilharzia Story' in the Central Malawi chapter).

Activities

On the south side of Nkhata Bay, the fabulous **Chikale Beach** is a popular spot for swimming and lazing on the sand. There are some places to stay nearby, and the beach also gets busy with day-trippers, especially at weekends.

For something more active, also on Chikale Beach, **kayaks** or **Canadian canoes** can be hired from Monkey Business (☎ 352365). You can go for a few hours, or take an organised trip along the lake shore for a few days (or longer depending on your own expertise and preference) for US$30 per day, staying at fishing villages or empty beaches along the way – highly rated by those who do them. Spectacular trips to Likoma Island, carrying the canoes on the *Ilala*, then paddling around the island and the Mozambican shore, are also highly rated. For more information you can contact Monkey Business through Tonga Tours (see Information earlier in this section).

If you want to learn **scuba diving**, Aqua Africa (☎/fax 352284, ✆ andy@aqua-africa.com) runs four-day courses for US$130, normally twice a week. Again, it comes highly recommended, and people who have done the course comment particularly on the attention to safety. You should try to book in advance, but if it's full you only have to wait a few days for the next course.

Tonga Tours (see Information earlier in this section) is an efficient, lively company running **tours** and **safaris** by vehicle to all parts of northern Malawi, including Vwaza, Nyika and Livingstonia from US$60 per person per day. The same destinations can also be reached on dedicated **mountain bike** tours, using a combination of bush camping and comfortable lodges. The 10-day trip to Livingstonia is popular, and shorter guided trips (eg, two or three days to Usisya) or just single-day rides around the local farmland

are also available. Alternatively, you can just hire a mountain bike and pedal around at your own pace. Another tempting option is the five day multiactivity trip, which includes kayaking along the lake shore, camping on remote beaches and a trek inland with the final two days returning to Nkhata Bay by mountain bike. This company is also involved in a scheme called Chiwila Eco-tours, in which local people in Nkhata Bay, Livingstonia and the surrounding area can benefit financially from tourism.

Places to Stay & Eat

Nkhata Bay has several places to stay and eat, all along the road into town (there's only one road in and out), and along the lake shore. Places in this section are described roughly north to south (ie, as you come into town).

As you come down the hill into the town centre, on your right, just past the post office, is the South African–run *Backpackers Connection* (☎ 352324), a busy place with good views over the bay. A bed in the dorm is US$2, singles/doubles with net and fan are US$3/4, camping is US$1 and there's a place to park vehicles if you're driving. There's also a bar, restaurant, clean bathrooms and a storage room for baggage if you want to travel light to Likoma Island or elsewhere. Down on the lake there's another bar and double chalets with bathroom for US$8.

On your left, and on the lake, are some other locally run places, including *Kupenja Lodge*, which are quieter, more simple and more local in feel – which some travellers prefer. At these places, rooms are US$1.50 per person, and food is only available if you order several hours in advance. Because these places are open to the lake, security has occasionally been a problem, so don't leave valuables in the rooms.

As this book was going to print we heard that *Africa Bay Backpackers* has been taken over by new management and is due for a major facelift, and possibly a change of name.

A little farther down the hill, on the right is *Jonathan's Juice Bar & Restaurant*, a mellow terrace under trees, with cool drinks from US$0.50, breakfasts and snacks from US$1, plus pizzas, pastas and stir-fries, including vegie options from US$2.50.

At the bottom of the hill is the bus stand, market and several shops. Opposite the market is the local style *Fumbani Restaurant* where cheap meals are available, but might need to be ordered long in advance. Nearby is a new locally owned place called *Ilala Lodge,* it has nice clean rooms with private bathroom from about US$10 per person. On the road west of the market is another local place – the *Cairo Hotel*, where plain rooms with smelly shared bathroom are not especially good value at US$2/3.

Beyond the market and shops you reach the *Yellow Submarine* with rooms for US$2.50/3 and a small private garden. Next door is the *Safari Restaurant*, a popular travellers' haunt with another great view across the bay, and selling omelettes and sandwiches for US$1, pizzas and moussaka from US$2 and pepper steak and chips or honey garlic chicken for US$3. Just past here is the ferry jetty, Aqua Africa and the end of the road.

If you turn right onto a dirt road just after the market, and go past Tonga Tours and Easy Money, then go right again, you'll reach the decidedly no-frills *Heart Hotel* – one of the few Malawian-run tourist places in town. Many budget travellers have recommended this place, although its village setting means a lot of people come and go, so you should be discreet with your valuables. You can sleep on the floor for US$0.60, or take the luxurious option of a bed for US$1 (with breakfast). Other meals are US$2. Mr Philip, the friendly proprietor, has opened a secluded budget camp site on the lake shore about 20km south of Nkhata Bay – ask at the hotel for details.

If you keep on the dirt road, you cross a bridge and head uphill and down dale (which always seems harder with a backpack) to reach several other places to stay. The first is the friendly *Mayoka Village* on a steep hillside over looking the bay, with simple but clean, mosquito-proof chalets for US$2.50/3. Camping is US$1. There's a bar, restaurant and free use of snorkel gear

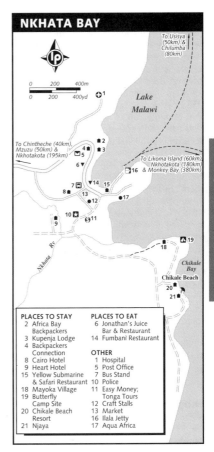

NKHATA BAY

Lake Malawi

To Usisya (50km) & Chilumba (80km)

To Chintheche (40km), Mzuzu (50km) & Nkhotakota (195km)

To Likoma Island (60km), Nkhotakota (180km) & Monkey Bay (380km)

Chikale Bay
Chikale Beach

PLACES TO STAY
2 Africa Bay Backpackers
3 Kupenja Lodge
4 Backpackers Connection
8 Cairo Hotel
9 Heart Hotel
15 Yellow Submarine & Safari Restaurant
18 Mayoka Village
19 Butterfly Camp Site
20 Chikale Beach Resort
21 Njaya

PLACES TO EAT
6 Jonathan's Juice Bar & Restaurant
14 Fumbani Restaurant

OTHER
1 Hospital
5 Post Office
7 Bus Stand
10 Police
11 Easy Money; Tonga Tours
12 Craft Stalls
13 Market
16 Ilala Jetty
17 Aqua Africa

and dugout canoes. Nearby, a new place called *Butterfly Camp Site* was under construction when we passed through and might be worth trying.

Chikale Beach Resort on Chikale Beach has nice-looking double chalets with bathroom for US$16/25 (less in the low season), including breakfast, but they're bare and functional inside. The bar and restaurant is bang on the fabulous beach, although this place is quiet in the evening – which some travellers prefer.

Njaya (℡/fax 352342, @ njayalodge@ compuserve.com) is a very popular place to stay, and a legend on the travellers' grapevine. The friendly management offers Asian-style reed and thatch chalets (which were all renovated in 1999) on Chikale Beach, and a range of cabins and bungalows on the hillside overlooking the lake. All rooms have mosquito nets and cost from US$3 per person in a simple hut with your own bedding, up to US$20 for a cottage with private bathroom. Camping is US$2. Security is good and there's safe parking for vehicles. The breezy bar overlooks the lake; there's satellite TV and good music in the evening, which makes for a lively atmosphere. In the restaurant, tasty food ranges from US$1 to US$3. Several readers have written to recommend the Sunday roast dinners, the Friday night barbecues and the wicked milkshake cocktails. You can get your laundry done, send email and there's a visa service if you're heading for Mozambique. Other services include massage, aromatherapy and reflexology, and for all you city slickers, credit cards are accepted. A transfer van runs between Njaya and the town centre a few times each day, and also meets the *Ilala* when it comes in to the jetty.

Most of the places to stay in Nkhata Bay can look after your baggage if you want to travel light across to Likoma Island (see Likoma Island later in this chapter).

Shopping

There's a PTC supermarket near the market. For wooden carvings and other souvenirs, there's an area of craft stalls on the narrow sandy street that runs behind the market, and another line of stalls at the junction at Mukwiya, a few kilometres from town, where the road down to Nkhata Bay turns off the main road. The carvers and traders have formed a cooperative, and pay a small percentage of their earnings into a local tree-planting scheme, which tourists are also encouraged to support.

Getting There & Away

Bus & Minibus All buses and minibuses leave from the bus stand next to the market. Travel to/from Mzuzu or Chintheche is US$0.75; to/from Nkhotakota costs US$2.

To reach Lilongwe, don't wait for the direct through bus (which sometimes never comes); it's far better to go to Mzuzu and change there.

Boat Many travellers also go to/from Nkhata Bay on the *Ilala* boat – for details see the Getting Around chapter earlier in this book.

AROUND NKHATA BAY

North of Nkhata Bay, the steep slopes of the Rift Valley escarpment plunge down to the lake and there's no room for a road alongside the shore. The villages here can only be reached on foot, by the *Ilala* or by local (and invariably overloaded) 'taxi-boats' that chug along the shore north of Nkhata Bay. At the village of **Usisya**, a new backpackers' hostel is under construction. You can get more details from the places in Nkhata Bay.

The territory on the east side of Lake Malawi, opposite Nkhata Bay, is Mozambique, but about 20km south of the Mozambican town Cóbuè is the **Manda Wilderness Area** – a community development and conservation project, which is easily reached from Nkhata Bay, or from Likoma Island (see Likoma Island later in this chapter). This place offers tented accommodation on the lake shore for US$50, including meals and guided walking safaris in the bush – which really is wilderness! It also offers canoe trips on the lake or along rivers.

Complete packages starting and ending in Nkhata Bay can be arranged through Tonga Tours (listed under Information in this Nkhata Bay section). If you're only going into this part of Mozambique for a few days, you probably won't need a visa; again Tonga Tours, or any of the backpacker lodges in Nkhata Bay, can advise you on this. You can also get information on the Manda Wilderness Area from Ulendo Safaris (listed under Travel Agencies in the Lilongwe chapter).

THE CHINTHECHE STRIP

Chintheche (chin-**tech**-ee) is a village about 40km south of Nkhata Bay. Although this place is unremarkable in itself (there are a few shops, a market, a mosque and a bank open twice a week), it's located near a long stretch of lake shore – known as the 'Chintheche Strip' – where several camp sites, hotels and lodges have been built, all with various styles and all catering for different types of visitors.

All the places to stay are situated about 2km to 5km east of the main north-south lake shore road (the M5) that runs between Nkhata Bay and Nkhotakota, usually involving a drive or walk along a sandy track through forest or farmland. Most of the places are signposted off the main road, but at minor junctions on the track there may be no signs (the local people seem to like them as decorations or firewood) so you may have to ask directions.

As with the rest of this chapter, places are described north to south. If you're travelling by bus, the Express services may not stop at every turn-off, so you may have to alight at the nearest place and walk or hitch the last few kilometres. Ordinary buses stop at more places. There are also minibuses along this road, which stop almost anywhere on request.

Places to Stay & Eat

In Chintheche village itself there are a few local resthouses, but a better option if you're short of cash is the under-used *Forest Resthouse*, where beds in functional and clean cabins cost US$2. Each room has two to four beds and its own bathroom. There's a lounge and dining area, with an outside kitchen where you can self-cater or ask the cook to prepare meals – but you must bring all your own food. There are also some basic rooms for US$1.50, and camping costs US$1. The resthouse is signposted down a track, 500m off the main road next to the large signpost for the Katoto Beach Motel (which was closed at the time of research). The only drawback with the Forest Resthouse is that it's not on the beach – you have to walk about 1km through the forest, but it's a pleasant stroll.

About 3km north of Chintheche is *Kawiya Kottages* (@ sosmalawi@malawi .net), two comfortable cabins, each with kitchen and bathroom, in a shady site on a private beach. This is good value at US$7 per person. Camping costs US$1.75. Nearby, another dirt track leads to London Cottages where single/double chalets with bathroom cost US$3/4. Camping is US$0.75.

About 2km down the main road and another 2km along a track is *Flame Tree Lodge* (☎ 357276), run by a very friendly English-Malawian couple on a beautiful promontory jutting into the lake, where smart chalets are US$15/25 with bathroom and breakfast (no extra charge for children sharing). Camping is US$2, and the showers are hot. This is a quiet place suitable for families or small groups. There's a bar, library and restaurant with meals from US$3. Breakfast (with home-made jam) is US$1.50. If you phone in advance they'll pick you up from Chintheche village.

Next along, about 2km farther south and 2.5km off the main road, is the turn-off to *Sombani Lodge* (☎ 357290), a line of cottages overlooking lawns with a nice beach and the lake beyond. This place lacks the Flame Tree's homey atmosphere, but prices are lower: rooms cost US$7/12, and family rooms cost US$18, all with private bathroom. Camping is US$1.50.

Another 1.5km along the main road, a tar road leads for 2km to the *Chintheche Inn* (☎/fax 357211, @ wildsaf@eomw.net, info@wilderness.malawi.net), a small and friendly mid-range place with stylish Mediterranean-style decor in the rooms, beautiful gardens, and thatched verandas overlooking the beach. There's also a swimming pool. Dinner, bed and full buffet breakfast costs US$90/150. The food in the restaurant, which has a nice terrace overlooking the gardens and the lake, is unpretentious, but very good. Young children in their parents' room pay for meals only. If you want to reserve a room and can't get through on the phone, ring Central African Wilderness Safaris (see Travel Agencies in the Lilongwe chapter) – it has a radio link with the inn. Chintheche Inn also has its own well-organised dive centre, offering courses and a range of excursions, which

NORTHERN MALAWI

include unique day-trips to Likoma Island that tie in with the chartered plane service.

Next to Chintheche Inn is a *camp site* run by the same management. It has flat grassy lawns, its own bar and restaurant. At US$5 per person this is steep compared to most other places locally, but worth it given the overall high standards, especially the hotel-quality showers and bathrooms.

Another 1km south down the main road is a signpost for the CCAP School (also called New Bandawe); go through here to reach the South African-run *Nkhwazi Lake Camp* overlooking a small sandy cove with a longer beach nearby. Camping costs US$1 per person. There are basic but clean ablution blocks, and a 'pub' with home-cooked meals around US$3 to US$5. Scuba gear and motorboats for anglers can be hired.

Continuing south down the main road you reach the turn-off to Bandawe (also called Old Bandawe) and *Makuzi Beach Retreat* (☎ 357296), another 3.5km down the track. This quiet and relaxing place offers camping for US$3, simple chalets for US$5, and cool comfortable chalets with bathroom for US$30 per person. Breakfast and lunch ranges from US$1 to US$4, with a set dinner for US$5, including lots of vegetarian options. Lara Jackson and other instructors run courses here in Reiki, yoga, massage, herbalism and similar pursuits.

About 7km from the Makuzi turn-off (55km from Nkhata Bay) is *Kande Beach Camp*, a legendary stop for overland trucks where beach life, good times and late night partying is the name of the game. Trucks get special rates, but individual drivers and backpackers looking to join in the fun pay US$1 for camping or US$10 for simple chalets. Also on site is a restaurant, large bar, games room and fully set-up dive centre where courses start at about US$150. Mountain bikes, canoes, kayaks and sailboards are available for hire.

Another 7km further south is *Mwaya Beach Lodge*, where the atmosphere is quiet and restful, and the entrance track designed to cross weak bridges and keep out the overland trucks! Simple chalets cost US$3.50 per person and camping is US$1.50. There's a bar, and food includes banana bread, beanburgers, pumpkin ravioli, or meals with chicken and fish for US$2 to US$4. Clean drinking water is free. You can stay here and learn to dive at Kande Beach for US$200, which includes the course at Kande Beach and all food and accommodation at Mwaya.

Old Bandawe & Makuzi Hill

Near Makuzi Beach Retreat is the site of Bandawe mission station. It was established by UMCA missionaries in the 1890s after they moved from their original position at Cape Maclear, before moving to the more successful site at today's Livingstonia. This site is often called Old Bandawe, to distinguish it from New Bandawe, built nearer the main road in the 1920s and still a thriving mission and secondary school today. All that remains today is a few huts and the church the missionaries built, which has a new roof and is still used on Sundays. It is a simple, square building with a series of low steps in a semi-circle facing the altar, instead of pews, contrasting sharply with the more European-style church later built at Livingstonia.

Also nearby is a graveyard where various missionaries are buried in a line facing the lake surrounded by a series of low white walls that seem to pen them in. A single grave lies outside the wall – our guide said it contained the body of a shipwrecked sailor who was not known to be a Christian.

Overlooking the lodge is Makuzi Hill, which has spiritual significance for the local people. For some unknown reason (geological, meteorological or magical) small bolts of lightning have been seen shooting a few metres *up* from rocks on this hill. There are also several caves, where the Tonga people would hide from Ngoni warriors or Swahili-Arab slave traders in the 19th century.

Lake Malawi's Islands

The islands of Likoma and Chizumulu are in the northern part of Lake Malawi, within the territorial waters of Mozambique, but they are part of Malawi, and linked to the rest of the country by the *Ilala* passenger boat service.

LIKOMA ISLAND

Likoma is something of an enigma: it's not a paradise isle in the usual sense, although it does have some excellent beaches. Instead it has a rather sparse beauty that not all visitors will appreciate. Some love it and stay for weeks; others are disappointed and leave as soon as possible. Either way, you'll meet few other tourists here.

Likoma measures 17 sq km, with a population of about 6000 people. The south is fairly flat, dry and sandy, with baobab trees a common feature. The north is more hilly and quite densely vegetated. The main settlement is Chipyela, and there are several other fishing villages dotted around the coast.

If you walk around the island, or visit beaches near villages, remember this isn't the Costa del Sol – the people here live a very traditional way of life, so keep your clothing and behaviour suitably modest.

Things to See & Do

Unless you charter a plane or boat, you're tied to the *Ilala* schedules, which means being here at least three days, so you'll have to relax whether you like it or not!

Likoma Island has some lovely, long sandy **beaches**, ideal for **swimming**, mostly along the southern coast but also notably at Yofu Bay in the north. A couple of islanders have been killed by crocodiles in recent years, so think twice about diving in, and ask for advice at the place where you stay.

For something more active, you can **walk** around Likoma; the island is easily small enough to explore on foot. The Akuzike Guesthouse in Chipyela has produced a map of the island, showing the best beaches, areas of interest and suggesting a number of walks.

Likoma Missionaries & the Cathedral of St Peter

European involvement on Likoma Island began in 1882 when members of UMCA (Universities Mission to Central Africa) established a base here. Leaders of the party Will Johnson and Chauncey Maples chose the island as protection from attacks from the warlike Ngoni and Yao people.

Maples became the first bishop of Likoma, but he died only a few months after being appointed, drowning in the lake off Monkey Bay. Despite the setback, missionary work on the island continued. Between 1903 and 1905 the huge cathedral was built and dedicated to St Peter – appropriately a fisherman. Today it remains one of Malawi's most remarkable buildings.

Measuring more than 100m long by 25m wide (for British travellers, that's the size of Winchester Cathedral), the cathedral has stained-glass windows and elaborate choir stalls carved from soapstone. The crucifix above the altar was carved from wood from the tree where Livingstone's heart was buried in Zambia. It was built at a part of the island called Chipyela, meaning 'place of burning', because the early UMCA arrivals had witnessed some suspected witches being burnt alive here. The island's main settlement grew up around the cathedral, and is still called Chipyela today.

The UMCA missionaries remained on Likoma until the 1940s. During that time they'd been hard at work – claiming 100% literacy among the local population at one point. The cathedral fell into disrepair, but was restored in the 1970s and 1980s, and local people are understandably very proud of it.

In Chipyela, the impressive **Anglican Cathedral of St Peter** should not be missed (see the boxed text 'Likoma Missionaries & The Cathedral of St Peter'). Nearby, the neat **market place** contains a few shops and stalls. There is also a bizarre tree in the square – a very old baobab that has been

NORTHERN MALAWI

Lake Malawi – Lake of Stars

Lake Malawi – formerly Lake Nyasa, and sometimes billed as 'The Lake of Stars' – is Malawi's single biggest geographical feature, and for most tourists it's the country's main attraction. See the Geography and Climate sections in the Facts about Malawi chapter; this boxed text deals more with the aesthetic side of things.

The lake is simply beautiful, with several long stretches of classic sandy beach, lapped by gentle waves and lined with palm trees, and ideal for relaxation. In other areas the steep western escarpment plunges straight into the lake, while the east side is fringed by the imposing hills and mountains of Tanzania and Mozambique, a vast dramatic backdrop, especially at sunrise and sunset. One of Malawi's great delights is to sit on the beach and watch the scenery change colour and texture hour by hour.

In the lake are several islands, mostly small and uninhabited. Some are no more than jumbled piles of rocks, but all provide useful homes for Malawi's famously colourful *mbuna* fish, and of course ideal sites for diving and snorkelling. This is one of the cheapest places in the world to learn to dive. Another activity is kayaking – a fascinating way to explore islands and parts of the shore inaccessible by road. The lake shore and nearby hills also offer several ideal bird-watching spots.

By day, views across the waters of the lake are further enlivened by the fishermen in rowing boats or dugout canoes paddling by. Many places to stay are near traditional fishing villages – an excellent opportunity to meet local people that you might not have elsewhere. At night, all you can see are the lanterns tied to boats, to attract fish, bobbing on the horizon. Often you feel that you're watching a scene that hasn't changed for centuries.

Different parts of the lake have different characteristics. To help you decide where to go, the following notes on various places – described north to south – will be useful. If you can't decide, then visit them all!

The Far North

Between the border and Chitimba there are long stretches of sandy beach, with spectacular escarpment behind. This area is less developed than farther south down the lake shore, and there are fewer opportunities for diving and water sports. It's a great place to relax, especially after arriving from Tanzania or walking down from Livingstonia.

Chitimba to Nkhata Bay

This whole section of lake shore can only be reached by boat – either the *Ilala* passenger boat or small local ferries. It's very undeveloped from a tourist angle, although a few small camps and backpackers have been built or are planned to be built.

overtaken by a strangler fig, and has rotted away from underneath so that it is now used by the locals as storeroom.

Down on the lake shore is the **fishing beach** where local boats come and go and the people wash and sell fish. Don't be surprised if some people greet you in Portuguese – traders come here from nearby Mozambique to sell firewood, vegetables and – bizarrely – fish to the locals.

From Likoma you can cross over to Mozambique for a day or two, just to visit the small town of Cóbuè and its Catholic cathedral (built by the Portuguese to be taller than the Anglican cathedral on Likoma Island) or maybe to visit Manda Wilderness Area, about 20km south of Cóbuè. For some information on this area see the Around Nkhata Bay section earlier in this chapter, or ask at the backpackers lodges in Nkhata Bay or on Likoma or Chizumulu islands. If you're only going into this part of Mozambique for a few days, you probably won't need a visa, although you must report to the Malawian immigration officials on the way out, and

Lake Malawi – Lake of Stars

Nkhata Bay

This is a vibrant market town tucked into the hills on a dramatic section of the lake shore. It has a strong local identity despite the influx of tourists. There are lots of places to stay, a lively backpacker scene, and plenty of diving and kayaking. Nkhata Bay is a major *Ilala* port, and an ideal gateway for Likoma and Chizumulu Islands.

Likoma & Chizumulu Islands

These large islands offer a choice of places to stay (top end and budget). There are beaches to die for and excellent diving. No vehicles are allowed, but there's fine walking to be had. Don't miss the huge and fascinating cathedral on Likoma.

The Chintheche Strip

This string of long sandy beaches and beautiful rocky coves is almost too perfect to be true. There are several camp sites, camps and lodges, catering for every taste and budget.

Nkhotakota

This busy fishing town and port has beaches and places to stay about 10km south. It serves as a gateway to the Nkhotakota Wildlife Reserve.

Senga Bay

Perhaps not the most spectacular part of the shore, Senga Bay still has good beaches, fishing and watersports, and plenty of places to stay. A major advantage is the easy access to/from Lilongwe.

Cape Maclear

This is the all-time classic backpacker destination. There's a big choice of budget accommodation, and a couple of good mid-range places too. The beautiful lake shore and scattered islands are located within Lake Malawi National Park. All the budget places to stay are in Chembe village, which is probably one of the best places on the lake to actually meet local people. It's also one of the best places for sailing, diving and kayaking.

Monkey Bay to Mangochi

More long golden sandy beaches are to be found here. There are some good top-end hotels here, and some fine budget options too. This area offers good access to/from Blantyre, and it's easy to tie in with a visit to Liwonde National Park.

---

return the same way. The backpackers lodges can advise you on this too.

Places to Stay & Eat

In Chipyela, the *Akuzike Guesthouse* is justifiably popular, with clean rooms around a courtyard at US$3 per person. There's running water, mosquito nets, a small restaurant (meals cost US$2 to US$3) and a map of the island on the wall, which is good for planning walks.

For cheap eats, try the *Women's Restaurant* near the market, or the nameless *food shack* on the fishing beach. Ordering meals in advance may prove rewarding, but don't expect a huge menu – the staples here are fish, nsima and rice. Fruit and vegetables are more limited.

Mango Drift, on a beautiful sandy beach on the west side of the island, charges US$1 for camping, US$2 for a dorm bed and US$3 per person in a simple hut. Lighting is solar powered and the open air hot water showers are reported to be 'worth getting dirty for!'. There's a bar with good sunset views and a restaurant serving meals from

US$1 to US$4. Comfortable double chalets with bathrooms are planned. Activities include sailing, canoeing and dhow (traditional Arabic sailing vessel) trips around Likoma and Chizumulu Islands, or across to Mozambique. The connected Two Island Divers scuba centre offers PADI open water courses for $150, which includes free accommodation. If you come on the *Ilala* from Nkhata Bay, there's time to do the course and catch the *Ilala* back again five days later. You can get more information on this place from the backpackers lodges in Nkhata Bay.

Your other alternative on Likoma is *Kaya Mawa*, a luxury lodge on the south side of the island, which is quite simply unique. Each chalet is different, designed with wild imagination, and has private access to the lake (the honeymoon suite even has its own islet). The bar and restaurant is balanced on the top of a huge rock buttress, with splendid views of sunrise and sunset. Rates are US$150 per person full board, including boat trips. This lodge's agent is Ulendo Safaris, listed under Travel & Tour Agents in the Information section of the Lilongwe chapter, and you can also get information from specialist travel agents overseas.

Getting There & Away

Air Air Malawi used to run regular flights to Likoma, but until these are resumed the only way to fly direct to Likoma is by charter plane. Alternatively, from June to October, an air charter company called Sefofane runs flights from Mzuzu to Likoma for US$55 per person one way. This plane connects with the daily Air Malawi service running between Lilongwe and Mzuzu. You can get more information from Ulendo Safaris or Central African Wilderness Safaris, listed under Travel & Tour Agents in the Information section of the Lilongwe chapter.

Boat Most people come to Likoma Island by the *Ilala* boat – see the Getting Around chapter for details. The boat usually stops for at least an hour or two, so even if you're heading elsewhere you might be able to nip ashore to have a quick look at the cathedral. Check with the captain first. However, it no longer stops at the fishing beach near Chipyela, but moors off another beach about 1km to the south.

The island is only about 10km off the coast of Mozambique, and dhows sail to the town of Cóbuè, from where you can continue through Mozambique. For more details see Mozambique in the Getting There & Away chapter.

CHIZUMULU ISLAND

Chizumulu Island is smaller than Likoma (and just a few kilometres away) and even more detached from the mainland – possibly the perfect lake hideaway. If you want to visit both islands, transport links make it best to go to Chizumulu first (see Getting There & Away later in this chapter). The main place to stay is *Wakwenda Retreat*, which has very friendly staff and a good beach near where the *Ilala* stops. Chalets cost US$3.50 per person, simple huts are US$2.50, and camping is US$1.50. There's a pleasant bar built in a baobab tree. You can also hire snorkel and dive gear. There are two *local resthouses* on the island where facilities are more basic, but rates are cheaper.

Getting There & Away

To reach Chizumulu from Nkhata Bay, the *Ilala* stops here before Likoma, once per week. Or you can get the dhow ferry that runs early every morning from Ulisa on the west coast of Likoma to Chizumulu (US$0.50), but it's a very choppy ride when the wind is blowing, and potentially dangerous if there's a storm.

Central Malawi

This chapter covers most parts of Malawi's Central Province (which has Lilongwe at its centre), with the addition of the Viphya Plateau. (Lilongwe is covered in its own chapter.) This chapter also covers the Nkhotakota Wildlife Reserve and Kasungu National Park, and the popular lake shore areas of Senga Bay and Cape Maclear. More details on the lake are given in the Lake Malawi box at the end of the Northern Malawi chapter. Places are described roughly north to south.

In this chapter there is also a section on South Luangwa National Park, in neighbouring Zambia. Many visitors to Malawi hop across the border to visit South Luangwa, as this is one of the best parks in Africa, and is very easily reached from Lilongwe or any other part of Central Malawi.

THE VIPHYA PLATEAU

The Viphya Plateau is a highland area, running like a broad backbone through north-central Malawi, from just south of Mzuzu down to Katate. Despite being called a plateau, this area is not flat but consists mostly of rolling hills, cut by river valleys and punctuated by occasional rocky peaks. Not surprisingly, the area is also sometimes called the Viphya Mountains.

Much of the Viphya Plateau is pine plantation or dense bush, but the journey through this area, along the main road (the M1) between Kasungu and Mzuzu is beautiful, especially if the sun is shining (but don't be surprised if there's dense mist and rain). If you've got a few days to spare, this is a good area to relax away from the hubbub of towns, or to cool down from the heat of the lake shore.

Places to Stay & Eat

Luwawa Forest Lodge (☎ *320897, 829725,* **@** *wardlow@malawi.net*) lies 10km east of the main road between Kasungu and Mzuzu. It used to belong to the Forestry Department, but it's now managed by the

Highlights

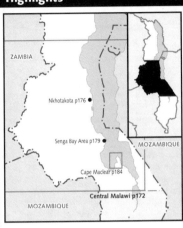

ZAMBIA

Nkhotakota p176 ●

Senga Bay Area p179 ●

MOZAMBIQUE

Cape Maclear p184 ●

Central Malawi p172

MOZAMBIQUE

- Hiking the Viphya Plateau, with its cool mountain air, cosy forest resthouses, good walking, mountain-biking and other outdoor activities

- Visiting Nkhotakota Wildlife Reserve – a frequently overlooked wilderness with top-quality bird-watching, plus a good chance of spotting elephants and lions

- Exploring Cape Maclear, the legendary traveller's byword for rest and relaxation; diving, snorkelling, canoeing, partying or just lying on the beach

- Wandering through Mua Mission Museum – a fascinating study of Chewa, Ngoni and Yao traditional beliefs and a journey deep into the soul of Malawi

- Travelling to Kasungu National Park, with its rich vegetation, excellent bird-watching and informative guides

- Meandering from Monkey Bay to Mangochi – the scenic strip of southern lake shore with beaches, palm trees, campsites, backpackers lodges, guesthouses, luxurious hotels and wonderful sunsets

CENTRAL MALAWI

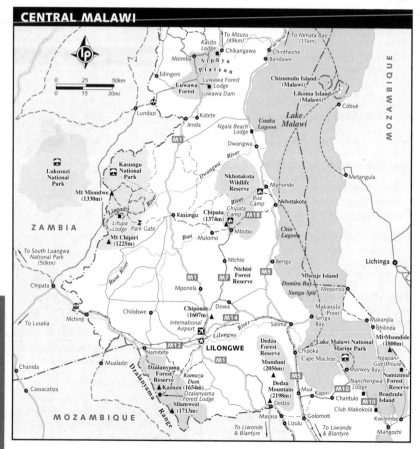

energetic George Wardlow, and offers comfortable accommodation in bedrooms sleeping up to four, with bathroom and kitchen, for US$15 per person (half price for children). Breakfast and lunch costs US$4, and a big three-course dinner is US$12. You'll soon wear off the calories – the lodge offers walking trails, mountain biking (US$20 per day), sailing, boating (US$5 per hour), fishing and several other activities. Keen hikers and mountain bikers will enjoy the long-distance wilderness walks and rides from Luwawa across the plateau and down the escarpment to Chintheche on Lake Malawi.

Bookings are preferred for the lodge, but are not essential.

Kasito Lodge (sometimes called Chikangawa Resthouse) is less than 1km west of the main road between Kasungu and Mzuzu. Because it is so close to the road, it is ideal for travellers without wheels, although it doesn't have the facilities or activities on offer at Luwawa Forest Lodge. There are five rooms with four beds in each with sheets and blankets. The shared showers are hot, the toilets are clean and lounge has a roaring wood fire. It costs US$3 per person – an absolute bargain. You must supply your own food, but there's a kitchen and the care-taker will cook (he's very good) and wash up, for which an extra tip is appropriate. Camping is US$1.50 per person, and the caretaker will probably allow you to use a bathroom inside. If you just turn up, and the place isn't fully booked, you can stay. Reservations are not required for camping. If the lodge is full, **Resthouse No 2** is nearby, and is cheaper but slightly less comfortable, and **The Annex** is even more basic again.

Getting There & Away

To reach Luwawa, there are three dirt roads branching eastwards off the main M1 north-south road. The ones to the north and south are just about passable with a 4WD, but the middle one is in good condition and can be used by any type of car. There's no public transport to Luwawa along any of these dirt roads, so if you haven't got wheels you'll have to get off the bus at the junction where the middle dirt road leaves the main road, and then walk – although you might be lucky and get a lift with another visitor or on a logging truck. Coming from the south, from Kasungu take the main road towards Mzuzu. About 110km from Kasungu you'll see a dirt road with a signpost pointing right (east) to Luwawa. Ignore this. Continue for another 9km until you see a sign that says 'Luwawa 10km'. Luwawa Forest Lodge is also signposted. Take this dirt road to reach the resthouse. Coming from Mzuzu, continue past the junction where the road from Mzimba joins from the right. After 8km you'll see a sign saying 'Luwawa D73'. Ignore this, and continue for another 8km to the 'Luwawa 10 km and 'Luwawa Forest Lodge' signs mentioned above.

To reach Kasito Lodge by car from the south, continue 27km beyond the Mzimba junction on the road towards Mzuzu; the lodge is signposted on your left. Coming from the north, you pass a large wood factory at Chikangawa village, and the turn-off to the lodge is a few kilometres beyond here on the right. Travelling by bus, ask the driver to drop you at the Kasito Lodge junction. Kasito Lodge is less than 1km to walk from here.

KASUNGU

Kasungu is a fairly large town just off the main north-south road (the M1) that runs through the middle of the country. Kasungu is a fairly large town, about 130km north of Lilongwe, just off the main north-south road (the M1) that runs through the middle of the country. This is where the roads east to Nkhotakota and west to Kasungu National Park branch off the main road. You may find yourself changing transport here, or overnighting on the way to the national park. There are no major attractions in the town, although the busy market off the main street is worth a look around. This is a place just to watch everyday Malawian life carrying on at its usual steady pace.

Note that the centre of town itself is about 2km off the main north-south road, which bypasses it to the west.

Places to Stay & Eat

The cheapest option is the none-too-clean **Council Resthouse**, on the main street opposite the National Bank of Malawi. The resthouse has a big room with mats on the floor where you can doss down for US$0.20, and rooms with two beds cost US$1.50.

More expensive but infinitely better is the quaint old **Chikambe Motel**, which was the former government resthouse. This motel charges US$7/11 for single/double rooms with bathroom and breakfast. It's out in the leafy suburbs of Kasungu, a 2km walk east of the centre.

The **Kasungu Inn**, at the eastern end of town, has clean and tidy rooms for US$20/30 with private bathroom and breakfast. Camping on the lawn is US$3 per person.

There are several cheap local restaurants on the main street and around the market. The **Golden Dish** is making an effort, with good food and reasonably clean surroundings. For a beer, try **Gab Pub** on the main street.

Getting There & Away

At the junction where the main street through town leaves the main north-south road there's a petrol station. A few minibuses stop here, but most public transport goes to/from the bus station in town, which is just north of the main street. The fare between Lilongwe and Kasungu is US$2.50, and between Mzuzu and Kasungu it's US$3.50. If you're heading for the lake shore, there are infrequent *matolas* (unofficial public transport in the form of a van or a truck) along the road through Nkhotakota Wildlife Reserve to Nkhotakota.

KASUNGU NATIONAL PARK

Kasungu National Park lies west of Kasungu town, along the border with Zambia. It covers more than 2000 sq km, making it the second-largest park in the country, after Nyika National Park. The landscape is mainly flat or gently rolling hills, with a few rocky outcrops rising above the plain. The soil is mostly sandy and the vegetation mostly *miombo* (dry and sparse) woodland interspersed by wide, marshy river courses, called *dambos*, where reeds and grasses grow. The park also has a small lake, called Lifupa Dam.

Although trees in miombo woodland are normally well spaced, allowing bush and grass to grow in between, the vegetation in Kasungu is relatively dense. This is because the park's population of elephants (who naturally act as 'gardeners' by keeping the growth controlled) has been seriously reduced since the 1970s by poaching. However, it's estimated that about 300 **elephants** still remain in the park, and the chances of seeing some are fairly good in the dry season. Other large mammals here include **buffaloes**, **zebras**, several **antelope** species and the dam contains a group of **hippos**. Predators include **lions** and **leopards**, but these are very rarely seen.

Since 1995, Kasungu National Park has been receiving aid money from the European Union to assist with anti-poaching efforts and management. Although there has been some definite progress since the dark days of the 1980s, and animal populations are recovering, the park cannot yet be termed a major wildlife-viewing destination.

But if you've come to Malawi for more than ticking off the 'big five', Kasungu is well worth a visit. The vegetation is lush and the birdlife is also excellent, with woodland and grassland species, as well as waders around the dam. The park also contains a number of historical sites. These include old iron kilns used by local people in this area before it was made a national park, and some very faint rock paintings that are assumed to be pre-Bantu.

Entry fees must be paid to go into the park (see National Parks & Wildlife Reserves in the Facts about Malawi chapter).

Activities

If you have your own vehicle you can tour the park on its good network of tracks, although most of these are closed during the rainy season and may not reopen until June each year. Alternatively you can go out to watch wildlife in a vehicle organised by the lodge (see Places to Stay).

Walking is also permitted in the park. A ranger (often called a 'scout') to act as guide is obligatory if you go beyond the confines of the lodge, but this is no problem as the guides always see more than you do on your own, and can explain about the animals, birds, and vegetation, helping you get more from your visit. For morning or evening walks of about two hours through the woodland around the dam, the hire of a guide costs US$10. You can also go for much longer walks – all day if you like – and really get a feel for the bush.

By foot or by car, a good place to aim for is Black Rock, about 4km north-west of the lodge, which is a good viewpoint (although the aerial on top spoils the feel of the wilderness). Other hills in the park include Miondwe, straddling the park boundary and the border with Zambia, and Wangombe (Hill of the Cow), about 23km north of Lifupa Dam.

Places to Stay

Lifupa Lodge has a tall thatched central bar and restaurant with a beautiful veranda overlooking the dam, where animals often come to drink. This is surrounded by luxurious twin-bedded chalets. Ownership was in flux at the time of research, so inquire about rates at a tour company or travel agent in Lilongwe. *Lifupa Camp* is nearby, where simple chalets with shared showers and toilets cost from US$30 per person. There's a kitchen where you can prepare your own food, or for a small extra fee the cook will do everything for you. Camping costs US$2.

Getting There & Away
It's 52km from Kasungu town to Lifupa Lodge and Lifupa Camp. There's no public transport, so without a car you'd have to hitch from Kasungu – the best place to wait is the turn-off to the park (signposted) near the petrol station on the main road.

If you're in your own car coming from the south, turn left (west) off the main road, just before the turn-off to Kasungu town. The road leads past a grand palace (built by former president Banda) and winds through farmland and villages. There are a few forks and junctions, but the park is signposted and local people will always point the way if you get lost. The park entrance is 35km west of Kasungu town, and from there it's another 17km by the shortest route to Lifupa Lodge and Camp.

The Central Lake Shore

DWANGWA
This town has grown up around a large sugar cane plantation established on the lake shore plain. There's a market, shops, a supermarket, a petrol station and a local *resthouse*. About 18km north of here is *Ngala Beach Lodge* (✉ ngala@malawi .net), formerly called Heidi's Hideout and still known by this name, which several travellers have recommended. Airy rooms and chalets with private bathroom cost US$18 per person, plus $7 for breakfast. Camping is US$2. There's a bar and a small restaurant, with a deck overlooking the lake. Dinner is around US$10. Canoes can be used by guests (free) to reach a nearby beach, and a motor boat or mountain bikes can be hired. The agent for the Lodge's is Ulendo Safaris in Lilongwe (see

Travel Agencies under Information in the Lilongwe chapter).

NKHOTAKOTA
Nkhotakota (nko-ta-ko-ta) is a town on the lake shore east of Kasungu, about 140km north of Salima, and about 200km south of Nkhata Bay. It was once the centre of slave trading in this region, and is reputedly one of the oldest market towns in Africa (although the market is nothing special these days).

The town is strung out along the main north-south lake shore road (the M5), and along a street that runs for about 4km down to the lake. The Stagecoach bus station is about 2km off the main road. From the bus station it's another 2km to the jetty on the lake shore where the *Ilala* passenger boat stops.

Things to see include the **mission**, with a huge church built with thick low walls and a high roof, presumably to keep congregations cool (it can get very hot on the lake shore, particularly just before the rains break). If you come on a Sunday the singing from the church is wonderful. In the grounds of the mission is a large **mango tree** called the 'Livingstone Tree' where the explorer David Livingstone (see History in the Facts about Malawi chapter) camped in the 19th century. Livingstone met a local chief called Jumbe here and tried to persuade him to abandon the slave trade. In the part of town called Kombo is another 'Livingstone Tree', and nearby yet another tree with historical significance – where an aspiring politician called Hastings Banda made speeches in the 1960s (see History in the Facts about Malawi chapter). The trees are nothing special, but the walk through the village-like outskirts is very pleasant.

Another possible attraction is the **hippo pool** at Jalo, a few kilometres north of town; local youths will show you the way. They may also try to show you the hot springs, 3km south of town on the main road, but this is not worth the bother.

Places to Stay & Eat
On the main north-south road, the *Nawo Guesthouse* is clean and quiet, and all

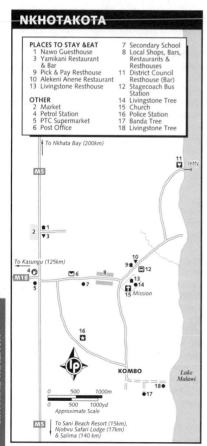

NKHOTAKOTA

PLACES TO STAY &EAT		7	Secondary School
1 Nawo Guesthouse		8	Local Shops, Bars,
3 Yamikani Restaurant			Restaurants &
& Bar			Resthouses
9 Pick & Pay Resthouse		11	District Council
10 Alekeni Anene Restaurant			Resthouse (Bar)
13 Livingstone Resthouse		12	Stagecoach Bus
			Station
OTHER		14	Livingstone Tree
2 Market		15	Church
4 Petrol Station		16	Police Station
5 PTC Supermarket		17	Banda Tree
6 Post Office		18	Livingstone Tree

To Nkhata Bay (200km)

M5

To Kasungu (125km)
M18

Jetty 11

10
9
12
13
14
15 Mission

16

KOMBO

Lake Malawi

18
17

0   500   1000m
0   500   1000yd
Approximate Scale

M5 To Sani Beach Resort (15km),
Njobvu Safari Lodge (17km)
& Salima (140 km)

rooms are good value at US$3 per room (single or double, with bathroom). Nearby is the market and the *Yamikani Restaurant & Bar*.

If you turn off the main north-south road and go into town along the main street towards the lake, about 1½km from the junction, you reach the mission. In the grounds is the *Livingstone Resthouse* with basic singles/doubles for US$2/3. There is also a kitchen where you can cook your own food. Naturally, as this is inside the mission grounds you should keep your behaviour suitably modest.

If you carry on down the main street towards the lake for another 500m, you reach the friendly and well organised *Pick & Pay Resthouse* (☎ 292459), which has clean rooms with nets from US$1.50 to US$3 and camping for US$1. There's also safe parking for vehicles. The food is good, although *Alekeni Anene Restaurant* next door keeps the competition fierce. The Stagecoach bus station is just opposite.

Another 2km down the main street, you reach the lake, the jetty, and the *District Council Resthouse*. The rooms here are disgusting and should be avoided at all costs, but there's a bar and the terrace that are worth visiting for a drink; it's a fine place for an evening beer overlooking the lake. Note also the terrace balustrade, which is built from crankshafts, axles and other old motor parts, while the windows on the staircase are still attached to the doors of the car they came from.

Getting There & Away

Bus & Minibus Stagecoach buses running along the main north-south lake shore road between Nkhata Bay and Salima swing in to the depot opposite the Pick & Pay Resthouse. Travel to Salima (hourly) costs US$1.50. For minibuses you have to go to the main road and wait at the junction opposite the PTC supermarket.

Boat You can go to/from Nkhotakota on the *Ilala* passenger boat that plies up and down the lake – see the Getting Around chapter. There's a jetty, but usually the lake is too shallow for the *Ilala* to come in, so small boats go out to ferry passengers ashore. If you arrive on the boat, it's a 2km walk from the jetty to the Pick & Pay Resthouse.

Around Nkhotakota

About 11km south of Nkhotakota is the turn-off to *Sani Beach Resort*, on the lake about 4km off the main road. It has smart single/double chalets for US$25/31 and simple huts for US$13/25, all including breakfast. Camping costs US$1.50 per person. There are boats and fishing gear available for hire, and the management are keen anglers.

CENTRAL MALAWI

Street life in Malawi. **Clockwise from top:** selling beans in Old Town Market, Lilongwe; a young boy playing *bano*, a popular Malawian pastime; shopping in Mwanza; a village shopkeeper with his merchandise

Malawi's colourful markets have produce for locals and crafts for visitors. **Clockwise from top:** vegetable stalls, Old Town Market, Lilongwe; woven replicas of overland trucks for sale; waiting for customers, Old Town Market, Lilongwe

About 13km south of Nkhotakota is the turn off to the smarter and more organised *Njobvu Safari Lodge* (☎ 292506, ✉ carole@ birdsafaris.co.uk), also on the lake about 4km off the main road. Nicely decorated chalets with bathroom cost US$30 per person, breakfast is included. Simple chalets are US$15 per person. Camping is US$2. There's a *bar* and *restaurant* (snacks around US$1.50, lunch US$4, three-course dinner US$11), and the owners are always happy to talk at length with guests. They're extremely informative about wildlife in the surrounding area.

About 15km south of Nkhotakota is the turn off to **Nkhotakota Pottery**, an offshoot of the famous Dedza Pottery, but with a better stock of wares, a nice beach and a small *restaurant*.

Chia Lagoon is a large bay linked to Lake Malawi by a narrow channel, crossed by a bridge near the main road about 24km south of Nkhotakota. Local people fish here using large triangular nets on poles, and seem resigned to having their photos taken by tourists on the bridge. Njobvu Safari Lodge organises boat trips into this 'mini Okavango' and to other points along the lake.

NKHOTAKOTA WILDLIFE RESERVE

Nkhotakota Wildlife Reserve lies west of the main lake shore road, covering a broad area of hills and escarpments. It's the largest reserve in Malawi but was virtually abandoned during the 1980s and early 1990s. Today, it's being rehabilitated, and although animals such as elephants and lions occur here, they're difficult to see in the dense vegetation. Walking is an excellent way to experience the reserve and sample some genuine wilderness. There's a mix of miombo woodland and patches of evergreen forest, and the reserve is crossed by several large rivers, so the birdlife is varied and rewarding.

For a place to stay, there are some dilapidated rondavels at *Chipata Camp*, the reserve headquarters, about 5km north of the dirt road towards Lilongwe, about 35km from Nkhotakota town. However, the best

place to aim for is *Bua Camp*, which is a beautiful clearing on the banks of a rocky river, where camping costs US$1. The turn-off to Bua is 10km north of Nkhotakota, then 15km on a dirt track, but without wheels your only way to get here is on foot. You can hire a reserve ranger to be a guide for walks, and reserve entry fees must also be paid (see the National Parks in the Facts about Malawi section earlier in this book).

If you don't have your own car, you can hire one at the Pick & Pay Resthouse in Nkhotakota for US$25 per day (see Places to Stay under Nkhotakota, earlier). Alternatively, properly organised day safaris to the reserve are arranged from Njobvu Safari Lodge (see Around Nkhotakota section), at US$50 per person, including transport, lunch, professional guide and entrance fees. Elephants are regularly seen. Bird-watching trips, night trips by vehicle to look for lions, and longer safaris for several days, can also be arranged. For more details see the Web site: www.birdsafaris.co.uk.

The Southern Lake Shore

SALIMA

The town of Salima is about 20km from the lake, where the road from Lilongwe meets the main lake shore road. Salima itself is nothing special, but it's the jumping off point for Senga Bay, a popular destination for visitors (see Senga Bay later in this chapter).

Places to Stay & Eat

If you get stuck in Salima for the night there are a few options – none very inspiring. The *Mai Tsalani Motel* near the PTC Supermarket, about a 10-minute walk from the bus station, has basic doubles with bathroom for US$3; singles are cheaper and the shared bathrooms not too bad. *Mwambiya Lodge*, across the railway from the bus station, has better singles/doubles for US$10/13 with breakfast. Both these places offer evening meals. There are several *bars* and *cheap eats* places near the bus station, and if you get stuck the *Malambi Inn* has bearable rooms for US$2/3.

Getting There & Away

To reach Salima from Lilongwe there are several buses, but it's easiest to take a minibus. The fare is US$1.50. There are also buses and minibuses between Salima and Mzuzu (which go along the lake shore road via Nkhotakota and Nkhata Bay). Buses and minibuses go to/from Blantyre for US$4. Local minibuses and matolas run between Salima and Senga Bay for US$1.

Most transport goes to/from the bus station in the centre of town, but if you're heading for Monkey Bay, wait for lifts or the bus at the junction about 2km west of the town.

Around Salima

On the escarpment between Salima and Lilongwe is **Tuma Forest Reserve**, which has been managed and protected by an organisation called the Wildlife Action Group since the mid-1990s. Elephants, buffaloes and some other large animals are sometimes seen, and the area is excellent for bird-watching. A small lodge is planned here, but for now you can arrange trips or get more information on the reserve or on the Wildlife Action Group from Safari Beach Lodge in Senga Bay.

SENGA BAY

Senga Bay is a large inlet at the eastern end of a broad peninsula that juts into the lake from Salima. The water is remarkably clear here, and the beaches are also good. The town of Senga Bay (marked simply as Senga on some maps) lies at the end of the road that runs east from Salima. Here, and stretched along the bay itself – over a distance of about 10km – are several places to stay, ranging from cheap camp sites to one of the classiest hotels in the whole of Malawi.

Activities

At Senga Bay, most of the lake shore establishments arrange **water sports**, such as windsurfing, water-skiing, snorkelling, diving and boat rides. A popular destination is the nearby island, known locally as Lizard Island, home to fish eagles, cormorants and, not surprisingly, huge monitor lizards. The whole island is spattered white with cormorant droppings, and it stinks, but don't let that put you off.

Alternatively, from Senga Bay town, you can go **hiking** in the nearby Senga Hills. There are a few trails but nothing well established, so they can be hard to follow if the grass is long. But the woodland is beautiful, and the viewpoints overlooking the lake are well worth the effort. It's best to hire a local guide from your hotel to show you the way (and also because there have been isolated incidents of robbery and harassment here). Go early morning or late afternoon: it's cooler, and the light is better for photographs.

You might also aim for the **hippo pools** about half an hour's walk up the lake shore beyond Steps Campsite, or reached by descending the north side of the Senga Hills. Again, a local guide is recommended. The hippos have a reputation for being timid, but aggressive when worried, so take care here.

Bird-watching in the area is excellent, with a good range of habitats in close proximity. You can travel into the hills mentioned above, or to the river (where the hippo pools are) which flows to the north of the hills and into the lake through a small marshy area.

If **fish-watching** is more your thing, Stewart Grant's Tropical Fish Farm (☎/fax 263165, 263407) is about 10km outside Senga Bay. It breeds and exports cichlids, and visits to the farm can be arranged if you're genuinely interested. Red Zebra Tours (✆ redzebras@malawi.net) is also based at the fish farm, offering one-day snorkelling trips, or multi-day fish-watching safaris (snorkelling or diving) around the lake, with an experienced guide, from around US$75 per day. For more information see the Web site www.lakemalawi.com.

If you prefer **shopping** to walking and wildlife, you'll also love Senga Bay. A few kilometres outside town on the Salima road are craft stalls with the best range of wood carvings you'll find anywhere.

Dangers & Annoyances

Take great care when swimming near the large rocks at the end of the beach at Steps Campsite; there are some tricky currents and a surprisingly strong undertow, and a tourist was unfortunately drowned here. The rest of the beach is fine.

As at most places along the lake shore, bilharzia exists here, and it can be very dangerous. See the Health section in the Facts for the Visitor chapter, and the boxed text on Bilharzia in the Cape Maclear section.

Many travellers, especially lone females, have complained about persistent hassle from touts and other local youths in Senga Bay, all wanting to be your 'guide', sell souvenirs or arrange boat rides. Beware especially of the enthusiastic guys at the craft stalls that offer to wrap your purchase – then charge more for this than you paid for the carving. And swapping your souvenir for a lump of wood has been tried more than once. Be polite and firm in your dealings and you should be OK.

Another scam that travellers have reported involves boat rides organised by the local youths. They take you across to Lizard Island, and then while you're having a swim or wander around, the guy in the boat goes through your day pack.

Places to Stay & Eat

There's a good choice of places to stay and eat in and around Senga Bay. The following places are described roughly west to east, reached as you come into town along the road from Salima (there's only one road in and out).

About 17km from Salima, as you head towards Senga Bay, a road on the right (south) turns off. This leads (after another 6km) to *The Wheelhouse*, where camping costs US$1 and boat rides are available. This place used to be famous for its circular bar on stilts out in the lake. Now the lake level has dropped, the bar stands stranded high above the sand, and loses some of its attraction, but it's still a popular overnight stop for groups on overland trucks, and anyone else with a vehicle (there's no public transport). The bar also serves pub food and snacks.

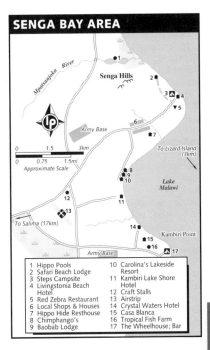

SENGA BAY AREA

0   1.5   3km
0   0.75   1.5mi
Approximate Scale

To Lizard Island (3km)

To Salima (17km)

Senga Hills

Army Base

Lake Malawi

Kambiri Point

Army Base

1 Hippo Pools
2 Safari Beach Lodge
3 Steps Campsite
4 Livingstonia Beach Hotel
5 Red Zebra Restaurant
6 Local Shops & Houses
7 Hippo Hide Resthouse
8 Chimphango's
9 Baobab Lodge
10 Carolina's Lakeside Resort
11 Kambiri Lake Shore Hotel
12 Craft Stalls
13 Airstrip
14 Crystal Waters Hotel
15 Casa Blanca
16 Tropical Fish Farm
17 The Wheelhouse; Bar

Stewart Grant's Tropical Fish Farm (see Activities earlier in this section) has a few *guest rooms*, but these are only for people taking fish-watching tours, or those with a genuine scientific interest in the fish that are bred here.

Near the fish farm is the small and cosy *Casa Blanca* that bills itself as a 'pension-bar-bistro', with Portuguese meals, and a few single/double rooms for US$12/18. Just 1km further is the dull and uninspiring *Crystal Waters Hotel*, where a double chalet is US$12. Again, this place can only be reached by those with wheels.

Back on the main road from Salima to Senga Bay, after a few more kilometres, another road branches off to the right, leading after 3km to the *Kambiri Lake Shore Hotel*. Somebody has made an effort here, with pleasant buildings and manicured grounds. The rooms, however, do not overlook the lake and are rather functional, and a touch on the pricey side (although

CENTRAL MALAWI

spotlessly clean) with singles/twins at US$22/28. Meals cost US$4 to US$7.

If you follow the main road from Salima all the way you'll reach the outskirts of Senga Bay town. At the western end of the main street a dirt road leads for 4km to *Carolina's Lakeside Resort* (☎ 261460, **@** *shelagh@malawi.net*), which is a smart and friendly place on a beach on the lake shore. A bed in a small dormitory is US$5, and chalets with bathroom are US$35 for one to three people. In a small block of apartments, plain rooms with shared bathroom are US$20 to US$30. Meals range from US$3 to US$5, and there's a bar, plus an outside terrace, and shady gardens (although Carolina, who planted them, has moved on to pastures new). You can hire boats for fishing, snorkelling or day trips. Bikes, sailboards and kayaks are free for guests.

Nearby is *Baobab Lodge*, a neat, low-key and friendly place with a shady bar overlooking the beach. Single or double rooms cost US$13, and triples US$21. Meals cost about US$3, and snacks US$1. Next door, the smaller *Chimphango's* has camping for US$0.50 and rooms for US$8.

Back in town and off the main street towards the beach, the basic *Hippo Hide Resthouse* is run by a group of local youths and has rooms for US$2.50/US$4. They can also arrange boat trips and hikes, and sell souvenirs or anything else you may (or may not) want. Some travellers rave about this place, others (again, especially lone women) complain of hard sell and harassment. You might want to get opinions from others before staying here.

The main street continues for 2km to the imposing gates of the *Livingstonia Beach Hotel* (☎ 263222, 263444, fax 263452, central reservations ☎ 620071) set in lush gardens, with picture-postcard views over the lake. Style and luxury don't come cheap though – rooms cost US$130/170, and chalets are US$170/185 including breakfast. The hotel has a tennis court, and also organises guided walks or drives to various places of interest in the area (such as Mua Mission – see Mua later in this chapter).

Be prepared for changes here; this hotel will come under the banner of Le Meridien hotel group in 2001, so a new look and new prices are likely.

Next door is *Steps Campsite*, which is clean and well organised, with flat pitches, electric hook-ups and spotless toilets and showers (but no hot water). Camping costs US$2.50. There's also a bar and a takeaway kitchen serving fast food (burgers US$3, chicken and chips US$6) and fresh bread. On the site is Scuba Do Dive School, offering dive courses, snorkel equipment and boat charter.

Just before the gates to Livingstonia Beach Hotel, a dirt road turns off left (north), and continues for 1km to *Safari Beach Lodge* (☎ 912238, **@** *safwag@ malawi.net*). This is the old forest resthouse, now renovated, and in a lovely spot. It is excellent for spotting local wildlife, and has a private beach. Rooms with bathroom cost US$35/55 including breakfast. You can arrange day safaris to Tuma Forest Reserve, where the same management team is involved in conservation management and plans to build another small lodge.

The best place to eat is *Red Zebra Restaurant*, at end of the main street, 500m from the Livingstonia Beach Hotel. It's open from 7am to 10pm, serving breakfast from US$1.50 to US$3, snacks from US$1 to US$2, burgers and omelettes for around US$3, and good main meals (such as fish and chips) for US$3.50. Or you can sit on the veranda and just have a beer, coffee or slice of chocolate cake (US$0.75).

Getting There & Away

Minibus & Matola From Salima local minibuses and matolas run to Senga Bay for about US$1, dropping you in the main street. If you want a lift all the way to Steps Campsite or Carolina's, you will have to negotiate an extra fee with the driver. Getting back from Senga Bay to Salima, minibuses and matolas leave from the main street.

Boat If you're travelling to/from Cape Maclear, you could consider chartering a speedboat, either from Carolina's or Scuba Do Dive Centre at Steps Campsite. This costs around US$100, but is not too expensive if you get a group of four or five together. It's also good fun, a pretty cool way to arrive at Cape Maclear, and it saves one hell of a trip on the bus.

CHIPOKA

This small town on the lake shore south of Salima is a port used by the *Ilala* passenger boat. It's also the nearest port to both Lilongwe and Senga Bay. It can be quite a busy place, and might be worth considering as a day trip from Senga Bay, although few tourists come here. If you decide to stay, there's a simple **resthouse** and a couple of cheap local-style **restaurants**.

MUA

Mua is a small town just west of the main road (the M5) between Salima and Balaka, consisting mostly of a large mission with a church, school and hospital, which has been here for around 100 years. There is also a fabulous **art and craft shop**, full of paintings and wood sculptures by local people who have been encouraged in their work by one of the priests at the mission. Some is of very high quality, and quite unusual, covering religious and secular subjects. Prices are reasonable. Nearby is a workshop where you can see the carvers in action.

For a deeper understanding of the ideas behind the sculptures, a visit to the **museum** is an absolute must. It concentrates on the three main cultural groups of the region – Chewa, Ngoni and Yao – and their approach to traditional beliefs, with exhibits from rituals and rites of passage. This is no dusty exhibition, but a journey deep into the very soul of Malawi. A guided tour is essential, takes three hours and costs US$5. The museum is open every day except Sunday. There are no places for visitors to stay or eat at Mua Mission, although you can buy soft drinks at the museum office. The nearest place to stay is Senga Bay or Salima, and it's easy to make a day trip from either place.

MONKEY BAY

Monkey Bay is a small town and port at the southern end of Lake Malawi, which most travellers pass through on the way to Cape Maclear. If you're in town for a while, go to *Gary's Cafe* (☎ 587296); the friendly people here offer snacks, meals and drinks at local rates. There is also a shop, art showroom, beer garden and camp site. Accommodation is planned. They can also advise on transport, changing money and anything else in the area. Opposite is *Ziwadi Resthouse* with fairly clean singles/doubles at US$2/2.50. Camping is allowed in the yard, but no fence means security is questionable.

Monkey Bay also has a market and PTC supermarket.

Just outside Monkey Bay, *Venice Beach* backpackers hostel and campsite was under construction when we passed through. The setting is beautiful. Ask for details at Gary's Cafe.

On the main road south of Monkey Bay, about 1km north of the Cape Maclear turnoff, the White Rock Shop is a small grocery store with a surprisingly good selection of food and drinks, both local stuff and imported goodies from Europe and South Africa.

Getting There & Away

Bus, Minibus & Matola From Lilongwe, there's one Stagecoach Express bus per day, which leaves around 8 am (but can be delayed until noon). It goes via Salima and the road around the southern lake shore between Mua and Monkey Bay (this road is called the Matakataka Road even though it doesn't actually go to Matakataka) and takes about seven hours. All other buses from Lilongwe to Monkey Bay go the long way round via Salima, Balaka, Liwonde and Mangochi, and take up to 12 hours. From Lilongwe you're probably better off going by minibus to Salima (US$1.50), from where you might find a minibus or matola going direct to Monkey Bay. If not, take a minibus towards Balaka, get off at the Matakataka Road junction near Mua (look out for the souvenir stalls), then take a matola (US$2) along the Matakataka Road to the main road between Monkey

The Great Bilharzia Story

Bilharzia (or schistosomiasis) is a disease that occurs all over Africa. It is transmitted by minute worms carried by infected humans and water snails. Both 'hosts' need to be present for the worms to transmit the disease. Bilharzia can be contracted if you swim or paddle in lakes, ponds or any shallow water, especially near villages or where reeds grow.

For many years Malawi's health and tourism departments stated that Lake Malawi was bilharzia-free. Only since the mid-1990s has it emerged that this claim was simply untrue – bilharzia is definitely present. A lot of people fell for it, including, it has to be said, Lonely Planet. Early editions of our *Africa on a shoestring* duly reported that Lake Malawi was free of bilharzia. Local tour companies were also hoodwinked, or went along with the pretence. A hotel on the shore of Lake Malawi sent its staff out early every morning to clear surrounding reeds of snails, without warning guests that the worms might still be present.

Although parts of the lake may be very low risk, in other areas – including some popular tourist destinations – you undoubtedly have a high chance of contracting bilharzia. There's no need to panic, and absolutely no reason to avoid coming to Lake Malawi – and once there, who could resist swimming in those beautiful waters?! But you must be aware of the risk. (You should also note that at some budget hotels the water in the showers may come straight from the lake.)

If you do decide to swim, and you do contract bilharzia, you might suffer from some symptoms almost immediately, in which case you should seek treatment fast. But usually symptoms do not show until the disease is well established – and this can be weeks or months after exposure.

Whether symptoms show immediately or much later, the long-term effects can be very harmful, so it is *absolutely essential* that you have a check-up for the disease when you get back home or reach a place with good medical services. Be sure your doctor is familiar with bilharzia, and be aware that the disease may have a long incubation period and may not be initially apparent, so you might need more than one test. For more information see Bilharzia under Health in the Regional Facts for the Visitor chapter.

Bay and Mangochi. Sometimes after heavy rain the Matakataka Road is impassable at its western end, in which case you have go from Mua to Golomoti, then north up a dirt road to meet the Matakataka Road at Kapiri. Another option if you're in a group is to charter your own matola. We heard from a group of travellers who hired a pick-up in Salima to take them all the way to Cape Maclear for US$100 – not a bad split between six people.

It's much easier to reach Monkey Bay from Blantyre: There's a daily Stagecoach bus via Liwonde and Mangochi for US$3.80. During the morning, minibuses also serve this route.

Your best option from Blantyre is the minibus especially for backpackers that runs straight to/from Monkey Bay and Cape Maclear a few times each week. Ask for details at Doogles (see Places to Stay in the Blantyre & Limbe chapter).

From Monkey Bay, a local pick-up shuttles to Cape Maclear a few times each day for US$1 per person. It usually meets the buses from Lilongwe and Blantyre. Otherwise, the people at Gary's Cafe will tell you when it's due.

Boat To avoid the bus hassles, many travellers use the *Ilala* boat to travel up or down the country to/from Monkey Bay (see the Getting Around chapter for details).

CAPE MACLEAR

Technically, Cape Maclear is a spit of land on the tip of an island at the end of the Nankumba Peninsula, jutting into Lake Malawi. It is about 20km by road from Monkey Bay. On the mainland shore nearby is a large bay and beach that everybody – but everybody – knows as Cape Maclear. The village spreading along the beach is officially called Chembe (it's Malawi's biggest fishing village), but this usually gets called Cape Maclear as well.

Technicalities aside, Cape Maclear is a travellers' byword for sun, sand, rest and recreation – the closest thing you'll find to an Indian Ocean beach in inland Africa – and many people passing through Malawi stay here at one time or another. Some never quite get round to leaving. Most travellers like it because it's cheap, friendly and beautiful. For others, the plentiful supply of 'Malawi Gold' (see Legal Matters in the Facts for the Visitor chapter) is another attraction. This is where you'll meet the friends you last saw in Cape Town, Nairobi, Zanzibar or wherever. It's the sort of place where you sit on the beautiful beach, have a few beers, and the next thing you know your visa's run out.

Despite an influx of visitors over the last few years, Cape Maclear hasn't lost its village feel, and amazingly, much of it seems completely unaffected by tourism. This is one of the best places in Malawi to actually meet local people. Most are friendly towards foreigners because outsiders bring money and jobs to the area. A few people, however, are less happy when they see their sons and daughters adopting unpleasant Western ways and when food prices are double what they are in non-touristy places.

Dangers & Annoyances

As at most places along the lake shore, the disease bilharzia exists here, and can be very dangerous. See the Health section in the Facts for the Visitor chapter, and the boxed text 'The Great Bilharzia Story' in this chapter.

Robberies occasionally happen on the beach at Cape Maclear (especially at night) or in the surrounding hills. Violence is very unlikely, but don't walk alone, and don't carry any valuables.

Scams to watch out for at Cape Maclear include the boys who take money in advance for a boat ride or barbecue and then disappear, or who take you on a boat then rifle through your day-pack while you're snorkelling.

Things to See

Much of the area around Cape Maclear and several offshore islands are part of **Lake Malawi National Park**, one of very few freshwater aquatic parks in Africa. The park headquarters is at Golden Sands Holiday Resort (see Places to Stay & Eat in this section). There's also a **Museum & Aquarium** at Golden Sands – it's aimed at visitors and local school children, and is well worth a visit to learn about the formation of the lake and the evolution of the fish. The information is non-technical and well presented.

Near the entrance gate to Golden Sands, a small path leads towards the hills overlooking the bay. A few hundred metres up here is a small group of **missionary graves**, marking the last resting place of Dr William Black and other missionaries (three European and one African) who attempted to establish the first Livingstonia Mission here in 1875 (see the History section in the Facts about Malawi chapter). Also near the gate is a large **baobab tree**. An 1888 photograph shows the tree looking exactly the same – almost branch for branch – which indicates how slowly these trees grow, and how long they can live.

On another historical note, Cape Maclear used to be a stopping-off point for **flying boats** (air liners that landed on water) between Britain and South Africa, via Egypt, Kenya and several other places. Unfortunately for flying boats, their era was short lived and the planes only landed here from 1949 to 1950. There are some old photos from this time in the Museum at Golden Sands.

Boat Trips

Local youths organise trips in fishing boats to nearby islands for about US$10 to US$40 per boat, or around US$5 per person, including snorkelling and lunch (fish and rice cooked on an open fire). Before arranging anything, check with other travellers for recommendations; some of the lads are very good, but others can be sharks.

Snorkelling

If you prefer to go snorkelling on your own, many places to stay rent gear (prices start at about US$2 – but check the quality of your mask). Otter Point, less than 1km beyond Golden Sands, is a small rocky peninsula and nearby islet which is very popular with fish and snorkellers. You may also actually see otters here.

Scuba Diving

There are four places organising diving at Cape Maclear: Scuba Shack, Lake Divers, Chembe Lodge and Kayak Africa. The instruction courses here are among the cheapest in the world, and there are plenty of options for experienced divers. The course prices at all four companies are similar (beginners from US$130 to US$150, advanced around US$120), but they all have other deals to attract clients. For example, Lake Divers includes accommodation, Kayak Africa has a beautiful offshore island base, and Chembe Lodge uses a catamaran. Talk to anybody who has done a dive course to get some personal recommendations. For those already qualified, shore dives are US$15, boat dives US$20 and night dives US$30.

Kayaking

One of the best ways to explore Lake Malawi is in a kayak. Kayak Africa (☎ 584456, ☒ kayakafrica@earthleak.co.za) has top-of-the-range kayaks (single and double) suitable for experts or beginners, which can be hired from around US$10 for a few hours. Day trips with guide and lunch cost from US$25.

The best option, if you've got the money, is to take a guided two- or three-day island hopping-trip, using Kayak Africa's delightful camps on Domwe and Mumbo Islands, which each take just ten guests. The charge is US$75 per person per night, and includes very comfortable furnished tented accommodation, good meals, hot showers, snorkel gear and park fees. We've had several letters from readers about this outfit, and everyone who's done the trip raves about it. You can either turn up and arrange things on the spot, or make arrangements in advance by email or through a tour agent in Lilongwe.

Sailing

You can go sailing with an outfit called Hello Afrika, which is based at Chembe Lodge (listed in Places to Stay). A sunset cruise on the eight-metre catamaran is US$8 per person, a full-day cruise US$20, and a stylish three-day cruise (including all meals) US$150. All trips can be combined with snorkelling or diving.

Hiking & Walking

There's a good network of paths in the hills that form a horseshoe around the plain behind the village. It's a good idea to get a

CAPE MACLEAR

1 Thumbi Island Camp
2 Golden Sands Holiday Resort;
   Museum & Aquarium;
   Lake Malawi National Park HQ
3 Emmanuel's Campsite;
   Sakondwera Restaurant & Shop;
   Kayak Africa; Chip's Bar
4 Top Quiet Resthouse;
   Stevens Resthouse;
   Scuba Shack
5 The Ritz; The Gap; Lake Divers;
   Bodzalakani Resthouse;
   Mayi Tsalani Resthouse
6 Fat Monkeys
7 Chembe Lodge; Hello Afrika
8 Mwala Wa Mphini
9 White Rock Shop

small group together for hiking, as going alone is not recommended – see Dangers & Annoyances earlier. If you're alone (or even if you are in a group) you can arrange a guide, either from the village or at the park headquarters at Golden Sands Holiday Resort. The park rate is US$10 for the guide for a full-day trip.

The main path starts by the missionary graves and leads up through woodland to a col below **Nkhunguni Peak**, the highest on the Nankumba Peninsula, with great views over Cape Maclear, the lake and surrounding islands. If you go up to the summit, it's about three hours each way. Plenty of water and a good sun hat are essential.

Another interesting place to visit on foot is **Mwala Wa Mphini** (Rock of the Tribal Face Scars), which is just off the main dirt road into Cape Maclear, about 5km from Golden Sands. This huge boulder is covered in lines and patterns that seem to have been gouged out by long-forgotten artists, but are a natural geological formation.

If you want a longer walk, a small lakeside path leads south-east from Otter Point, through woodland above the shore, for about 4km to a fishing village called **Msaka** (which has a small shop serving cold drinks). From here a track leads inland (east) to meet the main dirt road between Cape Maclear and Monkey Bay. Turn left and head back towards Cape Maclear, passing Mwala Wa Mphini on the way. The whole circuit is about 16km and takes four to five hours.

Places to Stay & Eat

In the last decade or so the number and variety of places to stay at Cape Maclear has grown considerably. Until the early 1990s the choice was Stevens Resthouse and Golden Sands Holiday Resort, and that was it. Now Cape Maclear has a huge choice of accommodation, with most at the lower end of the price scale, plus a couple of good mid-range options. Things change fast at Cape Maclear though, so more than anywhere else in Malawi, you should expect some new arrivals and some closures by the time you arrive. The places to stay

and eat in this section are described roughly west to east.

The main dirt road from Monkey Bay leads all the way to **Golden Sands Holiday Resort**, at the far western end of the beach. This is also Lake Malawi National Park HQ, and as it's inside the park you have to pay fees: US$1.20 per person, plus US$0.30 per car, both per day. The beach is cleaner and atmosphere generally quieter (one traveller said 'more sensible') than some other places in Cape Maclear; suitable for families, drivers and people who don't want to drink and smoke all night. Camping costs US$1 per person. Small rondavels, with private bathroom cost US$2/3/4 for one/two/three people. There's a small bar, but no restaurant. There's a **kitchen** where staff will prepare your food, or you can cook yourself. If you camp, watch out for the monkeys – they'll run off with anything edible. If you're in a group it's worth renting a rondavel to store your gear – you also get your own bathroom, which is in better condition than the communal ones. It's possible that Golden Sands may be privatised in the future, so don't be surprised if there's a brand new hotel here by the time you arrive.

Along the beach, about 1½km from Golden Sands, is **Emmanuel's Campsite**, charging US$1 per person in basic rooms, or US$0.75 for camping. It's clean and quiet, with a bar but no food available. They also run **Thumbi Island Camp** on the island opposite Cape Maclear beach, where large walk-in tents cost US$5.50 per person, including boat transfers and park fees. Meals are available and you can hire snorkel gear and kayaks.

Next along is **Sakondwera Restaurant & Shop**, where you can buy meals from US$1 to US$2, plus cheap beer, bread, tinned foods and groceries. The owner can advise on places to change money. (If you need more elaborate foodstuff there's a supermarket in Monkey Bay, and the White Rock Shop on the road between Cape Maclear and Monkey Bay – see Monkey Bay earlier in this chapter for details.)

Next door to Sakondwera Restaurant & Shop is Kayak Africa, and near here is

Chip's Bar which serves, naturally, deep fried potato pieces and other takeaway snacks – all at budget prices.

A bit farther along, set back slightly from the beach, is the relaxed and peaceful *Top Quiet Resthouse*. Its clean singles/doubles, around a sandy courtyard, are good value at US$1.50/US$2.10, or US$5 for a double with private bathroom. Very close to here is the legendary *Stevens Resthouse,* run by the Stevens family for as long as anyone can remember. This used to be one of *the* places to stay on the backpackers Cape to Cairo route, but there's stiff competition these days and it's lost some of its friendliness and atmosphere. Clean rooms are US$1.20/2.40. New double rooms with bathrooms and better beds cost US$5.

Breakfast is US$0.50, and other meals US$1 to US$2, although you can wait several hours between ordering and eating. The *bar* on the beach is a popular meeting place, but it's amazing that anyone able to build in such a fabulous position could come up with something so ugly.

Along the beach, *The Ritz* at Lake Divers is aimed mainly at people on dive courses, but anyone can stay. This simple place is well named; spotless rooms with lights, nets, sheets and towels and clean shared toilets are good value at US$7.50. They also have a dorm for US$2.50 per person. Next door is *The Gap*, a constantly popular beach bar serving breakfasts and snacks from US$1, and meals around US$3. This place is the social epicentre most evenings.

Cichlid Fish of Lake Malawi

There are over 600 species of fish in Lake Malawi. Most of these are of the family Cichlidae – the largest family of fish in Africa – and 99% of these cichlids are endemic to the lake. Chambo, familiar to anyone who has eaten in a restaurant in Malawi, are one type of cichlid. Others include the small utaka, which move in big shoals and are caught by fishermen at night. But Lake Malawi is most famous for the small, brightly coloured cichlids known as mbuna – of which there are many species. As well as being attractive to snorkellers and divers, mbuna are popular with aquariums, and for scientists they provide a fascinating insight into the process of evolution.

Cichlids have evolved over the millennia from one common species into many hundreds, yet they have continued to coexist. This has been achieved by different species developing different ways of feeding. Chambo eat phytoplankton that they filter out of the water through their mouths, but the different mbuna have developed a whole range of feeding mechanisms. Some mbuna have specialised teeth to scrape algae off the rocks; others scrape the algae off aquatic plants. There are also 'snail eaters', with strong flat teeth for crushing shells, 'sand diggers' that filter insects and small animals out of the sand, while 'zooplankton eaters' have tube-like mouths for picking up minute creatures. Other species include those that are plant eaters and fish eaters. All of these different feeding mechanisms depend principally on the shape and size of the cichlid head and mouth, and on the nature of the pharyngeal bone at the back of the throat. The evolution of these special adaptations have ensured that each species is able to deal with a particular type of food. Mbuna identification and classification is an ongoing process, and it is thought that many species of mbuna remain undiscovered, particularly around the north-eastern shore of the lake.

Equally fascinating is the cichlid breeding process. The male attracts the female with his bright colours, and if suitably impressed she starts to lay eggs, which she immediately takes into her mouth for protection. The male has a pattern near his tail resembling the eggs, which the female tries to pick up, at which point the male releases sperm into the water, which the female inevitably inhales. This process is repeated until all or most of the eggs are fertilised. The female keep the eggs in her mouth, and even when they become baby fish they stay there for protection. They emerge only to feed, but at the slightest sign of danger, the mother opens her mouth and the young swim straight back in.

Nearby are two very basic local places: the *Bodzalakani Resthouse*, charging US$0.75 per person in very basic rooms, and the similar *Mayi Tsalani Resthouse*, charging US$2 per person.

About 1km further on is *Fat Monkeys*, a huge camping ground aimed primarily at overland trucks and car-campers, with good security, showers, as well as a *bar* and a *restaurant*. Comfortable bungalows, simple cabins and dormitory accommodation for backpackers are planned.

At the far east end of Cape Maclear beach, a long way from all the other places (in distance and quality), is *Chembe Lodge* (☎/fax 584334, ☎ Blantyre 633489, ✉ hello-afrika@iafrica.com, tumbuka@ malawi.net), with large comfortable walk-in tents under thatch shelters, set in beautiful gardens, overlooking a very nice beach. Rooms cost US$29/33 including breakfast. Other meals cost US$3 to US$5, and there's a *bar*. The private and sheltered campsite is also good value at US$1.50 – tents are provided. Sailboards are free; water-skiing and sailing can also be arranged.

Getting There & Away

Bus & Minibus Using public transport, first get to Monkey Bay (see Monkey Bay earlier in this chapter). A local pick-up matola shuttles between Monkey Bay and Cape Maclear a few times each day for US$1 per person. It usually meets the buses from Lilongwe and Blantyre. Otherwise, the people at Gary's Cafe in Monkey Bay will tell you when it's due.

Boat From Cape Maclear, if you're heading for Senga Bay, ask around at the dive schools about chartering a speedboat. This will cost around US$100, which is not bad if split between a group, and the cruise across the lake is infinitely better than the long hard bus ride around.

Car If you've got your own wheels, from Mangochi take the sealed main road (the M15) along the lake shore. About 12km before Monkey Bay, you pass a turn-off on your left (west); this is the Matakataka

Road, towards Mua and Salima (Getting There & Away under Monkey Bay, earlier in this chapter). Keep on the main road, and about 6km further on, or 6km before Monkey Bay, the dirt road to Cape Maclear turns west off the main road. There are several craft stalls and shops at the junction (it's known locally as 'One-Stop Junction'). Many of the places to stay at Cape Maclear are signposted.

MONKEY BAY TO MANGOCHI

From Monkey Bay the main sealed road (the M15) runs along the lake shore south to Mangochi. Along this stretch of the lake are several places to stay, catering for all tastes and budgets. A selection is described here, arranged from north to south.

Leaving Monkey Bay, you pass the junction for Cape Maclear, then the junction of the Matakataka Road going west to Mua. Continue for another 18km to the turn-off for *Nanchengwa Lodge* (☎ 830062, fax 584417), 1½km west of the main road, which you reach by a dirt track winding through baobabs. This place is a very firm favourite for overland trucks and backpackers; the campsite is US$2.50 per person and a bed in the dorm is US$3.50, but the tree-houses on stilts, which sleep two for US$8, are most popular. Chalets cost US$15 for two people or US$35 for four on the beach.

There's a good *bar* and filling food available (with meals from US$2.50 to US$4), plus a whole range of activities such as **horse riding**, **sailing**, **snorkelling** and **diving**. The friendly and welcoming family which runs this place also have big plans to open a wildlife sanctuary (with the backing of local communities) in the wooded hills behind the lodge, where elephants, buffaloes and other wild animals are often seen.

About 3km south of Nanchengwa Lodge, and 1.5km off the main road, is the small and quiet *OK Lake Shore Hotel*, with very nice singles/doubles with private bathroom for US$15/20. No meals are available, but there's a kitchen and a chef – so it's ideal for self-catering. Also nearby is the *Florence Motel*, on the beach next to (overshadowed by) Club Makokola, with rooms at US$10/18 including breakfast.

Club Makokola (*☎ 584244, fax 584417, @ clubmak@malawi.net*) is about 50km south of Monkey Bay, near the southern end of Lake Malawi. This is a well-established luxury holiday resort with a range of comfortable and stylishly decorated rooms and chalets, costing from US$105/170, which includes a full buffet breakfast. Superior rooms with more facilites are available at a higher rate. Family chalets, with a separate room for children, are also available.

Club Mak (as it's known) recently enjoyed a lavish million-dollar renovation, but some rooms have yet to be done, so make sure you ask for a new one. Facilities at the club include two **swimming pools**, floodlit **football fields**, **squash**, **tennis** and **volleyball** courts, a 9-hole pitch-and-putt **golf course**, and a long strip of private beachfront.

The Club even has its own **airport**, served by daily Air Malawi flights to/from Blantyre and Lilongwe. There's a *bar* overlooking the swimming pool and beach, two *restaurants* where three-course evening meals are US$10, and lunches and snacks are also available. Based at Club Mak is Scuba Blue Dive Centre, offering scuba diving around nearby Boadzulu Island from US$30, and four-day dive courses from US$160. Also based at the club, Paradise Watersports offers a wide range of activities, including fishing and boat trips to the islands; you can also water-ski and wakeboard from US$10 a go. If all this sounds far too energetic, this resort has a large cabin cruiser that takes up to eight passengers on day trips, or for longer jaunts around the lake.

Just 1km down the road is another top-end establishment: ***Nkopola Lodge*** (*☎ 584444, central reservations ☎ 620588*), where cool and unfussy chalets and rooms in well-kept gardens overlooking a beach cost around US$100/150 including breakfast. The restaurant serves main meals from between US$5 to US$8, with special weekend buffets for US$12. Sailboards, canoes and small sailing boats are free for guests.

Other attractions include a **bird enclosure**, **petting zoo** and **casino**. About 1km further along the shore, the hotel also has no-frills chalets that are good value at US$46 (sleeping up to three people). Large double walk-in tents cost US$18 (one or two people). There's also a camping ground that costs US$8 per tent, or US$26 per caravan. The communal showers and toilets are clean, and there's a small bar and restaurant overlooking the lake.

North of Mangochi, ***Palm Beach Leisure Resort*** was established some years ago as a smart resort on lawns and a beautiful beach surrounded by (not surprisingly) a grove of palm trees. Chalets with private bathroom are now slightly dowdy, but fair value at US$16/30. Full breakfast costs US$4, and other meals cost between US$2 and US$4. Camping is US$1 per person. This place is quiet during the week, but livelier at weekends when people come from Blantyre and Lilongwe for boating and fishing.

MANGOCHI

Mangochi lies near the southern end of Lake Malawi, strung out between the main north-south lake shore road and the Shire River, which flows out of Lake Malawi and into Lake Malombe. This place was once an important slave market, and then an administrative centre in colonial days, when it was known as Fort Johnston. Relics of these times include a large **mosque** and the Queen Victoria **clock tower**. Even today the town has a vague Swahili-Arab feel, with a warm climate, palm trees, men in white robes and skull-caps and coconuts for sale in the street.

Other things to see include a memorial to the people who died when a steamer on the lake called the MV *Viphya* sank in a violent storm in 1946; the gun from HMS *Guendolin* (see the 'HMS *Guendolin* & Lake Malawi's Naval Victory' boxed text), and the large **cathedral**. The Shire Bridge is also scenic, and the excellent little **museum** is well worth a visit.

Facilities in Mangochi include several shops, supermarkets, banks, post office and telephone bureau.

HMS *Guendolin* & Lake Malawi's Naval Victory

The HMS *Guendolin* was a military boat made in Britain and assembled in Mangochi in 1899. For many years it was the largest boat on the lake (340 tons), with a top speed of 12 knots and was equipped with two powerful guns. The colonial authorities regarded such a show of strength necessary firstly to deter slave traders, who crossed the lake in dhows with their human cargo, and secondly because rival colonial powers Germany and Portugal had territory facing Lake Malawi (then Lake Nyasa) and were believed to have designs on increasing their influence in the region.

The Germans also had a gunboat, called *Herman von Wissemann*, but despite the territorial disputes of their respective governments the captains of the two ships were great friends and drinking partners, often meeting at various points around the lake for a chat and a few beers.

When WWI was declared in 1914, the *Guendolin* was ordered to destroy the German boat. The British captain knew where the *von Wissemann* would be, as they had previously arranged one of their regular get-togethers. But the German captain was unaware that war had broken out, and his ship was completely unprepared. The *Guendolin* steamed in and bombed the *von Wissemann*, rendering it unusable. The German captain and crew were then informed of the commencement of hostilities and were taken captive. This rather unsporting event happened to be the first British naval victory of WWI, and Lake Malawi's only recorded battle at sea.

In 1940 the *Guendolin* was converted to a passenger ship, and one of the guns was set up as a memorial in Mangochi, near the clock tower. Some years later the ship was scrapped. All that remains today is the gun, while the compass and the ship's bell are on display at the museum.

Places to Stay & Eat

There are several cheap dives in the part of Mangochi near the junction where the road through town branches off the main north-south road. The *Safari Resthouse* has grimy rooms for US$2, though the *restaurant* gets good reports. The nearby *Icecream Den & Restaurant* is more inspiring, with snacks around US$1, local food from US$1.20, fish and chips for US$2 and, of course, a range of ice-cream cones and sundaes.

Near the Shire Bridge and clock tower, the small and friendly *Mangochi Lodge* (formerly the Forest Resthouse) has clean singles/doubles for US$3/5. Other cheap options are the *Matimbe Shire View Resthouse*, where singles or doubles cost $1.75, and the *Domasi Resthouse*, next to the PTC supermarket, with singles (only) for $2.

The larger *Holiday Motel* has simple but clean rooms for US$2.50/3.50 and better rooms with bathroom for US$5/6, plus a cheap *restaurant*, big *bar* and good *bakery*.

Getting There & Away

All buses between Blantyre and Monkey Bay stop in Mangochi. The bus station is on the edge of the town centre, but minibuses on the main road stop at the petrol station near the junction where the road into town branches off the main north-south road. Minibuses to/from Blantyre cost US$3, Liwonde US$1.20, Zomba US$1.50. A mini-bus or matola to Ulongwe (for Liwonde National Park) costs US$1.

If you're heading for Mozambique, matolas to Chiponde (via Namwera) cost US$2 (see Mozambique in the Getting There & Away chapter).

AROUND MANGOCHI

The road south of Mangochi runs alongside **Lake Malombe** and is very scenic, although thick reed beds mean no beaches. However, there is a healthy **weaving industry** here, and you can buy baskets, mats, hats, chairs and all sorts of other curios made from grass, straw, reed and palm leaf at very good prices.

Another interesting area near Mangochi is **Mangochi Mountain**, on the east side of the Shire River, at the southern end of Lake Malawi. This is a hilly, tree-covered escarpment protected as a forest reserve.

There are ruins of an old colonial fort here, and small herds of elephants from the nearby Liwonde National Park sometimes migrate up into the forested hills during the rainy season.

If you *really* want to get away from it all, aim for **Ngapani Estate**, north of Mangochi in the strip of territory wedged between the lake's eastern shore and Mozambique. Nearby are Mt Msondole and Namizimu Forest Reserve – good for bird-watching. On the estate is the fully furnished *Ngapani Guesthouse*, which sleeps eight people, and can be hired from US$5 per person per night. Getting there is only possible for drivers: from Mangochi, go up the steep escarpment road through Kwilembe, then fork left (north) through Mchokola. You must book in advance with the estate owners, Sable Farming (☎ Blantyre 651799, 651646).

MCHINJI

Mchinji is about 115km west of Lilongwe, near the border with Zambia (for details on crossing the border see Zambia in the Getting There & Away chapter). If you get stuck here overnight this small town has several shops, a supermarket, some local *bars* and *restaurants*, a few *street food stalls* and some cheap and basic *places to stay*, although nothing very appealing. Best of a bad lot seems to be the *Tiyeseko Motel*, a few blocks off the right side of the road as you come in from Lilongwe, charging US$7 per room. There's safe parking in the yard, which is also used by local trucks and minibuses, whose drivers enjoy revving their engines very early in the morning.

Eastern Zambia

This section mostly covers South Luangwa National Park, which readers with a keen eye on the map will note is not in Malawi, but just over the border in neighbouring Zambia. Many visitors to Malawi also go to South Luangwa, as it's easy to reach, and is undeniably one of the best wildlife areas in the whole of Africa. Upmarket tourists can

fly here directly from Lilongwe, while budget travellers can use public transport. Another option, for visitors of all budgets, is to join one of the safaris offered by tour companies in Lilongwe (see Getting There & Away later in this section). This section also covers the town of Chipata, which for many travellers is the gateway to the park.

CHIPATA

Chipata is on the main road near Zambia's eastern border with Malawi. It's a lively, friendly town with a big market and several nice bars and cafes. Other facilities include supermarkets, shops, petrol stations, a telephone office, banks and moneychangers.

If you're coming from Malawi by public transport, it's possible to rush from Lilongwe to South Luangwa in one go. But neat bus connections are unlikely, and the journey is long and tiring, so it's worth considering a night's stopover in Chipata, and getting a minibus to South Luangwa early the next day.

Places to Stay

Shoestring travellers like *Kapata Resthouse*, near the bus station and market, 1km from the main street; it's safe, fairly clean and doubles cost US$6 (no singles). Food is available.

About 1½km from the bus station, the *camp site* run by the Zambian Wildlife Conservation Society charges US$2.50 per person. To get here, coming from Malawi, turn right off the main street at the BP petrol station, and continue for two blocks.

The nearby friendly *Kamocho Guesthouse* has doubles for US$20 (US$24 with private bathroom).

About 3km west of town, where the road to Luangwa turns off, the faded but friendly *Chipata Motel* has clean doubles with bathroom and breakfast for US$10 to US$15.

Further down the Luangwa road, 10km from Chipata, *Katutu Lodge* offers good clean singles/doubles with bathroom and breakfast for US$15/20, and very good value meals. Camping is US$5.

About 10km east of town, 1½km off the main road toward the border, *Sunnyside Farm Campsite* is a nice grassy site by a small lake, and has camping for US$2.50 per person. Bring all the food you need – and watch out for the mozzies in the toilet!

Getting There & Away

To reach Chipata from Lilongwe, see Zambia in the Getting There & Away chapter.

SOUTH LUANGWA NATIONAL PARK (ZAMBIA)

South Luangwa is quite simply beautiful – and full of animals. Vegetation ranges from dense woodland to open grassy plains, and mammals include lions, buffaloes, zebras, the endemic Thornicroft's giraffe and Cookson's wildebeest. The park also contains large herds of elephants and is noted for leopards. Antelope species include bushbucks, waterbucks, impalas and pukus. Birdlife is tremendous.

The wide Luangwa River is the lifeblood of the park – it flows all year, but gets very shallow in the dry season, when vast midstream sandbanks are exposed – usually covered in groups of hippos or crocodiles, basking in the sun. Animals prefer to drink at the park's numerous oxbow lagoons, formed as the river continually changes its course, and this is where wildlife-viewing is often best. All camps and lodges run drives in open-topped vehicles to watch wildlife (these are universally called 'game-drives') during the day or at night, and most also offer wildlife-watching walks for a few hours and longer walking safaris.

The main focal point is Mfuwe, where there's a large village (with shops and a market), the main gate into the park, a bridge over the river, the park gate (on the west side of the bridge), and several lodges and camps in the surrounding area. This part of the park can get quite busy with vehicles, but only because this is the best wildlife viewing area. And in Zambia everything is relative; if you've suffered rush-hour rally-style safaris in places like Kenya, you'll find it positively peaceful here.

Although South Luangwa is hard to visit on the cheap, there are more options for the budget-conscious here than other Zambian parks. Having said that, some shoestring

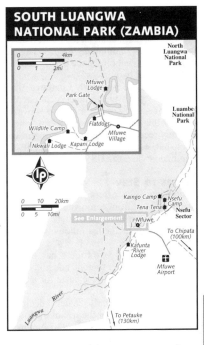

SOUTH LUANGWA NATIONAL PARK (ZAMBIA)

travellers who hitch in get a nasty surprise at the lack of real bargains. By the time you've paid for accommodation, your park fees and a couple of drives in the park, you're looking at about US$100. If you haven't got that, you won't get much from your visit, so it's probably not worth coming.

Entry Fees

Entry for tourists to South Luangwa is US$20 per person per day. A vehicle costs US$15.

Things to Do

All the places to stay have vehicles that can take you into the park to watch wildlife. Many also arrange wildlife walks, giving you a chance to sample the wilderness away from the confines of a car. At top-end lodges these activities are included with accommodation. At cheaper camps and camp sites you can arrange things on the spot. A morning or evening wildlife drive normally costs US$25. A night drive costs US$30.

This is based on three or four people in the car, and you should be able to team up with others – but don't bank on it. Alone, a drive will cost US$45 minimum. You also have to pay park fees, but only once per 24 hours – so this covers two drives.

There's more to South Luangwa than animals. If you want to meet local people, most lodges can arrange a visit to Kawaza, a real village (not a touristy set-up), where a highly recommended night staying in the guest-hut, eating, drinking and socialising Zambian-style costs US$40.

Places to Stay

South Luangwa offers a wide range of places to stay, from camp sites and budget huts through mid-range chalets to highly luxurious lodges; the list following is just a selection.

In the last few years there has been a move towards larger top-end and mid-range lodges in the park. These cater for around 30 guests, instead of around 10, which was the norm until recently. When deciding where to stay, consider the size of the lodge. It's not necessarily a question of quality – more one of atmosphere. Some visitors prefer the intimate exclusive feel of the smaller places; others prefer the facilities and livelier atmosphere of the larger places. When deciding where to stay, it's worth considering how long a lodge or camp has been operating in the park. Recent arrivals may have less experience when it comes to hospitality or, particularly, wildlife viewing.

Most lodges and camps within South Luangwa are on the banks of the river or an oxbow lagoon. Several lodges also have smaller 'bush camps' deep in the park, where they operate walks or drives away from the busier areas. Despite the rustic title most bush camps are very comfortable, with large tents, private bathrooms and excellent food.

Except for the cheaper chalets and camp sites, which don't need reservations, it's usually necessary to book accommodation in advance, either direct or through an agent in Lilongwe, Lusaka or overseas. For agents in Malawi, see Organised Tours in the Getting Around chapter or Travel Agencies in the Lilongwe chapter.

Several places to stay are just outside the park boundary, so you don't pay park fees when staying there until you go into the park. Note that some are open only in the high season – April/May to October/November – but those around Mfuwe are open all year, and rates are reduced in the low season. The prices listed here are per person high-season rates in double rooms.

Places to Stay – Budget & Mid-Range

Some shoestringers stay at the local-style *Cobra Resthouse* in Mfuwe village, particularly useful if you arrive after dark or need to catch a crack-of-dawn minibus out. (Lots of wild animals in the area makes walking around at night very dangerous.)

Flatdogs (@ moondog@super-hub.com), just outside the park near Mfuwe Gate, overlooking the river, gets consistently good reviews. There are separate campsites with excellent facilities for overlanders, self-drivers and backpackers, all at US$5 per person. Small 'cottage-tents' with bed and mozzie net cost US$10 per person. Imaginative and surprisingly luxurious self-catering chalets cost US$20 per person. There's a *restaurant*, a shop, a lively *bar* and quiet thatched shelters away from the camp where you can relax or watch wildlife. For families, a kids' menu and nanny service is provided. Wildlife drives are US$25 (US$45 for two drives). This place is run by Jake, a guy who understands backpackers and is a good source of local information.

About 6km west by road is the spacious and efficient *Wildlife Camp* (☎ 062-45026, @ miles@super-hub.com), with quiet and secluded self-catering chalets (sleeping up to three) for US$22 per person. Camping costs US$5, and there's a four-bed dorm or family room for US$16.50 per person. The bar also serves snacks and meals. Wildlife drives are US$20 (US$25 at night).

Places to Stay – Top End

South of Mfuwe Gate, just outside the park on the east bank of the river, is *Kapani*

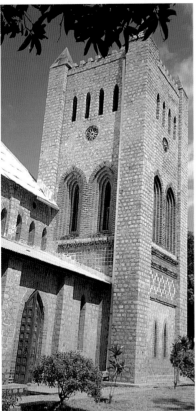

Malawi's historic churches show the powerful influence of the Christian missionaries. **Clockwise from top:** CCAP Cathedral, Blantyre; the clock tower (now a bookshop) and mission at Livingstonia; interior of Likoma Cathedral, Likoma Island; the imposing exterior of Likoma Cathedral

Catching the bus to Nkhata Bay

'Thank you for smoking'. Tobacco auction.

Fishing with traditional nets on Chia Lagoon

Mount Mulanje looms over tea estates. Tea is one of Malawi's major export crops.

Lodge (☎ 062-45015, **@** *kapani@super-hub.com*), a classic Luangwa camp, with cool thatched cottages overlooking a lagoon frequented by weed-munching hippos. Rates are US$290 per person all inclusive.

Farther along the river is *Nkwali Lodge* (☎ 062-45090, **@** *rps@super-hub.com*), run by Robin Pope Safaris, with tastefully designed walk-in tents and delightful open-air bathrooms, a *bar* and a *restaurant* overlooking the river and the camp's private waterhole; rates are US$250 all inclusive. This company also offers highly regarded walking safaris in the seldom visited northern reaches of the park. Robin Pope leads many personally, and past guests say his feel for the wilderness is addictive. But all addictions are expensive: from US$300 to US$470 per person per day.

A few kilometres further south, *Kafunta River Lodge* (☎ 062-45026, **@** *miles@super-hub.com*) has cool airy chalets and a vast *restaurant-lounge-deck* area offering a wonderfully open panoramic view over the river; the rate is US$280 all inclusive.

Just inside the park, near the main gate, is *Mfuwe Lodge* (☎ 062-45041, **@** *mfuweloj@zamnet.zm*), run by Malawi-based Club Makokola. This was completely rebuilt in 1998. The results are impressive: a central *restaurant* and bar area with gigantic thatched roof and open sides leading out onto a deck with swimming pool and splendid views over a lagoon where animals come to drink. The lodge sleeps around 36 people, with hotel-standard rooms in cottages (each for two or three people) lined along the lagoon with private verandas. They also have two bush camps in the southern section of the park, and offer a range of walking and vehicle safaris. Rates are US$300 per person. Their main reservation centre is Ulendo Safaris in Lilongwe (see Travel Agencies in the Lilongwe chapter) and they often offer special deals for this lodge.

North-east of Mfuwe Gate are some well-established top-end places. On the east bank is *Tena Tena* and *Nsefu Camp*, both run by Robin Pope Safaris and both overlooking beautiful wide bends in the river. Tena Tena

has a calm and unfussy atmosphere, and just four large walk-in tents under shady trees, each with veranda and private view. Nsefu was the first camp in Luangwa; the six double bungalows, although completely renovated, retain their historic atmosphere. This area is the Nsefu Sector – the only part of the park on the east bank of the river – which gives the lodges here some extra exclusivity, although again this has to be paid for: US$300 at Nsefu, US$325 at Tena Tena, all inclusive.

On the west bank of the Luangwa is *Kaingo Camp* (**@** *shensaf@satmail.bt.com*) run by highly respected safari guide Derek Shenton, owner of Shenton Safaris (☎ 062-45064, 053-62188). This place is small, exclusive, relaxed and friendly, with five delightful cottages surrounded by bush overlooking the river. Skilled guides run walks and wildlife drives, and there's also a bush camp that can be reached on a walking safari from the main camp. As always, quality comes at a price: US$300 per person (all inclusive).

Places to Eat

All the places to stay provide meals, from simple snacks at the camp sites to *haute cuisine* at the top-end lodges. There are also a couple of local eating houses in Mfuwe village.

If you come in or out by air, or with your own vehicle, take time to visit the unlikely but splendid *Moondogs Cafe*, which is just outside the Mfuwe airport terminal building, where good coffee, cold beers, tacos, waffles and salads grace the menu. They also have a radio link with Flatdogs and the other lodges.

Getting There & Away

Air Mfuwe airport is about 20km by road from the main gate, and is served by chartered and scheduled flights most days from Lusaka. From Lilongwe, Air Malawi flies to Mfuwe twice weekly (US$90 one way). It's also worth checking with travel agents about spare seats on chartered planes – a seat between Lilongwe and Mfuwe costs from US$150, and if you get a small group together to charter the five-seat plane it's even cheaper. Lodge vehicles meet all-inclusive clients with reservations.

Bus & Minibus First get to Chipata (for details see Zambia in the Getting There & Away chapter). From Chipata bus station, local minibuses run daily to Mfuwe village, mostly in the morning. They cost US$4 plus US$0.40 for a backpack, and leave only when full (which may take several hours). The journey can take up to five hours, depending on the state of the road. Once at Mfuwe village you can walk 1km to Flatdogs or hitch to the Wildlife Camp (we repeat – don't do this at night). Some travellers hitch to Mfuwe from Chipata: the junction by the Chipata Motel is the best place to wait for a lift. If you're in a group, to reduce waits and increase comfort, consider chartering your own minibus for a negotiable US$80.

To leave Mfuwe, minibuses to Chipata depart very early. Hitching with other tourists in their own vehicle is also a possibility. It's also worth asking around to see if any of the camps are sending supply vehicles to Chipata or Lusaka.

Car In your own vehicle, Mfuwe Gate and the surrounding camps are easily reached from Chipata. In the dry season the dirt road is usually in poor to reasonable condition, and the drive takes about three hours. In the wet season, it can take all day (or be simply impossible).

Organised Tours A wide range of tours are organised by companies in Lilongwe, ranging from luxury safaris using chartered planes and exclusive lodges, to budget group camping expeditions. For more details see Organised Tours in the Getting Around chapter.

Blantyre & Limbe

pop 490,000

Blantyre is the commercial capital and main industrial centre of Malawi. It is a large city by Malawi's standards, stretching for about 20km, and merging into Limbe – its 'sister city'. In colonial times Limbe was established as a smart European quarter, while Blantyre was considered less desirable. Today, however, there's little of interest for visitors in Limbe, and most people stay in Blantyre. Many visitors find that Blantyre has a bit more of a buzz than Lilongwe (if any of Malawi's sleepy cities can be said to buzz at all), but most stop only for a few days, mainly to send or receive mail, buy maps and books, or to pick up a Mozambican visa.

Regardless of this, Blantyre is a pleasant place with some interesting sights, several enjoyable restaurants and bars to while away the time and a fair selection of places to stay. Despite the sprawling suburbs and townships surrounding Blantyre, the city centre is very compact and most of the places of importance to travellers are well within easy walking distance. (Unless stated otherwise, all addresses in this section are in Blantyre, rather than Limbe.)

Orientation

Central Blantyre's main street is Victoria Ave. Along here are several large shops, the tourist office, the map office, banks, bureaus de change and travel agents. To the east is Haile Selassie Rd, which contains many smaller shops. At the northern end of Victoria Ave is a junction with Glyn Jones Rd and the landmark Le Meridien Mount Soche Hotel.

East of this hotel is a major traffic roundabout, from where the main road north-west leads to the airport, Mwanza and Lilongwe. This road has no official name but is known as 'New Chileka Rd'. About 500m farther east is another roundabout, with a clock on a concrete pedestal in the middle: from here ('old') Chileka Road leads north-east to the

---

Highlights

Around Blantyre p205

Greater Blantyre & Limbe p196

Blantyre City Centre p200

- Inspecting CCAP Church, a magnificent building hand-crafted by missionaries in 1891 and still standing proud
- Visiting the Carlsberg Brewery – famous for country-wide 'greens', interesting tours and free tastings
- Exploring Michiru Mountain, an edge-of-town forest reserve with walking trails, splendid views and good bird-watching

---

bus station and outer suburbs; and the main Chilembwe Highway leads south-east towards Limbe, where the main roads to Zomba (north-east) and Mulanje (south-east) branch. (Chilembwe Highway should not be confused with Chilembwe Rd in the centre.)

Maps Street maps of Blantyre and Limbe, on a folded sheet that also shows maps of Lilongwe, Mzuzu and Zomba, might be available at the Tourist Office. They're supposed to be free, but there may be a small charge. You can also get government survey maps of Blantyre, the surrounding area, and most

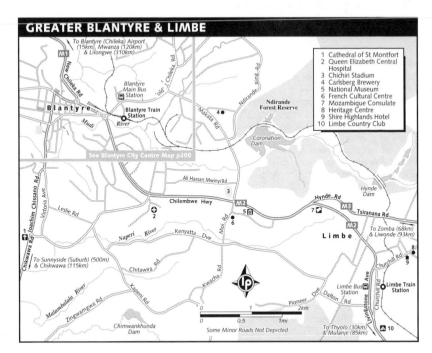

GREATER BLANTYRE & LIMBE

1 Cathedral of St Montfort
2 Queen Elizabeth Central Hospital
3 Chichiri Stadium
4 Carlsberg Brewery
5 National Museum
6 French Cultural Centre
7 Mozambique Consulate
8 Heritage Centre
9 Shire Highlands Hotel
10 Limbe Country Club

other parts of Malawi at the Department of Surveys Map Sales Office at the southern end of Victoria Ave. For more details on what's available, see Maps in the Planning section of the Facts for the Visitor chapter.

Information

Tourist Office The Tourist Office is on Victoria Ave and is open from 7.30 am to noon and 1 to 5 pm. There's not much in the way of leaflets and giveaways, but the people here make quite an effort to provide information and assistance. Even if they can't help you with something specific, they'll probably be able to put you onto someone who can.

Money There are branches of the National Bank of Malawi and the Commercial Bank of Malawi on Victoria Ave. (The National Bank has two branches within 100m of each other.) Banks are usually open 8 am to 1 or 2 pm weekdays. At the southern end of Victoria Ave are the Manica Travel and Finance Bank bureaus de change and there are two more private bureaus de change at the northern end, which often have competitive rates. If you've got time, shop around – rates and commissions can vary considerably.

Post Blantyre's main post office (GPO) is on Glyn Jones Rd, open Monday to Friday from 7.30 am to 4.30 pm, Saturday 8 to 10 am and Sunday 9 to 10 am. The poste restante is here. If you're using AmEx clients mail, the office is at Manica Travel, Victoria Ave.

Telephone & Fax For national or international calls and faxes, the Executive Telephone & Fax Bureau, on Henderson St, is open on weekdays from 7 am to 4 pm, Saturday 8 am to 2.30 pm and Sunday 9 am to 1.30 pm. Three-minute calls to anywhere outside Africa cost US$10. Reverse-charge (collect) calls are not possible.

Email & Internet Access For email and Internet access, Malawi.net Internet Bureau, next to Galaxy Travel on St George's St, charges US$4 for 30 minutes. But the best deal is at Tecktel Internet Bureau in the Fatima Arcade on Haile Selassie Rd, which charges US$1 for 45 minutes off-line, and US$1 for 10 minutes on-line. This is a highly competitive market, and prices are bound to change, so again, shop around.

Travel Agencies Most agencies are based on or just off Victoria Ave, including Airtour & Travel (☎ 622918), AMI Travel (☎ 624733) and Manica Travel (☎ 624533). Also worth trying is the switched on Galaxy Travel (☎ 633637) on Glyn Jones Rd. Most of the above deal mainly in outbound flights. Soche Tours & Travel (☎ 620777, fax 620440, ✆ sochetours@malawi.net), on Chilembwe Rd also arranges flights, coach travel, tours, safaris, car hire and hotel reservations. The efficient and organised Central African Wilderness Safaris (see Organised Tours in the Getting Around chapter) has a branch at Ryall's Hotel.

Bookshops There's a larger TBS bookshop on Victoria Ave and a smaller one at the Mount Soche Hotel. For a much wider selection, visit the Central Bookshop at the eastern end of Henderson St. They stock stationery, books and guides about Malawi, local language dictionaries and a good range of novels by local writers. There's also a pleasant coffee shop.

The Central Africana Bookshop, next to the PTC supermarket on Victoria Ave, specialises in antiquarian and specialist African titles and old prints and maps.

The Wildlife Society of Malawi giftshop at the Heritage Centre in Limbe (next to the Shire Highlands Hotel) specialises in books on natural history and national parks. Their prices are very reasonable.

Libraries & Cultural Centres Blantyre's main public library, the National Library, is off Glyn Jones Rd, near Mt Soche Hotel. The British Council library, on Victoria Ave opposite the Tourist Office, is open

Tuesday to Friday from 8 am to 5 pm, Monday afternoons and Saturday mornings to noon. Nonmembers can read books and magazines in the library but cannot borrow. Films are shown some afternoons and evenings – check the noticeboards for details. The French Cultural Centre is on Moi Rd, off Chilembwe Highway, towards Limbe.

At the Heritage Centre in Limbe, the Historical and Scientific Society of Malawi has a small library and reading room, with a quiet and wonderfully musty atmosphere. Nonmembers can read books here, but cannot borrow.

Medical Services If you have an embassy in Malawi and are able to contact them first, they will normally be able to advise on recommended doctors and dentists in Blantyre (embassies are listed in the Facts for the Visitor chapter). If this is not possible, some suggested places are listed here.

The Malaria Test Centre at the government Queen Elizabeth Central Hospital (☎ 630333), just south of Chilembwe Highway, charges US$1 for a malaria test. Ask for directions as the test centre is hard to find. For private medical consultations or blood tests, Mwaiwathu Private Hospital (☎ 622999) on old Chileka Rd is open 24 hours and is very good. A consultation is US$15; all drugs and treatment are extra. Overnight in a private ward is US$80, and before any treatment is given you must put down a US$220 deposit. For medical or dental problems a doctor's consultation at the Seventh Day Adventist Clinic (☎ 620488, 620006) costs US$6 and a malaria test is US$10.

For medicines and things such as shampoo, tampons and condoms, there's a large MPL pharmacy on Victoria Ave, and several smaller ones around the city centre.

Emergency The emergency phone number for the police and ambulance service is ☎ 199 (in Lilongwe and Blantyre only). See Emergencies in the Facts for the Visitor chapter for more information.

Dangers & Annoyances Parts of Blantyre can be dangerous at night, so you shouldn't walk around alone after dark. Some travellers walking between the city centre and Doogles (see Places to Stay later in this chapter) have been attacked at night where the road passes under the dark railway bridge near the roundabout. During daylight this route is fine, but after dark a taxi is recommended – from the centre to Doogles is US$4. (At night, taxi drivers will take you from the bus station to Doogles – all of 300m – but still charge US$1!) As always, watch your back in busy bus stations. Limbe is particularly crowded, so stay alert there.

Things to See & Do

The **Municipal Market** is just off Kaoshiung Rd and can be reached from there, but is most easily reached via the footpath that crosses the river from near the city centre Bus Station. The new buildings give it a more formal feel than the hectic market in Lilongwe, but it's still worth a visit even if you don't want to buy anything. Crafts and curios are not sold here – for details on where to find this type of stuff see Shopping later in this chapter.

Probably the most impressive building in Blantyre is the **CCAP Church**, just off Old Chileka Rd. For more details see the boxed text 'Blantyre's CCAP Church'. In the same area is a **clock tower** and a **cairn** marking the spot where the original missionaries camped before establishing the mission and church here.

Blantyre also has the **Cathedral of St Paul**, on Glyn Jones Rd, about 500m west of the Mount Soche Hotel, and the Catholic **Cathedral of St Montfort**, on Joachim Chissano Rd (the road towards Chikwawa and Nsanje), south of the city centre.

Other historical buildings of interest in Blantyre include the **Old Boma** (colonial administration office) near the junction of Victoria Ave and Haile Selassie Rd. This was originally the centre of government for the whole Nyasaland Protectorate, under the first commissioner, Sir Harry Johnston, until the capital was moved to Zomba in 1891.

Outside the centre is another colonial building: **Mandala House**, a large two-storey building that was the headquarters of the African Lakes Corporation in the late 19th century (see the boxed text 'Mandala & the African Lakes Corporation'). It is the oldest remaining European building in Malawi. The outside is quite interesting, but the interior (which is still used as offices) has been completely renovated, so there's little of interest inside.

The **National Museum** is midway between Blantyre and Limbe, just off Chilembwe Highway. There is a collection of traditional weapons and artefacts, exhibits relating to traditional dance, European exploration and slavery. Entrance is free.

There's also a small but fascinating museum at the **Heritage Centre**, next to the Shire Highlands Hotel in Limbe, which is

---

Blantyre's CCAP Church

The CCAP Church, officially called the Church of St Michael and All Angels, is in the mission grounds just off Old Chileka Rd beyond the bus station. It was built by missionaries of the Established Church of Scotland who came to Malawi a few years after their brethren of the Free Church had founded the first Livingstonia mission station at Cape Maclear (see History in the Facts about Malawi chapter). The settlement was named Blantyre, after the birthplace of David Livingstone, the famous explorer.

The leader of the missionaries was the Rev Clement Scott. With no training in architectural design or construction skills, and only local handmade bricks and wood available, Scott planned and then oversaw the building of this magnificent church, complete with dome, towers, arches and bay windows. Although Blantyre's CCAP Church was extensively renovated in the 1970s, what you see today is pretty much how it looked the day it was completed in 1891.

The Established Church of Scotland later became known as the Church of Central Africa Presbyterian (CCAP), and there are still CCAP churches and missions all over Malawi.

Mandala & the African Lakes Corporation

In 1878 a group of Scottish businessmen who had been involved in the Livingstonia mission expedition of 1875 founded the Livingstonia Central African Mission Company. This was designed to develop the route along the Zambezi and Shire Rivers and introduce trade to the area. The company appointed two brothers, John and Frederick Moir, as joint managers. They came to the Shire Highlands in 1878 and established a base near the Church of Scotland mission at Blantyre. The company's headquarters and trade name became known as Mandala, the local name given to John Moir because of the spectacles he wore (the word means something like 'pools of water').

Mandala trading posts were established along the

Mandala House, the oldest European building in Malawi

Shire River, in the highlands and along the lake shore. Even when the company changed its name to become the African Lakes Corporation in the early 20th century, the Mandala name was kept, and you can still see Mandala Group shops and garages all over the country today.

mainly concerned with early transport and other aspects of the colonial period.

PAMET (the Paper Making Education Trust) is an inspiring project that was set up to teach people how to recycle paper – an important issue in Malawi, where some people are too poor to buy school exercise books for their children. You can visit their workshop on Chilembwe St and arrange an informal tour. They also make beautiful paper from materials such as banana leaves, baobab bark, even elephant dung, and sell a lovely range of cards and other paper products.

Blantyre Sports Club offers daily membership for US$5. This allows you to enter the club and use the bar or restaurant. To use the pool or to play squash or tennis is another US$0.60. Nine holes of golf costs US$2.50. Equipment can be hired.

If you're of a less active inclination, a visit to the **Carlsberg Brewery**, off Makata Rd, east of the centre, may appeal. Tours go most afternoons for groups of four or more people. You must phone the public relations department (☎ 670022, 670133) to make an appointment but there's no charge. If you're alone you can join a group. The tour ends with a free tasting session. Some places to stay in Blantyre arrange transport here. Alternatively, you can walk or take a taxi.

Places to Stay – Budget

Camping Backpackers can pitch their tents for US$3 per person at Doogles (see Backpackers in this section), which also has room for a few trucks and cars with tents.

There's also a camp site and caravan park at the ***Motel Paradise***, which is about 4km from the centre of town on the road to the airport. It costs US$3 per person but, security isn't the best here, so take appropriate precaution if you leave your tent or vehicle to go into town.

A much better alternative for drivers is ***Limbe Country Club***, where you can park and camp on the edge of the playing fields for US$6 per person. This price includes club membership, so you can use the nice showers and ***restaurant*** inside. Otherwise, for most visitors, there's no need to stay in Limbe; all the other places listed in this Places to Stay – Budget section are in Blantyre.

Backpackers Overlanders, backpackers and independent travellers tend to rave about ***Doogles*** (☎ 621128, fax 634981, @ doogles@malawi.net) on the edge of the city centre and close to the main bus station (a bit too close when the station announcer's megaphone gets going at 5am!). A bed in the dorm is US$5 and double rooms with private bathroom cost US$15.

BLANTYRE & LIMBE

BLANTYRE CITY CENTRE

PLACES TO STAY
1 Kabula Lodge
3 Ryall's Hotel; Central
   African Wilderness
   Safaris; 21 Restaurant;
   Moir's Coffee Shop
8 Le Meridien Mount
   Soche Hotel; Michiru
   Restaurant; Gypsy's;
   Sportsman's Bar
15 Doogles; Bar
19 Nyambadwe Lodge
20 Grace Bandawe
   Conference Centre
21 Blantyre Lodge
36 Tumbuka Lodge
38 Hotel Training
   School

PLACES TO EAT
5 Hong Kong Restaurant
11 Home Needs
12 Chick Wings
27 L'Hostaria
28 The Royal Taj
42 Kips Cookin';
43 Ma's Cookin';
   Fiskini Takeaway
44 Alem Ethiopian
   Restaurant
47 Nando's
57 Cheap Food Stalls
58 Whistlestop Cafe;
   City Fish & Chips

OTHER
2 Cathedral of St Paul

4 ATC Supermarket
6 Air Malawi; Seventh
7 Day Adventist Clinic
9 Victoria Forex Bureau
10 National Library
13 Gindu Temple
14 Communications Centre
16 Petrol Station
17 Main Bus Station
18 Mwaiwathu Private Hospital
22 Fatima Arcade; Tektel
   Internet Bureau
23 South African Airways
24 Main Post Office
25 Malawi.Net Internet Bureau
26 Safari Curios;
   Galaxy Travel

29 Tourist Office
30 PTC Supermarket
31 Central Africana Bookshop
32 Commercial Bank
33 Colour Film Processors
35 Travellers Forex Bureau
37 Reserve Bank Building
39 Soche Tours & Travel
40 Building Society House;
   Immigration Office
41 TBS Bookshop;
   British Airways
45 Central Bookshop;
   Coffee Shop
46 Chimwewe Restaurant
48 Executive Telephone
   & Fax Bureau

49 National Bank
50 Manica Travel;
   Finance Bank
51 British Consulate
52 Legends
53 Pat's Nightclub
54 Kandodo Supermarket;
   Nico's Gelateria
55 National Bank
56 City Centre
   Bus Station
59 Old Boma
60 Map Sales Office
61 Blantyre Sports Club
62 Arizona Bar
63 Cactus Bar
64 Municipal Market
65 Mandala House

There's good security, and the friendly staff know a lot about travel in Malawi, transfer buses to Cape Maclear and Mulanje, and places to change money. They also provide a Mozambican visa service, and the walls are covered in maps and information. The *restaurant* serves snacks from US$1, lunch or dinner for US$4 to US$5, and the lively bar is very popular with local volunteer workers, expats and well-to-do Malawians. Clean drinking water costs US$0.20. You can make international phone calls for US$3 per minute and send email. Some budget tour outfits run excursions from here.

Guesthouses If Doogles is full you may be forced to take a room at *Blantyre Lodge*, the former Council Resthouse, which is near the train station. Rooms are around US$2 – although those in the new wing for US$6 are preferable. The shared toilets are filthy and anything you leave in your room may disappear. This is a place to bed down only.

A much better budget option is *Kabula Lodge* (☎ 621216) off Michiru Rd, northwest of the city centre. Small simple rooms with shared bathroom cost US$5, while more comfortable rooms (some with private bathroom) cost around US$10. The friendly Malawian woman who runs this place can prepare meals to order or you may be allowed to use the kitchen.

The *Grace Bandawe Conference Centre* (☎ 634267), on 'old' Chileka Rd about 2km from the city centre, is also a good choice. Quiet, clean singles/doubles cost US$7/12. Two rooms share a bathroom. Breakfast is US$1 and dinner (always chicken and rice) is US$2.40. A bed in the spartan dorm annex (over the road behind Phoenix School) costs US$3.

Places to Stay – Mid-Range & Top End

All rooms in this bracket have private bathroom and include breakfast unless otherwise stated. The Shire Highlands Hotel is the only place listed which is actuallyin Blantyre.

Guesthouses The cheapest in this range is *Nyambadwe Lodge* (☎ 633551). In a quiet

suburb off 'old' Chileka Rd, 3km by road north of the main bus station, it has clean and tidy singles/doubles from US$17/23 (or US$14/20 with shared bathroom). Camping costs US$10 per tent.

Further out in the north-western suburbs, on Chilomoni Ring Road, is *Michiru Lodge* (☎ 634038) where straightforward rooms are US$17/19 with bathroom and breakfast. Nearby, *Namiwawa Lodge* (☎ 636748) is in a nice leafy suburban setting and is quiet and spacious. It has good views from the garden and rooms from $12/15 (shared bathroom) to US$20/23 (private bathroom). A taxi to the city centre from either of these places is US$3 or US$4.

Very handy for the city centre, *Tumbuka Lodge* (☎ 633489, @ tumbuka@malawi .net) is a favourite among business travellers and better-off tourists, and deservedly so. It's in a quaint old colonial bungalow with big verandas, a shady garden and friendly efficient staff. Tastefully decorated rooms with bathroom cost US$72 (single or double) including a full breakfast. Drinks are served on the terrace and dinner costs around US$5. There's a TV lounge and you can make international phone calls or send email.

Hotels In the centre, the *Hotel Training School* (☎ 621866) on Chilembwe Rd has good single rooms for US$55 (but no doubles). The *restaurant* does three-course meals for US$4.10.

Le Meridien Mount Soche Hotel (☎ 620588, fax 620154) is a large block at the top of Victoria Ave and is favoured by business travellers. It was taken over by the international Meridien group in early 2000, and many changes are expected. Rates for superior rooms cost from around US$180/220, and standard rooms are cheaper. Facilities include a business centre, book shop, travel desk and swimming pool.

Nearby is *Ryall's Hotel* (☎ 620955), a smaller place with an interesting history. It has gardens and a swimming pool and a more personal feel. Rooms are around US$125/150. Following a takeover by the Protea hotel group in early 2000, this hotel

BLANTYRE & LIMBE

will be undergoing major expansion and renovation through 2001.

In Limbe, the **Shire Highlands Hotel** (☎ 640055, fax 640063) is an old colonial-style place, with rooms from US$120/140, including bathroom and breakfast. There's a swimming pool and a **restaurant** with snacks for around US$3, light meals for US$4 and main meals from US$6. (This hotel was also taken over by Protea, so changes and new prices are possible in the future.)

Places to Eat

Street Food & Snack Bars For cheap eats there are **food stalls** around the main bus station near Doogles and at the city centre bus station, which sell chips from US$0.30, grilled meat for US$0.40 and bowls of *nsima* (cooked maize flour) and sauce for around US$0.50.

Also near the city centre bus station, on Lower Sclater Rd, **Whistlestop Cafe** does good local dishes from US$1.20. Next door **City Fish & Chips** serves large portions for US$1.

Two more cheapie restaurants are **Fiskini Takeaway** (open every day) and **Ma's Cookin'** on the corner of Henderson St and Hanover Ave. Nearby is **Kips** – clean and friendly, with breakfasts from US$1 and meals around US$2 (open daily).

Home Needs, on Glyn Jones Road, is a South Indian snack bar and hardware shop. A slightly bizarre mix, but this place has good food, including vegetarian *masala dosas* (filled savoury pancakes) and other tasty snacks at cheap prices. This place is open lunchtimes and early evening only.

Top of the Western-style takeaways is **Nando's** on Haile Selassi Rd, with steak rolls and burgers at US$2.30 and good fried chicken and chips at US$4. You can get lemon sauce on your chicken, or risk sampling Nando's famously hot piri-piri sauce.

Chick Wings on Glyn Jones Rd is another takeaway – less flash, less tasty, and cheaper than Nando's.

Restaurants Popular for a splurge is **Nico's Gelateria**, where genuine Italian ice creams and cappuccinos are US$1.50

and pizzas around US$3. Up from here in the price bracket is another Italian-flavoured place – **L'Hostaria** (☎ 625052) on Chilembwe Rd. This is a popular place with a rustic terrace setting. Pizzas start at US$5, but at US$7 for small bowls of pasta and sauce the value is not great.

For some different flavours, go to **Alem Ethiopian Restaurant** on Victoria Ave (open lunch time only), where *injera* and *wat* (spicy meat served on a sourdough pancake) costs from US$4. You can also get 'normal' meals like chicken and chips or curry for US$1.50.

The **Hong Kong Restaurant** (☎ 620859) near the Mount Soche Hotel has all the usual Chinese dishes: you could pick a small selection of items off the menu, and have a meal for between US$5 and US$7, or you could splash out on a larger selection which will cost a total of about US$10 to US$15. Quality is very varied though – it seems care goes out the window on busy nights.

The Royal Taj (☎ 622376) on Livingstone Ave is reckoned by locals to be the best Indian restaurant in Blantyre, although it's not cheap: main courses are around US$5 to US$10.

The Green House (☎ 636375, 833518) is in the posh suburb of Sunnyside. It is open evenings only and has a European menu and fine food. Starters go from US$3 and main courses are around US$6 to US$8.

Hotel Restaurants The smart **Michiru Restaurant** at the Mount Soche Hotel has steak, fish and chicken dishes for around US$12 and specials such as prawns are around US$17. The restaurant has a good view, as it's on the top floor. In the same hotel, the less formal **Gypsy's** has main courses for around US$8.

The plush **21 Restaurant** at Ryall's Hotel is highly rated with main meals from around US$7 and specialities such as seafood for US$17. At **Moir's Coffee Shop** in the same hotel, the food is also recommended and more affordable.

Self-Catering Blantyre's market and supermarkets are listed under Shopping, later in this section.

Entertainment

Pat's Nightclub (in a yard set back from the junction of Victoria Ave and Independence Dr) is a serious drinking den in the day and evening, and is popular with a young crowd of poseurs at night. There's also a small snack bar here, which is open daytime and evening.

The *Chimwemwe Restaurant*, on the corner of Henderson St and Haile Selassie Rd, despite its name, is actually more like a bar, with snacks, music and gaming machines.

For more tranquil surroundings during the day, try the *garden terrace bar* at the Mount Soche Hotel where snacks are also available for around US$3. Also at this hotel, the *Sportsman's Bar* is favoured by local businessmen – only men seem to drink here – and other movers and shakers.

The liveliest bar in town is at *Doogles* (see Places to Stay – Budget), with a good blend of visitors, local expats and well-to-do Malawians. This bar closes at 10.30 pm, and people tend to move on to the *Cactus Bar*, on Lower Sclater Rd, which gets very lively late in the evening, and has a very distinct expat feel about it. The next-door *Arizona Bar* has a much more local flavour, but it can have a rough edge on some nights, and is not for the fainthearted, and definitely not recommended for single women.

Legends is a popular American-style bar and nightclub, which gets hot and busy after around 10 pm, particularly Thursday to Saturday. Entry is US$2 unless there's live music – when it's US$3.

Other occasional live music venues include the Mount Soche Hotel and Ryall's Hotel, where entry is also about US$3. There's also live music at *Blantyre Sports Club* on the last Friday of every month. To find out what else may be going on in the live music scene is easy: most events are publicised on fliers stuck to walls and lampposts all over town.

Spectator Sports

Blantyre's main sports venue is the Chichiri Stadium between the city centre and Limbe. This is also Malawi's national stadium: international football and other events are held here. There's no regular program, but matches are advertised in the newspaper and on billboards around town.

Shopping

Blantyre's main market is just off Kaoshiung Rd (also called Mandala Rd) south of the centre. You can buy fruit and vegetables here, plus (in case you should be searching) hardware, clothes, shoes, second-hand car spares and various household items.

As in many parts of Africa, you can also buy all kinds of pharmaceutical drugs – although Blantyre's market seems to have an especially good stock, mostly piled up unlabelled on stalls and counters. Stock is sold by the dealers (who don't seem to be pharmacists) to customers in tiny handfuls, wrapped up in twists of newspaper.

You can buy fruit and vegetables outside the main PTC supermarket on Victoria Ave, in the centre. This is one of the best supermarkets in Blantyre: as well as food, it sells many other goods useful for visitors, such as shampoo, batteries, cosmetics, tampons and baby food, much of it imported from South Africa or Europe and sold at similar prices as stock sold in Europe and South Africa.

A bit further down Victoria Ave is a Kandodo supermarket, where the stock is similar, but slightly cheaper and more limited. The ATC Supermarket on Glyn Johns Rd has a better selection, especially of imported food and other goods, but it is a bit pricier. Traders also sell fruit and vegetables outside the Kandodo and ATC supermarkets.

If you're looking for crafts and souvenirs, by far the best places to browse are the stalls outside the PTC supermarket on Victoria Ave. You can buy wooden carvings, basketware, jewellery, paintings, wire models and so on. The traders are eager to do deals, and the prices here can be quite reasonable. Smarter (fixed price) arts and crafts are available at Safari Curios on Glyn Jones Rd.

If you need film for your camera, Colour Film Processors at the north end of Victoria Ave has print film and can do passport photos on the spot. Developing and printing is also available. See Photography & Video in the Facts for the Visitor chapter for an idea of prices.

Overland drivers can refill their camping cylinders at the BOC depot on Johnstone Rd in the industrial area, off Chibembwe Hwy, near the Queen Elizabeth Hospital.

Getting There & Away

Air Blantyre's Chileka Airport is about 15km north of the city centre. Getting to/from the airport is covered in the Getting Around section below. For details on flights to international and regional destinations, or to other places in Malawi, see the Getting Around and Getting There & Away chapters.

Airline offices in Blantyre include KLM & Kenya Airways (☎ 620106) at the Mount Soche Hotel, British Airways (☎ 624333) on Victoria Ave, South African Airways (☎ 620629) on Haile Selassie Rd and Air Malawi on Robins Rd (☎ 620811).

Bus & Minibus The luxury Coachline service goes four times per day between Blantyre and Lilongwe (US$18, four hours). Note that it goes to/from the Mount Soche Hotel (the booking office is also there), not the bus station.

Blantyre's main bus station – for long-distance express and ordinary services run by the Stagecoach company – is on 'old' Chileka Rd, on the eastern edge of the centre. There are five Express buses each day between Blantyre and Lilongwe: two go direct via Zalewa (the junction with the Mwanza road – five hours; US$5); three go via Zomba (seven hours, US$6). Ordinary buses between Blantyre and Lilongwe via Zalewa go hourly (US$5). Blantyre to Zomba is US$1.50 on the express and US$1 by ordinary bus.

Other ordinary stopping services go from Blantyre to Mulanje (hourly, US$2), Mwanza (US$2.50), and to Monkey Bay (daily, US$3.80) via Liwonde and Mangochi (US$2 and US$3 respectively).

Other buses (ie, not run by Stagecoach), 'half-buses' and long-distance minibuses go from the bus station in Limbe. These mostly leave on a fill-up-and-go basis rather than to any timetable.

If you're heading for Zomba, Mulanje or the lake shore, rather than wait for a Stagecoach service in Blantyre, it's often quicker to get a local minibus to Limbe bus station and get a long-distance bus or 'half-bus' from there. Some sample fares are Zomba US$1, Mulanje US$1.50, Mangochi US$3.

For more details on Malawi's bus services see the main Getting There & Away chapter.

Getting Around

To/From the Airport Blantyre's airport is called Chileka Airport, and is about 15km north of the city centre. From the airport to the city is US$10 by taxi, but negotiate with the driver first, and expect to pay a 10% tip. Going the other way this can be negotiated down a bit. If your budget doesn't run to taxis, frequent local buses between Blantyre city centre bus station and Chileka town pass the airport gate. The fare is US$0.35.

Minibus Blantyre is a compact city so it's unlikely you'll need to use public transport to get around, during the day (see Dangers & Annoyances under Information earlier in this chapter) apart from the minibuses that shuttle along Chilembwe Highway between Blantyre city centre bus station and Limbe bus station. The one-way fare is US$0.25.

Taxi You can find private hire taxis at the Mount Soche Hotel or at the bus stations. A taxi across the city centre is around US$2. Between the centre and the bus station costs from US$3 to US$4. From Blantyre to Limbe costs around US$5.

Around Blantyre

Blantyre is surrounded by three large hills (officially labelled mountains) called Soche, Ndirande and Michiru. Once a year the Mountain Club of Malawi links all the summits in a 'Three Peaks' walk circuit, but you can walk to the top of the mountains at any other time of the year (weather permit-

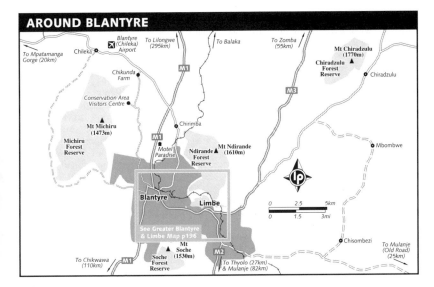

AROUND BLANTYRE

ting). The slopes of all three mountains have been declared forest reserves.

Further to the north-east, off the road to Zomba, is Mt Chiradzulu; the slopes of this peak are also contained in a forest reserve.

In the area to the east of Blantyre and Limbe, towards Mulanje and around Thyolo, are Malawi's main tea-growing plantations. This area is known as the Shire Highlands (for details on tea growing and places to visit see Tea Estates later in this chapter).

More details on all these places to visit around Blantyre are given in *Day Outings from Blantyre* (see Books in the Facts for the Visitor chapter).

MT NDIRANDE

Mt Ndirande lies north-east of Blantyre, in Ndirande Forest Reserve. The name Ndirande means Sleeping Man; when seen from Blantyre, the mountain looks like the profile of a man lying on his back.

The road to the mountain goes through an impoverished and rough part of Blantyre where outsiders may not be welcome; some walkers have been attacked on the mountain itself, so you should only go here with a switched-on local (preferably more than one).

MT SOCHE

Mt Soche is in Soche Forest Reserve to the south of Blantyre. The path up to the summit starts at Soche Secondary School, where you can find local schoolboys to act as guides for the one-hour walk to the top. The origin of this mountain's name is not clear. When we asked one lad where the name 'Soche' came from, he said it was named after the big hotel in town!

MT MICHIRU

Mt Michiru is by far the best of Blantyre's three peaks for hiking. To the north-west of the city the mountain lies at the centre of Michiru Forest Reserve, which is a well-managed conservation area administered by the Departments of Forestry and National Parks & Wildlife (with assistance from the Wildlife Society of Malawi).

There are several marked walking trails starting from the Forest Reserve Visitor centre and Education Centre on the east side of the mountain. You can buy a map of the area here, which also contains a lot of useful information on the trees and wildlife. Trails range from a short loop on the lower slopes to an all-day hike to the summit of

BLANTYRE & LIMBE

Mt Michiru (1473m). Both trails give excellent views of Blantyre and the surrounding area. Some of the trails have not been cut yet, although they are shown on the map, so check with the office staff about what actually exists on the ground. A ranger (often called a 'scout') can be hired if you'd prefer a guide. The reserve contains monkeys, bushbucks, klipspringers and even leopards, but you're unlikely to see much wildlife. The variety of birds is much more rewarding – over 400 species have been recorded here.

Getting There & Away

The conservation area visitors centre office (where the trails start) is 8km out of Blantyre. There's no public transport from Blantyre, so you'll have to walk or take a taxi if you don't have your own car. From near Ryall's Hotel, take Kabula Hill Rd northward, then take the first left onto Michiru Rd. This section is sealed and passes through a select suburb and then through a township area. At the end of the sealed section (about 3km from Blantyre) a dirt road leads through the lightly forested area at the foot of the mountain. There are several turns to the left, but ignore all these until you reach one signposted 'car park and nature trails'. This takes you to the visitors centre.

If you don't want to get a taxi the whole way, you could take it to the end of the end of the tar road. The walk from here through the forest to the office (5km) is interesting in itself. After visiting the reserve or walking some trails you may be able to get a lift back to Blantyre with other visitors to the reserve.

Another option is to approach Michiru from the main road between Blantyre and Chileka airport. Take any bus or minibus from the city centre heading towards the airport and Chileka town (the settlement near the airport) and get out at the turn off to Chikunda Farm (the fare to here, or Chileka, is about US$0.35). From here a small track leads southwards along the eastern flank of the mountain. Follow this until you see the sign for the 'car park and nature trails', which points you towards the visi-

tors centre. There are many other tracks and paths in the area, so the route can be confusing, but there are always people around who can show you the right direction.

TEA ESTATES

South and east of Blantyre, on the rolling hills of the Shire Highlands, where the climate is ideal for growing tea, the area is covered with plantations (or 'estates'). The first tea bushes were imported from India during the early days of the Nyasaland colony, and tea production quickly became a major industry. Growing tea is a very labour intensive form of agriculture – it's only viable in countries where wages for manual workers are low. Tea is a major export crop (along with tobacco and sugar) for Malawi and provides thousands of people with jobs.

Travelling on the main road between Limbe and Mulanje you'll see the seemingly endless fields of tea, with vivid green bushes in neat lines covering the hillsides. The tea pickers (men and women) work their way slowly down the lines, picking just a few leaves and a bud from the top of each bush and throwing them into a large basket they carry on their backs. At the end of each shift, the baskets of fresh tea leaves are taken to a collection area where they are weighed and each worker's wages are calculated. The leaves are then transported to a tea factory, where they are trimmed and dried before being packed in bags and boxes ready for export. Only a small proportion of low-quality tea stays within the country to be sold locally.

If you have a genuine interest in tea production, it may be possible to arrange a tour of an estate and factory. There is no established setup; you simply phone an estate and ask a senior manager if it would be possible to visit. You'll probably need your own vehicle, or will have to take a taxi, as most estate offices are off the main road and are difficult to reach by public transport. The best place to start is Satemwa Estate (☎ 472233), near the small town of Thyolo (**cho**-low) on the main road between Limbe and Mulanje. The estate is home to

Chawani Bungalow (☎ *472356*), which can be hired for US$65 per night. It sleeps up to eight in four double bedrooms and the price includes the services of a caretaker/cook. From the bungalow you can walk through the tea estates or go through the evergreen forest remnants on nearby Thyolo Mountain, which is a popular bird-watching spot.

Other tea estates that may allow visits include British African Estates (☎ 472266) and Namingomba Estates (☎ 472300, 472492). The latter also has a ***guesthouse***, which charges US$7 per person (self catering). The tourist office on Victoria Ave in Blantyre might be able to help with more suggestions.

Southern Malawi

The Southern Province of Malawi, with Blantyre roughly at its centre, lies between the south end of Lake Malawi and the far southern tip of the country. This chapter includes the main features of the province, namely Zomba town and the Zomba Plateau, as well as Malawi's flagship wildlife area, Liwonde National Park. It also covers the highland wilderness of Mount Mulanje and the rarely visited Lower Shire area, with Lengwe National Park and Majete Wildlife Reserve. Places are described roughly north to south. (Blantyre and Limbe are discussed in a separate chapter earlier.)

The Upper Shire Valley

The Shire River flows out of Lake Malawi, through Lake Malombe, then cuts west of the central highland region around Zomba and Blantyre. This area is called the Upper Shire Valley – essentially a section of the Great Rift Valley wedged between the higher ground of Malawi's central plateau and the mountains of western Mozambique. Just beyond the small settlement of Matope, in the area of Zalewa (where the main road between Blantyre and Mwanza crosses the river), the Shire starts to descend via a series of scenic but rarely visited rapids, waterfalls and gorges, which eventually come to an end near Majete Wildlife Reserve, the start of the Lower Shire area, which is also described in this chapter.

BALAKA

This small town just north of the main road between Lilongwe and Zomba is unremarkable (although the splendid modern basilica church is worth a look), but you may find yourself here if you travel to/from Mozambique by rail via Liwonde and Nayuchi. For details see the Getting There & Away and

Highlights

Southern Malawi p209

MOZAMBIQUE

Liwonde National Park p211

The Zomba Plateau p216
(Southern Section)

Zomba p213
Mount Mulanje p222

MOZAMBIQUE

- Spending time in Liwonde National Park – Malawi's premier park, situated on the scenic Shire River; an excellent place for spotting elephants from a boat

- Hiking in Mount Mulanje – sheer cliffs, high peaks, endless views and good-value mountain huts

- Strolling through Zomba, a colonial town with a large and colourful market, over-looked by a dramatic mountain

- Braving the Lower Shire area, Malawi's hot and seldom visited 'Far South', with wildlife reserves and historical monuments

Getting Around chapters. For a place to stay, there's a basic local *resthouse* near the bus and train stations.

LIWONDE

You may visit Liwonde town if you're heading for Liwonde National Park or going to Mozambique by rail (the train to the border passes through here). The town is divided by the Shire River, flowing south from Lake Malombe, which is crossed by

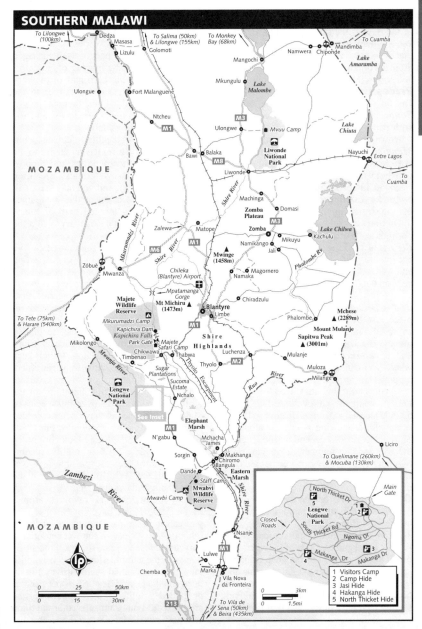

SOUTHERN MALAWI

To Lilongwe (100km)
To Salima (50km) & Lilongwe (155km)
To Monkey Bay (68km)
To Cuamba

Dedza
Masasa
Lizulu
Golomoti
Namwera
Chiponde
Mandimba
Lake Amaramba

Ulongue
Fort Malanguene
Mkungulu
Lake Malombe
Mangochi

Ntcheu
M1
M3
Ulongwe
Mvuu Camp
Lake Chiuta

Bawi
Balaka
M8
Liwonde National Park
Nayuchi
Entre Lagos

MOZAMBIQUE
Liwonde
To Cuamba

Machinga
Zalewa
Matope
Zomba Plateau
Domasi
M3
Zomba
Mikuyu
Kachulu
Lake Chilwa

Zóbuè
Mwanza
M6
M1
Shire River
Mwinge (1458m)
Namikango
Jali
Phalombe Rv

Chileka (Blantyre) Airport
Namaka
Magornero

Mpatamanga Gorge
Mt Michiru (1473m)
Chiradzulu
Mchese (2289m)

Majete Wildlife Reserve
Blantyre
Limbe
Phalombe
Mount Mulanje

To Tete (75km) & Harare (540km)
Mkurumadzi Camp
Kapichira Dam
Kapichira Falls
Park Gate
Majete Safari Camp
Shire Highlands
Luchenza
Sapitwa Peak (3001m)

Mikolongo
Chikwawa
Thabwa
Thyolo
M2
Ruo River
Muloza
Milange

Timbenao
Sugar Plantations
Sucoma Estate
Mulanje

Lengwe National Park
Nchalo

See Inset
Elephant Marsh
M1
N'gabu
Mchacha James
To Quelimane (260km) & Mocuba (130km)

Sorgin
Makhanga
Chiromo
Bangula
Liciro

Dande
Staff Camp
Eastern Marsh
North Thicket Dr
Main Gate

Mwabvi Wildlife Reserve
Mwavbi Camp
5
Lengwe National Park
1
2

MOZAMBIQUE
Zambezi River
Closed Roads
South Thicket Rd
Ngoma Dr
3

Nsanje
Makanga Dr
4
Makanga Dr

Lulwe
Marka
Vila Nova da Fronteira
1 Visitors Camp
2 Camp Hide
3 Jasi Hide
4 Hakanga Hide
5 North Thicket Hide

Chemba
213
To Vila de Sena (50km) & Beira (435km)

0   25   50km
0   15   30mi

0   3km
0   1.5mi

the main road on a barrage. On the east side of the river is the railway station, the market, a supermarket, several shops and a few places to stay. On the west side are some more accommodation options.

Places to Stay

On the east side of town, the *Market Square Motel* has good singles/doubles with bathroom and breakfast for US$5/10.

Down by the river is the strangely titled *Manpower Shireside Lodge* where simple but clean rondavels (circular bungalows) with hot water, nets and fan are fair value at US$8.50/13 for singles/doubles. There's a *bar* and a *restaurant* in a garden overlooking the river. Camping is allowed.

On the west side of the river, the rather optimistically named *Liwonde Holiday Resort*, just off the main road, is basic but acceptable, with clean shared bathrooms and a friendly owner. Rooms cost US$1.50 per person.

Another 1.5km off the main road is *Kudya Discovery Lodge* (☎ 532497); this place is a bit rundown, with tatty rooms from US$16/20 that are not worth the money. But it does have a swimming pool and a *restaurant* overlooking the river where you can always see a big group of hippos.

If you can't stay in Liwonde National Park, a company called Waterline (☎/fax 532552), based at Kudya Discovery Lodge, runs wildlife-viewing boat trips along the Shire River. Prices depend on the length of the trip and the number of people, but a two-hour tour for two or three people costs US$22 each.

Getting There & Away

Liwonde town is on the main road that runs between Lilongwe and Blantyre (via Zomba). All public transport stops here, on both the west and east side of the river. Note that if you're on the bus between Lilongwe and Blantyre that goes via Zalewa, this does not go through Liwonde town. If you're heading straight for Liwonde National Park, see the Getting There & Away information in that section.

LIWONDE NATIONAL PARK

Liwonde National Park is the best in Malawi. The scenery varies, and is very beautiful, while the park is well managed and has an increasing number of animals – especially in the northern half of the park and along the river. The park lies to the south of Lake Malawi, and includes part of Lake Malombe, the Shire River and the eastern Upper Shire Plain.

There is a very healthy elephant population and the Shire River seems to be overflowing with crocodiles and hippos. Antelopes such as waterbucks are often seen near the water, and you may see small herds of beautiful sables on the floodplains. Liwonde also has a small herd of rhinos that are protected in a sanctuary within the national park.

Some visitors are disappointed by the lack of animal variety, but Liwonde's setting is unsurpassed, and as long as you are not desperate to tick off the 'big five' it would be hard not to enjoy it. Having said that, through 2000 and 2001, the park will be restocked with more species, including buffalo, eland, Niassa wildebeest, reedbuck, zebra, roan and hartebeest, which may in turn attract lions and other predators; visitors keen to spot a wider range will also be rewarded.

The combination of rich riverine, mopane and grassland habitats means birdlife is very varied – over 400 species of Malawi's 650 species have been recorded here. All in all, after a slump in the 1980s and early 1990s, the future looks bright for Liwonde and a visit is highly recommended. Entry fees are payable (see National Parks & Wildlife Reserves in the Facts about Malawi chapter).

Tourism in the park revolves around Mvuu Camp. If you have your own vehicle you can tour the park's network of tracks (although they close in the wet season and vary from year to year, so check the situation with the camp). Alternatively, wildlife viewing tours (called 'game drives') in an open-top 4WD vehicle (US$18 per person) or guided wildlife walks (US$10) can be arranged at Mvuu Camp. To enter the rhino sanctuary costs an extra US$2, and the money goes directly to this project. Most rewarding and enjoyable are boat rides (US$18) on the river which go from (and can be easily arranged at) Mvuu Camp, morning or evening, when you're virtually guaranteed to see elephants, hippos, crocodiles and a whole host of birds.

Places to Stay & Eat

Mvuu Camp, managed by Central African Wilderness Safaris (☎ 771153, ☎/fax 771397 in Lilongwe, *@ info@wilderness.malawi .net*), is deep in the northern part of the park on the banks of the river. Comfortable chalets are US$42, big walk-in tents are US$39 or you can camp in your own tent for US$8 (all charges are per person). The shared showers and toilets are the cleanest we've seen north of the Limpopo, and there's a fully equipped kitchen (with staff on hand to help) if you want to self-cater. Or you can eat at the airy thatched *restaurant* that overlooks the river; breakfast is US$8.40, lunch US$11 and dinner US$15. There's also a bar-lounge area. Full board in a chalet (including meals, wildlife drives, boat rides etc) costs US$130 per person. Children between four and 12 are charged half price, but those under six are not allowed on wildlife drives.

A short distance upriver is *Mvuu Wilderness Lodge*, also managed by Central African Wilderness Safaris. This is a top-quality place and has large luxury double tents with private balconies overlooking a waterhole where wildlife and birds are active. There's a maximum of only ten guests, so this place is relaxed and intimate, with attentive staff and excellent food. There's also a small swimming pool. Luxury comes at a price though – US$230 per person per night, which includes full board, park fees and all wildlife drives, boat rides, bird walks etc. You can book through a travel agent in Malawi or abroad. Otherwise, contact Central African Wilderness Safaris (in ADL house) at the main office in Lilongwe or the branch at Ryall's Hotel in Blantyre.

At least two new places are planned to open in Liwonde by 2001. These include a new *lodge*, to be operated by Makomo Sa-

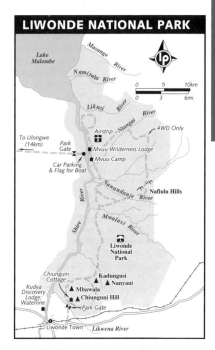

LIWONDE NATIONAL PARK

faris (see Organised Tours in the Getting Around chapter), contact them for more information; and *Chiunguni Cottage*, which was closed to the public for some years, and is due to be operated by the Wildlife Society of Malawi. Accommodation in Liwonde National Park remains open all year, as places in the south are always accessible; the places in the north can be reached by boat, even if rain closes some of the park tracks.

Getting There & Away

Liwonde National Park has an airstrip and some visitors to the park (especially those staying at the top-end Mvuu Wilderness Lodge) fly straight in. There are no scheduled flights, but charter flights are operated by Sefofane (represented by Central African Wilderness Safaris and Ulendo Safaris, see Travel Agencies in the Lilongwe chapter). Planes fly on demand for two or more, and a one-way flight between

Lilongwe and Liwonde is US$160. For more details see Air in the Getting Around chapter.

The main park gate is 6km north-east of Liwonde town. It's straightforward (and signposted) if you're in your own vehicle, but there's no public transport from the town to the park, although hitching with other visitors is not impossible. From the gate to Mvuu Camp is 28km by park track (except the first 5km or so, this track can be closed in the wet season).

Another way for vehicles to reach the park is via the dirt road (open all year) from Ulongwe, a village between Liwonde town and Mangochi. This leads for 14km through local villages to the western boundary, where there's a park gate. About 1km beyond here, near the riverbank, there's a car park (with a watchman) and, just beyond here, a jetty; you hoist a flag and a boat from Mvuu Camp comes to pick you up. This service is free if you're staying at the camp.

For those without wheels the best option is to get any bus or minibus between Liwonde town and Mangochi and get off at Ulongwe (make sure you say this clearly, otherwise the driver will think you want to go to Lilongwe). In Ulongwe, local boys wait by the bus stop and will take you by bicycle to the park gate or all the way to the boat jetty and flag. This costs US$2 to US$3, although if you've got a big pack there may be an extra charge or you may need two bikes.

'The hour-long cycle ride through the villages is superb, with a great commentary from your pedalist. However, do not leave it too late. At dusk elepants come much nearer to the track – and so the cyclists demand extra money. We had a very close encounter with three elephants and without the bikes we would have been flattened.'

George Casley, UK

Another option is the boat transfer service along the Shire River offered by Waterline (☎/fax 532552), based at Kudya Discovery Lodge (see Liwonde earlier in this section). They will drop you at Mvuu Camp, and return to pick you up, for US$72 each way (the price is for the boat for one to three passengers), or US$20 each for groups of four to five. If you make an advance reservation for Mvuu Camp (through the office in Lilongwe), you can also arrange a transfer on the camp's own boat from Liwonde town to the camp for US$20 per person (minimum four). Approaching Mvuu by river is very enjoyable – along the way you're likely to see elephants and certain to see hippos.

The Zomba Region

ZOMBA

With a population of approximately 75,000, the large town of Zomba was the capital of Malawi until the mid-1970s, and the seat of parliament until 1998. Although the politicians have moved to Lilongwe, on the outskirts of Zomba is Chancellor College – the University of Malawi's main campus. There's also a large army camp here (which, locals say, accounts for the town's low crime rate). About 10km outside Zomba is Mikuyu, a notorious jail for political prisoners in President Banda's day, which was closed in 1994 and which is now open to the public as a memorial to those who were detained here.

Zomba is a large busy place, with all the attractions of a town and none of the downsides of a city. At its heart is the vibrant market and shopping area (the largest market in the country), which is a great place to do your shopping or simply to wander around and watch Africa at work. The scenic backdrop to the town is the Zomba Plateau; a walk through the suburbs on the lush and peaceful foothills reveals faded but still impressive colonial and government buildings – a reminder of Zomba's historical importance.

Zomba is not a place for wild parties, and you won't see that many other tourists, but the town somehow encapsulates what Malawi is all about, and a visit here is highly recommended.

Places to Stay

The *Council Resthouse* opposite the bus station has beds in a big room for US$0.50 and singles/doubles for US$1.50/2, but the shared bathrooms are disgusting.

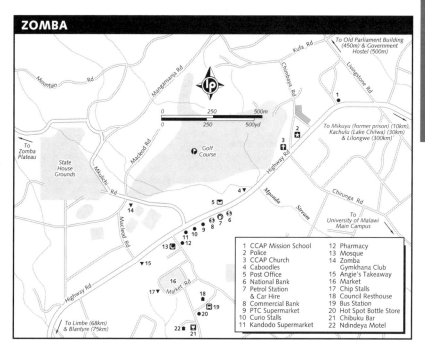

ZOMBA

1 CCAP Mission School
2 Police
3 CCAP Church
4 Caboodles
5 Post Office
6 National Bank
7 Petrol Station
   & Car Hire
8 Commercial Bank
9 PTC Supermarket
10 Curio Stalls
11 Kandodo Supermarket
12 Pharmacy
13 Mosque
14 Zomba
   Gymkhana Club
15 Angie's Takeaway
16 Market
17 Chip Stalls
18 Council Resthouse
19 Bus Station
20 Hot Spot Bottle Store
21 Chibuku Bar
22 Ndindeya Motel

Much better is the nearby *Ndindeya Motel*, where large rooms with clean shared bathrooms cost US$3/6 or US$7/10 with bathroom. The restaurant is good, with breakfast from US$1 and meals from US$2. To get here, go south from the market and turn right (west) onto a dusty side-street just before the brightly painted Chibuku Bar.

Up the hill and price scale from here is the *Government Hostel* in the house of the first colonial governor. Rooms cost US$35/40 with bathroom and breakfast. Staff will assume you'll want one of the more modern rooms in the garden, but those in the old house have more character – try for the room in the atmospheric west tower. Main dishes in the restaurant are US$3 to US$5, and the set menu is US$10.

Places to Eat

There are plenty of cheap restaurants – *Angie's Takeaway* on the main street is probably the best. Around the market area

are several *chip stalls* serving up deep fried potato chips. One or two of them serve grilled meat as well as other street food.

For a splurge, *Caboodles* on Highway Rd serves good coffee and sticky cakes for US$1.50, ham and salad or BLT rolls for US$2 and pizza and salad for US$3.

At the *Zomba Gymkhana Club*, a fine but faded colonial relic just north of Highway Rd, you can get meals and drinks in pleasant surroundings.

For picnics, camping or self-catering, there are two supermarkets on Highway Rd.

Getting There & Away

Zomba is on one of the main routes between Lilongwe and Blantyre, and there are frequent Stagecoach buses. The Express to/from Lilongwe is US$4.50; to/from Blantyre is US$1.50. Note that if you're on the Stagecoach bus between Lilongwe and Blantyre that goes via Zalewa, this does not go through Zomba. If you're coming from

Blantyre in the south, there are minibuses (US$1) every hour or so to Zomba from Limbe bus station. From Zomba, minibuses to Limbe cost US$1. To Liwonde, bus or minibus costs US$0.80.

AROUND ZOMBA TOWN

Around Zomba town are some interesting places to visit. The main one is the **Zomba Plateau** (see later in this chapter). The other two, Lake Chilwa and Namaka Postal Museum, are a touch more esoteric and may only appeal to ornithologists or philatelists.

Lake Chilwa

Lake Chilwa is the second largest of Malawi's lakes, lying about 30km east of Zomba town. Forget about beaches though; this shallow lake is surrounded by reed beds, swamp and marsh. This makes for excellent bird-watching territory, and an interesting place to visit if you just want to get off the main track for a day or two. A booklet on the birds of Lake Chilwa has been produced by the Wildlife Society of Malawi and is available in the small shop at the Ku Chawe Inn on the Zomba Plateau (see the Zomba Plateau later in this chapter), or from the Wildlife Society of Malawi giftshop at the Heritage Centre in Limbe (see the Blantyre & Limbe chapter).

By far the easiest way to get to Lake Chilwa is along the road from Zomba town which branches off the main road between Zomba and Lilongwe about 5km from the centre of Zomba. This leads to the peaceful lakeside fishing village of Kachulu. There's a couple of basic local ***resthouses*** here, but not much in the way of food, so you're probably better off bringing some supplies from Zomba in case you can't find a meal in Kachulu.

You can either stroll along the shore or local fishermen will be happy to take you out in a boat. Rates seem vague as very few visitors come here and boat rental is a new concept; about US$5 for a morning or afternoon trip would be fair.

Namaka Postal Museum

At Namaka, about 30km south of Zomba on the main road towards Blantyre, is a slightly incongruous but well kept and fascinating Postal Museum. It is also called the Mtengatenga Museum, after the *tenga-tenga* (porters) who were the first mail runners in the country at the end of the 19th century – see the boxed text 'The Mail Runners'.

The museum is a converted resthouse, originally built for the runners on the route between Blantyre and Zomba. It contains various exhibits including samples of stamps and postmarks from the earliest days of the protectorate to the present time, pictures of early postmen and post offices, and a fine collection of post boxes. Entry is free.

THE ZOMBA PLATEAU

The Zomba Plateau is divided into two halves by the Domasi Valley. The southern half has a road to the top, a hotel (the landmark Ku Chawe Inn), a camping ground, several picnic places and a network of drivable tracks and walking paths that wind through pine forest or patches of indigenous woodland. There are also several narrow ridges along the edge of the escarpment, with viewpoints overlooking the plains below. The plateau also has streams, waterfalls and a couple of lakes, where fishing is allowed. Some people prefer to drive around, but Zomba Plateau is also a good place for hiking or mountain biking (mountain bikes can be hired from Zomba Forest Lodge – see Places to Stay & Eat later in this chapter). Whatever you do on the Zomba Plateau, the cool air makes a welcome change from the heat of the lowland areas.

'Zomba is far gentler than Mulanje, and also far more accessible, cultivated and lush. During and after the rainy season, it's also a wild fruit fanatic's dream – strawberries, rhubarb, yellowberries and blackberries grow in abundance.'

Richard Carr, UK

Things to See

About 2km by road from the Ku Chawe Inn are **Mandala Falls**, which are not as impressive as they used to be, since **Mlunguzi Dam** was significantly enlarged in 1999. The area downstream from here is worth avoiding for a few years, as the landscape

The Mail Runners

From the late 19th century, the colonial authorities administering Malawi (which was then called the British Central African Protectorate) developed a well-organised and far-reaching postal service. At the time the main 'gateway' to the country (and to much of the surrounding region) was Chiromo on the Lower Shire River. Steamers from the Indian Ocean would come up the Zambezi River through Portuguese territory (which later became Mozambique), then up the Shire River and would unload at Chiromo. The country's first post office was built here in 1891. Mail would be distributed from here to Chikwawa, Blantyre, Zomba and other settlements throughout the protectorate, including various points on Lake Nyasa (where steamers were also used), and further beyond Karonga into southern Tanganyika (which later became Tanzania), Northern and Southern Rhodesia (which were later divided into Zambia and Zimbabwe) and the Belgian Congo (later Zaïre, and still later named Congo again).

There were very few roads at this time, so the post was carried by mail runners – local Africans who would literally run between post offices with a bag of mail on their heads. These journeys obviously took many days to complete, so post offices doubled as resthouses for the runners. Other resthouses were built at roughly 30km intervals along the main routes, and a system of relays was developed to reduce lost time. The route between Blantyre and Zomba (the two main settlements) was busy, and surprisingly fast. The runners would meet at Namaka resthouse – the halfway point, now the museum – exchange bags, then return the same way. Using this method, post took just a day. By 1896 the runners were going at night, so that letters posted in Blantyre in the evening were delivered next morning in Zomba (ironically a record sadly unmatched by today's postal service).

The first mail runners wore uniforms of white tunics and shorts and ran in bare feet. It was soon realised that white does not stay white long when the wearer runs through the African bush for days at a time, so the uniform was later changed to blue. At first the runners were allowed to carry spears as protection against wild animals; they were later issued with rifles. As early as 1894, the postmaster general, one Ernest Harrhy, wrote the following report: 'In February, two carriers carrying mail bags between Mpimbi and Zomba were confronted by several lions. Deeming discretion to be the better part of valour, they sought safety in the high branches of a friendly tree, and waited until their leonine majesties condescended to move on to pastures new.' A later report noted that 'cases have occurred where mail men have been driven to take refuge in a tree, and leave the bags at the foot to be smelled and pawed and discarded as inedible by disappointed beasts of prey...'.

Despite these dangers, and the colonial officials' rather casual attitude towards the safety of their employees, the mail runners continued pounding the tracks of Nyasaland until the mid-1930s, when bicycles were issued. Roads were also being improved by this time and the first postal van was introduced in 1942.

recovers from the construction. A nature trail leads from Mandala Falls upstream through some beautiful indigenous forest and a trout farm to **Williams Falls**, another picturesque cascade.

A popular place to visit is **Chingwe's Hole**, on the western side of the plateau. It is supposedly bottomless and the basis of various local legends, although it is now overgrown and not especially impressive. Nearby, however, is a splendid viewpoint looking westward over the Shire Valley.

For even more impressive views, head for the eastern side of the plateau, where **Queen's View** (named after Queen Elizabeth, wife of King George VI, who visited Zomba in 1957) and **Emperor's View** (after Emperor Haile Selassie of Ethiopia, who came here in 1964) overlook Zomba town and out towards Mount Mulanje.

Hiking

The southern half of Zomba Plateau is ideal for hiking. Using the map in this book, and

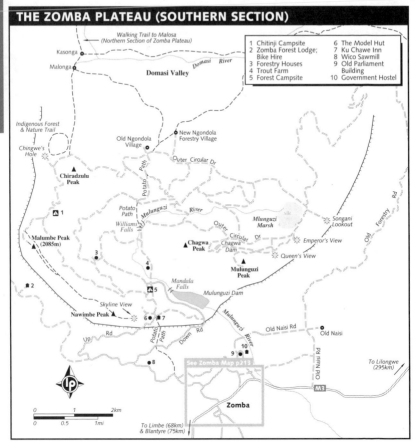

THE ZOMBA PLATEAU (SOUTHERN SECTION)

Walking Trail to Malosa
(Northern Section of Zomba Plateau)

Kasonga

Malonga

Domasi River

Domasi Valley

1   Chitinji Campsite
2   Zomba Forest Lodge;
    Bike Hire
3   Forestry Houses
4   Trout Farm
5   Forest Campsite

6   The Model Hut
7   Ku Chawe Inn
8   Wico Sawmill
9   Old Parliament
    Building
10 Government Hostel

Indigenous Forest
& Nature Trail

Chingwe's
Hole

Old Ngondola
Village

New Ngondola
Forestry Village

Outer Circular Dr

Chiradzulu
Peak

Potato Path

Potato
Path

Mulunguzi   River

Williams'
Falls

Outer

Circular

Dr

Mlunguzi
Marsh

Songani
Lookout

Malumbe Peak
(2085m)

Chagwa
Peak

Chagwa
Dam

Emperor's View

Queen's View

Mulunguzi
Peak

Mandala
Falls

Mulunguzi Dam

Skyline View

Nawimbe Peak

Up   Rd

Potato
Path

Down   Rd

Mulunguzi River

Old Naisi Rd

Old Naisi

Old Forestry Rd

Old Naisi Rd

10

9

To Lilongwe
(295km)

See Zomba Map p213

M3

Zomba

0   1   2km
0   0.5   1mi

To Limbe (68km)
& Blantyre (75km)

the list of features in Things to See, you can plan your own route. The network of tracks and paths can be confusing though, so for more help with orientation, there's a 3-D map of the plateau in the 'Model Hut' by the Ku Chawe Inn, and a visitors book where hikers and travellers have added comments and advice.

If you want more detail on hiking routes, *A Guide to Zomba Plateau* is a single sheet map with information on the back, including several suggested hiking routes. It is produced by the Wildlife Society and is available in Blantyre and the Ku Chawe Inn

for around US$1.50. For more detailed information, the Zomba Plateau is covered in Lonely Planet's guide *Trekking in East Africa*.

Really adventurous hikers may find the northern half of the plateau more interesting. There are few tracks here, and no pine plantation – the landscape is reportedly similar to that on Mount Mulanje and Nyika.

The Potato Path This path, used by local people, links Zomba town to the Domasi Valley across the southern half of the plateau. The section from town up on to the

Warning

Some travellers have reported being hassled by 'ruffians' when walking on the plateau. Locals say these are not people from Zomba but outsiders working on the Mlunguzi Dam construction site. Whoever they are, to avoid trouble you should consider arranging a guide with the forest officer stationed at the Model Hut.

plateau is described in Getting There & Away later in this section.

From near the Ku Chawe Inn, the Potato Path goes straight across the southern half of the plateau, sometimes using the park tracks, sometimes using narrow short-cut paths, and leads eventually to Old Ngondola Village. From here it descends quite steeply into the Domasi Valley.

The Domasi Valley is noted for its fertile soil, plentiful water and good farming conditions, so the local people grow vegetables (especially potatoes) and take them along the Potato Path (hence the name) down to Zomba town to sell in the market.

Places to Stay & Eat

This section deals with options on the actual mountain. For options in Zomba town itself, see Zomba earlier in this chapter.

Camping On the plateau, the aptly named *Forest Campsite* is on a flat grassy site among large pine trees. Camping here costs US$1 per person. There are toilets and wood-fired hot showers. It's one of those places that is beautiful in sunlight and a bit miserable in mist (you've got a fifty-fifty chance).

Alternatively, go to *Chitinji Campsite* near Malumbe Peak, which has been completely renovated by an enterprising local called Nasiv Jussab. This is now an excellent place to stay at US$3 per person, although it is even more likely to be shrouded in mist. The building of cabins is planned. Nasiv has also taken over the running of the Trout Farm, and plans another campsite there. He can also advise on hikes in the surrounding area, and is especially keen to help people who want to explore the

wilderness zone on the northern section of the plateau.

If you're camping you should bring most of the food you need from Zomba town, as there's no shop on the plateau. There is only a local style *tea room* and some *stalls* selling fruit, vegetables and (sometimes) bread between the hotel and the Forest Campsite.

Guesthouses The charming *Zomba Forest Lodge* is on the western slopes of the plateau, 6km along a winding dirt road off the Up Road. This is the former Kachere Forest Resthouse, which has now been nicely renovated and has a kitchen for self-catering and comfortable rooms with private bathroom at US$18 per person. Mountain bikes can be hired. For more information, see Land & Lake Safaris under Organised Tours in the Getting Around chapter.

Fans of obscure historical facts may like to note that this building was originally the home of a colonial officer serving on board HMS *Guendolin*, the ship involved in Malawi's only recorded battle at sea (see the boxed text 'HMS *Guendolin* and Malawi's Naval Victory' in the Central Malawi chapter).

Hotels The *Ku Chawe Inn* (☎ 514253, 514211, central reservations ☎ 620071, fax 514230) is a top-quality hotel built right on the edge of the plateau escarpment with excellent views and very comfortable singles/doubles from US$100/154 with breakfast. Evening meals cost around $9.

There is a good *restaurant* and *bar*, where they keep a fire going on cold nights, and the terraced gardens are particularly pleasant. Nonguests can drink in the bar or eat dinner here, or enjoy the buffet breakfast for US$6.50. Be prepared for changes; this hotel will come under the banner of the Le Meridien hotel group in 2001, so new looks and new prices are likely.

Getting There & Away

A sealed road leads steeply up the escarpment from Zomba town to the top of the plateau (about 8km). After the last junction, it's narrow and one way only, and is called the Up Road. There's a separate Down Road, which has been widened and now takes traffic both ways. Ku Chawe Inn is at the top of the Up Road.

There's no bus up to the plateau, but you can try hitching or waiting for a *matola* (unofficial public transport, usually a van or a truck) by the junction on the main street in Zomba opposite the Kandodo supermarket (you'll see a crowd of local people waiting here). Alternatively, you can take a taxi from town to the Ku Chawe Inn or Forest Campsite (negotiable from around US$8).

If this is beyond your means, you can get a taxi part way through the suburbs, say as far as the Wico Sawmill, or the Zomba Forest Lodge turn-off, then simply walk up the Up Road. There are excellent views that are often missed by drivers who have to concentrate on the narrow turns.

Alternatively you can walk all the way from Zomba town to the top of the plateau via the Up Road or the Potato Path. The latter route is signposted at a sharp bend on the road up to the plateau about 2km from the outskirts of Zomba town. The path climbs steeply through woodland to reach the top of the plateau near the Ku Chawe Inn. Allow two to three hours for the ascent, and about 1½ coming down, but note that there have been reports of occasional attacks on lone hikers using the Potato Path. You are advised to go in a group or take a local companion. (For a description of the route onwards from the Ku Chawe Inn across the plateau, see Hiking earlier in this section.)

Mount Mulanje

Mount Mulanje (also called the Mulanje Plateau) rises steeply from the undulating plain of the highlands, surrounded by escarpments and near-vertical cliffs of bare rock, many of which are over 1000m high. The cliffs are dissected by vegetated valleys, where rivers drop in spectacular waterfalls. It is often misty here and Mount Mulanje's high peaks sometimes jut out above the cloud, giving the mountain its local name – The Island in the Sky.

Mulanje measures about 30km west to east and 25km north to south, with an area of at least 600 sq km. On its north-east corner is the outlier Mchese Mountain, separated from the main massif by the Fort Lister Gap. The massif is composed of several bowl-shaped river basins separated by rocky peaks and ridges. The highest peak is Sapitwa (3001m), the highest point in Malawi and all Southern Africa north of the Drakensberg.

Some visitors come to the base of the mountain just for a day visit, to fish in the streams, picnic on the rocks, or maybe walk up to the top of the escarpment and back down again. But the stunning scenery, easy access, clear paths and well-maintained huts make Mulanje a fine hiking area and many people spend at least a few days walking on the mountain.

Walking through the valleys and river basins is fairly straightforward, although some of the ridge crossings are steep. Several other peaks on the massif are above 2500m, and you can reach most of the summits without needing to be a rock climber, although some of the ascents are very steep, and potentially serious for inexperienced hikers, especially when you sometimes need to use your hands as well as your feet to go up. We've had letters from many readers in the past who reckon Mulanje to be one of the highlights of their trip.

INFORMATION
Regulations

Hiking on Mount Mulanje is controlled by the Likabula Forest Station (☎ 465218, PO Box 50, Mulanje) at the village of Likabula (also spelt Likhabula), about 15km from Mulanje town. It's open every day from 7 am to noon and 1 to 5 pm (including weekends and most holidays); it is run by a very friendly lady called Dorothy. You must register here and make reservations for the mountain huts (you can also phone or write in advance). This is also the best place to arrange guides and porters.

Camping is only permitted near huts. Open fires are not allowed, which is especially important during the latter part of the dry season, when there is a serious fire risk. Also forbidden is the collecting of plants and animals.

Guidebooks & Maps

The *Guide to Mulanje Massif*, by Frank Eastwood, which is available at bookshops in Blantyre and Lilongwe, has information on ascent routes and main peaks plus a large section on rock-climbing, but nothing on routes between huts. There's more detail on Mulanje in Lonely Planet's *Trekking in East Africa*, which also covers Nyika and Zomba.

If you need detailed maps, Mulanje is covered by the government survey 1:50,000 sheet number 1535 D3 which shows most paths, and all the huts (except Minunu Hut, which is at approximate grid reference

826377). The 1:30,000 *Tourist Map of Mulanje* covers a similar area and is over-printed with extra information for walkers. These maps are usually available from the public map sales offices in Lilongwe and Blantyre (see Maps in the relevant chapters), but don't rely on this as stocks sometimes run dry.

Guides & Porters

Porters are not obligatory, but they do make the trekking easier, especially for the first day's steep walk from Likabula Forest Station (they will also help guide you through the maze of paths). Most porters will act as guides on the routes between huts, but you need a guide or a porter with proper guiding experience if you plan to go up some peaks.

Pines on Mulanje

The pine plantations on Mulanje were first established by the colonial government in the early 1950s, mainly around Chambe. The sides of the massif are too steep for a road, so all the timber is cut by hand and then carried down on a cableway (called the skyline) or by forest labourers. As you're going up the Chambe Plateau path you'll see these incredibly hardy guys walking downhill, sometimes running, with huge planks of wood balanced on their heads.

The plantations provide employment for local people and wood for the whole of southern Malawi. A side effect, apart from plantations being ugly, is the tendency of pine trees to spread slowly across the natural grassland as seeds are blown by the wind. These introduced trees disturb the established vegetation balance – always precarious in highland areas.

JENNY BOWMAN

Labourers have to carry huge planks downhill on their heads.

As you arrive in Likabula (or Mulanje town), you'll be besieged by hopeful locals looking for work. However, you should only arrange porters at Likabula, as the Forest Station keeps a list of registered porters who are known to be reliable. Some porters are not on the list but are 'cleared' by the office staff. (We have heard from travellers who did deals with porters not on the list. For some of these people their trek went well, but others have reported porters going on strike, getting most of their pay up front and then disappearing, and even demanding extra pay with menaces at the end of the trip.)

The Forestry Department and porters have a standard charge of US$4 per day per porter, payable in kwacha. You should avoid hiring porters who undercut this price in their eagerness to get work. The maximum weight of the pack each porter carries is 18kg. If your porter also guides you up peaks (if he has the relevant knowledge), an extra fee may be payable. Before agreeing to anything, check with the Forestry Office that the porter is familiar with the routes.

The total fee for the whole trip should be agreed before departure, written down and then paid at the end of the trip. From this money porters will provide their own food, so about 25% may be required in advance. Make sure porters bring everything they need, and tell them no other food can be provided. Even if you do this, you'll still feel guilty when you stop for lunch and the porters sit and watch you eat, so take a few extra packets of biscuits for them.

You may want to tip your porter if the service has been good. A rule of thumb is to pay something around an extra day's wage for every three to five days.

Supplies

There is nowhere to buy food on Mount Mulanje, so you must carry all you need. At Likabula village there is a small market, but you're better off getting supplies at Chitikali (where the dirt road to Likabula turns off the main sealed Blantyre-Mulanje road), which has shops, stalls and a small supermarket, or in Blantyre.

DANGERS & ANNOYANCES

Mount Mulanje is a big mountain with notoriously unpredictable weather. After periods of heavy rain, streams can become swollen and impassable. Do not try to cross them. Wait until the flood subsides (sometimes a few hours) or adjust your route to cross in safety further upstream.

Even during dry seasons, it's not uncommon to get rain, cold winds and thick mists, which makes it easy to get lost. Between May and August periods of low cloud and drizzle (called *chiperones*) can last for several days, and temperatures drop below freezing. None of this is a problem as long as you've got warm, waterproof gear and don't get lost. Otherwise, you risk suffering from severe exposure. This is no idle warning: In 1999 an ill-prepared traveller got lost and unfortunately died up here.

The massif is criss-crossed with firebreaks, some of which are followed by paths, but some of which are not, and are mistakenly followed by hikers. Some firebreaks can become overgrown or new ones made; be prepared for 'extra' or 'missing' firebreaks in route descriptions. Some footpath junctions are signposted, but you shouldn't rely on this as signs may be destroyed by fire or simply go missing.

PLACES TO STAY

This section deals with places to stay on the actual mountain. For details of places to stay in Mulanje town itself see Mulanje later in this chapter.

Likabula

At Likabula Forest Station, where most hikes start, the Forest Resthouse is spotlessly clean and has a kitchen, a comfortable lounge, several twin bedrooms and a clean shared bathroom for US$3.50 per person. A cook will prepare your food and wash up etc. Camping in the grounds costs US$1.

The nearby *Guesthouse* at the CCAP Mission has rooms and good self-catering chalets for US$2.50 per person. Camping costs US$0.75 per tent.

We've heard rumours that a luxury lodge may be built in the Likabula area, so if this is your style, ask around for details when you arrive.

On the Mountain

On Mulanje are seven *forestry huts*: Chambe, Lichenya, Thuchila (**chu**-chil-a), Chinzama, Minunu, Madzeka and Sombani. Each is equipped with benches, tables and open fires with plenty of wood. Some have sleeping platforms (no mattresses); in others you just sleep on the floor. You provide your own food, cooking gear, candles, sleeping bag and stove (although you can cook on the fire). A caretaker chops wood, lights fires and brings water, for which a small tip should be paid.

Payments must be made at Likabula Forest Station, and you show your receipt to the hut caretaker. The huts cost just over US$1 per person per night – an absolute bargain, although this may rise in the future. Some huts may be full at weekends, but you can normally adjust your route if this is the case. As the reservation system doesn't require a deposit, some local residents book and then don't turn up. It's worth checking to see if this has happened. Camping is permitted outside the huts (US$0.60 per person).

Some hut improvements (such as mattresses and a piped water supply) may be introduced in the future.

The only other place to stay is the *CCAP Cottage*, on the Lichenya Plateau. It's similar to the forestry huts, but there are utensils in the kitchen, plus mattresses and blankets. For this extra luxury you pay US$1.25 per night. You can make reservations at the CCAP Mission in Lkabula.

HIKING ROUTES

There are about six main routes up and down Mulanje, three of which (the main ascent routes) start at Likabula Forest Station. These are the Chembe Plateau Path (also called the Skyline Path), the Chapaluka Path, and the Lichenya Path. Other routes, more often used for descent are Thuchila Hut to Lukulezi Mission, Sombani Hut to Fort Lister Gap, and Minunu Hut to Lujeri Tea Estate. The route from Madzeka Hut to Lujeri is very steep; the wooden ladders required

to cross the steepest sections have rotted away, making it effectively impassable. On the south-western side of Mulanje, the Boma Path and the path from Lichenya to Nessa are both dangerously steep and very rarely used.

Once you're on the massif, a network of paths links the huts and peaks, and many different permutations are possible; some choices are outlined below. It normally takes about three to six hours to walk between one hut and the next, which means you can walk in the morning, dump your kit, then go out to explore a nearby peak or valley in the afternoon.

A Mulanje Traverse

There are many ways to traverse the Mulanje Massif. The route described briefly here, from Likabula to Fort Lister Gap, is one of several options, although it seems to be the most popular. It can be done in four days, but there are several variations that can extend this period, and plenty of opportunities for sidetracking to take in a few extra peaks and ridges.

Stage 1: Likabula Forest Station to Chambe Hut This stage takes you up onto the plateau. There are two options: the Chembe Plateau Path, which is short and steep (two to four hours); and the Chapaluka Path, which is less steep and more scenic (3½ to five hours). (The Chambe Plateau Path is also called the 'Skyline Path' after the 'Skyline' – the aerial cableway that carries wood down from the plantations on the plateau.)

Whichever path you take, you'll spend most of the time going uphill, but don't forget to look as the spectacular views across the plains open out behind you. The last hour or so is through plantation, which may be dense pine trees or an ugly cleared wasteland, depending on where cutting is taking place. You pass near Chambe Forest Station and then reach Chambe Hut.

The hut is one of the largest on the plateau, and there's a patch of ground for camping nearby. From the hut veranda there are good views of the south-east face of Chambe Peak (2557m).

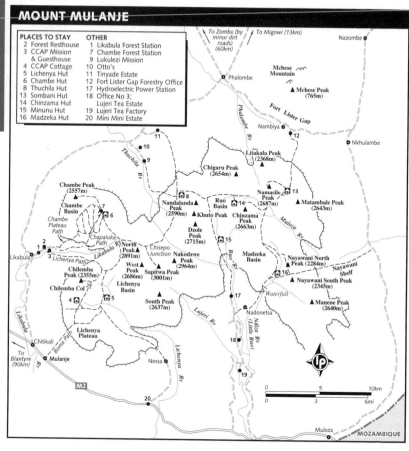

MOUNT MULANJE

PLACES TO STAY	OTHER
2 Forest Resthouse	1 Likabula Forest Station
3 CCAP Mission	7 Chambe Forest Station
& Guesthouse	9 Lukulezi Mission
4 CCAP Cottage	10 Otto's
5 Lichenya Hut	11 Tinyade Estate
6 Chambe Hut	12 Fort Lister Gap Forestry Office
8 Thuchila Hut	17 Hydroelectric Power Station
13 Sombani Hut	18 Office No 3;
14 Chinzama Hut	Lujeri Tea Estate
15 Minunu Hut	19 Lujeri Tea Factory
16 Madzeka Hut	20 Mini Mini Estate

Sidetrack: Chambe Peak If you fancy conquering this spectacular peak on the same day as your ascent of the plateau, leave Likabula early; it will take you five to seven hours from Chambe Hut to get to the top and back. The path is not always clear, so you may need a guide. It might be better to start very early and do this peak before walking to your next hut; or stay at Chambe Hut for two nights, doing the peak on the day in between.

From Chambe Hut, a path leads northwest through plantation, and then goes up a ridge on the eastern flank of the peak. About two to 2½ hours from the hut, you reach a large cairn on a broad level part of the ridge at the foot of the main face. You may be happy just reaching this point, which offers excellent views over the Chambe Basin to the escarpment edge and the plains far below. The next stage of the route requires some steep scrambling on bare rock – which can be intimidating – and should definitely be avoided after rain.

If you decide to push on, the summit of Chambe Peak is marked by a large concrete and metal beacon, which is not visible until you're almost on it. The views from the summit of Chambe Peak in clear weather are superb; you can see most of Mulanje's main peaks, and much of the western side of the massif. Long stretches of the escarpment that surrounds the massif can also be seen, and below this the plains stretch out towards the Zomba Plateau in the north and the mountains of Mozambique in the south. It is often possible to see the waters of Lake Chilwa, to the north-east. On very clear days Lake Malombe, at the southern tip of Lake Malawi, can also be spotted.

To get back to Chambe Hut, retrace the route. Go slowly on the way down; it's easy to go off the route, and just as easy to slip and fall on some of the steeper sections.

Stage 2: Chambe Hut to Thuchila Hut
This stage is 12km and takes four to five hours. The start can be complicated to find as there are several paths in this area; if you haven't got a porter ask the hut caretaker to put you on the right track. After an hour or so, you cross a narrow ridge that joins the Chambe Basin to the main massif, but steep drops on both sides are hidden by dense vegetation. Continue on the path until you reach a junction (about 1½ hours from Chambe Hut) where you go straight on, up a steep path. (The path to the right leads to Lichenya Hut.) To the left are fine views down into the Thuchila Valley.

About two hours from Chambe Hut you reach Chisepo Junction, where a path leads up to the summit of Sapitwa Peak. The main path takes you across the edge of the Thuchila basin – a very scenic section, which crosses several streams with wonderful pools ideal for swimming – to reach Thuchila Hut.

A return option, if you're short of time, is to descend from Thuchila to Lukulezi Mission, past an old building called Otto's, which porters use as a landmark, to reach the dirt road that runs between Likabula and Phalombe. From here you can walk (or wait for a matola) back to Likabula.

Sidetrack: Sapitwa Peak
The summit of Sapitwa is the highest point on Mulanje, at 3001m. You can walk to the top, but it's a toughie, and the upper section involves some scrambling and tricky walking among large boulders and dense vegetation. From Chisepo Junction you should allow three to five hours for the ascent and two to four for descent. From either Chambe or Thuchila, add another four to five hours onto the times for doing the peak itself, or plan to spend a night at the very basic Chisepo shelter. Perhaps not surprisingly, Sapitwa in the local language means 'don't go there'.

From the junction, the route is clearly shown for most of the way by red marks painted on the rocks. This spoils the feel of untouched wilderness, but it stops a lot of people from getting lost. There are also a few marks missing, just to keep you on your toes. As you get near the summit you can see the top, but the route winds tortuously through an area of huge boulders and dense vegetation.

The views from the top, when you do finally make it, are worth the slog. On a clear day you get a panoramic vista of the whole plateau, the other nearby peaks, the edge of the escarpment and the plains far below.

Stage 3: Thuchila Hut to Sombani Hut
The path from Thuchila Hut takes you quite steeply up a valley to a small col, which you reach about one hour from the hut. Just past the col the path to Minunu Hut branches off right (south). Continue straight on, down into the Ruo Basin, the top of the large Ruo River valley. At a clear junction, about two hours from Thuchila Hut, turn right to drop down into the valley and cross two streams and climb steeply up to reach Chinzama Hut after another 10 minutes. (You could stay here if you want an easy day.)

From Chinzama Hut aim eastward as the path climbs up the valley side, through grass and bush and across patches of rocks, to reach a small col. Cross into the next valley and drop through rolling grassland to reach a junction. Take the left path (the right path leads to Madzeka Hut) and go through grassland to cross a wooden bridge and some small streams to reach Sombani Hut, about two hours from Chinzama Hut.

Sidetrack: Namasile Peak
Namasile is the large mountain that dominates the view directly opposite Sombani Hut. To get to the

top of this peak takes 2½ to three hours, 1½ to 2½ hours descent. The path to the summit, which is steep and strenuous in places, spirals round the north side of the mountain and approaches the summit from the west (the 'back' of the mountain when viewed from Sombani Hut).

From the hut, aim north down a clear path to cross the stream in the valley bottom on a wooden bridge. On the opposite bank is a fork. Keep straight on (right leads towards the Fort Lister Gap) up a firebreak to its end. From here the path is marked by occasional cairns, but you should have a map or a guide for this route, as getting lost is a real possibility.

The route takes you below the main cliffs of the peak (about 1½ to two hours from the hut) and then up a broad vegetated gully. When you see the summit beacon you'll think you're nearly there, but now comes the hard bit. The path crosses bare rock and enters an area of large boulders and dense vegetation before zigzagging up over boulders and grassy slopes approaching the summit (2687m) from the north-east.

Views from the summit of Namasile Peak, over the north-eastern side of Mount Mulanje, are excellent, stretching across the Ruo and Madzeka Basins and the upper part of the Sombani River valley. To the north-east the escarpment drops to the Fort Lister Gap, with the separate peak of Mchese beyond.

Return to Sombani Hut by the same route. Take care on the way down; it is all too easy to miss cairns and go off the route.

Stage 4: Sombani Hut to Fort Lister Gap This stage is 5km, and takes about three hours. It takes you off the plateau, heading in a northerly direction. The path leads through some patches of indigenous forest, with great views over the surrounding plains. Although it keeps descending, it is not as steep as the Chambe path coming up. There are many forks, so a porter is useful to show you the way, but if you're on your own the rule of thumb at every fork is to take the path that keeps going down. For the last section you follow a dirt track, past Fort Lister Forest Station.

From the Fort Lister Gap it's another 8km along the dirt road to Phalombe village. There's little or no traffic, so you'll have to walk (about two hours), but it's pleasant enough. Most porters include this in the fee you pay for the final day. From Phalombe you can get a matola back to Likabula or Mulanje town.

Alternative Descents From Sombani Hut you can extend your trek by another day or two and go to Madzeka Hut. From here you might be able to descend steeply beside the Ndiza River (also called the Little Ruo River) to Lujeri Tea Estate. This is so steep it includes ladders for some sections, and some of these get damaged during rainy seasons and may not be replaced, which makes the route impassable. The staff at Likabula will know if this route is open or not. If the route is open it takes three to five hours from Madzeka via Nadonetsa (a scattered village) to reach Office No 3, a landmark at Lujeri Tea Estate, where you might be able to find transport to the main road (as described later). Even if this descent route is closed, it's well worth considering an out-and-back leg to Madzeka Hut, because this is a beautiful part of the mountain.

Another alternative from Sombani Hut, Chinzama Hut or Thuchila Hut is to go to Minunu Hut, stay your last night there, and descend to Lujeri Tea Estate beside the ('Big') Ruo River. From Minunu Hut to the hydroelectric power station takes about three to four hours. From there to Office No 3 is 10km on a good dirt road (allow another three hours).

From Office No 3 it's still 13km until the main road to Mulanje town and Blantyre. You may be lucky and find somebody in the office with a car or a tractor who can help you with a lift. If you're out of luck, you'll have to start walking. From the office, follow the dirt road through the tea plantation. After 3km, keep the tea factory on your left, go over a large river bridge, turn left, and follow this road for about 9km to reach the main sealed road. Wait here for a bus (there are several each day) or try hitching.

Kayaking is one of several water sports enjoyed on Lake Malawi.

Impala lilies in flower

A clear view over Lake Malawi from the small town of Livingstonia

Sunset with mosquito nets

Keep on truckin'. Overlanding to and through Malawi is popular.

DAVE HAMMAN

A bachelor herd of impalas on the alert

JASON EDWARDS

Eland with corkscrew horns

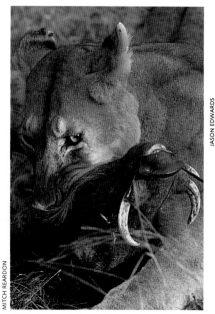

MITCH REARDON

Making a meal of a warthog

ANDREW MACCOLL

Scavenging jackals and a hyaena feeding

MITCH REARDON

Leopards can be spotted in Nyika National Park

The Chambe-Lichenya Loop

This short but beautiful route is not an officially named trail, but it's recommended for a good taste of Mulanje if you haven't got time for a traverse of the whole massif. It starts and finishes at Likabula Forest Station, and takes three days and two nights, but could be shortened to two days.

Stage 1: Likabula to Chambe Hut This section of the route is the same as Stage 1 of the Mulanje Traverse (see A Mulanje Traverse earlier in this chapter). The optional sidetrack up Chambe Peak is also described in that section.

Stage 2: Chambe Hut to Lichenya Hut or CCAP Cottage Follow the directions in Stage 2 of the Mulanje Traverse described earlier in this chapter. At the junction about two hours from Chambe Hut, turn right (straight on leads to Thuchila), and descend through natural forest. The path levels out and crosses several small streams, which are the headwaters of the Likabula River. Down to the right is the Likabula Valley, while up to the left are North Peak and West Peak, outliers of Sapitwa. Continue into the Lichenya Basin to reach the newly rebuilt Lichenya Hut, which is about four hours from Chambe Hut. Alternatively, continue for about another hour to reach the CCAP Cottage.

Stage 3: Lichenya Hut or CCAP Cottage to Likabula From the CCAP Cottage a path climbs steeply up towards a col on the east side of Chilemba Peak. You can side-track up the ridge to the peak for some excellent views over the western side of the Mulanje massif. Return to the col by the same route.

From the col, the path drops to a junction. Go left, then downhill through forest, to eventually reach the Likabula River. Wade through, or jump from rock to rock, and go up the far bank to reach the dirt track between the Mulanje-Phalombe road and the Likabula forest station. From the other side of the river, there is also a short cut which takes you straight to the CCAP Mission (if that's where you're staying) but you'll probably only find it if you've got a guide or porter.

This whole stage takes four to five hours, depending on where you started, plus 1½ to 2½ hours if you do the sidetrack up Chilemba Peak.

Getting There & Away

To reach Mount Mulanje, take any transport heading from Blantyre or Limbe heading for Mulanje town (described in the section following). A bus from Blantyre to Mulanje costs $2, from Limbe is $1.50. More details on transport from Blantyre are given in the Blantyre & Limbe chapter.

The dirt road to Likabula turns off the main sealed road between Blantyre and Mulanje town at a large village called Chitikali, about 2km west of the centre of Mulanje town (ie, before Mulanje town if you're coming from Blantyre). At the junction is an old 'to Phalombe' signpost. If you're coming from Blantyre on the bus, ask to be dropped at Chitikali. From here, irregular matolas run to Likabula for US$0.50. If you're in a group, you can hire the whole matola to Likabula for around US$10. Alternatively, you can walk (10km, two to three hours); a pleasant hike through tea estates with good views of the south-west face of Mulanje on your right.

MULANJE

At the foot of Mount Mulanje, the small town of Mulanje is the centre of Malawi's tea-growing industry. You may stay here overnight if you're going to Mozambique (see Mozambique in the Getting There & Away chapter), but most travellers come on the way to hike on Mount Mulanje (as described earlier in this section).

Places to Stay & Eat

Camping is possible at *Mulanje Golf Club*, on the eastern side of town, for US$2.50, which includes membership so you can use the showers and *bar*.

The *Council Resthouse* has doubles from US$1.50, but the *Mulanje Motel*, down from the bus station, is better with double rooms for US$3. Next door is the smarter *Mulanje View Motel*, with a wide choice: from US$3 for a simple single to US$7 for a double with bathroom and breakfast. There's a *bar* and good-value food in the *restaurant*, and you can pitch a tent for US$1.

Getting There & Away
Buses and minibuses go to/from Blantyre and Limbe throughout the day for around US$2. If you're heading for the Mozambique border, a minibus or matola to the border is US$0.60 from Mulanje town.

The Lower Shire

The southern limit of the Shire Highlands area, with Blantyre at its heart, is marked by the Thyolo Escarpment (also called the Shire Escarpment). Beyond here, the land falls to the Lower Shire Valley area, usually shortened to The Lower Shire, and sometimes simply called the 'far south' – a thin spine of territory jutting deep into Mozambique.

The main road south from Blantyre plunges down the escarpment in a series of hairpin bends with excellent views over the Shire River and out towards the Zambezi on the hazy horizon. Even when it's cool in Blantyre and on the highlands, it can be blisteringly hot down here – the sharp change of temperature and landscape, in less than 30km, is striking.

For tourists this is one of the least-visited areas of Malawi and is very different from the rest of the country. The main features are Lengwe National Park, Majete and Mwabvi Wildlife Reserves, and the Elephant Marsh – a vast area of seasonally flooded swampland. Lengwe, Majete and Mwabvi are often overlooked, but plans are afoot to improve the infrastructure and facilities here, so things may change in the future. Around the small towns of Chikwawa and Bangula are some sites that may appeal to aficionados of obscure historic monuments.

MAJETE WILDLIFE RESERVE
Majete Wildlife Reserve lies west of the Shire and is mainly miombo woodland with dense patches of forest along the river. Animals recorded here include elephants, sables, kudus and hartebeest, but very few remain because of heavy poaching. It's best to forget about mammals and appreciate the reserve simply as a beautiful wilderness area; you're almost certain to have the place to yourself. Bird-watching is good, and walking is allowed, with a ranger (often called a 'scout'), although the standard entry fees that must be paid at the gate (see National Parks & Wildlife Reserves in the Facts about Malawi section) seem a little steep here.

Just past the gate, a short track leads east to the spectacular Kapichira Falls, although the view is tarnished slightly by the vast dam and power station under construction here.

The main track in the reserve, which is also the only drivable one, runs parallel to

The Majete Crossover

From Mkurumadzi Camp, hardy hikers could consider continuing north alongside the Shire River to Mpatamanga Gorge, just to the south of where the old road between Mwanza and Blantyre crosses the river on a bridge. This means crossing the Mkurumadzi River, which can be dangerous if the water is high (not to mention the possibility of crocodiles), and the route is not clear; you'd be well advised to arrange a guide at the gate or at Majete Safari Camp. At the end of the hike, where the old road between Mwanza and Chileka crosses the river, you can find occasional matola transport going to Blantyre.

Perhaps the best way of walking this route is to try and link up with the Mountain Club of Malawi (see Activities in the Facts for the Visitor chapter). Every year members arrange a walk called the Majete Crossover in which two groups of walkers set out from opposite ends of the route between Mpatamanga Gorge and the entrance gate to Majete Wildlife Reserve. They meet at Mkurumadzi and camp overnight there, not forgetting to swap car-keys so the vehicles left at either end can be collected and brought back to Blantyre.

the Shire River (although not near enough to see it) until its confluence with the River Mkurumadzi, where there's a ranger post called Mkurumadzi Camp. If you're in a car, this track crosses some deep gullies, so high clearance is essential. If you're walking you can go from the gate to Mkurumadzi in a day, stay the night and walk back (or continue north – see the boxed text 'The Majete Crossover').

Places to Stay & Eat

Inside the reserve you can pitch a tent at the *Mkurumadzi Camp ranger post*. It's a nice setting, on the confluence of the Shire and Mkurumadzi Rivers, but the camp itself is a bit tatty, and there are no facilities whatsoever.

A better alternative is the friendly *Majete Safari Camp*, just outside the reserve on the west bank of the river, a few kilometres from the reserve entry gate. The service is relaxed and the camp has seen better days, but the chalets with bathrooms from US$7 per person are fair value, and camping is US$3. There's a *bar*, a kitchen for self-catering, or you can buy *meals* (US$1.50 to US$3) if you order long in advance. Motorboat hire for fishing or bird-watching costs US$1.50 per hour. The camp overlooks the Shire River and the Matitu Falls, southernmost of the Shire Cataracts, of which Kapichira Falls are the largest and best-known. The Shire Cataracts were the notorious barrier to Livingstone's 1858 expedition. (Livingstone camped in this very spot – see the History section in Facts About Malawi for details.)

Getting There & Away

Majete Safari Camp is 15km north of Chikwawa, on the road to Majete Wildlife Reserve. By bus, the nearest you can get to the reserve is Chikwawa (US$1); there are several per day to/from Blantyre. From Chikwawa, matolas run to Kapichira village. (This is on the east bank of the river – there's a bridge below the dam at Kapichira Falls. It was once a tiny village, but it's grown considerably in the last few years, mainly to house and cater for staff at the dam and power station.)

The Majete Chapel

An interesting feature of Majete Safari Camp is the small chapel, built by the owners in 'Afro-Saxon' style and dedicated to the wilderness, rather than to a saint. It deliberately has no door, so people (and birds, bats and frogs) can come and go as they like, and there's a large open window looking out across the river. When Livingstone camped just below Matitu Falls in 1858, he wrote that he wished to 'hear a church bell ring out across the Shire River'. He was probably speaking metaphorically – he wanted to bring Christianity to the whole area – but the chapel at Majete reminds us of his words.

LENGWE NATIONAL PARK

Lengwe is Malawi's southernmost park. Much of the area surrounding the park has been turned into sugarcane plantation, but the natural vegetation – mixed woodland and grassy *dambo* – is protected here. Mammals include nyalas – at the northern limit of their distribution in Africa – as well as bushbucks, impalas, duikers and kudus, but sightings are harder here than in some other parks because of dense vegetation and also because numbers have been reduced by poaching. You're better off admiring the large and varied bird population.

Standard entry fees (see National Parks & Wildlife Reserves in the Facts about Malawi section) must be paid at the main – and only – entrance gate. Only the eastern section of the park (measuring some 100 sq km, but still a relatively small part) is open to visitors, and even here many of the tracks for vehicles are often impassable. Rather than driving around, it's more rewarding to walk in the park or spend some time at the viewing hides overlooking water holes; there's one within easy walking distance of Visitors Camp.

Places to Stay & Eat

The only place to stay is *Visitors Camp* which is in a beautiful setting under big shady trees, about 2km from the main entrance gate. Camping costs US$1 per person and double chalets are around US$7 (for one or two people). Shared bathrooms are basic and the kitchen for self-catering is virtually unusable (some chalets have their own kitchen and bathroom – these are better). You must bring all your own food.

If you've got a car and prefer more comfortable accommodation, you can stay at *Sucoma Sports Club* (☎ 428200 extension 287), a social club for managerial staff of the Sucoma sugar plantation, which is 8km east of the small town of Nchalo – the main entrance to the sugar estate. (Nchalo is about 25km south of Chikwawa, and about 18km from the national park gate.) At the club, comfortable chalets overlooking the river cost US$5.50 per person. There's a bar, and meals are also available.

If the club sounds a bit neocolonial for your tastes, in Nchalo itself is a *Government Resthouse* and a couple of other very basic lodging houses. There's also a bank, a *bakery* and a supermarket.

Getting There & Away

If you're travelling by car, take the main road from Blantyre south towards Nsanje. If you're on public transport, take a bus from Blantyre to Nchalo or Nsanje. Whatever your means of transport, you go down the zigzag escarpment road and over the Shire River on a bridge near Chikwawa (see Getting There & Away under Majete Wildlife Reserve earlier in this chapter). About 20km south from the bridge a signpost indicates Lengwe National Park to the right. If you're in a car turn right (west). If you're on the bus, ask to be dropped here. The park entrance is another 10km to the west through seemingly endless sugar plantations. If you're without wheels you may be able to hitch this last bit on a tractor.

To reach Sucoma Club, continue down the main sealed road towards Nchalo, Bangula and Nsanje. In Nchalo village you cannot fail to see the large main entrance gates to the sugar estate on your left (east). Go through the gates, then drive through the estate for 8km, passing the huge factory and following signs to the Sports Club (not the

Shire Club). This option is only really possible for drivers, as there's no public transport to the club.

MWABVI WILDLIFE RESERVE

In the southernmost tip of Malawi, Mwabvi is the country's smallest and least-visited wildlife reserve (under 350 sq km). It has a genuine wilderness atmosphere, consisting of low hills covered by mixed woodland and has numerous streams in rocky gorges. The scenery is quite unlike any other part of Malawi, and there are spectacular views over the Shire and Zambezi Rivers. The reserve's western boundary is the border with Mozambique.

Mwabvi was virtually abandoned in the 1980s and early 1990s (probably because of its remote location) and it suffered from the ravages of poaching. Rhinos and lions were once recorded here, but apart from a few buffaloes and nyala it's unlikely that any large animals remain today. Also during this period, local people moved into the edges of the reserve and built huts or established small plots for growing crops. They have been allowed to remain, and these parts of the reserve have been effectively 'written off', so its area is smaller than shown on most maps.

At the time of writing, access was possible only with a car or great determination; the reserve office is reached from the main road between Chikwawa and Nsanje, from just east of the village of Sorgin, about 10km west of Bangula. The Wildlife Society of Malawi is currently involved in projects to protect the reserve by encouraging local people to benefit from its resources. This may also improve access for visitors, so it would be worth inquiring about the latest situation at the Wildlife Society shop in Limbe (see the Blantyre & Limbe chapter).

BANGULA

This small town (or large village) is on a junction where the road from Blantyre splits: one branch continues south to Nsanje and the Mozambican border (see the Getting There & Away chapter); the other branch goes north-east to Chiromo and

Makhanga. There's no bus station, but all transport stops at the junction. If you need to overnight here, the *Aska Resthouse* has simple but clean rooms for $4.50, and the *Halal Restaurant*, appropriately opposite the mosque, serves local dishes. Other facilities include shops, bottle stores, and a post office (confusingly called Chiromo Post Office – even though it's in Bangula).

THE ELEPHANT MARSH

The Elephant Marsh is a large area of seasonally flooded plain on the Shire River about 30km downstream from Chikwawa, just south of the vast Sucoma sugarcane estates. Despite the name there are no elephants here any more, although vast herds inhabited the area less than 100 years ago. Some hippos and crocodiles still lurk in quiet areas, but the main draw is the spectacular selection of birds – predominantly water species. This is one of the best bird-watching areas in Malawi, so most visitors are keen spotters, but it's well worth considering a visit here if you simply want to sample a peaceful and very unusual landscape. The marsh is well off the beaten track, but its eastern side is not too difficult to reach. For more details on vegetation and wildlife, a copy of the *Day Outings from Blantyre* booklet produced by the Wildlife Society of Malawi is very useful.

Traditionally, local people from the surrounding area came to the marsh in drought periods when water was scarce on the higher ground. Rice, maize and other crops grow in these conditions (which is why the sugar plantation was established on the northern edge of the marsh). It is also an important fishing area. In recent years, pressures on land elsewhere have caused the temporary human population of the marsh to increase and become more permanent. Through the 1990s, the Wildlife Society of Malawi was involved in various schemes to help local people continue to harvest the marsh without destroying it through overuse, or by the introduction of grazing animals such as goats.

Places to Stay & Eat

As mornings and evenings are the best time to see birds (it's also not so hot), it may be more convenient to stay near the marsh – especially if you don't have your own vehicle. The best place is at the village of Makhanga, about 10km north-east of Bangula. The *Makhanga Leisure Centre* has cheap rooms, and *New Makhanga Restaurant* does cheap food. If you have a car you could stay at *Sucoma Sports Club* (see the Lengwe National Park section earlier).

Getting There & Away

The only way to see the marsh properly is by boat. The usual way of doing this is to hire a local boat at a small village called Mchacha James (where the Department of Fisheries has a jetty), on the south-east side of the marsh, north of Bangula, about 5km from Makhanga.

First you need to get to Makhanga; this is less straightforward than it used to be since the road and railway between Bangula and Makhanga got completely washed away. Coming from the north by car, your only option is to turn left (east) at Thabwa (the bottom of the escarpment), about 30km from Blantyre, and go along the north bank of the river. Matolas run along this road too, so you can get off from the bus running between Blantyre and Nchalo or Nsanje here and get a matola to Makhanga.

Alternatively, by public transport, get the bus from Blantyre all the way to Bangula then walk 3km to the point where the road is washed away, get a canoe across, and then take a matola through Chiromo to Makhanga. A final option to consider might be the train from Limbe to Makhanga – see under Train in the Getting Around chapter earlier in this book.

Once in Makhanga you need to aim northwards on the road towards the village of Muona. After 2.5km a dirt track leads west for 4.5km through villages and small fields to the Department of Fisheries jetty at Mchacha James. The route is not signposted, so you'll have to get directions; it might be worth arranging a local guide in Makhanga. If you don't have a car you can walk, or get a bicycle taxi to take you there for around US$1.50. Bizarrely, there's a guy in Makhanga with a tandem; you can sit on the back seat and pedal to Mchacha James for US$2. Alternatively, you can rent a bike and ride it yourself, or charter a matola – there are normally one or two parked by the railway tracks. A final option is to visit the Department of Fisheries office in Makhanga, on the Muona road, about 1km west of the railway tracks – the staff here have motorbikes and might be able to help you with a lift to the jetty.

When you finally get to Mchacha James, local boat owners may offer to take you in dugout canoes, but there's also a couple of more stable rowing boats for hire owned by two brothers called Willis and Coaster Saidi. These friendly guys speak good English and can tell you a lot about the birds and people of the marsh. Their rates are extremely negotiable; around US$10 for two people for a morning or afternoon trip seems to be fair.

THE EASTERN MARSH

We heard from a keen travelling bird-watcher who reported that an area called the Eastern Marsh, downstream of the main Elephant Marsh, was easy to reach and worth a visit. About 3km east of Bangula, south of Chiromo, on the west side of the Shire River (the east side is in Mozambique) an old railway embankment leaves the road and runs through the edge of this small marsh. You can walk along this embankment; it provides good views over the marsh. The embankment continues for about 10km towards the main road between Bangula and Nsanje, and used to meet it near a village called Phokera, about 9km south of Bangula. But the final section has

---

Early Missionary Graves

The Shire River was the gateway for early explorers, missionaries, settlers and those in colonial service who came to the area now called Malawi; the far south of the country is dotted with the graves of these early arrivals.

Near Majete Safari Camp, at the site where Livingstone and subsequent travellers were forced to end their journey by boat (see History in the Facts about Malawi chapter), is the grave of one Richard Thornton, a British explorer and geologist who travelled with Livingstone on the Zambezi River in the late 1850s before going freelance for a while and working for a German expedition on Kilimanjaro in today's Tanzania. He rejoined Livingstone in 1862 on the Zambezi and Shire expeditions, but died of dysentery in 1863.

Downstream a few kilometres, near the bridge over the Shire River east of Chikwawa, is the grave of the Rev Carter Scudamore, an early Universities Mission in Central Africa (UMCA) missionary who also died here in 1863. He was buried alongside the mission physician Dr J Dickinson, and the site is marked by a gravestone. Also on the banks of the Shire is a grave to Herbert Rhodes, brother of the more famous Cecil J, who died here in the 1890s. The gravestone by the bridge is easy to find, but the others take local knowledge – if you're staying at Majete Safari Camp, they can help.

Near Chiromo, on the south-west side of the Shire, is another graveyard. This takes some searching out, as it is now completely overgrown. Coming from Chiromo, heading towards Bangula, it's on the left, 1½ km from the bridge just after a small group of huts called Chikanzi. The inscriptions make sober reading, and remind today's visitors of the less-glorious aspects of colonial ambition in Africa:

Charles Carvin, Gunner, HMS Mosquito, died 1891;
Samuel Hodges, Stoker, HMS Herald, died 1890, age 28;
CW Joubert Pauw, died 1906, age 25;
Dennis O'Connel, Her Majesty's Customs, died 1907, age 27;
'Wee Archie', beloved son of Agnes Todd and WK Keiller, born May 1896, died November 1896.

been washed away by a tributary of the Shire River, and you need to find a local person with a boat to ferry you across. It might be easier just to walk out and back from the northern end of the embankment.

CHIROMO

For dedicated historians, Chiromo could be worth a visit. This small village, about 5km north-east of Bangula, was an important staging post in the days of the early British settlers in Malawi, and the site of the protectorate's very first post office.

Through the late 19th century and into the early 20th century, foreign travellers heading for Lake Malawi or the highlands around Blantyre would come from the Indian Ocean port of Quelimane (then in Portuguese East Africa) and the smaller port of Chinde (a British 'concession'), then go by boat up the Zambezi and into the Shire River. For about 80km the Shire formed the border between British and Portuguese territory, but at Chiromo the border followed another large river called the Ruo (which rises in Mount Mulanje) and the Shire flowed through wholly British territory. Thus Chiromo became an important gateway to the whole British Central African region. Passengers on boats would alight at Chiromo and continue their journey by road or rail. (See History in the Facts about Malawi chapter for more details.)

In the early 20th century a railway was constructed between Blantyre and the Portuguese colonial port of Beira. The line crossed the Shire River at Chiromo and ran roughly parallel to the river as it flowed southwards. (The line crossed the Zambezi at Vila de Sena in Mozambique – still a major crossing point today.)

The original railway bridge has been replaced, but the one that remains is probably 50 years old – and quite impressive – designed to carry cars and trains over the river. There's also some ancient traffic lights that warn vehicles of approaching trains, but the bulbs were last replaced some time before independence. Today a man with a flag does the job, but he hasn't had much employment since the railway was washed away by floodwater and all trains now stop at Makhanga.

The old train station and original post office at Chiromo have fallen down, but you can walk among some of the other ruined buildings, which date from colonial times. The jetty where the steamers used to land has also gone, but it is possible to reach the confluence of the Shire and Ruo Rivers for a good view of the bridge and a peek across the border into Mozambique.

For details on transport into Mozambique from this part of Malawi, see the Getting There & Away chapter.

Language

CHICHEWA

Chichewa is a complex language: word pre-fixes and suffixes change according to context, so one single word cannot always be given for its English equivalent. In this guide the most common form is given, but do remember that by using these words and phrases you may not be speaking 'proper' Chichewa. Most importantly, however, you'll be understood, and Malawian will be pleased to hear even a few words of their language spoken by a foreigner.

Note that, as in many African languages, the sounds for l and r appear interchangible in Chichewa. For example *zambire* (many) is usually pronounced *zam-bi-li*. Malawians speaking English also sometimes interchange these sounds, hence Malawi's most popular beer (a Carslberg Green) may be pronounced *gleen*.

Greetings & Civilities

Mazungu means 'white person', but is not derogatory. *Bambo* literally means 'father' but is a polite way to address any Malawian man. The female equivalent is *Amai* or *Mai*.

Hello.	*Moni.*
Please.	*Chonde.*
Thank you.	*Zikomo.*
Thank you very much.	*Zikomo kwambile/ Zikomo kwambiri.*
Excuse me.	*Zikomo.*
Good/Fine/OK.	*Chabwino.*
Good night.	*Gonani bwino.*
Hello, anybody in?	*Odi.*
Come in/Welcome.	*Lowani.*
How are you?	*Muli bwanji?*
I'm fine.	*Ndili bwino.*
And you?	*Kaya-iwe?* (to one person)
	Kaya inu? (to several people)
Goodbye. (to person staying)	*Tsala bwino.* (lit: 'stay well')
Goodbye. (to person leaving)	*Pitani bwino.* (lit: 'go well')

What's your name?	*Dzina lako ndani?*
Where are you going?	*Ukupita kuti?*
I'm going to Blantyre.	*Ndikupita ku Blantyre.*

Useful Phrases

Yes.	*Inde.*
No.	*Iyayi.*
I want ...	*Ndifuna ...*
I don't want ...	*Sindifuna ...*
How much?	*Ntengo bwanji?* or *Ndalama zingati?*
many	*zambile*
enough/finish	*bas*
Why?	*Chifukwa?*
I don't understand.	*Sindikunva.*
What's this?	*Ndi chiani?*
What's that (far away)?	*Icho ndi chiani?*
Where?	*Kuti?*
Here.	*Pano.*
Over there.	*Uko.*
I'm tired.	*Ndatopa.*
today	*lero*
tomorrow (early)	*m'mara*
tomorrow	*mara*
yesterday	*dzulo*
Women	*Akazi*
Men	*Akuma*
to eat	*kudya*
to sleep	*kugona*
to buy	*kugula*

Food

Bring me ...	*Mundi passe ...*
bread	*buledi*
chicken	*nkhuku*
coffee	*khofi*
eggs	*mazira*
fish	*somba*
fruit (one)	*chipasso*
fruits (many)	*zipasso*
lake perch	*chambo*
meat	*nyama*

Tumbuka & Yao Phrases

Tumbuka is widely spoken in Malawi's north, and Yao is widely spoken in the south. Nearly all Tumbuka and Yao people speak Chichewa, and many also speak English, either of which they may use as common languages.

English	Tumbuka	Yao
Hello.	*Yewo.*	*Quamboni.*
How are you?	*Muliwuli?*	*Iliwuli?*
Fine.	*Nilimakola.*	*Ndiri chenene.*
And you?	*Manyi imwa?*	*Qualinim we?*
What is your name?	*Zinolinu ndimwenjani?*	*Mwe linachi?*
Where do you live?	*Mmukukhalankhu?*	*Ncutama qua?*
My name is John.	*Zinalane ndine John.*	*Une linaliangu John.*
I live in	*Nkhula ku ...*	*Gutama ku ...*
Thank you (very much)	*Yewo (chomene).*	*Asante (sana).*
Goodbye.	*Pawemi.*	*Siagara gani ngwaula.*

milk	*mkaka*
potatoes	*batata*
tea	*ti*
vegetables	*mquani*
water	*mazi*

In restaurants *nsima* is stiff maize porridge served with a sauce of meat, beans or vegetables.

Numbers

Chichewa speakers talking together will normally use English for numbers and prices. Similarly, time is nearly always expressed in English.

1	*chimonzi*
2	*ziwili*
3	*zitatu*
4	*zinayi*
5	*zitsano*

Note however, that Chichewa speakers talking together will normally use English for numbers and prices. Similarly, time is nearly always expressed in English.

Glossary

Although English is widely spoken in Malawi, visitors from other English-speaking countries will notice many words which have developed different meanings locally. There are also many words which have been borrowed from Afrikaans, Portuguese and indigenous languages. This Glossary includes many of these 'Afro-English' words, as well as other general terms and abbreviations which may not be understood.

In African English, repetition for emphasis is common: something that burnt you would be 'hot hot'; fields after the rains are 'green green'; a crowded minibus with no more room is 'full full', and so on.

af – derogatory reference to a black person, as bad as 'nigger' or 'abo'

AFORD – Alliance for Democracy, a Malawian political party strongest in the north of the country

ANC – African National Congress

animist – various definitions, but the most useful seems to be: 'beliefs based on the existence of the human soul, and on spirits that inhabit or are represented by natural objects and phenomena, which have the power to influence human life for good or ill'

apartheid – 'separate development of the races'; a political system in which peoples are segregated according to ethnic background

askari – guard; Yao person who served in The King's African Rifles regiment

bakkie – (pronounced 'bukkie') utility or pick-up truck

BCAP – British Central Africa Protectorate, the colonial-era name for Malawi prior to the adoption of the name Nyasaland

beni – traditional dance of the Yao people

bhundu – the bush, the wilderness

bilharzia – waterborne disease caused by minute worms which are passed on by freshwater snails

biltong – dried and salted meat that can be made from just about anything from antelope or ostrich to mutton or beef

boerewors – spicy Afrikaner sausage of varying consistency

boma – in Malawi and some other countries, this is a local word for 'town', or more specifically town centre, or area containing government buildings. In East Africa the same word also means fortified stockade. It is not an indigenous African word, and may be derived from the early colonial term BOMA (British Overseas Military Administration) which was applied to any government building, such as offices or forts.

braai – barbecue

BSAC – British South Africa Company; led by Cecil Rhodes, this company was hugely influential in shaping Southern Africa in colonial times

buck or **bok** – any kind of antelope, also part of many species' name: reedbuck, bushbuck, springbok etc

chamba – Malawian term for grass, marijuana

chapa – Mozambican term (*chapa-cem*) used in Malawi, often shortened to chapa, a pick-up van or truck converted to carry passengers

chibuku – local mass-produced beer, stored in tanks and served in buckets, or available in takeaway cartons.

chiperone – damp misty weather which affects southern Malawi

chitenjas – sheets of brightly coloured cloth worn by Malawian women, readily available in markets

dagga – (pronounced dakha) South African term for grass, marijuana

dambo – area of grass, reeds or swamp alongside a river course

Difaqane – (also called Mfecane) forced migration by several Southern African tribes in the face of Zulu aggression in the early 19th century; translates as 'the scattering of the tribes'. Mfecane, a Zulu word, means 'the crushing'.

donkey boiler – watertank positioned over a fire and used to heat water

drift – river ford

euphorbia – several species of cactus-like succulents which are endemic in Southern Africa

game – formerly used for any animal hunted, now means larger mammals. Hence 'game-drive', 'game watching', 'game scout' etc.

Gule Wamkulu – traditional dance of the Chewa people

half bus – a bus with about 30 seats, to distinguish it from a big bus or a minibus

inselbergs – isolated rocky hills common to Southern Africa; literally means 'island mountains'

Izzit? – rhetorical question which most closely translates as 'Really?' and is used without regard to gender, person, or number of the subject. Therefore, it could mean 'Is it?', 'Are you?', 'Is he?', 'Are they?', 'Is she?', 'Are we?' etc. Also 'How-zit?', for 'How are things?', 'How's it going?' etc. Originates in South Africa but used by people of European descent all over Southern Africa.

just now – reference to some time in the future but intended to imply a certain degree of imminence – it could be half an hour from now or two days from now, ie, 'at the appropriate time'

kaffir – derogatory reference to a black person

kloof – ravine or small valley

kopje – pronounced, and sometimes spelt, 'koppie', an isolated hill or rocky outcrop which translates from Afrikaans as 'little head'

kwacha – currency of Malawi and Zambia

LMS – London Missionary Society

make a plan – 'sort it out'; this can refer to anything from working through a complicated procedure to circumventing bureaucracy

Malawi shandy – nonalcoholic drink made from ginger beer, Angostura bitters, orange or lemon slices, soda and ice

mambilira – xylophonesque instrument with wooden keys

mapilenga – see beni

marimba – African xylophone, made from strips of resonant wood with various-sized gourds for sound boxes

maseche – percussion instrument; rattle or shaker attached to dancers' legs

matola – vehicle, usually a pick-up van, acting as an unofficial public transport service

mazungu – white person

mbira – thumb piano; it consists of 22 to 24 narrow iron keys mounted in rows on a wooden sound board

MCP – Malawi Congress Party; led by Dr Hastings Banda, this party ruled Malawi as a one-party state from 1964 until 1994

miombo – dry open woodland, also called brachystegia woodland

now now – not the present moment, but pretty soon after it – sometime sooner than *just now*

nsima – maize porridge; black African staple (called *ugali* in East Africa and *mealie meal* in South Africa)

pan – dry flat area, often seasonal lake-bed

peg – mile post

pint – small bottle of beer or can of oil (or similar) usually around 300 to 375 ml (and not necessarily equivalent to a British or US pint)

pronking – leaping, as done by several species of antelope, apparently for sheer fun

relish – sauce of meat, vegetables, beans, etc eaten with *nsima*

rondavel – round, African-style hut

shebeen – an illegal township drinking establishment

sjambok – whip

slasher – hand tool with a curved blade used to cut grass or crops, hence 'to slash' means 'to cut grass'

squaredavel – see *rondavel* and work out the rest

tackies – trainers, tennis shoes, gym shoes

tambala – minor Malawian unit of currency: 100t equals 1MK (*kwacha*)

UDF – United Democratic Front, Malawian political party that won the 1994 elections, led by Bakili Muluzi, returned to power in elections in 1999

ulimba – hand-held drum made from a gourd

veld – open grassland (pronounced 'felt') – lowveld, highveld, bushveld, strandveld

veldskoens – comfortable shoes made of soft leather (also called 'vellies')

vlei – any low open landscape, sometimes marshy (pronounced 'flay')

vila – town

vimbuza – curative dance performed by traditional healers

zeze – violinesque instrument

LONELY PLANET

You already know that Lonely Planet produces more than this one guidebook, but you might not be aware of the other products we have on this region. Here is a selection of titles that you may want to check out as well:

Africa on a shoestring
ISBN 0 86442 663 1
US$29.99 • UK£17.99 • 199FF

Read This First: Africa
ISBN 1 86450 066 2
US$14.95 • UK£8.99 • 99FF

East Africa
ISBN 0 86442 676 3
US$24.99 • UK£14.99 • 180FF

Southern Africa
ISBN 0 86442 662 3
US$27.99 • UK£16.99 • 189FF

Mozambique
ISBN 1 86450 108 1
US$19.99 • UK£11.99 • 139FF

Southern Africa Road Atlas
ISBN 1 86450 101 4
US$14.99 • UK£8.99 • 109FF

Trekking in East Africa
ISBN 0 86442 541 4
US$17.95 • UK£11.99 • 140FF

Tanzania, Zanzibar & Pemba
ISBN 0 86442 726 3
US$17.95 • UK£11.99 • 140FF

Available wherever books are sold

 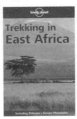 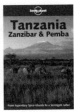

ON THE ROAD

Travel Guides explore cities, regions and countries, and supply information on transport, restaurants and accommodation, covering all budgets. They come with reliable, easy-to-use maps, practical advice, cultural and historical facts and a rundown on attractions both on and off the beaten track. There are over 200 titles in this classic series, covering nearly every country in the world.

 Lonely Planet Upgrades extend the shelf life of existing travel guides by detailing any changes that may affect travel in a region since a book has been published. Upgrades can be downloaded for free from **www.lonelyplanet.com/upgrades**

For travellers with more time than money, **Shoestring** guides offer dependable, first-hand information with hundreds of detailed maps, plus insider tips for stretching money as far as possible. Covering entire continents in most cases, the six-volume shoestring guides are known around the world as 'backpackers bibles'.

For the discerning short-term visitor, **Condensed** guides highlight the best a destination has to offer in a full-colour, pocket-sized format designed for quick access. They include everything from top sights and walking tours to opinionated reviews of where to eat, stay, shop and have fun.

CitySync lets travellers use their Palm™ or Visor™ hand-held computers to guide them through a city with handy tips on transport, history, cultural life, major sights, and shopping and entertainment options. It can also quickly search and sort hundreds of reviews of hotels, restaurants and attractions, and pinpoint their location on scrollable street maps. CitySync can be downloaded from **www.citysync.com**

MAPS & ATLASES

Lonely Planet's **City Maps** feature downtown and metropolitan maps, as well as transit routes and walking tours. The maps come complete with an index of streets, a listing of sights and a plastic coat for extra durability.

Road Atlases are an essential navigation tool for serious travellers. Cross-referenced with the guidebooks, they also feature distance and climate charts and a complete site index.

LONELY PLANET

ESSENTIALS

Read This First books help new travellers to hit the road with confidence. These invaluable predeparture guides give step-by-step advice on preparing for a trip, budgeting, arranging a visa, planning an itinerary and staying safe while still getting off the beaten track.

Healthy Travel pocket guides offer a regional rundown on disease hot spots and practical advice on predeparture health measures, staying well on the road and what to do in emergencies. The guides come with a user-friendly design and helpful diagrams and tables.

Lonely Planet's **Phrasebooks** cover the essential words and phrases travellers need when they're strangers in a strange land. They come in a pocket-sized format with colour tabs for quick reference, extensive vocabulary lists, easy-to-follow pronunciation keys and two-way dictionaries.

Miffed by blurry photos of the Taj Mahal? Tired of the classic 'top of the head cut off' shot? **Travel Photography: A Guide to Taking Better Pictures** will help you turn ordinary holiday snaps into striking images and give you the know-how to capture every scene, from frenetic festivals to peaceful beach sunrises.

Lonely Planet's **Travel Journal** is a lightweight but sturdy travel diary for jotting down all those on-the-road observations and significant travel moments. It comes with a handy time-zone wheel, world maps and useful travel information.

Lonely Planet's eKno is an all-in-one communication service developed especially for travellers. It offers low-cost international calls and free email and voicemail so that you can keep in touch while on the road. Check it out on **www.ekno.lonelyplanet.com**

FOOD & RESTAURANT GUIDES

Lonely Planet's **Out to Eat** guides recommend the brightest and best places to eat and drink in top international cities. These gourmet companions are arranged by neighbourhood, packed with dependable maps, garnished with scene-setting photos and served with quirky features.

For people who live to eat, drink and travel, **World Food** guides explore the culinary culture of each country. Entertaining and adventurous, each guide is packed with detail on staples and specialities, regional cuisine and local markets, as well as sumptuous recipes, comprehensive culinary dictionaries and lavish photos good enough to eat.

OUTDOOR GUIDES

For those who believe the best way to see the world is on foot, Lonely Planet's **Walking Guides** detail everything from family strolls to difficult treks, with 'when to go and how to do it' advice supplemented by reliable maps and essential travel information.

Cycling Guides map a destination's best bike tours, long and short, in day-by-day detail. They contain all the information a cyclist needs, including advice on bike maintenance, places to eat and stay, innovative maps with detailed cues to the rides, and elevation charts.

The **Watching Wildlife** series is perfect for travellers who want authoritative information but don't want to tote a heavy field guide. Packed with advice on where, when and how to view a region's wildlife, each title features photos of over 300 species and contains engaging comments on the local flora and fauna.

With underwater colour photos throughout, **Pisces Books** explore the world's best diving and snorkelling areas. Each book contains listings of diving services and dive resorts, detailed information on depth, visibility and difficulty of dives, and a roundup of the marine life you're likely to see through your mask.

OFF THE ROAD

Journeys, the travel literature series written by renowned travel authors, capture the spirit of a place or illuminate a culture with a journalist's attention to detail and a novelist's flair for words. These are tales to soak up while you're actually on the road or dip into as an at-home armchair indulgence.

The new range of lavishly illustrated **Pictorial** books is just the ticket for both travellers and dreamers. Off-beat tales and vivid photographs bring the adventure of travel to your doorstep long before the journey begins and long after it is over.

Lonely Planet **Videos** encourage the same independent, tough-minded approach as the guidebooks. Currently airing throughout the world, this award-winning series features innovative footage and an original soundtrack.

Yes, we know, work is tough, so do a little bit of deskside dreaming with the spiral-bound Lonely Planet **Diary**, the tearaway page-a-day **Day-to-Day Calendar** or a Lonely Planet **Wall Calendar**, filled with great photos from around the world.

TRAVELLERS NETWORK

Lonely Planet Online. Lonely Planet's award-winning Web site has insider information on hundreds of destinations, from Amsterdam to Zimbabwe, complete with interactive maps and relevant links. The site also offers the latest travel news, recent reports from travellers on the road, guidebook upgrades, a travel links site, an online book-buying option and a lively traveller's bulletin board. It can be viewed at **www.lonelyplanet.com** or AOL keyword: lp.

Planet Talk is a quarterly print newsletter, full of gossip, advice, anecdotes and author articles. It provides an antidote to the being-at-home blues and lets you plan and dream for the next trip. Contact the nearest Lonely Planet office for your free copy.

Comet, the free Lonely Planet newsletter, comes via email once a month. It's loaded with travel news, advice, dispatches from authors, travel competitions and letters from readers. To subscribe, click on the Comet subscription link on the front page of the Web site.

LONELY PLANET

Guides by Region

Lonely Planet is known worldwide for publishing practical, reliable and no-nonsense travel information in our guides and on our Web site. The Lonely Planet list covers just about every accessible part of the world. Currently there are 16 series: Travel guides, Shoestring guides, Condensed guides, Phrasebooks, Read This First, Healthy Travel, Walking guides, Cycling guides, Watching Wildlife guides, Pisces Diving & Snorkeling guides, City Maps, Road Atlases, Out to Eat, World Food, Journeys travel literature and Pictorials.

AFRICA Africa on a shoestring • Cairo • Cairo City Map • Cape Town • Cape Town City Map • East Africa • Egypt • Egyptian Arabic phrasebook • Ethiopia, Eritrea & Djibouti • Ethiopian (Amharic) phrasebook • The Gambia & Senegal • Healthy Travel Africa • Kenya • Malawi • Morocco • Moroccan Arabic phrasebook • Mozambique • Read This First: Africa • South Africa, Lesotho & Swaziland • Southern Africa • Southern Africa Road Atlas • Swahili phrasebook • Tanzania, Zanzibar & Pemba • Trekking in East Africa • Tunisia • Watching Wildlife East Africa •   Watching Wildlife Southern Africa • West Africa • World Food Morocco • Zimbabwe, Botswana & Namibia
Travel Literature: Mali Blues: Traveling to an African Beat • The Rainbird: A Central African Journey • Songs to an African Sunset: A Zimbabwean Story

AUSTRALIA & THE PACIFIC Auckland • Australia • Australian phrasebook • Australia Road Atlas • Bush-walking in Australia •Cycling New Zealand • Fiji • Fijian phrasebook • Healthy Travel Australia, NZ and the Pacific • Islands of Australia's Great Barrier Reef • Melbourne • Melbourne City Map • Micronesia • New Caledonia • New South Wales & the ACT • New Zealand • Northern Territory • Outback Australia • Out to Eat – Melbourne • Out to Eat – Sydney • Papua New Guinea • Pidgin phrasebook • Queensland • Rarotonga & the Cook Islands • Samoa • Solomon Islands • South Australia • South Pacific • South Pacific phrasebook • Sydney • Sydney City Map • Sydney Condensed • Tahiti & French Polynesia • Tasmania • Tonga • Tramping in New Zealand • Vanuatu • Victoria • Walking in Australia • Watching Wildlife Australia • Western Australia
Travel Literature: Islands in the Clouds: Travels in the Highlands of New Guinea • Kiwi Tracks: A New Zealand Journey • Sean & David's Long Drive

CENTRAL AMERICA & THE CARIBBEAN Bahamas, Turks & Caicos • Baja California • Bermuda • Central America on a shoestring • Costa Rica • Costa Rica Spanish phrasebook • Cuba • Dominican Republic & Haiti • Eastern Caribbean • Guatemala • Guatemala, Belize & Yucatán: La Ruta Maya • Healthy Travel Central & South America • Jamaica • Mexico • Mexico City • Panama • Puerto Rico • Read This First: Central & South America • World Food Mexico • Yucatán
Travel Literature: Green Dreams: Travels in Central America

EUROPE Amsterdam • Amsterdam City Map • Amsterdam Condensed • Andalucía • Austria • Baltic States phrasebook • Barcelona • Barcelona City Map • Berlin • Berlin City Map • Britain • British phrasebook • Brussels, Bruges & Antwerp • Brussels City Map • Budapest • Budapest City Map • Canary Islands • Central Europe • Central Europe phrasebook • Corfu & the Ionians • Corsica • Crete • Crete Condensed • Croatia • Cycling Britain • Cycling France • Cyprus • Czech & Slovak Republics • Denmark • Dublin • Dublin City Map • Eastern Europe • Eastern Europe phrasebook • Edinburgh • Estonia, Latvia & Lithuania • Europe on a shoestring • Finland • Florence • France • Frankfurt Condensed • French phrasebook • Georgia, Armenia & Azerbaijan • Germany • German phrasebook • Greece • Greek Islands • Greek phrasebook • Hungary • Iceland, Greenland & the Faroe Islands • Ireland • Istanbul • Italian phrasebook • Italy • Krakow • Lisbon • The Loire • London • London City Map • London Condensed • Madrid • Malta • Mediterranean Europe • Mediterranean Europe phrasebook • Moscow • Mozambique • Munich • the Netherlands • Norway • Out to Eat – London • Paris • Paris City Map • Paris Condensed • Poland • Portugal • Portuguese phrasebook • Prague • Prague City Map • Provence & the Côte d'Azur • Read This First: Europe • Romania & Moldova • Rome • Rome City Map • Russia, Ukraine & Belarus • Russian phrasebook • Scandinavian & Baltic Europe • Scandinavian Europe phrasebook • Scotland • Sicily • Slovenia • South-West France • Spain • Spanish phrasebook • St Petersburg • St Petersburg City Map • Sweden • Switzerland • Trekking in Spain • Tuscany • Ukrainian phrasebook • Venice • Vienna • Walking in Britain • Walking in France • Walking in Ireland • Walking in Italy • Walking in Spain • Walking in Switzerland • Western Europe • Western Europe phrasebook • World Food France • World Food Ireland • World Food Italy • World Food Spain
Travel Literature: Love and War in the Apennines • The Olive Grove: Travels in Greece • On the Shores of the Mediterranean • Round Ireland in Low Gear • A Small Place in Italy • After Yugoslavia

LONELY PLANET

Mail Order

Lonely Planet products are distributed worldwide. They are also available by mail order from Lonely Planet, so if you have difficulty finding a title please write to us. North and South American residents should write to 150 Linden St, Oakland, CA 94607, USA; European and African residents should write to 10a Spring Place, London NW5 3BH, UK; and residents of other countries to Locked Bag 1, Footscray, Victoria 3011, Australia.

INDIAN SUBCONTINENT Bangladesh • Bengali phrasebook • Bhutan • Delhi • Goa • Healthy Travel Asia & India • Hindi & Urdu phrasebook • India • Indian Himalaya • Karakoram Highway • Kerala • Mumbai (Bombay) • Nepal • Nepali phrasebook • Pakistan • Rajasthan • Read This First: Asia & India • South India • Sri Lanka • Sri Lanka phrasebook • Tibet • Tibetan phrasebook • Trekking in the Indian Himalaya • Trekking in the Karakoram & Hindukush • Trekking in the Nepal Himalaya
Travel Literature: The Age of Kali: Indian Travels and Encounters • Hello Goodnight: A Life of Goa • In Rajasthan • A Season in Heaven: True Tales from the Road to Kathmandu • Shopping for Buddhas • A Short Walk in the Hindu Kush • Slowly Down the Ganges

ISLANDS OF THE INDIAN OCEAN Madagascar & Comoros • Maldives • Mauritius, Réunion & Seychelles

MIDDLE EAST & CENTRAL ASIA Bahrain, Kuwait & Qatar • Central Asia • Central Asia phrasebook • Dubai • Hebrew phrasebook • Iran • Israel & the Palestinian Territories • Istanbul • Istanbul City Map • Istanbul to Cairo on a shoestring • Jerusalem • Jerusalem City Map • Jordan • Lebanon • Middle East • Oman & the United Arab Emirates • Syria • Turkey • Turkish phrasebook • World Food Turkey • Yemen
Travel Literature: Black on Black: Iran Revisited • The Gates of Damascus • Kingdom of the Film Stars: Journey into Jordan

NORTH AMERICA Alaska • Boston • Boston City Map • California & Nevada • California Condensed • Canada • Chicago • Chicago City Map • Deep South • Florida • Great Lakes • Hawaii • Hiking in Alaska • Hiking in the USA • Honolulu • Las Vegas • Los Angeles • Los Angeles City Map • Louisiana & The Deep South • Miami • Miami City Map • New England • New Orleans • New York City • New York City City Map • New York City Condensed • New York, New Jersey & Pennsylvania • Oahu • Out to Eat – San Francisco • Pacific Northwest • Puerto Rico • Rocky Mountains • San Francisco • San Francisco City Map • Seattle • Southwest • Texas • USA • USA phrasebook • Vancouver • Virginia & the Capital Region • Washington DC • Washington, DC City Map • World Food Deep South, USA • World Food New Orleans
Travel Literature: Caught Inside: A Surfer's Year on the California Coast • Drive Thru America

NORTH-EAST ASIA Beijing • Beijing City Map • Cantonese phrasebook • China • Hiking in Japan • Hong Kong • Hong Kong City Map • Hong Kong Condensed • Hong Kong, Macau & Guangzhou • Japan • Japanese phrasebook • Korea • Korean phrasebook • Kyoto • Mandarin phrasebook • Mongolia • Mongolian phrasebook • Seoul • Shanghai • South-West China • Taiwan • Tokyo
Travel Literature: In Xanadu: A Quest • Lost Japan

SOUTH AMERICA Argentina, Uruguay & Paraguay • Bolivia • Brazil • Brazilian phrasebook • Buenos Aires • Chile & Easter Island • Colombia • Ecuador & the Galapagos Islands • Healthy Travel Central & South America • Latin American Spanish phrasebook • Peru • Quechua phrasebook • Read This First: Central & South America • Rio de Janeiro • Rio de Janeiro City Map • Santiago • South America on a shoestring • Santiago • Trekking in the Patagonian Andes • Venezuela
Travel Literature: Full Circle: A South American Journey

SOUTH-EAST ASIA Bali & Lombok • Bangkok • Bangkok City Map • Burmese phrasebook • Cambodia • Hanoi • Healthy Travel Asia & India • Hill Tribes phrasebook • Ho Chi Minh City • Indonesia • Indonesian phrasebook • Indonesia's Eastern Islands • Jakarta • Java • Lao phrasebook • Laos • Malay phrasebook • Malaysia, Singapore & Brunei • Myanmar (Burma) • Philippines • Pilipino (Tagalog) phrasebook • Read This First: Asia & India • Singapore • Singapore City Map • South-East Asia on a shoestring • South-East Asia phrasebook • Thailand • Thailand's Islands & Beaches • Thailand, Vietnam, Laos & Cambodia Road Atlas • Thai phrasebook • Vietnam • Vietnamese phrasebook • World Food Thailand • World Food Vietnam

ALSO AVAILABLE: Antarctica • The Arctic • The Blue Man: Tales of Travel, Love and Coffee • Brief Encounters: Stories of Love, Sex & Travel • Chasing Rickshaws • The Last Grain Race • Lonely Planet Unpacked • Not the Only Planet: Science Fiction Travel Stories • Lonely Planet On the Edge • Sacred India • Travel with Children • Travel Photography: A Guide to Taking Better Pictures

Index

Text

Boxed Text

MAP LEGEND

CITY ROUTES				REGIONAL ROUTES		BOUNDARIES	
Freeway	Freeway		Unsealed Road		Tollway, Freeway		International
Highway	Primary Road		One Way Street		Primary Road		State
Road	Secondary Road		Pedestrian Street		Secondary Road		Disputed
Street	Street		Stepped Street		Minor Road		Fortified Wall
Lane	Lane		Tunnel				
	On/Off Ramp		Footbridge				

TRANSPORT ROUTES & STATIONS

	Train		Ferry
	Underground Train		Walking Trail
	Metro		Walking Tour
	Tramway		Path
	Cable Car, Chairlift		Pier or Jetty

HYDROGRAPHY

	River, Creek		Dry Lake; Salt Lake
	Canal		Spring; Rapids
	Lake		Waterfalls

AREA FEATURES

	Building		Market		Beach		Campus
	Park, Gardens		Sports Ground		Cemetery		Plaza

POPULATION SYMBOLS

✪ CAPITAL	National Capital	● CITY	City	● Village			Village
◉ CAPITAL	State Capital	● Town	Town				Urban Area

MAP SYMBOLS

■	Place to Stay	▼	Place to Eat	●	Point of Interest

✈	Airport	✉	Embassy, Consulate	◖	Mosque	✚	Police Station
⑤	Bank	⊥	Gate	▲	Mountain	✉	Post Office
◉	Border Crossing	卍	Hindu Temple	⌒	Mountain Range	◲	Pub or Bar
❑ ❒	Bus Stop, Terminal	✛	Hospital	血	Museum	✖	Shopping Centre
◭	Camping Ground	❍	Internet Cafe	✦	National Park	◱	Taxi Rank
◲	Chalet	✳ ✉	Lookout	)(	Pass	☎	Telephone
✇	Church	⚑	Monument	◉	Petrol or Gas Station	❶	Tourist Information

Note: not all symbols displayed above appear in this book

LONELY PLANET OFFICES

Australia
Locked Bag 1, Footscray, Victoria 3011
☎ 03 9689 4666 fax 03 9689 6833
email: talk2us@lonelyplanet.com.au

USA
150 Linden St, Oakland, CA 94607
☎ 510 893 8555 TOLL FREE: 800 275 8555
fax 510 893 8572
email: info@lonelyplanet.com

UK
10a Spring Place, London NW5 3BH
☎ 020 7428 4800 fax 020 7428 4828
email: go@lonelyplanet.co.uk

France
1 rue du Dahomey, 75011 Paris
☎ 01 55 25 33 00 fax 01 55 25 33 01
email: bip@lonelyplanet.fr
www.lonelyplanet.fr

World Wide Web: www.lonelyplanet.com *or* AOL keyword: lp
Lonely Planet Images: lpi@lonelyplanet.com.au